THE FUR TRADER AND THE INDIAN

THE

FUR TRADER

AND THE

INDIAN

by Lewis O. Saum

UNIVERSITY OF WASHINGTON PRESS

Seattle and London

Library of Congress Catalog Card Number 65-23915
ISBN 0-295-73793-X (cloth)
ISBN 0-295-74031-0 (paper)

FOR JOANNE

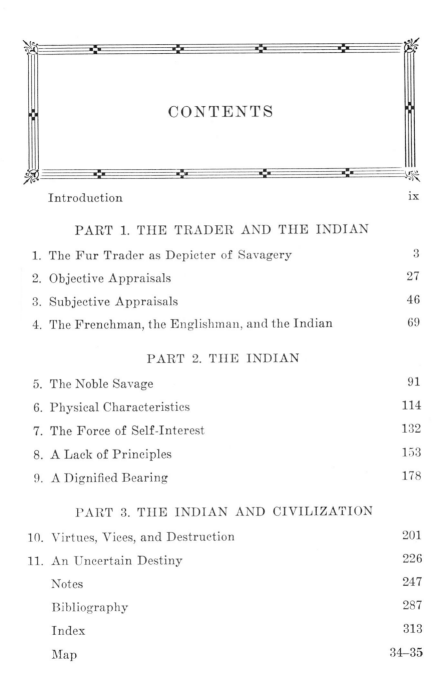

CONTENTS

INTRODUCTION

A RECENT SCHOLAR HAS SUGGESTED, PERHAPS PLAYFULLY, THAT ONLY anthropologists and children perpetuate an interest in Indians.[1] Though the dictum has a degree of plausibility, the present study assumes the legitimacy of a similar concern on the part of historians. This work is not a study of Indians per se. It does reflect the dissatisfaction expressed by such men as Daniel Boorstin and Bernard DeVoto with the inadequacy of historical awareness of the red man. Recently Boorstin argued that our history has failed by too often lumping the natives with "the inclement weather, the wild animals, and the unknown distances, among the half-predictable perils of a wilderness."[2] And DeVoto, who studiously avoided depicting the natives as stage props against which white men enacted their roles, protested against the tendency to view our past

. . . as if history were a function solely of white culture—in spite of the fact that till well into the nineteenth century the Indians were one of the principal determinants of historical events. Those of us who work in frontier history—which begins at the tidal beaches and when the sixteenth century begins—are repeatedly nonplused to discover how little has been done for us in regard to the one force bearing on our field that was active everywhere.[3]

This study analyzes the image of the Indian that impressed itself upon the consciousness of the earliest white men among them. It may, to some degree, help fill the void of which DeVoto wrote. Conceivably, it may clarify our understanding of frontier thinking and actions, and to a lesser extent, the thinking of America generally.

Historians of the fur trade have done surprisingly little to indicate how traders viewed the people with whom they dealt. Indeed, in many cases they treat the Indian much as do general works on the frontier advance, that is, as a feature of the terrain, albeit an economic terrain. In nearly all accounts, economic and expansive aspects of the trade receive greatest attention. In his still usable pioneering study, Hiram Martin Chittenden presented specific incidents, most notably the spread of smallpox up the Missouri in the 1830's, in such a way that one can infer his estimate of basic attitudes. Similarly, E. E. Rich's excellent work on the Hudson's Bay Company describes policy so perceptively that one gains additional understanding as to how traders looked upon their tawny customers. Both authors, however, described attitudes toward the Indian largely in the impersonal terms of trade policy. From reading them, one would suspect that the Indian rarely entered the consciousness of the trader except as an object concerning which a policy had to be devised. In the latest major work on the trade, Paul C. Phillips' *The Fur Trade,* the Indian approaches the condition of being "conspicuous by his absence." The present study seeks to add a further dimension—the traders' conception of the Indian—to these and other works.

In an essay on Indian relations, Howard Peckham concluded that only since the closing of the frontier have efforts been made to discuss the red man with anything approaching objectivity.[4] He referred solely to historical presentations. Before the late nineteenth century, however, writers of all kinds showed less interest in describing the Indian than in using him as a device. Roy Harvey Pearce characterized American thinking as bent upon destroying the natives, thereby removing an impediment to progress and stilling guilt-ridden apprehensions of what the Americans might become if they did not themselves progress. Conversely, if Pearce is wrong and if the views of those who lauded savagery were in fact dominant, truth was no better served. The Indians used by John Heckewelder to emphasize Christian virtues, by Thomas Jefferson to refute the Count de Buffon, by Baron Lahontan to assail the religious establishment, and by Benjamin Franklin to tease the French court are more pleasing but no more real.

Though their attitudes did not nicely and necessarily reflect the objective realities of Indian nature, traders showed an awareness of the wide range of prevailing conceptions and often sought a balanced view. Thus, Minnesota trader Henry Hastings Sibley noted the disparity between the two most common evaluations. Truth, he remarked, lay somewhere between the Indian as ''the impersonation of the chivalry of olden times, proud, hospitable and gallant'' and the Indian as ''revengeful, implacable and bloody minded.''[5] Similarly, Edwin Denig recognized ''two sets of writers both equally wrong, one setting forth the Indians as a noble, generous, and chivalrous race far above the standards of Europeans, the others representing them below the level of brute creation.''[6] The comments of Sibley and Denig do more than indicate extremes of sentiments in uninformed outsiders. They represent an ambiguity in the traders themselves, an inclination to see in the aborigine both the reprehensible and, to a lesser extent, the admirable. Though it is too neatly balanced, the following comment of Henry Boller reflects this duality, as well as evidencing a sound perspective:

I could "paint" you, were it not for the constant interruptions . . . two pictures:

The One would represent the bright side of Indian Life, with its feathers, lances, gayly dressed & mounted "banneries", fights, buffalo hunting &c.

The other, the dark side, showing the filth, vermin, poverty, nakedness, suffering, starvation, superstition, &c. *Both would be equally true—neither exagerated, or distorted; both totally disimillar!*[*]

To the trader, the Indian represented far more than a part of the wilderness landscape. He was a very human being with a nature, a character, whims, foibles, strengths, and weaknesses, all of which bore investigation, pondering, and exposition for altruistic reasons as well as selfish ones.

Though many have assisted me in one way or another during

* Henry A. Boller Papers (MSS in the North Dakota Historical Society, Bismarck), Boller to a brother, July 15, 1859. In order to convey the flavor of their writings, I have preserved the fur traders' original spellings. Trusting to the reader's faith and understanding, I have dispensed with what could have become an almost ubiquitous *sic.*

the preparation of this work, I must single out Professor Lewis E. Atherton of the University of Missouri. His advice and encouragement have been immensely helpful. The Floyd Calvin Shoemaker Fund for Research in Missouri History facilitated my efforts in the early stages of investigation. Later, a grant from the Johnson Fund of the American Philosophical Society enabled me to travel to several repositories of original documents. A lightened teaching load at Southwest Missouri State College in Springfield, Missouri, during the second semester of 1965 allowed me to work the final revisions of the manuscript with much more expedition than would otherwise have been the case. My wife, Elizabeth Gillette Saum, bore several of the burdens attendant upon such a project.

PART 1
THE TRADER AND THE INDIAN

1. THE FUR TRADER
AS DEPICTER OF SAVAGERY

IN EVALUATING THE NATURE AND CHARACTER OF THE FUR TRADERS as a group, one historian identified two major types. On the one hand he pictured the ever present free-lance traders, men devoid of morality and principle and at heart more savage than the primitives with whom they dealt. On the other, he portrayed licensed traders and those connected with large commercial concerns. The latter were not, he insisted, " 'solitary frontier heroes,' " nor were their methods at all above reproach. They were, however, men of substance and character.[1] To a large degree this duality applies to all of the fur-trade domain. Almost without exception, the men considered here fall into the second category, largely because they alone left records.

In the late nineteenth century Charles Pierre Chouteau of St. Louis gave to the state of Illinois a statue depicting his father's fur-trade associate, Pierre Menard.* Assuredly, *Menard,* which stands on the state capitol grounds in Springfield, was meant to do full justice to the man whose memory it perpetuates. Nevertheless, the two-figure work affords an instructive symbolic intimation of the role which traders prescribed for themselves in the wilderness. Menard stands atop a granite pedestal, looking down with calmness and gravity into the upturned face of a seated Indian. The latter has a fox pelt draped over his lower arm, and one can suppose that the Kaskaskia trader explains economic intricacies. The tasteful elegance of the trader's garb denotes a man of substance who knows civilization and bears its trappings gracefully and with dignity in the presence of the savage. His dress, his posture, and his attitude evince a reluctance to submit to the atavistic compulsions of primal

* See frontispiece. Photograph by David E. Beatty.

circumstances or fawningly to curry rapport with the primitive by discarding the marks of cultural attainment. The red man possesses a fine physique and a strikingly craggy visage, on which there appears a gratifying glimmer of comprehension. Menard's, however, is the overwhelmingly dominant presence. The look of somber awe on the savage's face conveys the impression of the white man's mastery, as well as the Indian's subtle awareness of it. And, almost crudely, the physical arrangement strengthens the effect. The standing trader and the squatting red man (neither high enough to compete nor low enough to jar artistically) illustrate graphically a wilderness ascendancy that traders sought and often felt they had attained. *Menard* may well represent an ideal conjured up in the minds of an artist, a latter-day Chouteau, and a committee choosing a design. However, it also embodies to an impressive degree the traders' own ideal of conduct, as well as their studied and seemingly successful effort to withstand the erosion of their sophistication in the face of barbarism.

In 1796 fur-trade veteran James Mackay penned a letter of advice to John Evans, a frontier neophyte setting off into upper Missouri Indian country. The trader urged, among other things, that the young Welshman maintain dignity: "On all occasions be reserved with your detachment as well as with the savages; always give to your conduct the air of importance and show good will toward everyone white or red." [2] The stereotype of the trader as a moral degenerate who participated with wild abandon in the activities of native life, bacchanalian and otherwise, has some validity in regard to small, independent operators. In regard to men of any stature working for established firms—the men who left records of their actions and attitudes—the very opposite was the ideal, if not universally the reality.

Perhaps influenced by Edwin Denig, whose fear of appearing common in the eyes of the Indian kept him from wearing frontier garb, Rudolph Kurz reasoned that Indians respected the white man only insofar as he showed traits or talents they did not possess. The native could never respect a white man as a hunter or warrior, for instance. To copy the Indian's life, habits, and dress only invited his derision. Relying upon Denig's information, the young intellectual used Robert Meldrum and some of his subordinates at Fort Sarpy as examples of the futility of attempting to gain the Indian's admiration by doing as he did. Meldrum's ability as a fighter and hunter had won him no real influence, and only his "prodigal liberality" kept the Crows at Sarpy. James Chambers, a Fort Sarpy employee possessing scant inclination to emulate the natives, substantiated Kurz's view of Meldrum, his men, and, by inference, Indian nature. In his journal of 1855 Chambers expressed disgust for both the unseemly generosity and the indecorous conduct of his superior and his peers. On this occasion a band of Crows came in to celebrate the killing of a few Blackfeet. Meldrum praised the warriors for having done well, and then, wrote Chambers, "he presented a squaw with a dress & ninety strands of beads   Old fellow   thinks I   goods are scarce & you might have saved them & traded for robes." Then, even more reprehensibly, "Big Six," a fellow employee of Chambers, "steps in to the ring with three dollarsworth of beads & kisses Miss Tramps on her foot   a dirty lousy whoring slut   oh the fool." [3]

Meldrum and Big Six seem to have been exceptions to the rule, however. A young traveler on the Santa Fe trail, Lewis Garrard, allowed himself to be "magnetized, spirited away" by O-ne-o, daughter of Se-hak, into the revelries of a Cheyenne scalp dance; but he justified his neglect of proprieties on the grounds that he was only a sojourner and, unlike the men with whom he traveled, he had no stake in the fur trade. Thomas Fitzpatrick fulminated against those who, like Garrard, dropped their dignity; Fitzpatrick insisted that no course of action better suited the white man in his dealings with Indians than "the very rules of decorum which govern a gentleman in civilized society. . . ." Judging from fur-trade records, most traders accepted the kind of advice given by James Knight, governor in chief of Hudson's Bay, to a party bound for the Churchill area in 1717. If they encountered Indians, the men must "treat them civilly not Useing to much familliarity with them for that will make them prove Saucy & impudent but carry your Self wth Gravity and Solidity." Almost as an afterthought, Knight made certain that not even the lowliest member of the group would prejudice the white men's image. The leader of the expedition should see that the apprentice boy, Richard Norton (who later became governor of Churchill and whose half-breed son, Moses, gained similar rank), "doth not Play the Rogue with them wch you know he is to Often Addicted to." [4]

Just as traders consciously guarded their dignity, so too they sought to maintain their refinement. Frederick Jackson Turner held that for a time the frontier environment proved too much for the white man: "It strips off the garments of civilization. . . . Before long . . . he shouts the war cry and takes the scalp in orthodox Indian fashion." Self-evident and attractive as this logic may appear, the fur trade provides numerous illustrations which contradict it. Louis B. Wright seems more nearly correct in contending that the "forces of light," however fiercely contested by the "powers of darkness," managed to prevail almost from the outset. To be sure, traders themselves occasionally intimated that the wilderness had an injurious effect upon their veneer of cultivation. Often, however, they made such comments ironically, facetiously, or with an apparent intent of contriving dramatic impact. W. F. Wentzel, a seemingly cultured Norwegian, satirically explained to Roderic McKenzie that he had failed to write to McKenzie's son because "I am an Indian, he is a Christian. . . ." Similarly, an anonymous polemicist—evidently a fur trader—cited an abuse in the government factory system and sarcastically shammed ignorance of the effects of such practices. "I am but demi-civilized . . . ," he explained. Late in life Henry Hastings Sibley theorized that civilized men backslid in the wilderness, and did so because savagery was the "normal condition" of man. The idea would have carried more weight had not its spokesman become, after a twenty-year career in the trade, a territorial representative in Washington and ultimately the first governor of Minnesota. [5]

On a fundamental level, the fur trade, because it was a civilized economic apparatus, presupposed a basic command of civilized forms. It ill behooved the company trader to discard the methods of his culture. Recognizing this reality, Alexander Fisher, a veteran of Hudson's Bay Company service, wrote a series of yearly letters of encouragement and advice to Henry Fisher, his nephew in the trade, urging him to better himself through study. The older man concluded his letter of 1832 by recommending that Henry read in both French and English—"lay by the Fiddle and take to Books. . . ." Sometime during the ensuing twelve months the uncle received sobering word from the young man's superior to the effect that he was neglectful and would "hardly keep an Indian account as it ought." In the years thereafter, though, the uncle's admonitions seem to have taken effect, and in 1837 he wrote in a tone of congratulation. Now the young man's superior reported him doing well in his affairs and spending time in study. However, because Henry's education was inadequate, he must continue to strive. "Take up a Book and Read," Alexander exhorted, concentrate on spelling and secure a copy of "Johnsons Dictionary." Charles W. Borup must have felt similar motivation in arranging for a governess to be sent to his post on western Lake Superior. Writing to company president Ramsay Crooks in 1840 to acknowledge the woman's safe arrival and to thank Crooks for his efforts in securing her, the well-educated Dane showed an understandable and civilized concern for the training of his brood. "You have a family yourself," he wrote, "and well know the anxiety a parent must feel for his childrens education——" [6]

The wilderness also impelled traders to preserve the marks of their refinement as a defensive gesture, as a means of vicariously escaping boredom, drudgery, and perhaps even physical danger. Thus, one trader told his employer of being a "downright Exile" among "a Barrel of drunken infamous fugitives," and pleaded for a shipment of books. Martin McLeod of the Minnesota trade spelled out such motivation in more detail. In a diary entry of November, 1840, he insisted that no life was more "dull & monotonous" than that of a trader in the winter season. Particular circumstances at his St. Peters River post compounded the painfulness of a naturally bad situation. McLeod shared a fifteen-by-twenty-foot cabin with another trader, an interpreter, and the latter's "b——h of a wife & 2 d——d noisy rude children." He would have to suffer this condition, not to mention the ''annoyance of hosts'' of natives, until April—''a pleasant *prospect* God wot; n'importe, I have a few books, a dog & a gun.—some patience—and *so,* and *so* I suppose I must be resign'd.'' McLeod resigned himself first of all to Byron, whom he rated the superior of Shakespeare, and, with the month not yet over, he had enjoyed *The Giaour, The Corsair,* and *Parasina.*[7]

But most important of all, traders carried a fair amount of refinement into the wilderness, and during their sojourn beyond the civilized world they patterned their actions in accord with that attainment. Thus, one must not suppose that Martin McLeod, for example, was driven by desperation alone to flirt with good literature. On his initial trip west while part of the quixotic scheme of the Universal Indian Liberator James Dickson, he spent time aboard a Great Lakes vessel with Xenophon's *Cyropaedia,* and on another occasion during the same trip he ''Pass'd the day reading 'Tacitus'.'' Only by overestimating the primordial persuasion of the wilds would we be surprised then to find him a few years later in his uninspiring surrounding on the St. Peters River taking up Byron. His veneer of civilization seems to have worn quite well. In that same trying winter McLeod reread John Gibson Lockhart's seven-volume *Life of Sir Walter Scott,* none of which had been published for more than four years, and again he found it a delight. After a long absence he returned to the Bible, the historical parts of which he considered ''highly instructive and interesting.'' He was vastly pleased when fellow trader Joseph Laframboise turned over to him a complete history of England in nine volumes. It would provide ''quite a feast.'' But not everything met his approval. In a memorandum book containing references to Schoolcraft, Latrobe, and others, he made the following note of evaluation:

Irving's tour on the Prairies
~~Read~~   *Poor production* [8]

In civilization or out of it, McLeod possessed a degree of polish. It was completely in keeping with his inclinations that he named his son Walter Scott McLeod, notwithstanding the fact that the child's mother bore the unlikely name, Ouitonna.

Although McLeod provides a striking illustration, his case is by no means singular. In 1839 Ramsay Crooks forwarded from the New York office to the Philadelphia editor of the *Catholic Herald* a five-dollar subscription payment for Mackinac trader, Samuel Abbott. Such transactions, which appear with surprising frequency in the American Fur Company papers, certainly evidence no weakening in the fiber of sophistication. Henry Hastings Sibley's theory that man regressed in nature was belied by the prominence of his own later life; and Sibley violated his principle just as thoroughly while yet a trader. With eleven years of wilderness existence behind him, he wrote an 1840 letter to company president Crooks requesting shipment of some rather elegant clothes and three works which are hardly symptomatic of savagery—"Nicholas Nickleby," "The life & writings of Geo. Washington" by Jared Sparks, and "De Tocqueville on America." Even the debauchee, Francis Chardon, in expressing revulsion at the desolate loneliness of the high plains, did so with a passage from Laurence Sterne's *A Sentimental Journey Through France and Italy,* only slightly misquoted. Through ratiocination, Sterne had reduced the Bastille from a symbol of horror to "simply a confinement." But immediately thereafter the cries of a caged starling devastated his finely spun logic. Suffering the spiritual and physical stifling of midwinter imprisonment on the "dreary, Savage waste," Chardon identified with the plight of that bird, and so invoked the insights of its artistic creator: "Disguise thyself as thou wilt, Oh Slavery, Still thou art a bitter draught, and though thousands in all ages have been made to drink of thy cup, it is no less bitter on that account." For all the celebrated grossness and materialism of frontier circumstances, it is comprehensible to find trader Hugh Heward invoking the humanistic ideal—"consider your Body only as the Servant of your Soul." [9]

The fur trade called for men of various practical talents. Some individuals, such as George Simpson, became powerful administrators of the wilderness. Others—such as Alexander Henry, Peter Skene Ogden, John Work, and Edwin Denig—spent their years as company traders. The fur trade of the Rocky Mountain West, relying as it did only incidentally upon furs harvested by Indians, employed white men as trappers. This unexalted role was filled by such familiar figures as "Old Bill" Williams, "Uncle Dick" Wootton, Jim Beckwourth, and others. Because fur trading occurred on the earliest of frontiers, the roles of fur trader and explorer often defy clear distinction. Many of the early French explorers—for example, Pierre Esprit Radisson, Samuel de Champlain, and Pierre de La Vérendrye—utilized trade in furs either as basic motivation or as a means of supporting other projects. Similarly, Hudson's Bay Company traders such as John Rae, Thomas Simpson, and Samuel Hearne undertook exploratory ventures at the behest of the company. The fact that so many frontier merchants occasionally or recurrently dabbled in the trade compounds the problem of definition. Men such as William Morrison of Kaskaskia apparently considered the fur trade only one facet of their diversified economic endeavors. On the eastern seaboard at the outset of American development, the propensity of any and all to engage in Indian trade precludes nice definition. The activities of Henry Hudson, Captain John Smith, and William Byrd of Westover illustrate the nature of the problem. This consideration compels greater emphasis upon trans-Appalachian sources, in reaches where "fur traders" more nearly lent themselves to efforts at identification.

In addition to fur traders, a considerable group of men observed the fur trade at first hand without participating directly themselves. This class includes the young and curious traveler on the Santa Fe trail, Lewis Garrard; the translator and minister plenipotentiary between civilization and savagery, Conrad Weiser; army man B. L. E. Bonneville; the extraordinary and mysterious Englishman, George Frederick Ruxton; and the prospective or novice participant in the trade, Nathaniel Wyeth. Arbitrary choice alone has kept this group from growing to unworkable size. Almost without exception they enter into this study not to expound their own views of the Indian, expert or ignorant as they may have been, but instead to express the concepts of the Indian held by men who engaged in the fur trade. In this context one final individual demands mention—Rudolph Friederich Kurz. As a young Swiss romantic traveling up the Missouri River, he exposed his preconceptions of noble savagery to the crude realities of primitive life. Here he falls into the category of those, like Garrard, who described the thinking of others. Later, as a part-time clerk for the Upper Missouri Outfit, Kurz's views of the Indian merit consideration as those of a fur trader.

To consider the traders' qualifications as observers of the Indian involves two basic questions. First, to what degree did they have a knowledge of the primitives? This question would loom larger were one working in anthropology or ethnology. In that case he would seek to determine whether traders had the necessary information to convey a reliable picture of the objective realities of Indian existence. However, for a study of attitudes, already fraught with non-objective aspects, such a consideration diminishes in importance. Still it has significance. It could, for example, suggest leads and information to those in anthropological disciplines. As a group, fur traders had the earliest extensive contact with the Indians. Moreover, they had to study the people with whom they dealt, for fur trading consisted of more than dragging a keg of cheap liquor into the woods and returning rich. Even the immensely busy George Simpson, whom Frederick Merk called "a typical nineteenth-century captain of industry," prided himself on examining native ways with "some attention." [10] Traders should, therefore, qualify as tolerably good sources of objective information. Indeed, their accounts should be employed more widely. One might, for example, ponder the absence in fur-trade literature of recognizable references to the institution of the potlatch on the Northwest coast. And while that ritual—so subject to anthropological attention in modern times—went unnoted, the earliest fur-trade accounts indicate that the totem pole, a cultural article generally assigned to the period following white contact, had obvious precursors of cruder design. Conceivably, the potlatch, instead of reaching its much-heralded proportions indigenously, developed analogously to the totem pole—after the influx of European goods made it more practicable.

The objective reliability of fur-trade statements about the Indian more nearly concerns people in other academic areas. For the historian, the subject—the fur trader—has central interest. Thus, the second, and for this study the more important question to ask of the qualifications of the trader as observer is a subjective one. How well did he express himself?

In turn, this question breaks down into several components. In the first place, to what degree did these men as a group possess the intellectual acumen to express their attitudes on paper and thus to posterity? Traders were not intellectuals. However, considering their historical context, they did possess good educations. They came largely from American, lower Canadian, Scotch, French, and British middle classes, and enjoyed the educational opportunities open to such people. In discussing the almost ubiquitous Scots in the Canadian trade, one writer made the following high assessment of their character:

These Scottish boys were ideal types for the fur trade service. Having the basis of a classical education, the Shorter Catechism, and the Westminster Confession of Faith for sheet anchors, they carried their unbending principles into their careers. What they may have lacked in exuberance of spirits they made up in loyalty and moral qualities.[11]

This, of course, represents a fond description; but the presence of "moral qualities" among traders was certainly widespread.

The Virginian, James Clyman, who wrote readable poetry, intelligible discussions of time-space concepts, and far too little about Indians, had an exceptional intellect. But men such as Edwin Denig, the knowledgeable son of a Pennsylvania physician; David Thompson, a poor boy of Welsh extraction educated in mathematics and geography at the Grey Coat School, Westminster; Peter Skene Ogden, a wandering member of a prominent United Empire Loyalist family; Jean Baptiste Trudeau, an impoverished school teacher; and Peter Garrioch, who attended Kenyon College for a year, then tried pedagogy, only to flee that calling because of "dolts and dunderheads"—such men appear often in the annals of the trade. When Edwin Denig viewed with indelicate levity Rudolph Friederich Kurz's sketch of an "ideal human figure," the young romantic understandably took umbrage. However, in spite of his superior's obscene remarks and nonaesthetic desire to have a copy of the production—offenses which must have cut the sensitive artist deeply—Kurz attested to the generally worthwhile nature of Denig's ideas, however strongly expressed.[12] Even the irreverent and dissolute Francis Chardon showed evidence of perceptive, though gloomy, introspection. Similarly, James Chambers' chronicle of viciousness and ugly debauchery at Fort Sarpy, though regrettably deleted in editing, contains glimmerings of knowledge along with a heady but not gratuitously obscene humor.

Although Chambers operated in a less elevated position than the Thompsons, Denigs, and Ogdens, his humorous vignettes show abundant perspicacity. Nothing, for example, portrays better the tendency of the Crow nation toward pilfering than Chambers' delightful allegory involving the departure of a Crow war party in search of the Sioux:

. . . lo & behold   it appeared that each & every one of them [the white men at the post] had unknowingly a substitute on the War path One's Blanket being martialy disposed had trotted off in quest of the Sioux Another's Coat concluded to cover the shoulders of a "Brave.["] Big Six's Comb was under the impression that a richer trapping ground could be found elsewhere . . . two Wolf Skin of Valles Vamosed the Ranche & your Humble Servants Shirt, cut stick & put off to the wars   the war party returned   the cold weather put a damper on the red "Sons of Mars" but cold had no efect on the representatives of F. Sarpy   they still kept on the war path, if not they certainly would have returned. On interrogating the Crows about each of thier representatives, it appall'd the Boys to hear that the Warriors knew nothing of the Absconding parties from F. Sarpy.   the Boys are in despair   they are alarmed for the safety of Brigadier Coat, Col Blanket, Sergeant Comb, Corporal Mug & the rank, in No. 3 Bug row surmises & suspicions are rife. . . .

Chambers' lengthiest and most delightful entries came after New Year, on which day "Our little band of Brothers are celebrating the day with a vengeance." If the frivolity and alcoholic consumption of the season helped inspire these midwinter entries, the diary seems to have suffered little for it. On the third of January, following brief comments on the business of the day, Chambers began immediately to relate an affair centering around Mose, a Negro from Virginia, and "Big Six," a vicious and depraved fellow native of the Old Dominion. After asking theatrically, " 'What noise is that in Ethiopia, has some rascally savage maltreated the Ethiop . . . ?,' " the puckish trader divulged that Mose's Crow wife had gone away with "Bucks   Young Crow Bucks   At that the worse possible kind of bucks. . . ." After editor Anne McDonnell's deletion of obscenity the account continues:

Big Six disinterested good soul that he is, is doing all that lays in his power to console the Bereaved husband quoting Scripture to Mose to prove that his afflictions are for the best "Oh Six you do not know how I loved that woman. . . . Six sugested that perhaps his color did not suit   Mose Became indignant & replied that he was lighter than an Indian, if I was not says he could I get as light a child as that "Oh says Six doubts exist about your being the Father of that child. where is the kinks   I can see none the child's hair is straight & your hair is wool. dont say so Six   dont trifle with the feelings of a man in misfortune & that, a man the same as yourself away from "Old Virginny   tis true say Six that I have a warmer feeling for Virginians than any others   providing their hair is straight . . . etc.[13]

Nothing is known of Chambers' background, but he evidently lacked extensive formal education. He possessed a greater sense of the comic than many of his fellow traders, but most traders who left written records were similarly competent in expressing their attitudes in writing. For example, William Maxwell mused over his life by way of allegory. He had, he wrote, served several "Generals." For a time he was a "Son of Mars," but, though he never received a scratch, he had left that leader long ago with no intention of returning. Next he entered "Venuses service" wherein he was less fortunate: "I recd some flesh wounds that give me a great deal of Trouble for some Time, but time and a good constitution got the better of them without paying one Shilling to the Doctor." Finally, Maxwell enlisted in "Bachus Service" in which he still remained, and in which he was faring indifferently.[14]

To a noteworthy extent, traders not only had the ability to express themselves; they had the inclination as well. On one occasion in 1848 Robert Stuart apologized to his daughter for his failure to correspond and noted, apparently as extenuation, his "utter abhorrence of even the sight of pen, ink & paper." Earlier in life—as an Astorian thirty-five years before—Stuart had written copiously, but age and a career of continual administrative letter-writing had replaced vigor with revulsion. Most traders did not share this disgust of an old man who had but six months to live. More typically, on New Year's Day of 1843 Peter Garrioch set about making amends for neglecting to record his affairs of the past eight months:

To allow eight months to slide off into Eternity without preserving a single memento, for probable Old age to advert to in the days when such things would be memorials and hand-maids to the memory, is to leave one in absolute doubt, wheather he spent that period of life in the active discharge of those duties Connected with any Calling in this life, or wheather the whole routine of his functionaries were then reduced to a state of such domnant stupor, which the great blank in his life-book would intimate. That he was perfectly unconcious of existence during that period.—That would be ridiculous! To avoid the odium of such a charge, is what induces me, for my own satisfaction however, to fill up that vacuum of my active life which lapse of eight months unnoticed, has caused.[15]

Men of the organized fur trade possessed and sought to maintain mental alertness. They had the ability to express themselves. But an even more difficult question remains. To what degree do fur-trade accounts reflect the views and insights of the writers rather than the inclinations of the companies employing them, the expansive tendencies of nations, or any one of a myriad of other possible influences? The question defies clear determination. However, one thing appears certain. Many traders had the freedom of spirit to avoid merely reflecting their employers' pecuniary instincts.

To be sure, a George Simpson could write in remarkable understatement that "Philanthropy is not the exclusive object of our visits to these Northern Regions."[16] And very likely, the Indian appeared often, as he did to Simpson, as little more than a pawn in an economic game. From this perspective—and no one utilized it more than Simpson—the native had scant meaning except insofar as he comported himself in harmony with the designs of the fur trade.

Hugh MacLennan recently suggested that deep in Simpson's soul there existed a suppressed but viable trace of "the old wildness that never quite leaves the pure Scot." As evidence he cited the fact that, although cargo space was at a premium, Simpson carried with him in his *canot du maitre* two bagpipers. "Underneath his brutal surface callousness," according to MacLennan, "the primitive heat burned, and hence that pair of pipers." But Simpson represents an unlikely choice to demonstrate an independent spirit on the part of fur traders. Whatever aesthetic urges he may have felt, he evidently justified the bagpipers on economic grounds—they awed the Indians. As Chief Factor Archibald McDonald put it while traveling with Simpson, "the sound of the bugle, the bagpipes, Highland Piper in full dress, the musical snuff box, &c., excited in them emotions of admiration and wonder." Evidence of the "primitive heat" of Simpson's soul is strangely absent from his published narrative, journals, reports, and letters. On the contrary, he seems to have been a peculiarly soulless person, with little awareness of anything outside the interests of the Hudson's Bay Company and the confines of his own rather crabbed and petty sense of dignity. He would have found a comfortable niche in the character-depriving anonymity of modern administrative hierarchies. George Bryce, an early and fond historian of the company, attempted to breathe some life into a walking repository of Hudson's Bay Company interests by intimating that Sir George had an eye for the ladies, but it is only an intimation.[17]

All of this is by way of preface to the regrettable fact that a man of Simpson's spiritless temperament should loom so large as a symbol of the organized fur trade. Judged by his views of the Indian, Simpson seems little more than an anthropomorphism of a giant, mindless economic concern. He uttered slightly humanized translations of the pecuniary reflexes of the Hudson's Bay Company. Many of his fellows did much more.

These others were not debauched *bon vivants* or reckless fools, but they were men of more human proportions. Of course, no fellow trader ever insulted Simpson for jeopardizing profits by going on a prolonged drunk, as apparently happened to the intelligent and perceptive Edwin Denig. And Simpson never flirted with hopes for the Indians' future based upon patently unrealistic appraisals of the red men, as did such men as John McLean and John Long. Simpson could chide the confused syntax and prolixity in the writing of Samuel Black, formerly his *bete noir* in the North West Company, but Black's account contains a streak of scientific curiosity and of near-genius (or madness) entirely missing from the writings of Sir George. During the decisive winter of 1820 and 1821 at Fort Wedderburn on Lake Athabasca, Simpson recorded in his journal what he saw as the ruffianly and desperate character of his opponent, Samuel Black. In commenting on this judgment, R. M. Patterson has pointed out that Sir George showed no indication of realizing that Black—the "strangest man" Simpson ever knew—may well have been pondering the origins of the varying beach levels of the lake or trying to explain the success of kitchen gardens on geologically new soil.[18]

Traders, of course, entered the wilderness for economic reasons, and at times their written expressions seem circumscribed by mundane economic boundaries. Fur-trade administrators urged and expected their subordinates to assume a properly commercial outlook and conduct. Writing to Ramsay Crooks in 1824, Robert Stuart predicted poor returns from the Green Bay sector because the men there lacked "the *main* features in the character of a Trader"—"enterprize, industry & economy." Green Bay notwithstanding, men in the field often fulfilled just such mercenary expectations. After noting that only some traders had the requisite education to portray savage life, Edwin Denig conceded regretfully that they often refrained from doing so by design in order to keep the trade veiled in a more profitable mystery. Edward Umfreville attested to crass inclinations in others when he complained that his predecessors at a Saskatchewan River post had been "too much actuated by the impetuous desire of accumulating wealth, to allot a small portion of their time to the advancement of useful knowledge. . . ." By intimation, his own breadth of vision suffered no such limits. John Askin of the early Detroit trade demonstrates less explicitly the practical bent of some traders. Whatever heady notions about Indian society or about the scheme of things that may have entered his mind, he limited his written expressions to such uninspiring realities as the following diary entries: "The poor Blk Sow took Boar———the first hen laid yesterday. . . . Potatoes may be planted on Stubble ground with Dung." Occasionally, traders' commentaries took on the proportions of gross materialism. Thus, an Indiana trader who had far more interest in laying out town sites than in pondering Indian nature referred to the creation of a new firm which would be organized "with an 'eye single' to this glorious speculation." [19]

But these men gave evidence of being more than mere ciphers in vast economic operations. Some, of course, could not meet the exacting standards of "enterprize, industry & economy." John Lawe, evidently responsible in part for prejudicing the American Fur Company efforts at Green Bay in 1824, received a stern letter from Robert Stuart indicating his failure to meet the measure. Stuart softened the reprimand by couching it in terms of a report which had reached his ears: *"That John Lawe is as good a fellow as ever lived, but must soon ruin himself, for the Whiskey bottle is never off his table. . . ."* The report may have been exaggerated, Stuart obligingly conceded; but hereafter, he advised, let your friends speak of you "with *dry throats* and *sound heads.*" Human weakness certainly kept some men from attaining the ideal commercial standard. Others, however, manifested a conscious unwillingness to fit or be described in the desired mercenary pattern. Thus, when "Rev. Mr. Potter" made some slighting remarks in the *Missionary Herald* about traders, Martin McLeod fired off an angry rebuttal. McLeod considered Potter's comments especially injurious because of the inferences which would be drawn from them by persons entertaining "uncharitable prejudices against indian traders whom they verily believe to be little if any better than *Horse dealers. . . ."* [20]

The businessman, whether in the wilderness or elsewhere, has not, of course, enjoyed universally tender treatment in the twentieth century. Meridel Le Suer, a veteran of literary communism, provides an extreme but appropriate illustration. In a short story titled "The First Farmers' Revolt," she portrays conditions in Minnesota at the time of the 1862 Sioux uprising. Her protagonist, a young white boy, tells of having "had the grandeur and the freedom of being in the wilderness before it was spoiled. I rode a horse. I was soothed and rocked in the grand cradle of nature. I went to the Indian camps. I saw them living, dancing, living deep in the land. The land was their mother." Having depicted an idyll, she introduces the inevitable marplots. The homesteaders and the simple red men could have lived in harmony if, as the boy's father tells him, "it had not been for the trader and mercantile class that exploited both of us." As Martin McLeod's resentful comments indicate, traders sensed this indictment, which represents the ultimate in criticisms, and they reacted to it. At trying junctures Peter Skene Ogden, a friend and kindred spirit of Samuel Black, mightily damned the Indians, pondered the advisability of extermination, and grumbled that their perversity inhibited success of the trade and the advance of traders. These expressions, however, are the manifestations of the spleen and simple humanity of an intelligent though turbulent individual, not the purposeful reactions of an economic man. In his published narrative Ogden intimated in a defensive fashion that traders did more than mirror the material aspirations of their companies. He minimized the contribution of "drawing-room authors" and those who traveled for pleasure or for scientific pursuits in comparison to those like himself who "encounter these hardships for vile lucre." [21] Defensive and petulant as his remark seems, it indicates that he, and no doubt many others, felt wronged for being stigmatized as uncomprehending mercenaries. The point that needs to be made is not that these men kept economic considerations from coloring their attitudes, for time and again they allowed that very thing. More importantly, however, they wrote a great deal about the natives out of sheer curiosity.

Ogden did not contrive his resentment. His defense of men in the trade appears genuine and justified, at least in part. Although commercial activities determined the broad outline of traders' affairs, they possessed the curiosity of fairly intelligent men and often extended their thinking beyond everyday practicalities. The Indian, their human counterpart in the wilderness, represented a logical object of that interest, as well as a being whose nature it was worth while to know. Thus, John Porteous appears unusual in admitting to a relative that "I rely nearly as much on the acco⁺ of Indian Sojourners as yourself. . . ." Traders valued their knowledge of the red men. It served them day by day and could work to their advantage thereafter. Late in life Robert Stuart, for example, sought the office of Commissioner of Indian Affairs. In correspondence with Senator William Woodbridge of Michigan he noted his qualification of "long and general knowledge of Indian relations." When opponents of his appointment charged Stuart with abolitionism, he denied it, calling his previous belief a mere flirtation with an impossible ideal. However, when they charged also that he had overmuch influence in the wilderness, Stuart followed a different tack. Far from denying it, he considered it a merit—one *"equal to about six Regiments of Infantry."* [22]

Most traders, of course, were unconcerned with prerequisites for exalted positions. Their motivation for knowing and describing the Indian stemmed from other sources. Donald Mackenzie, for example, hoped to end his days in a snug cottage with book and pen, as well as dog and gun, providing the world a "full-narration" of fur-trade life. In this Mackenzie failed; but others succeeded. And even when the impulse was less pretentious, traders showed an interest, if not always an engrossment, in the red man. This interest, no matter what its source, often found expression in fur-trade records. John McLean noted that he composed his lengthy narrative mainly "to while away many lonely and wearisome hours which are the lot of the Indian trader. . . ." In a discussion of the journals and debt books kept at Hudson's Bay Company posts, former trader Isaac Cowie indicated some reasons, or instigations, for commenting on the natives. These records not only apprised successors of the characters of individual Indians, they served as safety valves for weary tempers as well. A trader could afford a vicarious and harmless airing of "his private opinion of some influential and unbearable Indian'' via the written word. In addition to this, their superiors often prodded men in wilderness posts. Inspired by Sir John Sinclair's statistical studies of Scotland, Roderic McKenzie devised a pamphlet to be circulated among the wintering partners of the North West Company. With the pamphlet to guide their gathering of information, they would become the counterparts of the parish clergy in Sinclair's efforts. The printer failed to complete the pamphlets, which would have run to fifty or sixty pages; but McKenzie provided his subordinates with synopses of it. The first sections dealt with plant life, animal life, and geography. But McKenzie, himself a fur-trade veteran, devoted most space to the aborigines:

The *Natives,* the Origin and meaning of the names of Tribes, Whence they Came, How far Distant, in what direction, by what means, their ancient and present State of Population, the cause of their increase and decrease, Number of Families, Number of Men, Women and Children in each Family, and the Number of Souls in all—Their Morals, Principles, Statures, Superstition, Idols, Ceremonies, Traditions, Amusements, Disposition, Qualifications, Occupations, Government, Police, Regulations, manners, Customs, Industry, Economy, Food and manner of Preparing it, Habitations, Utensils, Vessels, Dresses, Ornaments   Arms, Instruments, manner of making War, Tombs, Monuments, Advantages and Disadvantages, Means of Improvement—Eminent Men—General Character of each Tribe.[23]

This, of course, would scarcely please a modern anthropologist. Nevertheless, it represents a large order upon the curiosity of wilderness businessmen.

Traders did, however, at times rather maddeningly avoid generalization or elaboration. When George Davenport, for example, reported to his superior a sanguinary encounter between the Sioux and the Sac-Fox, he limited himself to description. Though he wrote extensive comments, and though he had added inducement in the reported involvement of some white cattle drovers, not an adjective or an adverb betrayed his sentiment or attitudes. In such cases, significance (though a somewhat imponderable one) most likely resides in the absence of telling words, phrases, or intimations. Occasionally, this forbearance assumes truly amazing proportions; witness Hugh Faries' Rainy Lake diary entry in which he noted, with seeming *savoir-faire*, that during the previous night's debauch "the Cancre had his testicles pulled out by one of his wives, through jealousy." Aside from the terse observation that "the Cancre" would probably die, Faries did not surrender to what would appear to be an overwhelming inducement to expatiate on Indian nature.

An obvious explanation is that the man's sensibilities had become so jaded that the import of the affair was lost to him. True as this may have been in some cases, other explanations for reticence present themselves. Lack of time, as well as faulty physical circumstances, restricted the diary-keepers' comments. Thus, a great difference exists between the skeleton-like journals of David Thompson, containing little beyond geographical information, and the lengthy narrative in which he took time to elaborate. Francis Chardon set down the problem of deciding the noteworthiness of occurrences he witnessed, but left the solution to a higher tribunal. In his Fort Clark journal for February 24, 1836, he noted: "Can find nothing to record worthy the attention of Posterity—unless the fact of an Indian horse falling down the bank and breaking his neck may be so considered—This however I leave to be decided by the learned." [24]

The descriptive and narrative nature of traders' writings seems to have stemmed in part from conscious design. This is apparent, for example, in Alexander Mackenzie's introduction to his narrative of explorations:

I have described whatever I saw with the impressions of the moment which presented it to me. The successive circumstances of my progress are related without exaggeration or display. I have seldom allowed myself to wander into conjecture; and whenever conjecture has been indulged, it will be found, I trust, to be accompanied with the temper of a man who is not disposed to think too highly of himself. . . .

Mackenzie's work falls into the general category of travel literature, and in the above comment he probably performed a ritualistic insistence upon accuracy. As Percy G. Adams has shown, the sting of Dean Swift's closing parody in *Gulliver's Travels* on the veracity of travel writers dictated that such men make an inordinate profession of innocence, "as if they had been caught in the company of shady characters." Given the excellence and generally unembellished tenor of this trader-explorer's book, however, he has done more than engage in a compromising formality. Beyond a stated intent to adhere to the descriptive on the part of men like Mackenzie, awareness of individual differences among Indians probably accounted for the notable lack of generalization in the writings of some traders. The truth expressed by Peter Skene Ogden, that "every Indian is not a hero, nor every female a Penelope," must have kept many traders from uttering comprehensive statements, though it did little to deter Ogden.[25]

Because homogeneity is too often imposed upon the thinking of past ages, the individuality of perspective among fur traders bears mention. They were not of a piece in origin, sophistication, circumstances, success, or temper. An intriguing demonstration of this appears in the traders' reactions to a particular primitive phenomenon—the cedar bark strip skirts worn by women on the lower Columbia. In his first reference to the Chinooks, Alexander Henry briefly mentioned this garb, remarked that its wearer was "by no means shy," and went on to other things. Similarly, David Thompson, an admirer of the ankle-length dresses of the plains women, only mentioned this "rude kilt" but added that the women who were dressed "looked much better" than those going naked. Astorian Robert Stuart also contented himself with simple description of Columbia River fashions, but others felt called upon to go beyond this. In his recollections, the Irishman Ross Cox evidenced moral outrage in writing that the Chinook dress "in calm weather, or in an erect position, served all the purposes of concealment, but in a breeze, or when indulging their favorite position of squatting, formed a miserable shield in defence of decency. . . ."[26]

With tolerance, a bit of frivolity, and conceivably a commentary on those like Cox, Alexander Ross described the garment as praiseworthy for "its simplicity, or rather for its oddity, but it does not screen nature from the prying eye; yet it is remarkably convenient on many occasions. In a calm the sails lie close to the mast, metaphorically speaking, but when the wind blows the bare poles are seen.'' Finally, Gabriel Franchère made a positive defense of the bark strand, knee-length skirt by noting that when the women were standing ''it drapes them fairly enough; and when they squat down in their manner, it falls between their legs leaving nothing exposed but the bare knees and thighs.'' Fur traders, like the rest of humankind, saw things with their own eyes, not precisely with the eyes of their culture.[27]

Finally, preference of sources deserves some mention. With few exceptions the authenticity and validity of published fur-trade journals appear to be above question. However, because fur-trade narratives roughly fit the genre of travel literature, they partake of the failings common to that type of writing. Percy G. Adams' recent analysis of these works indicates the frequency with which travel authors borrowed from one another. To a limited degree, traders plagiarized. A book by John Dunn uses a great deal of material from Alexander Mackenzie and Thomas Simpson, only part of which is identified as to origin. Edward Umfreville seems to have lifted an example of trader-Indian discourse from a manuscript written years before by James Isham but not yet published when Umfreville wrote. Reprehensible as it may strike the modern reader, borrowing does not loom overly large in the context of this study. So long as a prospective fur-trade author followed the logical course and plagiarized fellow-traders, the practice does not nullify the value of any particular work.[28]

Occasionally, however, a work excites suspicion on other grounds. At times, traders seemed to challenge their readers' credulity with tales that bear the marks of fabrication. In the first section of his two-part work, Alexander Henry the elder included a lavish portion of cannibalism, impressive Indian oratory, and personal hair-breadth escapes. Indeed, he sorely tempts his readers to mutter an ''amen'' to his reference to these affairs as being ''more like dreams than realities, more like fiction than truth!'' Milo Milton Quaife's insistence that the Henry narrative must be irreproachable because Francis Parkman relied heavily upon it does not still one's skepticism. Conceivably, Henry made a compromise between crude and uninspiring fur-trade realities and the demands of the reading public by incorporating some lurid tales in his "Part One" while making "Part Two" a conventional narrative of the wilderness life he knew. Similarly, in the case of John Long, one can hope that his description of the "turkey snake" serves only as an indicator of his aptitude for portraying reptiles. According to Long's narrative, this unique creature decoyed wild turkeys by mimicking them, pierced them with its spearlike tail when they approached, and quickly devoured them with its double row of teeth. Most people have forgiven Long his "turkey snake": Reuben Gold Thwaites, who edited his narrative, remarked only that such a species "cannot be identified," and a recent bibliographer did not allow Long's singular snake to keep him from calling the work "the most valuable record of Indian life and the fur trade of the period." Most authorities accept these works, for there is the ring of plausibility about those parts of Long that do not dwell on "turkey snakes" and those of Henry that do not recount cannibalism or other sensational activities.[29]

From the perspective of this study, the most notable group of questionable fur-trade sources are those purporting to be the works of the mountain men of the far West. In the middle and late nineteenth century many of these appeared. Some, of course, merit honest consideration. The writings of Warren Angus Ferris, Osborne Russell, and Zenas Leonard appear reliable. Even these, however, occasionally try the most flexible credulity. At one point Leonard quoted the hardened mountain man, Thomas Fitzpatrick, as saying by way of description of an encounter with Indians: " 'My noble steed than him, I would defy the whole Indian world to produce a stouter, swifter, or better, was now brought to the test. He started with the velocity of the reindeer. . . .' " [30] Fitzpatrick was literate, but he probably would have relied upon less exalted phraseology to describe a close brush with death at the hands of Indians. Other works deserve only guarded use—the reminiscences of "Uncle Dick" Wootton and Jim Beckwourth, for example. One might argue that even the mendacious Beckwourth never conjured up a "turkey snake" and that by such criteria he deserves as much attention as Long. However, Long became fanciful only rarely and was in this respect far outdone by the mulatto, Beckwourth.

In a recent essay William Goetzmann reasoned that the mountain man is more accurately portrayed as "Jacksonian Man" than as offcast of civilization or as wilderness hero of mythical proportions. Utilizing the terminology of Richard Hofstadter and Marvin Myers, Goetzmann viewed these men as "expectant capitalists" and "venturous conservatives," men who went into the great West to make a stake in civilized life and who to a surprising degree succeeded in doing it.[31] This reassessment, while cloaking the mountain man in the unaccustomed garb of substance, does not erase the shortcomings of their writings as sources for this study. The mountain men occupied an atypical position in the fur trade. Because they usually acted as trappers, not as traders, their relations with the natives were different from those of other men in the business. Their perspective—generally a more tenuous and hazardous one—colored their thinking, and not to the red man's advantage. This condition, along with America's lurid fascination with its closing frontier, helps to account for the deplorably sanguinary character of their published works. Moreover, various of the mountain men relied upon amanuenses. Whatever their aspirations and accomplishments in the sphere of liberal capitalism, many lacked training adequate for the clear expression of sentiments and beliefs. When ghost writers took up their burden, posterity could only guess whose feelings had been depicted. Consequently, the mountain men appear hereafter in a supporting role—not to expound their own views of savagery, but to lend an impressionistic substantiation to the views of others. The educated, middle-class traders, upon whose evidence the bulk of this study is based, had little trouble expressing themselves. While active, they wrote meaningful journals and letters. And later, if they desired to elaborate such efforts into frontier narratives, they possessed the ability to turn out readable if not inspired works.

2. OBJECTIVE APPRAISALS

IN MARCH OF 1831 AN UNIDENTIFIED TRADER RECORDED IN THE FORT
William journal his feelings regarding a singularly outrageous
Indian act. Under the severe deprivation of a far North winter, a
red man had been journeying toward the post with his family.
Feeling that his wife and children impeded his own progress toward
safety, he abandoned them, and then managed to reach Fort William,
reporting that the unfortunate ones had perished along the
way. Though a party from the post found that some of the group
had died, others had endured to give the lie to the Indian's
seemingly foolproof rationale for going on alone. In the post record
the unknown chronicler showed the man no mercy. "Unnatural
wretch," "inhuman wretch," and "unnatural miscreant" appeared
in one brief entry excoriating the nature of that particular
native. Sorely pressed as he may have been, however, the trader did
not generalize; he limited his comments to that one "unnatural
wretch," and did nothing to suggest that such conduct was representative.[1]

In a similar, though not unique instance, William Aitkin of the
early Minnesota trade penned an anguished letter to his superior
relating the apparently unprovoked murder of his son by natives of
the area. The aggrieved father had bitter things to say; but he
avoided what must have been the compelling temptation to dwell
upon the universal dastardliness of Indian character. He argued
that red men had been shown overmuch indulgence, but only the
murderers of his son were labeled "monsters." Recently, Dorothy
Johansen has commented on a like reluctance of Rocky Mountain
trappers and traders to make blanket condemnations of the red race:
"Unlike the small farmers who carried civilization into Kentucky's

bloody ground, drove the Cherokees from their lands, and finagled the reduction of Oregon's reservations, the mountain man could and did distinguish between friend and enemy, good Indian and bad.'' Basically, this held true for all the fur-trade frontier. Moreover, the distinctions went beyond a simple alignment of friends and enemies. Traders made differentiations of greater variety and wider scope. Unlike the waves of American people who followed them, fur traders possessed sufficient understanding of the Indians to recognize the almost endless variety within their way of life.[2]

Objectively, the traders categorized Indians according to observable characteristics of person and culture. Their objectivity did not, of course, equal the formalized or scientific methodology associated with the term in modern times. They were largely men of action, not men of thought. They were as lacking in philosophical objectivity as most men. Nevertheless, they frequently transcended opinionated narrowness. George Simpson (a man little given to introspection) readily recognized the influence of subjective determinants upon his views, though he rarely allowed sufficiently for them. Late in his two-volume narrative, which chronicled a trip around the world as well as describing wilderness conditions, Simpson remarked on the posthouse at Kamishloff, the first station inside Russia after leaving Siberia. Finding the posthouse ''filthy and wretched,'' the fur-trade administrator and his party sought shelter in a peasant's hut. ''As a curious instance of the extent to which a traveller's feelings influence his opinions,'' Simpson observed, ''I set down this village as 'miserable' in the first draft of my journal; while Captain [John Dundas] Cochrane, who had here 'received the kindest attentions,' lauded it as 'pretty.' ''[3] Simpson's perceptive recognition was by no means singular. In regard to the Indians, traders often displayed a more or less conscious reliance upon criteria of categorization without the self—thus describing the *object* rather than reflecting the *subject*.

For all the differences that traders saw in the aborigines, they made no great effort to demonstrate that dissimilar racial stocks were involved. Among those who expressed themselves on the subject of Indian origins, some subscribed to the Judaic theory popularized by James Adair, while others held to the later substantiated position that the Indians had migrated from northeastern Asia. The consistently jaundiced James McKenzie of the North West Company favored the former, noting of the Israelites: ''. . . they were ungrateful, so are the Indians.''[4] However, some traders, whose ideas did not fit neatly into either of these theories, did detect racial diversity among the North American natives.

In his description of the Nipigon country, Duncan Cameron noted that all of Indian society shared a common root—''except the Esquimaux, who by their long beards and filthy ways of living quite differ from all the Indians.'' Those traders who went far enough north to see the Eskimo doubted that his ethnic background was the same as that of the Indian. He was neither Jew nor Asiatic. Thomas Simpson, trader and explorer for the Hudson's Bay Company, recognized the marked distinctions among Indians generally, but did not ascribe disparate racial beginnings to them. However, late in the 1830's at the mouth of the Coppermine River he encountered Eskimos and tellingly compared them to the Indians in his party:

The slender, agile figure of the latter was strikingly contrasted with the square, rugged forms of these natives of the sea. It seemed as if . . . I had together before me descendants of the nomadic Tartar and the sea-roving Scandinavian, two of the most dissimilar and widely separate races of the ancient world.

David Thompson and John McLean, two intelligent men with many years' experience in the far North, concurred in Simpson's judgment; both considered the Eskimo racially separate and a product of northern Europe.[5]

A few traders saw ethnic differences elsewhere in the Indian world. Peter Pond, who was instrumental in pushing trade into the extreme Northwest, felt that the disparate-origins theory explained much of the strife that typified what he called the Indians of the East and those of the West. The people who had populated North America came from two distinct stocks, one most likely European, the other probably Siberian. Indeed, Pond went so far as to describe a line which separated the two—a line running from northwestern

Missouri to the middle of the northern border of British Columbia. For all its apparent simplicity, Pond's explanation contains bothersome discrepancies. Elsewhere in his memoir one gets the impression that he meant to describe a line more nearly paralleling the Rocky Mountains, a construction which would have accorded with the thinking of various later observers. Moreover, his line did not impose meaning upon as much inter-Indian conflict as he implied. It did nothing to explain, for instance, the sanguinary struggle raging in the western Great Lakes region between Siouan and Algonquian tribes. The following statement in regard to the inhabitants of the "Plaines immenses" almost defies explanation: "All of these tribes appear to have the same origin, and they speak a language which has much affinity with that of the Eskimos of the coast of Labrador." That Pond saw a relationship between the Algonquian Nascopies of Labrador—not the Eskimos—and the Algonquian plainsmen—such as the Arapaho, Cheyenne, and Blackfeet—is probably the most generous interpretation one can make of this statement. In the view of his contemporary, Roderic McKenzie, Pond "thought himself a Philosopher and was odd in his manners." Nevertheless, he seriously considered the sources of the North American peoples.[6]

James Mackay, a shadowy but nonetheless important figure in both the Canadian and American trade around the turn of the nineteenth century, also attempted to differentiate racially among tribes other than the Eskimos. He wrote that the Indians "seem to be Descendants of Different nations from different parts of the Earth." Observers such as Simpson distinguished between Eskimo and Indian largely on the basis of obvious physical differences, but Mackay drew racial distinctions among peoples lacking such striking bodily dissimilarities. He granted that the rudeness of the Indians' condition made them all appear the same; but their languages, upon which he centered his analysis, were as divergent as those of "Otaheite and Siberia." Although Mackay categorized in an unclear fashion, some things are evident. He considered the Eskimo completely distinct, human only in bodily form (even in that deficient) and a migrant from northwestern Europe. As Mackay worked his way south into groups about which he probably knew much more, he lumped some of the major tribes of the Algonquian stock into a race and credited them to northeastern Asia. Tribes farther to the south had racial distinctness also, but he did not hazard a guess as to their geographical source.[7]

With Mackay on the 1795 expedition into Indian country that inspired his notes on Indian tribes was a young Welshman named John Evans, who may have worked an exotic influence on Mackay's thinking. Because of a revival in the popularity of the Madoc story—the tradition that Prince Madoc of Wales had colonized somewhere in North America in the twelfth century—Evans came to America to identify and re-Christianize the ''Welsh'' Indians. Mackay's document does not make clear whether the ''Madocians'' of that time were Comanches or Mandans; but, whichever it was, their comprehension of the Welsh language was found to be miserably lacking. Notwithstanding Evans' failure, some things in Mackay's document smack of the young foreigner's thinking. His reference to the then recently popularized ''Otaheite'' suggests more nearly the parlance of London salons than the terminology of a wilderness businessman. The theory of disparate origins itself would allow for the Madocian theory. Indeed, Mackay described a tribe, apparently the Comanches, in terms reminiscent of the Welsh thesis:

They are more honest, peaceable & sincere in all their transactions—friendly to each other & courteous to strangers   Their manners more approaching civilization, their skin more fair, their countenance more open and agreeable & their features in a Great Degree, resembling that of white people.[8]

Mackay, one would suppose, would certainly be disappointed that Evans, armed with a full command of oral and written Welsh and a dictionary of the language, failed to communicate with a group so admirable. Moreover, Mackay's reluctance to designate a point of origin for the tribes south of the Algonquian peoples may have been a result of Evans' inability to identify the Welsh Indians. Perhaps he did not wish to presume knowledge where a scholar had failed.

Beyond such rare efforts to categorize racially, traders far more frequently attempted to categorize by environment. In correspondence with Henry Rowe Schoolcraft, Thomas Fitzpatrick drew analogies between the American Indians and the ancient Israelites. The possibility of an ancestral connection evidently appealed to the Rocky Mountain trader. He paired the medicine lodge with the tabernacle; noted the avoidance of women at unclean times of their life; and suggested an identity between the two elaborate systems of sacrifices, anointings, ablutions, and purifications. But, however intriguing, Fitzpatrick considered the ethnic tie more apparent than real. It failed to satisfy him, and he took a fairly sophisticated position in arguing to Schoolcraft that "where a barbarous people have been found, I have come to the conclusion that man in that state is pretty much the same sort of being throughout, except what difference may naturally arise from the physical adaptation of the country they inhabit in supplying their wants." [9]

That Indians varied according to the conditions under which they lived was clearly evident to fur traders. Indeed, those subscribing to an environmental explanation of Indian differences occasionally employed an amazingly simple form of anthropogeography. They held that Indians differed according to the latitude in which they lived. James Adair, operating in the mid-eighteenth century in what was to become the southeastern United States, felt that at least physical attributes were determined by distance from the tropics. Thus, the Chickasaw were far taller and stronger than the more southern Choctaw, though only two degrees of latitude separated them and despite the fact that their languages indicated close kinship in the recent past. Adair's readers might well have questioned the physical superiority of the Chickasaw, for whom the author had unbounded respect, because later in his book Adair stated that the Choctaw, for whom he had great contempt, were unexcelled as runners and ballplayers. Such a minor inconsistency, however, would not hamper a man who used most of a lengthy work to prove the Judaic origins of the American Indians. [10]

Philip Turnor of the Hudson's Bay Company posited an idea similar to Adair's in his discussion of the relations between the Crees and the Chipewyans farther to the north. When these groups met, the Crees habitually provoked quarrels and ultimately emerged victorious, even when outnumbered by their stouter and more hardy northern neighbors. Turnor felt justified in generalizing his observations into a formula, for the Chipewyans in turn treated the Eskimos who bordered them on the north in a similarly harsh fashion, while Crees suffered ill treatment at the hands of tribes to the south of them. *"I believe it has been found,"* he concluded, *"that the farther North the more Peaceable the Indians."* [11]

Others felt that severity of climate and condition, regardless of latitude, did much to determine the nature of the Indians. Most obviously this would apply to the natives of the Great Basin, who continually triggered the contempt and the pity of those who came among them. Most of the men who recorded their impressions of these people felt that their inferiority resulted from their environment, not that their environment had been forced upon them because of their inferiority. Rufus Sage, for example, cited as evidence of this a "Digger" child raised away from the rigors of the Great Basin who developed into completely normal, indeed apparently superior, manhood. Similar logic appears in the writings of David Thompson, who, in explaining the distinct differences that he saw among the Crees, noted that those living along the margins of Hudson's Bay were smaller and less manly than those who enjoyed the milder climate farther inland.[12]

Where Turnor, Thompson, Adair, and others may have obtained such concepts, except from observation, is hard to say. Having had training suitable for geographers, Turnor and Thompson may have encountered the ideas of such eighteenth-century thinkers as Giovanni Vico and Charles de Montesquieu who stressed the importance of geography and climate in influencing culture. Moreover, environmentalism has a lengthy and impressive lineage, being evident at least from the time of Herodotus. Thus, the environmental notions of these frontiersmen were a rather common part of the intellectual baggage of the contemporary culture.

Although traders occasionally used a narrow anthropogeography, they more commonly rested their environmental classifications upon the distinctions between fisher and hunter, woodsman and plainsman. They saw that cultures differed according to accommoda-

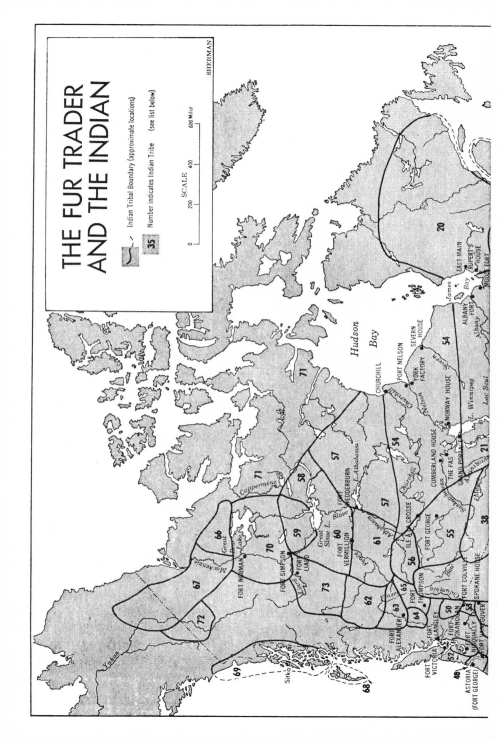

THE FUR TRADER AND THE INDIAN

Indian Tribal Boundary (approximate locations)

35 Number indicates Indian Tribe (see list below)

SCALE

0   200   400   600 Miles

SHERMAN

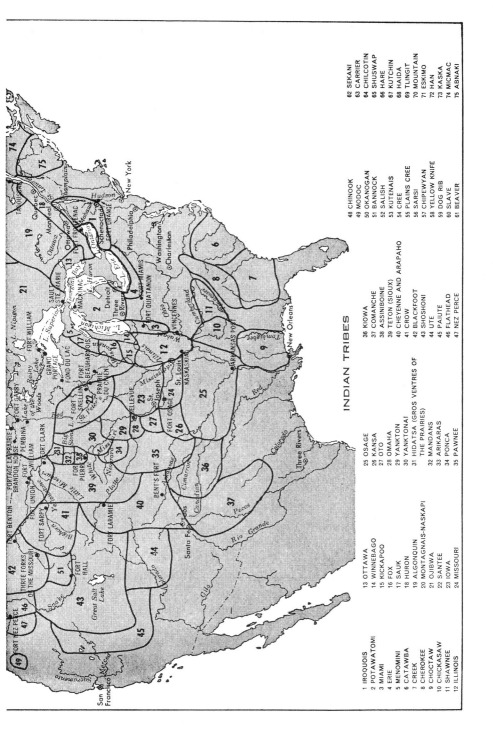

INDIAN TRIBES

1 IROQUOIS
2 POTAWATOMI
3 MIAMI
4 ERIE
5 MENOMINI
6 CATAWBA
7 CREEK
8 CHEROKEE
9 CHOCTAW
10 CHICKASAW
11 SHAWNEE
12 ILLINOIS

13 OTTAWA
14 WINNEBAGO
15 KICKAPOO
16 FOX
17 SAUK
18 HURON
19 ALGONQUIN
20 MONTAGNAIS-NASKAPI
21 OJIBWA
22 SANTEE
23 IOWA
24 MISSOURI

25 OSAGE
26 KANSA
27 OTO
28 OMAHA
29 YANKTON
30 YANKTONAI
31 HIDATSA (GROS VENTRES OF
    THE PRAIRIES)
32 MANDANS
33 ARIKARAS
34 PONCA
35 PAWNEE

36 KIOWA
37 COMANCHE
38 ASSINIBOINE
39 TETON (SIOUX)
40 CHEYENNE AND ARAPAHO
41 CROW
42 BLACKFOOT
43 SHOSHONI
44 UTE
45 PAIUTE
46 FLATHEAD
47 NEZ PERCE

48 CHINOOK
49 MODOC
50 OKANOGAN
51 BANNOCK
52 SALISH
53 KUTENAIS
54 CREE
55 PLAINS CREE
56 SARSI
57 CHIPEWYAN
58 YELLOW KNIFE
59 DOG RIB
60 SLAVE
61 BEAVER

62 SEKANI
63 CARRIER
64 CHILCOTIN
65 SHUSWAP
66 HARE
67 KUTCHIN
68 HAIDA
69 TLINGIT
70 MOUNTAIN
71 ESKIMO
72 HAN
73 KASKA
74 MICMAC
75 ABNAKI

tions to environment and that the characters of the peoples within these separate cultures were markedly diverse. The fisher not only lived differently from the hunter; he thought, acted, and appeared differently as well. Environment and way of life, then, far more than race, or even tribal stock, accounted for variations among tribes. George Simpson expressed this outlook when he wrote:

The Sarcees, now inhabiting the banks of the Bow River, were originally Chipewyans from Athabasca; and they resemble rather the Blackfeet than their own original stock. Again, the Crees, on migrating from the bush into the plains, exchanged the characteristics of their race for those of the tribes among which their southerly advance placed them.[13]

The Columbia River basin and the highlands to the east best illustrate the hunter-fisher dichotomy the traders saw. Fur men frequently traveled through this area, and it afforded them an opportunity to pass quite rapidly from tribes that lived almost solely by fishing to those that lived by the chase. Most of the men who wrote at any length of their experience in this region noted cultural dissimilarities. And these variations went beyond the physical equipment of the peoples involved. To the trader, a Nez Perce and a Clatsop were not the same person, one with a bow, one with a net. Thomas Fitzpatrick, for example, intimated that coastal tribes such as the Chinooks could with "greater propriety be arranged and placed with the Islanders of the Pacific, than with any of the inland tribes. . . ." The trader sensed a correlation—whether coincidental, influential, or causative—between the way of life of a given tribe and that tribe's nature and character. For an extreme example, William Hardisty's comment that tribes living on flesh were darker-skinned than those living on fish admits of varying interpretations. However, Hardisty did recognize a connection between natural setting and human condition.[14]

The Astorian, Robert Stuart, writing of the natives he had seen in the Pacific Northwest, concluded that in spite of an evidently common origin, "no race of people in the world . . . can exhibit a greater variety, with regard to size and appearance. . . ."[15] And this was not random variety; those who lived in one way obviously varied from those who lived in another. In addition to size and appearance, these natives differed in ways more nebulous and less easy of objective determination. Having drawn quasi-scientific distinctions, such observers went on to make others that were more subjective. They expressed likes and dislikes, and the degree of antipathy mounted as the trader made the transition from hunting to fishing cultures. The journey from Flathead country high in the Rockies to Chinook country at the mouth of the Columbia involved not only a physical descent; for the trader, it involved an anthropological descent as well.

Degeneration of respect for the natives that accompanied the trip from mountains to sea appears often in the daily journals kept by traders. On a journey down the Columbia in the summer of 1811, David Thompson remarked on July 6 of having contact with "these friendly Indians," and on the eighth approved of a dance in his honor by the Shahaptin women, only two of whom were naked. But as his down-river course continued, his revulsion mounted. By the eleventh, celebrations at his arrival had become a bit disorderly, and he noted that the Indians were the least regular in behavior of all that he had encountered. On the next day he contemptuously wrote the natives off as "fat, brawny, and naked." [16]

Other men indicated more explicitly their increasing disapprobation as the natives inclined more and more toward a fishing culture. In one of his published works, Alexander Ross, a man of vast experience in the area, compared the tribal subdivisions of the Snake nation. He described the Shoshonis, who subsisted by hunting buffalo, as a tall, slender people who fought and dressed well, were clean of camp and of person, and bold and independent of action. The Snakes proper seemed far different to the Astorian. They lived largely by fishing; they fought and dressed poorly; and they allowed filth to mar their dress and camp. They differed so greatly from the Shoshoni as to appear "as if they had been people belonging to another country." At Celilo Falls, Ross Cox encountered both mounted hunters and pedestrian fishers, and his assessment matched perfectly that of Alexander Ross. "In language, dress, and manners, they appeared to belong to distinct nations," he

concluded. Cox and Gabriel Franchère, both members of the Astoria
venture, exemplify the traders who compounded the indictment by
detecting a decline of morality as they descended the Columbia and
came among people less given to the chase. And well over a hundred
years earlier Pierre Esprit Radisson, after having been abandoned
by Indians south of Lake Winnipeg, reasoned that "those that liveth
on fish uses more inhumanities than those that feed upon flesh." [17]

Traders who used the plainsman-woodsman dichotomy seemed no
less certain of the existence of real differences in character and
culture than those who distinguished between hunter and fisher. As
Edwin Denig put it, "the habits of the prairie Indian differ
essentially from the Indian of the forest. . . ." However, traders
showed far less certainty that one category was superior, the other
inferior. David Thompson probably stated the woodsman-plainsman
duality most clearly. In terms prophetic of Walter Prescott Webb,
he wrote of the Blackfoot confederation that "these great Plains
place them under different circumstances, and give them peculiar
traits of character from those that hunt in the forests." Thompson
then narrowed his scope to include only the Piegans, whose position
in the vanguard of the confederation's advance southwestward made
them somewhat exaggerated specimens of all plains Indians. According to Thompson, they possessed extraordinary fighting ability,
chivalrous bearing, and a martial spirit. Peter Pond, "the caustic
Yankee with the flamboyant spelling," recorded a similar sentiment
in his wonderfully unique orthography: "Ye Yantonose are faro-
shas and Rude in thare Maners Perhaps Oeing in Sum masher to
thare Leadig an Obsger life in the Planes." But the environment of
the plains Indians, even more than their aggressiveness, made them
a fortunate people—"the affluent," as Robert Stuart called them.
They exhibited an independence—like "the air they breathed or the
wind that blew"—and leaders in the trade recognized and sought
to circumvent that self-sufficiency. [18]

Looking off into the subarctic which has never yet yielded the
story of his ultimate fate, crotchety James Knight told that "them
Natives to the Norward are more Savage and brutelike than these
and will drink blood and eat raw flesh and fish and loves it as well as

some does Strong Drink.'' And less dramatically, John McLean, after noting the close tribal affinity between the Crees and the Saulteaux, indicated that they were nonetheless as easily distinguishable ''as an Englishman from a Frenchman.'' [19] Traders knew that to see one Indian was not to see all. The plainsman differed from the woodsman, and he had to be dealt with differently. The fisher differed from the hunter, the Eskimo from the Algonquian, and the Sioux from the Ute. By using methods objective in theory, if not always in application, the trader saw the rich variety within Indian society. To a surprising and commendable degree, he possessed the understanding which allowed him to avoid the handy psychological mechanism of the stereotype. To paraphrase Walter Lippmann, the fur trader tended to see first and then define, not to define first and then see.

One final means of objectively classifying red men, which calls for at least brief attention, involves the brutally simple logic that, as General Philip Sheridan put it, the good Indian was the dead Indian. Excepting the ghost-written, journalistic exercises of the Rocky Mountain trappers, who of course were not traders, there should be little reason to suspect such an attitude among fur men. One might readily assume that economic interest alone would have precluded such a sinister outlook. However, Frederick Merk, in his essay introducing some of George Simpson's journals, seemed to argue the prevalence of that very attitude. According to Merk, it permeated the American fur trade. Since St. Louis, itself a frontier community, served as a nucleus, men in the field had no contact with moderating or nonfrontier influences. The leaders of this trade, operating ''in the midst of its harsh realities,'' knew ''the sordidness and cruelty of savage life, and . . . had little compunction in profiting by its weaknesses and vices.'' Across the boundary to the north, native Canadians shared these harsh convictions about the red men. And even the subject of the work, George Simpson, harbored similar feelings during his early years in the wilderness. Ultimately, according to Merk, the benevolent paternalism of the Hudson's Bay Company moderated Simpson's heartless frontier outlook. However, without outside supervision, Merk wrote, the

Governor would have been as "realistic and hard-bitted as any American or Nor'Wester," that is, he would have felt that "the only good Indian is a dead Indian." "London paternalism and St. Louis individualism gathered each its own fruit." [20]

Many traders showed an utter disinterest in the Indians' welfare. Humanitarianism certainly did not flourish in those surroundings. After remarking that his party refused to buy an Arikara girl who aspired to marriage rather than concubinage, John Luttig closed the day's entry with the following supremely flippant notation: "–chastity.—got this day 21 chickens." In a tone of mordant mockery Francis Chardon compared the death plunge of an old woman to the feats of a contemporary athlete: "One of Sam Patch's leaps, was performed by an Old Woman at the Village this Morning, Who, to Out-do-Sam, instead of Jumping, over the Falls into the water, Made a pitch from the bank of the Village on to the rocks below–Sam beat that if you can–." And Alexander Henry the younger left some classic statements indicating a total lack of concern. At one point in his journal he wrote, "Grande Gueule stabbed Perdrix Blanche with a knife in six places; the latter, in fighting with his wife, fell in the fire and was almost roasted, but had strength enough left, notwithstanding his wounds, to bite her nose off." If one naïvely suspects that Henry may have been trying to bring order out of this chaos, he will be properly disabused by a later passage: "Grande Gueule stabbed Capot Rouge, Le Boeuf stabbed his young wife in the arm, Little Shell almost beat his old mother's brains out with a club, and there was terrible fighting among them. I sowed garden seeds." [21]

Moreover, beyond this indifference to the fate of the natives, traders subjected them to a tremendous amount of written abuse. The literature of the trade fairly teems with blistering diatribes, ordinarily centering on such overworked epithets as "scoundrel" and "rascal." At times these heated verbal exercises became euphemistic if not overt expressions of the chilling sentiment of the frontier tradition. For example, in Labrador in 1799 James McKenzie's party encountered some Indians who told of deaths within their ranks. This, McKenzie noted, "rids the world of a number of rascals," and then added that those remaining were "stupid fellows who unworthily survived the fate of all the rest.'' At the Mandan post in September of 1834 the highly dyspeptic journalist, Francis Chardon, recorded that three of the post's Indians had been killed by enemies while picking fruit along the Missouri. He reacted with the acerbic comment, ''Oh! Plumbs & Cherries! May success attend you–.'' Writing to a business partner from Mackinac, Isaac Todd had occasion to mention approvingly the ''Pasport to the other World'' recently given to an otherwise-minded red man near the post. The theme received rather more precise statement from Francois-Victor Malhiot, a North West Company trader. He readily admitted that there were some good Indians; but he went on to conclude that ''in general if I were able to put them all in a bag and know that Lucifer wanted them, I would give them all to him for a penny!'' [22]

These utterances, however, execrable as they may be, more nearly represent callousness and indifference in the face of human suffering than murderous intent. Spilling ink had far more to recommend it than spilling Indian blood. It was safer, easier, and cheaper. Most importantly, it relieved exasperation without too greatly violating the civilized moral precepts which traders took with them into the wilderness. Thus, Francois-Victor Malhiot, the source of the statement about selling every Indian to the devil for a penny, informed his superiors that though his judgments of the Indians might seem harsh, it was not caused by hatred. ''But, no! May God preserve me from feeling that way toward anyone on earth whatever. . . .'' Similarly, Bela Chapman at Grand Portage looked back upon, reconsidered, and tempered acrimonious commentaries on his Indians. In a letter headed ''Misery Dec'. 11th'' Chapman wrote: ''My Hogs have all come back and cheat and lie and steal, the Devil is not a match for them–.'' Nine days later the ''Fort Misery'' letter book reveals that the harassed trader had sent his ''hogs'' away, adding hopefully ''may they never return.'' On February 4 of the following year, after forbearing to continue an ill-humored essay on a red man for fear of wasting ink and paper, Chapman recognized that in recent entries he had cast some ''bad reflections.'' For these, he wrote, ''I humbly beg pardon and acknowledge my fault for it was in the heat of my passions."²³ Most often, when bedeviled traders indulgently savored the prospect of a general Indian demise, they tellingly resorted to the obliqueness of euphemism. Chardon's applauding "Plumbs & Cherries" and Malhiot's hypothetical transaction with Lucifer suggest that these blunt and unapologetic men tended to accept, with the mind if not always with the heart, the red man's right to existence.

On those rare occasions when traders did straightforwardly counsel decimation of Indian society, they pleaded extenuating circumstances. While leading a Hudson's Bay Company brigade in the Snake country in 1827 and 1828 Peter Skene Ogden wrote menacingly:

Acting for myself, I will not hesitate to say I would willingly sacrifice a year or two to exterminate the whole Snake tribe, women and children excepted. In so doing I could fully justify myself before God and man. Those who live at a distance are of a different opinion. My reply to them is this: Come out and suffer and judge for yourselves if forbearance has not been carried beyond bounds ordained by Scripture and surely this is the only guide a Christian sh'd follow.²⁴

Here it should be recalled, even in the face of our colossal impatience with such misanthropy, that the traders would not have needed a defense or "rationalization" if they had truly believed their own tirades. Nor does it seem likely that in such a statement Ogden contrived disingenuity in order to weaken or circumvent the greater humanity of someone else. In their journals traders essentially soliloquized; in their letters they spoke to men who shared closely their own predilections. They had little reason to dissemble. When men such as Ogden attempted to explain away their occasionally murderous intents, they did so because such designs were as unpalatable to them as to outsiders.

Unlike other frontiers, the fur trade had little place for dead Indians. Almost universally the native was an integral part of the fur-trade operation. He brought in the bulk of the pelts and robes; and, while a person fulfilling that function might never have captured the trader's outright sympathy, his right to existence surely would have gone largely unquestioned. Thus, John Thomas of Moose Fort was by no means fatuously sentimental in informing a fellow trader of his deep concern at the death of the Indian, Otis,qua,keeshick. That he should go on to instruct his colleague to "succour his widow and fine family of little sons" appears no more unusual. Thomas admitted that the Indian was to be lamented, "as he's a great loss to the Honorable Company," and that his wife and children should be aided, "as they may hereafter become of great Service." [25] Certainly, these telling qualifications take the happy glow from our appreciation of the trader's humanity. Nevertheless, if John Thomas did not act precisely in accord with a beneficent ideal, we can at least take comfort in the obvious fact that his serving of mundane, material considerations necessitated solicitous treatment of the survivors of Otis,qua,keeshick. Evidently, traders often served humanity and decency coincidentally with their efforts to follow sound business principles. The American trade of the Rocky Mountains, wherein brigades of trappers scoured the streams for beaver and dealt with the Indians only peripherally, may well be an exception. Even under that system, however, the natives contributed to the harvest of furs.

Aside from the coldly economic concern for the red man, there seems to have existed an interest in him fully as vital, if not as continual. That interest sprang from the recurrent necessity to cooperate for survival. Just as a threat of Indian skulduggery erased the superficial differences between the employees, say, of the Hudson's Bay Company and the American Fur Company, so the specter of starvation minimized the very real disparity between red man and white. And threats to survival were more than isolated or occasional phenomena. The North American wilderness, far from maintaining a happily predictable fullness, often took on fickle and difficult proportions. The literature of the fur trade abounds with instances of famine and outright starvation. One scholar has noted of the Hudson's Bay domain that "the threat to the Company's servants was not from the Indians, whom they so often befriended, and with whom they shared their scanty rations, but from nature." [26]

Under such circumstances, a sanguinary view of Indian society, however repressed and guarded, would have amounted to sheer folly, a luxury the traders could not afford. The stingily capricious character of the Canadian wilderness made this doubly true. Thus when Questach, "Captn. of our Goose Hunters," died at Albany Fort on James Bay in 1784, his passing occasioned real concern. Edward Jarvis, a former London surgeon with thirteen years' service as a trader, had a coffin built and confided in the post journal that, "Myself with all the Indians on the plantation attended the remains of old Captn. Questach to a wooden tomb built in a very permanent manner; he was buried with more solemnity and cere-mony than ever I saw upon like occasion; Gave him the colour half mast high." No doubt, trade policy dictated some of this con-cern, or at least the manifestation of concern; but in a harsh land the loss of Questach was honestly felt—as captain of the goose hunters if not as an individual. When a particularly trusted and helpful Indian at Fort William had been frozen to death, the trader made little display of his feelings. In his journal, however, he could not finish his "melancholy account without expressing my sincere regrets for his loss. . . ."[27]

Of course, these evidences of care stemmed at least partly from self-interest. One cannot enjoy certainty in separating altruism from egoism; but, even maintaining a discreet distance from naïveté, one encounters frequent expressions of apparently uncon-trived regard for fellow humankind. For all the shortness of their tempers, traders did not revel in the misfortunes and hardships that befell the aborigines. In 1828 Green Bay trader John Lawe, for example, wrote to a nearby Indian agent pleading the case of an aged and helpless Menomini who was on his way to ask assistance. In his memoirs, John McLean wrote that once in an altercation he had felled an Indian with a club, and it had appeared that the man would die as a result. This had alarmed McLean: "Was I indeed guilty of the blood of a fellow creature? The thought chilled me with horror." When the company's conservation policy, designed to save fur resources—"the cursed *cruel* Ta boo that is on the Beaver"—de-prived the Indians of the far Northwest of a salable product, J. L. Lewes at Fort Simpson protested. In a heated letter to a fellow trader, he asked rhetorically "is it to be expected that I am to tell the Indians starve, die and be d-m-d but let the Beaver live   any such that may expect that of J. L. L. will be most egregiously mistaken.'' And after viewing the effects of starvation among the Indians of western Oregon, the often irascible Peter Skene Ogden extended complete sympathy : ''It is distressing to see human beings suffer in this way while others are enjoying life subject but to few of its inconveniences, a reward is said to await the deserving . . . at the great day . . . [These Indians] may be found to merit it if not our chance is not great.'' Ogden's solicitude should cause no surprise. Nor was it out of character for James Chambers, whose contempt for the red men seems unexcelled, to confide in his New Year's Day entry that he wished them well in the days ahead.[28]

However much they may have irritated each other, the trader and the Indian shared a community of interests. No doubt, one must view with vigorous skepticism Ramsay Crooks's self-righteous statement of this condition when noting ''the inclination of the 'powers that be' to gag everybody who would protect the Indians. . . .'' His concern here, in the context of a recent government treaty with the natives, sounds maudlin, petulant, and, worst of all, hypocritical. On the other hand, it would be difficult to gainsay the same man's honesty of interest when mentioning governmental arrangements designed to allow ''our 'Red brethren' to reach their hunting grounds in time to do good both to themselves & to us.'' In 1830 Pierre Menard, at the time doubling as fur trader and as Indian subagent, declared to Congressman E. K. Kane that ''you know me well enough to know . . . that I will do justice to the Indians as well as to the Government.''[29] The Congressman may well have accepted the reminder.

The transitory nature of the wrathful and sinister judgments passed upon natives by traders, either straightforwardly or by intimation, indicates that they were products of gross irritation. The tirades reflected the fact that the traders were perturbed far more than they were cognizant of any demonstrable condition in the beings they damned. The speakers revealed themselves and their own circumstances more than the apparent object of their fury, the Indian. Thus, the good Indian–dead Indian hypothesis partakes only superficially of objectivity. For the fur trader, it had little meaning, and that in a subjective context, which consideration will be treated in the following chapter.

3. SUBJECTIVE APPRAISALS

WHEN PETER SKENE OGDEN REMARKED ON THE "STATELY INDEPEND-
ence" which is "morally distinctive of the native hunter of the wilds
of North America" and which distinguished him from the "ignoble
fisher of its waters,"[1] his preference was based on an objective
criterion. Such criteria appear often in the fur-trade literature, but
even more frequently traders tended to distinguish and evaluate
Indians, not in terms of what they really were, but in terms of their
relationship with the fur traders. As noted earlier, the trader by
essentially objective methods perceived the diversity within Indian
life. However, an even fuller variety presented itself when he cast
off the demands, restrictions, and pretensions of objectively judging
the red men and gave rein to his hopes, interests, and preferences.

The fur trade was an economic endeavor, and because economic
interpretations of human actions have so long been a major theme in
historical writing, it is appropriate to examine first those distinctions drawn among groups of Indians on the basis of economic
realities—distinctions made in terms of how well a given tribe fitted
into the scheme of the fur trade. The fur trader was prone to see the
worst in tribes that fitted poorly into the trade and conversely
thought highly of those that fit well.

Harvesting furs represented the Indian's most evident and direct
means for harmonizing with the economic spirit of the trade.
Duncan M'Gillivray bluntly stated this fundamental fact: "With
respect to the Fur trade, whatever peculiarities each tribe of Indians
may have, and however various their customs manners and language
may be, they are divided by the North West Company into two
classes; those who have furs and those who have none." This is, first
of all, a policy statement of a harshly realistic business enterprise;

and it defines a basically objective means of distinction, for quantity of furs possessed is measurable and demonstrable. Often, however, this discrimination manifested itself in a less pointed and more subjective form. M'Gillivray, never one to sugar-coat things, stated elsewhere that the Indians' reception by the traders was exactly proportionate to their fur-getting performance. The trader met those who came empty-handed with indifference and contempt. Men of less candor and indifference, and possibly less brutality, than M'Gillivray withdrew to the more discreet haziness of subjectivity. Edward Umfreville of the early Canadian trade showed less respect for the Sarsis than any other tribe discussed in his book—their women, for example, were the "most ordinary" of any he had seen, though liberal with their favors. As a possible if unintended explanation for his dislike, Umfreville commented revealingly in the same context that, "they bring us very few peltries, and those ill drest." Such men would not declare that the only good Indians were those who had furs. Their evaluations were, however, colored by this consideration.[2]

For a variety of reasons, the lists of "have" and "have-not" tribes fluctuated greatly—tribal areas were continually changing in reaction to frontier pressure, good beaver grounds were soon denuded, fashions were fickle, and Indians were sometimes well-disposed and sometimes not. Some groups, however, acted as perennial drags on the trade. The Arikara tribe was always the *bete noir* of the American trade, at least in part because it was unable or unwilling to make good beaver hunts. Daniel Lamont of the Upper Missouri Outfit, writing to Pierre Chouteau, Jr., inveighed against the Arikaras for their outrages, suggested a governmental policy of extermination for them, and added significantly, "their trade has ever been a losing one."[3]

Economic considerations must also have entered into the consistently disparaging appraisals of the far West river-and-coast tribes. These peoples placed little emphasis upon hunting. They excelled in fishing and trading, and in the latter capacity they acted as gatherers and middlemen when Russian, British, and American traders first operated on the upper Pacific coast. From the early fur-trade perspective, they fulfilled a useful function. By 1793, however, Alexander Mackenzie had pushed overland to the ocean, and within a few years white traders were in the high reaches of New Caledonia at the source of the furs. Thus, the coast tribes's role as gatherers and middlemen diminished in importance, and traders probably lost respect for them proportionately. However, available sources do not demonstrate positively that the loathing and disgust these people elicited in the nineteenth century represented a deterioration.

Until the mid-1820's, when buffalo "robes" became fashionable, the Indians of the high plains at least roughly fit the category of "have-not" tribes. Consequently, though not as evidently as with the Pacific coast tribes, disapproval of the plains peoples appears, at times, to have clearly economic grounds. For example, Alexander Henry the younger, who found little to admire in any Indian, distinguished between the woodland Crees and their brothers of the plains. The former could buy the things they needed, while the latter comprised a "useless set of lazy fellows—a nuisance both to us and to their neighbors." In an account of the Red River country in the last decade of the eighteenth century, John McDonnell of the North West Company expressed a similar sentiment in regard to the Assiniboines. They took no beaver or otter—only wolf, fox, and buffalo robes. McDonnell had little trouble in recognizing their unsavory attributes, and it seems evident that these stemmed from the fact that they constituted the "worst hunters" of any Indians in the Northwest trade.[4]

George Simpson, however, felt that judgment of the plains Indians should be reserved. He believed that their independence born of comparative abundance—and not their miserable performance as hunters or the barrenness of their land—explained the bad fur returns of the plains Indians. The elder Alexander Henry, who visited the Assiniboines in the 1770's, carried the same theme even further. Henry found some good things to say about these Indians, possibly because, unlike the Crees with whom he had traded previously, they would exchange valuable skins for trinkets. The buffalo furnished their wants, and they could afford to be generous if so inclined. This admission notwithstanding, the practical outcome seemingly was consistent: according to an explicit statement by Duncan M'Gillivray, the Indians of the plains met less generous treatment from the trader, at least in the early years of the trade. It seems reasonable to assume that this was a general practice.[5]

The causative relation between furs and affection, although patent, is not as simple as it appears. Not only was the Indian without furs unappreciated; this lack of regard also caused him to do even more to alienate the traders' affections. Furs bought things—liquor, weapons, baubles. The Indian without furs received none of these things, and he could become an active nuisance and a threat to the trader who distributed the bounty so inequitably. Such an Indian could be an easy prey for a traditional enemy bearing modern weapons traded for furs. This at least partially explains the Iroquois's decimation of their western neighbors, the Crees's terrorizing of the Chipewyans, the Chippewas' expulsion of the Sioux from their forest homeland, and other power realities of the Indian frontier. To be without a trader—either because of remoteness or barrenness—put the red man in an unenviable position; to be in the power of such Indians put the trader into a circumstance fully as unenviable. The jealousy, hatred, and vengeful spirit of the "have-not" Indians, constant realities of the fur-trade frontier, elicited little comment, although they are occasionally mentioned, as in Ross Cox's *The Columbia River*.[6] When he wrote his memoir, Cox had long since left the trade and was a newspaperman in Ireland. The men actively engaged in the fur trade could scarcely be expected to justify the hatreds of people who despised them.

Traders, then, tended to distinguish subjectively between Indians with furs and Indians without. However, they considered other economic factors, also. The Indian from a barren domain or with long-established cultural patterns which prevented the taking of furs was uncooperative because of circumstances and not necessarily because he was contrary. But when the red men displayed an outright malice of intent in their failures to cooperate, their actions evidently colored the traders' appraisals and rendered those appraisals wrathful.

It can be argued that such obloquy was a product of the moment, that the trader unburdened himself with the awareness that he was speaking from pique, and that he really did not believe that the uncooperative tribe was literally more filthy, licentious, thievish, lazy, or dishonest than any other group. But in the fur-trade literature these diatribes appear without explanation of mitigating factors, although sometimes from context it can be inferred that obstruction of the trader's designs and not reasoned judgment triggered the outburst. When Edwin Denig, usually a calm and perceptive observer, insisted that the Arikaras, whom he heartily despised, possessed along with all their other shortcomings a uniquely large and prolific species of lice, it seems reasonable to suppose that he spoke from passion.[7] Since he did not footnote this interesting revelation, hinting that the reader should view it with skepticism, he meant it to stand. The size of their lice was included in Denig's appraisal of a specific tribe; and, because it does not lend itself to material demonstration (at least from our perspective), it has to be considered part of a subjective evaluation. That observation does not tell much about vermin, and perhaps even less about the Arikaras; but it does tell something about Denig's attitudes.

Beyond lacking furs, the native practice of exacting duties on trade goods passing through their territory caused traders to view red men with disdain. Under this system, when the hearts of the red men were especially bad, the tariff—generally in the form of a bribe to a powerful chief—might mature into a full-blown embargo or even simple pillaging. These devices posed especially knotty problems in the traders' gradual ascent of the Missouri in the years, roughly, between 1790 and 1830. In thus obstructing the trade the Indians thought not only of gaining booty for themselves but also of depriving enemies, or even friends, in more remote areas of white men's goods. As the vanguard of the trade approached the Otoes, Omahas, Poncas, Pawnees, Sioux, and various others, these tribes practiced various forms of extortion and took their places in history as incorrigible rascals. But the Arikaras had the worst reputation. While they could halt the traders and exact bribes, they did; and long after that tactic was ineffective they continued to harass and commit desultory outrages at any opportunity. The literature teems with heated denunciations of the Arikaras; they might easily be considered the most despised of western tribes.

A contrarily inclined tribe could, of course, raise itself in the estimation of the trader. Cooperativeness, like possession of furs, fluctuated. George Simpson indicates how a tribe could plumb the depths of disrepute and then restore itself to grace. In the violent days preceding the merger of the Hudson's Bay and North West companies, Simpson, who was at Lake Athabasca (the focal point of the final crisis), vilified the Chipewyans of the surrounding territory. He could not see a solitary good trait in their nature. They exhibited a low cunning; they were false, cowardly, covetous, treacherous, and had not a particle of honor: "In short I conceive the Chipewyan character disgraceful to human nature." The Governor made a vastly different assessment seven years later in 1828, when he assumed a posture which for George Simpson seems fawning. The Chipewyans, he wrote, were not only fine hunters but were exceptionally provident as well—they took the beaver with such care and wisdom that the animal was on the increase in their lands. They never asked for liquor, wrote Simpson, and they had agreeably accepted the termination of the credit system in favor of barter.[8]

During the last tragic years of competition between the two companies, the Chipewyans had done what all Indians did when white men quarreled around them: they played the situation to the utmost and made themselves perfectly abominable. With the conflict past and order restored, the Governor saw a much different Chipewyan. Contrary to what Frederick Merk argued in *Fur Trade and Empire,* London paternalism did not mellow George Simpson during these years. Instead, trade realities had changed from chaotic to orderly. Simpson admitted as much in his appraisals of the Chipewyans. He had conceded in 1821 that, while the North West Company, his dire enemy, had held sovereign control over these Indians, they were "timid, simple and tractable." At the time of writing, however, they acted with an unseemly independence, treated the traders with indifference, neglected the hunts, and practised all the vices they had learned. And directly after his warm endorsement of the same group in 1828 the Governor commented that only a few years earlier the Chipewyans had been almost unmanageable owing to "the bad habits contracted in the hottest opposition ever known in the Indian Country." [9]

Edwin Denig distinguished among Indians in a unique way. He employed a "great man" theory. In his essay, "Of the Sioux," he wrote, "The conduct of all and every band of Indians takes its nature from the chief who, if a good and reasonable man, has wise regulations and given [gives] prudent advice to his soldiers, has consequently good followers who in course of time become tractable and well disposed by the force of habit and example." The seeming objectivity of that statement disappears when Denig goes on to say in the next sentence, "What is here meant by good Indians are those well disposed toward whites and not disturbing the order of other bands by depredations or rebellion against local privileges." [10] Not the object but the subject of the judgment takes pre-eminence. Among fur traders, Denig seems to have stood alone in subscribing to this interpretation, although it appears obvious and cogent to the modern reader. Certainly, our popular culture, which is inclined to see Sitting Bull's fanatic bellicosity as the cause of the Little Big Horn debacle, has an acute awareness of the theme.

At times, the Indians' national and religious leanings influenced the judgments passed on them. The reader of fur-trade sources remains uncertain whether the red man was degraded by contact with the French, the British, the missionary, and so forth, or whether he gravitated to them because he was degraded in the first place. But such an Indian was invariably reviled. In his remarks on the Indians of Lake Huron's northern shore—"the most uncouth, savage-looking beings I ever beheld"—John McLean illustrated the tendency simultaneously to comment on the red men and, by indirection, on an alien element of civilization. The horrid and brute-like aspect of this particular tribe came, he reasoned, from "natural deformity" compounded by "American whiskey." George Simpson's statement before a Parliamentary committee that the

Blackfeet were "primarily American Indians"—a thought which would have outraged the men working out of St. Louis—suggests that the two, Blackfoot and American, somehow deserved each other. With similar intent and less delicacy, Peter Garrioch of Red River colony indicted the Missouri River tribes and the United States at the same time. The conclusion of this ex-teacher's account of shocking depravity at Fort Pierre makes it clear that the lasciviousness of the Mandans, Gros Ventres, and Arikaras nicely complemented the lechery of the nation that held sovereignty over them. To illustrate the "sublime doings" Garrioch told of a "miserably duped libertine" who, having contracted for the company of a fair one, was brought under cover of darkness an aged hag "leaning on the verge of her grave." By the "glorious morning Sun, who is the test and touchstone of all beauty" he discovered the deception. "The duped wretch, unconscious of guilt, shame, decency, or honour, paid her off her hire and sent her away with a glee. Fifty percent premium for the hind-quarters of old women of the Mo.!! –Better than any Bank in the United States. Go it Yankees!" [11]

Though the intimations of Simpson and Garrioch are not singular, Indians tainted by foreign influences appear far more commonly in the hacked-out captivity narratives and the spurious memoirs of "old hunters" than in valid sources. One such work contains amazingly varied fare: a twice-repeated tale of the hero's salvation from burning at the stake by the comely sixteen-year-old daughter of a chief, a diatribe on the evils of Mormonism, an essay on the past evils of slavery, and a lengthy encomium on the wonders of the Salvation Army. In this exercise in didactic and ethnocentric miscellany the author indicated clearly from his supposed adventures in the Columbia River area that "British Tribes" far surpassed American in deviltry, being "exceedingly hostile and cruel." [12] Appropriately enough, a "British" tribe captured and ill treated him before his rescue by the lass who, seemingly, was less "British" than her father. The writer of bogus frontier narratives had no need, even if he had the desire or ability, to describe the Indian qua Indian. Instead he used the aborigine as a convenient and sensational literary device. In this he had solid precedent, for men such as

Thomas Jefferson and Benjamin Franklin had done much the same thing, except to them the red man was a philosophical rather than a literary tool. The Indian provided the means to flail Georges de Buffon, or to mock the French court, or (as in the above illustration) to titillate the baser passions of undiscriminating readers.

The possibility of uncovering subjective distinctions based on the criterion of the trader's class background is an intriguing prospect, but the sources do not lend themselves well to such an effort. The social derivations of many of these men appear lost beyond recovery. Moreover, the literate, record-keeping men of the trade about whom something is known seem largely of a piece in regard to class origins. They came from the middle ranks. In short, it would be difficult to compare the thinking of traders from one social class with that of traders from another; even tentative conclusions would necessarily be formulated on the basis of very inferential evidence. However, in following such a tack, it may be worthy of note that Peter Garrioch's "miserably duped wretch"—whose precise interest in the Indians Garrioch seemed not to share—filled the unexalted role of cook. The wag whose ribald sense of the ludicrous victimized the cook was himself a lowly freeman. More explicitly, George Simpson in a classic statement damned the American trappers in the Rockies as "people of the worst character, run-aways from Jails, and outcasts from Society." Such a " 'Motley crew' " rarely failed to antagonize friendly Indians by "indiscreet" conduct. In a similar vein, Edward Umfreville remarked on the coarse and overly familiar posture assumed by lower-class French-Canadians in the trade, noting how it often brought them to grief. The meaning seems patent, and the theme pervades fur-trade literature: it required men of some stature and propriety to go among the natives. Compelling as this line of reasoning may be, however, its subjective haziness and complexity seem so compounded as to defy untangling. The truly low-class men in the trade did not speak to posterity for themselves. And, in all three of the above illustrations the fur-trade spokesmen wrote from motives beyond the apparent. Difficult as it may be to assess traders' attitudes toward Indians while bearing in mind subjective determinants, it becomes frighteningly more so when attempting to describe traders' judgments of yet other peoples' attitudes while keeping in mind subjective factors at both removes. Umfreville's insistence that the stolid and proper demeanor of lower-class Orkneymen put them in good stead with the red men suggests the intricacy involved.[13]

By means subjective and objective, selfish and scientific, the trader could see the diversities within the Indian world. To some degree this recognition of variety lends itself to schematization. Taking these men as a group and looking at their judgments of Indian society as a whole, one can detect a real scale of preference. Obviously, this was a fluctuating scale, for the constantly changing circumstances of the trade placed the Indian in various lights. Human evaluations being what they are, however, the surprising thing is that a pattern emerges at all.

Aside from the "Diggers" of the Great Basin, who were often considered to be little more than animals, the Arikara probably occupied the lowest position on this scale—"universally hated" according to Annie Abel. As has been seen, they clashed too often with the economic projects of the fur companies to gain anything except hatred. Yet the Arikaras were as proficient as other tribes in taking buffalo robes, which had become the major item of trade long before the close of operations. Until the very end of the fur-trade era, however, the Arikaras remained the most despised tribe of the upper Missouri. Over the years, conflict and disease had worked attrition upon them, thus negating their contrary inclinations. Nevertheless, as late as the 1830's the Upper Missouri Outfit sought ways to get rid of them. Traders suggested removal, as well as extermination at the hands of government forces or of other Indians, most of whom were perfectly willing but quite unable to oblige in the task. Almost thirty years later, with the Civil War only a year away, the Arikaras' sinister reputation continued to thrive, for young Henry Boller noted their abiding hatred of white men, told how a party of them had recently " 'raised hell' " in the post, and named them "the meanest Indians in the country." It is possible, of course, that the Arikaras were thoroughgoing rascals without provocation. Seemingly, causes other than economic resulted in the sobriquet, "The Horrid Tribe." [14]

Such groups as the Winnebago of the Great Lakes area, the Blackfoot confederation of the Rocky Mountains, and several tribes on the upper Pacific coast fell into the same general classification. Thus, a good representation of the linguistic groups appeared in the ranks of the unpopular—the Arikara were Caddoan, the Blackfeet were Algonquian, the Winnebago were Siouan, and the coast tribes were Athapascan and Penutian. At the outset of the far western fur-trade era, the traders who encountered the Blackfeet considered them to be a fine set of Indians. Both Anthony Hendry in the 1750's and Matthew Cocking in the 1770's attested to their kindness and hospitality—and both felt them to be more reminiscent of Europeans than of savages. Apparently because of an unfortunate clash with the Lewis and Clark expedition, however, these nomads reconsidered, and they soon became Ishmaelites of the first order. In 1810 Pierre Menard, an important member of one of the first large ventures into the heart of Blackfoot country, had good reason for referring to "la barbarie des pied noire." In this he set the tone, for throughout the remainder of the fur-trade period the Blackfeet attracted unrelieved loathing. Their murderous propensity represented a weighty smirch in itself—one which, according to Menard, kept the expedition "de faire une petite fortune." The traders' reaction to the Blackfeet differed from their feeling toward the Arikaras, however, in that the Blackfeet aroused their hatred, the Arikaras their hatred and contempt.[15]

Traders in areas other than the Great Plains experienced Indian difficulties as well. Men who worked in the far West considered some of the upper Pacific coast tribes to be contemptible ineffectuals; they were to learn that the malignant character of other tribes was active rather than passive. The *Tonquin* massacre represented only the most celebrated of their depredations. In 1857 when Lord Stanley of the Select Committee on Hudson's Bay asked George Simpson whether the company encountered more trouble west of the Rockies than it did east, Sir George replied, "Much more trouble. They are difficult of management.'' Twenty years earlier, in explaining to an archbishop the company's hesitance in allowing a Catholic mission west of the Rockies, Simpson pointed out that the population there was ''more barbarous, ignorant and treacherous than any with whom we have dealings.'' [16]

The journals of John Work, a Hudson's Bay man of many years' experience, evidence the trials to which these people subjected the traders. Work ordinarily chronicled his movements in an uninspired fashion, rarely setting down anything but the most prosaic and unadorned facts of the company's business. Even when working through Blackfoot country he seemed little moved, though aware of the dangers. However, in 1835 when he led a maritime trading venture up the coast of New Caledonia, his journal fairly bristled with fulminations against the natives.[17] The Blackfeet had left him unruffled, but the Stikines and other coastal tribes worked him into a passion. Of course, in the comfort and leisure of his compartment on a company ship between trading sessions Work probably unburdened his soul of more than he did while toiling through plains and mountains. Moreover, he met far more unmerciful and irksome competition from ''Yankee'' traders on the coast than he ever did inland. Thus, he may have had more inclination and opportunity to vilify the coastal natives. And one can readily imagine that ulterior motives colored George Simpson's above-mentioned evaluations. Nevertheless, the upper Pacific tribes often appeared abominable in the eyes of their traders.

Some groups remained consistently at the other end of the scale. All traders, perhaps, had favorite tribes; but almost without exception the men who had experience in the far West developed a respect, sometimes a fondness, for some of the Rocky Mountain people. This attitude centered upon the Nez Perces and Flatheads, especially the latter. All that was good about Indian society seemed embodied in these tribes. Their kindness, generosity, and reverence impressed many traders. Peter Skene Ogden, a man of devastating realism, chose the Flatheads as his favorites. Not only were they praised, as by Ogden, they were defended against detractors, as well. When a captivity narrative of dubious authenticity described bondage, torture, and indignities at the hands of the Flatheads, William H. Ashley wrote an indignant letter to the editor of a St. Louis newspaper. Operating on ''a desire to do justice to those who have it not in their power to vindicate themselves,'' this fur-trade innovator challenged the integrity of the author and then went on to give a generous and heartwarming character reference for the Flathead tribe.[18]

One would like to believe that such praise stemmed from honest recognition of human virtues, and certainly that was in part the case. But there was more. In a harsh and cruel land the nobility of a friend—and the Flathead was consistently that—may well have become magnified. Along with the Shoshonis, who also enjoyed a generally favorable reputation among the traders, the Flatheads and the Nez Perces maintained a traditional animosity for the Blackfeet, and where those scoundrels were concerned it probably was easy to subscribe to the idea that the enemy of my enemy is, indeed, my friend. As early as 1810 in a letter from Blackfoot country to his brother Meriwether, trader Reuben Lewis mentioned the possibility of working in conjunction with the Flatheads to offset Rocky Mountain hazards.[19] Traders soon realized this informal league, and they continued it for many years.

The Hudson's Bay Company men, though they always recognized the virtues of tribes such as the Flatheads, never allowed themselves to become quite as maudlin as their American counterparts. Peter Skene Ogden balanced his praise of the Flatheads with some criticisms of what he considered to be Indian-like traits.[20] Two things probably account for this discrepancy between American and British attitudes. First, contrary to Simpson's testimony before a Parliamentary committee, the British traders came closer to a *modus vivendi* with the Blackfeet than did the Americans. Thus, their trade and their lives probably depended less upon a fawning cordiality with traditional enemies of the Blackfeet. Also, the fur-trade literature of the American West, unlike that of Canada, includes abundant highly questionable sources—sources which seized upon, magnified, and distorted the Flatheads' established reputation for right living. The belief that there had to be a noble savage lurking about somewhere died slowly; and the Flatheads in their mountain fastness seemed the last, best hope. Two factors—the prevalence of the noble savage convention in spurious sources, and the popularity in the United States of a shoddy western literary genre—must color any evaluation of the thinking of American fur men. North of the border, the obstacles to accurate reconstruction of fur-trade views seem less formidable.

In the collective fur-trade opinion, as might be expected, the vast bulk of the tribes were classified somewhere between the Arikaras and the Flatheads. Some ranked comparatively high—the Cheyennes, for instance, who seemed to be a generally clean and friendly people, or the Spokans and Walla Wallas who bore some resemblance to the Flatheads and Nez Perces. Others fell nearer the bottom: for example, the Chipewyans, who were noted for parsimony, and the Pawnees, who had too many of the qualities of their fellow Caddoans, the Arikaras. In other cases there was little concurrence. Commentaries on the Crows differed greatly. Traders strongly liked or disliked them, rarely hated them, and forgave their trespasses to a surprising degree. Perhaps the variation of opinion exists because the Crows had too great a flair for the dramatic—or the sensational—ever to be simply ignored.

The trader, then, recognized a high degree of tribal diversity and to some extent schematized the variations. Even better evidence against a stereotyped fur-trade view of the Indian lies in the traders' frequent acknowledgment—sometimes tacit, sometimes explicit—of *individual* differences among Indians. Looking back over his many years of contact with the red men, David Thompson wrote: ". . . on becoming acquainted with them there is no want of individual character, and almost every character in civilized society can be traced among them, from the gravity of a judge to a merry jester, and from open hearted generosity to the avaricious miser." Isaac Cowie discounted "the idea of those unacquainted with Indians, that all of them are alike. . . . There is a great deal of human nature in an Indian, and they vary individually nearly as much as every other race and nation." [21]

Abundant inferential evidence indicates that the trader neither

considered all Indians to be the same nor treated them alike. The
Isaac Cowie statement above appears in the context of a discussion
of the Indian debt book, a Hudson's Bay Company record of two
factors—the debt, and the individual character of Indians coming to
the posts. A report for the Rainy Lake region illustrates this recognition of differences. The author of the document listed the adult
male Indians, indicated such things as the number of women and
children with them, and then made revealing commentaries on individuals: Flat Mouth—"Good for Nothing"; Premier's oldest son—
"Conceited but a tolerable hunter"; Premier's stepson—"A poor
Hunter and a Great Rascal"; Little Gun—"a good hunter but a
rogue"; Little Scioux—"a good hunter & honest"; Sluggard—"his
name is his character." In their affairs with the aborigines, traders
translated these vague differentiations into hard policy. Thus,
" 'Ne-shoot', the Buck's son" faced the prospect of a niggardly
welcome on his next visit to Fort Ellice, the post trader having been
advised not to give him "a *pipe* of Tobacco or a load of ammunition." On the other hand, when "Illinois" and his band arrived at
Fort William, paid their debts, and requested a keg to keep the
occasion, good character told. The man in charge at first attempted
to delay until the arrival of the Chief Trader, "however rather than
displease a good Indian I yielded. . . ." And an Indiana trader
explained to his superior that he took a particular Indian's furs at
an uncommonly high price because the individual was "a friend and
old customer, and I took his skins at hazard. . . ."[22]

The tendency to draw distinctions in character was not limited to
men such as David Thompson, who had a demonstrable sympathy
for the natives, or to shadowy, unknown figures, such as those
mentioned immediately above. Traders who held Indian society in
general contempt had little more inclination to resort to stereotypical descriptions. At the end of a journey hard-bitted Simon M'Gillivray paid his red guide with unusual liberality, noting simply that
he was "a worthy old man." In early 1795 at Fort George on the
Saskatchewan, Simon's kinsman, Duncan, engaged Gun Case and
Sitting Badger to do the hunting for the post during the summer,
noting that they were "brave, resolute Indians" who were unlikely

to desert in the face of adversity. At the Crow post James Chambers, who had been there long enough thoroughly to despise those happy warriors, confided in the Fort Sarpy journal that the "Crow Indians are a lousy, thieving, Beggarly set of Rascals," and added some fiery particulars to prove his thesis. Only lines later, however, he admitted that Dogs Head, a Crow, was the best Indian on the upper Missouri.[23]

The trader showed preferences on the basis of culture, generally choosing the hunter over the fisher and the nomad over the villager; and he made similar preferential distinctions in regard to the Indian's position vis-à-vis the trade. One might suppose that the latter determinant was overwhelmingly important. For example, Champlain explained to a band of Indians that Chomina, one of their number, was so much appreciated by the whites because in time of need he readily volunteered aid, in time of privation he practiced compassion rather than extortion, and at all times his loyalty to the French, unlike that of some of his fellows, stayed firm. Similarly, Francois-Victor Malhiot, who would have seen the devil take every red man, described L'Epaule-de-Canard in the following terms: "He is a sobre, brave savage, liked by the others, liking the French, capable of sacrificing himself for them; a good man for errands; he does not ask for things, is satisfied with everything that is given him and is a famous hunter." Putting the economic even more overtly Duncan Cameron of the North West Company expressed regret over the death of an Indian who, "though he was a d. . . .d rascal, both with white people and with Indians . . . was a good hunter, from whom I had above a pack last year. . . ." Such a performance could cause one to overlook some peccadilloes. Certainly, in the eyes of the traders these were good Indians.[24]

Telling as such evidence is, another means of distinction and preferential classification outranked the economic: it involved the age-old concept that familiarity breeds contempt. The primary, though not sole, qualification of a good Indian consisted in his being well removed. This theme will be further developed in chapters seven and eight, but it requires some treatment here.

Traders made it a working principle that Indian respect for them diminished with contact. Thomas Fitzpatrick and Doctor John McLoughlin employed the adage itself, and many others developed precisely the same idea in their discussions of how best to maintain awe in the natives. That the reverse was also true—that the trader became less fond of the Indian—appears far more infrequently, at least in any explicit fashion. Its recognition would have required a rather scrutinizing self-examination on the part of traders. Inferentially, however, this motif pervades their writings. Rudolph Friederich Kurz recognized the working of the mechanism in his superior at Fort Union—"he is always in the best humor with Indians when none are around." However, Kurz apparently failed to perceive the same thing in himself. His early ardor to portray "the romantic mode of life" of the red men gave way to impatience and ultimately to a preference for studying and sketching the animal life of the high plains. Even the romantic artist seemed gradually to discover that the savages had feet of clay.[25]

If familiarity did beget contempt in fur-trade affairs, the explanation for it lies in several circumstances. First of all, the overenthusiasm with which neophytes anticipated contact with the red race had almost no chance of survival. Here, of course, we encounter that seemingly inappropriate complex of ideas centering on primitivism and noble savagery—subjects which will be dealt with at length elsewhere. Also, as has been noted above, traders believed, probably correctly, that the natives' respect for them suffered by contact, a situation which no doubt reduced the Indians' inclinations to please the fur men, and the traders logically must have reciprocated. Cumulative causation of this nature could quickly render mutual regard practically nonexistent.

Beyond problems of trade relations and lack of sympathy resulting from cultural contrast, the trying circumstances of their profession must have jaundiced the traders' outlook. Physical hardship and deprivation pervaded their lives. One harassed trader opened a letter to his Detroit employer with this matter-of-fact observation: "Dear Sir I am in possession of nothing at present, but my Life. . . ." The trader at a Hudson's Bay Company post closed a letter in this classically revealing fur-trade fashion: "My Indians are drunk, my Accompts backward and our other work likewise. . . ." Describing his surroundings to a mother in the East, an upper Missouri trader used an earthy frontier expression to convey his meaning. He worked, he said, in "the country where a man eats sh–t and goes naked." Indecorous and impressionistic, one might say, but not wholly inaccurate.[26]

The vexations involved in dealing with people of a very alien culture weighed heavily on the men at the posts. Alexander Ross later wrote that he never answered a call at the gate until he had walked back and forth across the enclosure twice. This induced a properly settled state of mind for meeting tawny visitors who, beyond their usual begging and threats, might summon the trader and, when the gate was opened, laugh in his face and stalk away. Exacerbating as this may have been, it appears mild beside Ross's treatment at the hands of a Columbia River native who agreed to carry his burden over a difficult portage in return for some coat buttons, then immediately flung the heavy parcel over a two-hundred-foot precipice, howled in derision as Ross struggled to rescue it, and finally came forward to ask as payment the coat as well as the buttons. Ross suppressed a powerful inclination to give the "rogue" some buttons of "another mould"; indeed, he paid the amount originally set. However, that the incident left Ross's image of the natives unchanged would be hard to conceive. In matters of trade itself Indians provided equal exasperations. Rudolph Kurz told how on one occasion his superior, Edwin Denig, with endurance all but annihilated, was hounded by an amazingly persistent and beggarly native. After fleeing only to be ferreted out, Denig made his stand, the essence of which Kurz recorded:

"Now say at once what it is you want," Mr. Denig interposed before the former could speak. "First?"

"A calico case for my pipestem," Le Gras began, "long enough to hang over at both ends."

"Second?" Mr. Denig went on, counting off on his fingers.

"Eyewater."

"Third?"

"Tobacco."

"Fourth?"

At this point the brazen Indian recognized the humor of the situation and began to laugh, thus allowing the harassed trader again to withdraw before an apparently superior force. When competition prevailed, the actions of the red men could threaten a trader's very equilibrium. Thus a Hudson's Bay man at York Fort in 1778 found that the influence of the Montreal "Pedlars" made the natives "so exceedingly insolent, that flesh and blood is to weak to bare it . . . my life is almost a burden to me." [27]

Other, more unsavory characteristics ill suited the fur-trade frontier for the development of mutual esteem. Violence and drunkenness abounded, though certainly not to the degree portrayed in popular treatments. Licentiousness was often rampant. That kind of familiarity which could indeed breed contempt appears in the following excerpt from a fur-trade journal: "Committed fortification today and got a Whipping from my beloved *Wife,* for my trouble– Oh poor me–." The general atmosphere surrounding the incident contains little that is extraordinary, though the consequences for the trader are somewhat unique. Similarly, Peter Garrioch's description of the "rutting business" at Fort Pierre, though it is extreme, illustrates the disgust and outrage that many traders must have felt when they encountered life reduced to the least common denominator. This sensitive and perceptive man recognized that his written portrayal contained terminology which "ought in justice to be applied to the brute creation alone." Under the circumstances, however, he considered it appropriate and let it stand.[28]

Aside from unattractive contacts with the natives, other realities of fur-trade life augured ill for the development of generous sentiments. Martin McLeod evidenced this in one way by writing that there was no existence "more dull & monotonous" than that of a trader during the winter months. A Hudson's Bay man in the far Northwest considered these drawbacks so great as to justify a unique request. In a letter to the Bishop of St. Boniface he sent five pounds' sterling credit to the Providence Mission, and then took the "great liberty"—"which under other circumstances might be improper and unseemly"—of asking the divine to send him three gallons of Jamaica rum or brandy. It would serve no improper use, he assured the bishop, and it would brighten the holiday season for men who lead "dull and lonesome lives." One frequently finds in fur-trade correspondence a nostalgic melancholy, a harking back to friendlier scenes irretrievably removed. At Christmas of 1833 Martin McLeod composed or transcribed a poem, "Sigh not for Summer Flowers." Though it may strike one as incongruous, it has in reality a characteristic tone. The same poignant gloominess appears in Cuthbert Cumming's gentle remonstrance to a fellow Scotsman in the trade, who as years passed tended more and more toward brevity in his letters. Probably to motivate his countryman to greater efforts, Cumming invoked the days "o Lang Syne" when "we twa sat by the ingleside and so discordantly tuned our pipes to that national air. . . ." For a moment he mused in recollection but then jarred himself back to the gray present by noting that "them days are gone bye & I feel a presentiment never to return. Fare thee well my friend & if for ever   still for ever   fare thee well." [29]

Much has been said of the optimism of the frontier mind. Frederick Jackson Turner ascribed "buoyancy and exuberance" to it. The fur-trade literature, however, provides almost no evidence to support this view. The loneliness and monotony that typified traders' lives made for a morbidity and pessimism of outlook which in the nineteenth century was probably heightened by a prevalent romantic sentimentalism. These wilderness operators seem to have been peculiarly given to dark brooding and painful introspection, moods they had ample opportunity to indulge during recurrent periods of absolute boredom. The impact of the overwhelming winter solitude can be seen in David Thompson's recollection of the time when the devil sat down across the checker table from him at Cumberland House on the Saskatchewan. The unexpected visitor—whose features were those of a Spaniard and who had two short black horns and a body covered with hair to the waist—lost every game to the well-practiced young trader; but he maintained his aplomb, only becoming "more grave." In spite of his excellent showing in the face of an impressive antagonist, Thompson seems never to have given his onetime opponent another chance. He eschewed checkers forever, as well as other diversions wherein Satan might seek a test of strength. Martin McLeod apparently never had such an awesome caller, but he assumed a commonly pensive tone in his brief and random essay on "the *life of man*." "How vain our hopes," he began, "how futile our aspirations." Alexis Bailly, a contemporary of McLeod in the Minnesota trade, confessed that his strongest wish had been "to obtain greatness." In this, of course, he met frustration, and his fretful soliloquizing evidences a sense of persecution as well as a self-satisfied feeling of modest accomplishment in the face of a world bent on his ruin. Were one to indulge in analytical excesses, he could readily brand Bailly with some form of complex or neurosis. Nevertheless, this scion of a prominent French-Canadian family expressed the mood of many of his fellows in one of his patently egocentric reflections: ". . . like a lonely tree transplanted from its native soil into a barren wilderness, he seems to stand alone exposed to every blast. . . ." [30]

These doleful sentiments, typical of men in the trade, appear so deeply stamped on Francis Chardon of the upper Missouri trade as to make him a caricature of his fellows. Thus he provides us with a comprehensive facsimile of the common fur-trade disposition. Looking out upon the "dreary, Savage waste" that is now western North Dakota, this jaded ex-Philadelphian wrote on January 27, 1836:

No news from any quarter—*lonesome*   One single word *lonesome*—would suffice to express our feelings any day throughout the Year—We might add—discontented—but this would include the fate of all Mankind. It is a Melancholy reflection when we look forward into futurity—and know that the remnant of our days *must* be spent in toilsome and unavailing pursuits of happiness. And that sooner or later we must sink into the grave without ever being able to attain the object for which we have toiled and suffered so much . . . the past . . . is no less gloomy. It is like a dreary expansive waste—without one green verdant spot on which Memmory loves to linger. . . . The little experience that time has given only teaches us to Know,   , That Man was Made to Mourn, . . .

Chardon, of course, spoke in the abstract. But the repeated economic reverses and manifest uncertainties of the trade often translated the abstract into the concrete, transformed a vague and general discontent into particular irritations. "La plus grand douleur" occasioned by the loss of a keel boat loaded with furs put Francois Chouteau in a proper state of mind for noting specifics. His present grievous situation, he indicated, only compounded the ordinary exasperations of the absence of family, the tribulations of travel, and "de trouble et de vexation avec les sauvage." [31] Thus, a common fur-trade frame of mind would have qualified, if not precluded, recognition and admission of the better qualities in others.

Not all the hazards to kind sentiments stemmed from the actions of the natives or from the difficult physical circumstances. White men tried each others' patience fully as much in the wilderness as they did elsewhere. Even where the competition of rival firms was absent or was kept from deteriorating into violence, traders continually indulged in quarreling, jealousy, and backbiting. A St. Louis trader, for example, received the following reminder and suggestion from a business associate: "Fits of madness are frequent with you, but you ought to vent them on those who are the cause of your wrath. . . ." An 1826 letter from Robert Stuart to subordinate Jean Baptiste Beaubien reveals a typical fur-trade purport, as well as an administrator's effort to install the reign of harmony among his underlings. Beaubien and John Kinzie operated together for the American Fur Company in the Chicago area, but they evidently did so with much discord. To mitigate the situation Stuart became very stern and noted that both men should be more concerned with the company's interests than with who was to be "le grand Bourgois." Understandable as these problems are, they could scarcely have done other than aggravate already trying conditions.[32]

A final factor connected with, if not directly causing, a diminution of respect for the Indian emerged from the belief—sometimes honestly held, sometimes hypocritically—that the Indian was a worse person for his contact with civilization. Although developed more fully elsewhere (see pp. 201–15), it deserves mention here. The trader, as a product of white civilization, saw the debasing of the Indian happening directly around him. Thus the contempt which familiarity bred was not alone a matter of knowing the red man better and, consequently, seeing his true character. While the trader was coming to know the Indian, the Indian was changing. With passage of time the Indian not only *seemed* more contemptible, he actually *was,* from the fur-trade perspective, more contemptible. The deterioration of the trader's regard for Indians as he came to know them implies yet another method of distinction: the good Indian was the one unknown by the trader or as yet unexposed to white civilization.

Unlike the later frontiersman, the trader's attitudes toward the natives did not hinge upon a spiteful and murderous brutality. The trader showed a rather admirable awareness of the myriad mores of the wilderness dwellers and a marked degree of tolerance for these alien ways. However, given recent assumptions about human relations, one might detect an element of paradox in the trader's views, perhaps even a sourly misanthropic note. For all their intimate knowledge and understanding, their acceptance was clearly noncommittal. Their hearts did not grow fonder; knowledge did not engender admiration. Indeed, the more they knew, the less they respected. Familiarity bred a coldly realistic discernment that scuttled esteem. As James Adair, an occasional trafficker in noble savages, pointed out, the Indian, like fire, was best admired from a distance.[33] Two things about the natives especially warmed the trader's heart—his furs and his absence, particularly the latter. And perhaps such a state of affairs should occasion no surprise. A vast cultural gulf separated the trader and the red man, and lacking fond, modern suppositions about the brotherhood of man, the trader may have done unusually well.

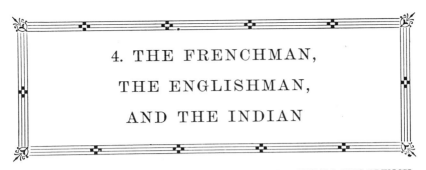

4. THE FRENCHMAN,
THE ENGLISHMAN,
AND THE INDIAN

A COMMON CONCEPTION OF FRONTIER REALITIES REVEALS THE FRENCH-man as far superior to his English competitor in dealing with the Indian. By this portrayal the Frenchman entered easily and quickly into understanding and rapport with the native of the wilderness while the Englishman and the Indian went on sharing their mutual suspicion. Implicitly or explicitly, it is argued that the product of British culture was too unbending, maintained his aloofness to too great a degree, and allowed patronization and condescension to manifest itself in his relations with the aborigines. While intolerance typified the English attitude toward the natives, French policy at least occasionally reflected an enlightened spirit, and the actions of French individuals showed an easy acceptance of the red man. Francis Parkman stated this disparity in outlook in the early chapters of the *Conspiracy of Pontiac*. The French, he noted, had a "plastic and pliant temper" which allowed them to humor, cajole, and understand the natives. "They met the savage half way," he wrote, "and showed an abundant readiness to mould their own features after his likeness." On the other hand, a "thorny and impracticable barrier" divided the English from the Indians, and relations between them were marked by "scorn on the one side, and hatred on the other. . . ."[1]

This prevailing conception of Indian-white relations has gone beyond the level of popular attitudes or even of historical writings. The noted authority, A. L. Kroeber, placed the imprimatur of anthropological scholarliness upon this view in a 1939 publication by noting that "the English attitude toward natives was . . . less tolerant than that of the French and Spaniards." In *Patterns of*

Culture Ruth Benedict spoke simply of "traditional Anglo-Saxon intolerance." [2]

For all its general acceptance, however, this view of frontier relationships seems not to be entirely satisfactory. The literature of one frontier stage—the fur trade—hardly substantiates this generalization. The dichotomy between tolerant Frenchman and bigoted Anglo-Saxon—a contradistinction that one might well expect would loom large in the expressions of the fur-trade era—does not manifest itself for the reader. This is not to say that the opposite is more nearly correct—that the English showed a finer humanity—but rather that, as a body, the first-hand accounts and recollections of the generally candid and unapologetic men of the fur trade do little to bear out the common conception.

By way of preface it bears noting that the authors of the major secondary works on the fur trade have been reluctant to employ cultural or national origins as a touchstone of individual or group attitudes. Most works on the fur trade have dealt with its economic and expansive aspects while virtually ignoring the tenuous subject of how the trader conceived of his red customer. The latest major study, that of Paul C. Phillips, leaves most to be desired in this regard. The Indian receives little mention in this two-volume work. Happily, some works—Hiram Martin Chittenden's sixty-year-old classic and E. E. Rich's history of the Hudson's Bay Company, for example—present fur-trade actions in such a way that fur-trade attitudes can, to some degree, be inferred. Still, they say little explicitly about how the trader viewed the Indian and thus give small indication that a man from one cultural background looked upon the natives much differently than did a man from another. In a discussion of the fascination of Indian life for white men in the wilderness, Chittenden noted simply that, for all his faults, the red man "was . . . not disliked by those who knew him most nearly." He made no effort to indicate that this rule applied more to one nationality than to another. Even Bernard DeVoto, who generally subscribed fully to Parkman's formula, felt called upon to temper somewhat the view of his nineteenth-century predecessor in the writing of epic, frontier history. After quoting Parkman to the effect that the English "scorned and neglected" the Indian while the French "embraced and cherished him," DeVoto added that "the generalization is something less than true."[3]

Secondary sources on the fur trade do not provide the solution to the problem, however. The question at hand involves attitudes, and the above authors, DeVoto excepted, did not actually address themselves to the task of depicting such things. Their hesitancy in using the common categorization gives some inferential weight to the view that questions it. More substantial evidence must come, however, from the sentiments expressed by traders themselves.

First of all, one might ask if the primary sources frequently, or even occasionally, state in a conscious and explicit fashion that the Frenchman enjoyed a greater success with the natives. Did the English-speaking trader express anger, envy, or frustration over the fact that his Gallic competitor outshone him in dealing with the red men? Conversely, did the Frenchman at times indulge his self-satisfaction by pointing out the inadequacies of his opponent in this regard? And did men in the trade account for the success or failure of themselves or of their competitors by the comparative degree of tolerance and acceptance afforded their tawny customers?

In each case the answer is no. Although Monsieur Jérémie, a trader of French background, argued in a rare instance that Indians liked and respected the French while distrusting the English, he made no effort to demonstrate that this sprang from French tolerance or English bigotry. Jérémie, who was active on the western shores of Hudson's Bay around the turn of the eighteenth century, believed that the Indians held the English in low regard because of the deceitfulness of the English. According to him, Indians despised lying. For men such as Jérémie, who were actually involved in wilderness pursuits, it must have been difficult to hold to any hard and fast principle contrasting the character of relations between Frenchman and Indian and those between Englishman and Indian. Only a few pages after giving qualified evidence in support of the rule, he admitted that, in spite of their friendliness for the French, the Indians near Bourbon had treacherously slain a French hunting party of eight men. By the same token, La Vérendrye informed

Governor Marquis de Beauharnois that the Indian trade on Hudson's Bay could be taken from the English, basing his argument largely upon native derision of English cowardice. According to the explorer-trader, the Indians felt that "le français est bien différent ne craignant rien." [4] It goes almost without saying that La Vérendrye's best interests would have been served by having Beauharnois and the French court believe that such was indeed the case—that the red men did not see the white men on the bay as "hommes comme le français."

Writing in the mid-eighteenth century, Joseph Robson, a former Hudson's Bay Company employee, stated that the French received better treatment from the natives "because the french have taken more pains to civilize their manners, and engage their esteem." Robson's testimony stands almost alone, for all the familiarity of its ring, and it occasions very real doubts. He worked for the company as a carpenter, and his knowledge of Indian-white relations may have been somewhat limited. More importantly, he wrote expressly as a critic of his former employer with the intent of destroying the company's dominance in British America. In the heat of his disquisition he made such interesting revelations as that subarctic Canada had great agricultural potential and that the natives were a "white people." Forty years later Edward Umfreville, like Robson a disgruntled former employee of the British firm, engaged in similar polemics; but he came to strikingly different conclusions about French as opposed to English relations with the Indians. For all the shortcomings of the firm he attacked, "it however must be owned, that the Hudson's Bay traders have ingratiated themselves more into the esteem and confidence of the natives" than have their French rivals from lower Canada. According to Umfreville, the Hudson's Bay men conducted themselves so prudently that the red men respected them and had not killed one of their number for fifteen years past. Conversely, the French traders evoked "detestation and contempt" due to unseemly familiarity, deception, drunkenness, and "commerce with Indian women." Consequently, scarcely a year passed without one or more falling victim to natives filled with "abhorrence and disgust." In closing his discussion of

this subject Umfreville pointed out that he had digressed because of
the "frequent encomiums" passed on the Gallic traders. Though his
own efforts were consciously directed at destroying the Hudson's
Bay Company, he wished to set the record straight "in regard to
these *Messieurs Voyageurs*." [5]

The trader of Anglo-Saxon origins often indulged his dislike for
Latin or Gallic cultures. When Philip Turnor, a geographer-trader
for the Hudson's Bay Company, described a Chipewyan near Great
Slave Lake as being "quite a Frenchefied fellow," he certainly
disparaged things French quite as much as this particular Indian.
Turnor registered the general antipathy which English traders had
for French culture. But this commonly felt disregard did not stem
from the reputed facts that French traders showed the red men
greater toleration, or that French traders had greater acumen in
wilderness dealings. After all, the sweep of historical events had
provided ample reason for products of these two cultures to eye each
other with hostility. The Spaniard was as detested by the American
fur traders of the far West as was the Frenchman elsewhere. Here
too, however, the hatreds seem more a product of American westward expansion and Spanish efforts to halt it than of differing
approaches to the Indians. When Stanley Vestal had Kit Carson say,
" 'If Spaniards warn't made for shootin', what are rifles for'?," it
appears that the animosities of the Texas Revolution and the
Mexican War took precedence over diverse attitudes toward the
Indian. Some similar consideration must have colored the thinking
of Charles Larpenteur, himself a product of French culture, when
he took into his upper Missouri post an unfortunate Mexican and his
Indian wife. Because of her hardships in a recent childbirth,
Larpenteur pitied the woman, but he resolved "to ship off" her
spouse—"Mexicans being only fit to herd horses. . . ." [6]

If white men of differing backgrounds held each other in contempt for their comparative acceptance of and success with the
Indians, they chose a peculiar means of expressing it. Time and
again in their writings traders of all origins called upon the Indian
as an obliging witness to the perfidy and dastardliness of those who
were outsiders—nationally, religiously, or commercially. Fur-trade

literature abounds in instances where the simple red man acts as a dispassionate and judicious accuser or as an active confounder of, say, the Frenchman, the priest, or the opposition trader. This usage appears most frequently—almost *ad nauseam*—in those questionably reliable narrative recollections of American mountain men. But sources of unimpeachable authenticity contain abundant examples. James McKenzie, for example, recorded an incident wherein some Labrador Nascapees—Indians, by the way, whom he thoroughly despised—cleverly confounded a priest in his efforts to explain the Trinity.[7] McKenzie obviously felt that the reactions of what to him were depraved and almost subhuman creatures to the teachings of the priest lent added weight to his own reservations about Catholicism. In instances cited earlier, Monsieur Jérémie argued, in essence, that Englishmen practiced deceit; and La Vérendrye accused them of pusillanimity. Jérémie and La Vérendrye intimated that others gave potent substantiation to their opinions and relied upon what amounted to a higher tribunal: the Indians, they said, recognized the false and timid nature of the English as well. Englishmen and Frenchmen alike, then, laid claim to the testimony of the Indian in heaping derision upon adversaries. If Englishmen felt handicapped by their own intolerance or aloofness, or by the absence of the same in Frenchmen, they took pains to avoid committing their concern to writing.

The idea that the French had better relations with the Indians than the English connects tolerance with effectiveness in practical matters. The Frenchman, supposedly, enjoyed greater success, and by this logic his success came at least partly from the mutual acceptance between himself and the natives. But traders almost universally subscribed to a view of Indian nature and counseled methods of dealing with the natives that have a far different ring from these happy assumptions. One of the most prevalent ideas about the Indians in fur-trade writings holds that they were motivated almost solely by self-interest in their dealing with others. Edwin Denig did most to describe this facet of Indian nature. Others recorded the same sentiments in more succinct fashion. Two centuries earlier Samuel de Champlain expressed the typical outlook when he made a mockery of Indian generosity by noting simply that "they give nothing for nothing." After haranguing some Indians on the virtues and grandeur of the French empire, La Vérendrye put the material stamp of validity upon his remarks by arranging a feast of fish and corn and concluded with stark realism that "without the pot one has no good friends."[8]

According to the trader, the key to Indian actions lay in self-interest. Maintaining friendly and profitable relations with him necessitated keeping him at a distance. Doctor John McLoughlin, who directed the Hudson's Bay Company affairs on the Pacific slope, noted simply that "familiarity begets contempt," and throughout the fur-trade domain men reiterated the essence, if not the precise words, of Aesop's maxim. Pierre-Antoine Tabeau of the upper Missouri trade found that newly contacted tribes were always easiest to deal with because they stood in awe of the whites. Unfortunately, he noted, "a little familiarity destroys this illusion." Tabeau went on to schematize Indian-white relations in terms of three stages: ". . . the age of gold, that of the first meeting; the age of iron, that of the beginning of their insight; and that of brass, when a very long intercourse has mitigated their ferocity a little and our trade has become indispensable to them." A logical corollary of this outlook held that Indian transgressions against whites must be met by predictably stern firmness. Allowing humanity to stand in the way of retaliation would only invite ever greater outrages. This represented a universal rule of the wilderness. Whether expressed by Daniel Duluth's pleading necessity after busting the skulls of suspected Indian murderers or Joshua Pilcher's wrathful accusations when a punitive expedition failed, the principle demanded observance.[9]

Given these assumptions about the Indian, one is hard pressed to see how a trader could ascribe his own success or that of his opponents to benevolence or tolerance. In 1795 Jean-Baptiste Trudeau (or Truteau) bemoaned the fact that the French and Spanish traders of the Missouri had little success and noted that if the English controlled the river the trade would be a going concern. From this one must infer either that the French traders, such as himself, were no more tolerant than their opposite numbers in the Hudson's Bay or North West companies, or that tolerance counted for little. Whatever the merits of the former possibility, traders generally subscribed to the latter. On one occasion crusty Duncan Cameron, a United Empire Loyalist formerly of Schenectady, recorded a recruiting raid that he made on a Hudson's Bay Company establishment. His efforts to seduce some of their better Indians into the North West Company trade met with success and left the red men drunk and disaffected with the Hudson's Bay people. After noting the insolence and aggravation that "the English" had forborne through the hectic night, Cameron went on to generalize as follows:

Those people have the patience of Job and are real slaves to the Indians who come to their forts. We keep them at a greater distance, which makes them more respectful to us than to the English. . . . I know that they treated them much better than we could afford to do, but they had not the art of convincing the Indians of that.

Those who have interpreted the supposed French successes in gaining the practical cooperation of the Indians as evidence of French toleration may have operated upon a questionable assumption. When, for example, Robert de La Salle deigned to spend time visiting a chief on the lower Mississippi, he did not, as his comrade and champion Henry Tonty pointed out, do so as a warmhearted gesture of brotherhood. Rather, the sight of a woman with a pearl necklace and "the hope of obtaining some merchandise" motivated him. Seemingly, the ability of white men to marshal the aborigines in some economic or imperial design could as easily indicate cynicism and opportunism as racial tolerance.[10]

Little overt evidence exists in fur-trade literature to show that men of one cultural background excelled those of another in dealing with Indians. If such was the case, traders by and large failed to register it. There is little to indicate that success, when achieved, hinged upon benevolence or understanding. Indeed, success in practical relations could have precluded such generous postures. This does not argue the inherent rightness of the traders' rather misanthropic outlook; it does suggest that such a view was almost universally held.

Going beyond the assumptions upon which trade relations were based and looking at the traders' conscious appraisals of native life, the reader notices first of all their degree of interest in the Indian. Though fur traders are often pictured as unreflective mercenaries and exploiters, they did in fact possess a great deal of honest curiosity. Of course, journals of the trade were often kept under circumstances that must have discouraged speculation of any sort. Still, the workings of inquiring minds gave rise to a good deal of descriptive material. For example, Jacob Halsey, a dissipated clerk for the Upper Missouri Outfit, enlivened the Fort Pierre journal with sketches of the Mandan and Arikara tribes.[11]

Material of greater length, if not greater significance, appears in the narrative writings of these men. When traders looked back upon a career in the wilderness, they rarely failed to include a generous amount of commentary on the aborigines. After examining the fur-trade literature, one can hardly fail to understand, if not entirely to sympathize with, the somewhat petulant complaint of Peter Skene Ogden, who late in life wrote a book about the Indians. At the outset of this work he took a gratuitous slap at "those who travel in pursuit of amusement or science" and who then presumed to inform the world of the true nature of the red man. These "drawing-room authors," Ogden argued, should, before evaluating the Indian, repeat the experiences and gain the insights of "men like us who only encounter these hardships for vile lucre." [12]

Traders possessed a lively, scientific curiosity about the American primitive. And that curiosity characterized French traders no more than it did non-French traders. In commenting upon Henry Kelsey's pioneering trek from Hudson's Bay to what is now the prairie provinces in the years around 1690, Bernard DeVoto argued the uniqueness in attitude of this youthful fur-trade explorer. According to DeVoto, Kelsey's fellows in the "caste-bound, quintessentially British Company" must have looked much askance at his unseemly interest in the savages. Indeed, his desire to travel inland among them may well have brought his sanity under question.[13] That interpretation of attitudes, however, has enjoyed more reiteration than demonstration.

First of all, probably no fur-trade commentators outdid such men as James Adair, David Thompson, Edwin Denig, Samuel Hearne, James Isham, or Alexander Ross in terms of simple volume allotted to discussion of the natives. Denig wrote two book-length accounts of the high plains tribes, both of which ultimately appeared in print under the aegis of modern anthropologists. Adair produced a "history" of the American Indians, and the others injected generous treatments of the natives into their writings. If cultural background served as a determinant of how thoroughly traders discussed Indian life, it seems not to have acted as the traditionally accepted interpretation would lead one to believe. The trio of narratives centering upon the establishment of Astoria provides a good illustration of this similarity in amount of treatment given the red men. Gabriel Franchère, a product of French culture, has no more to say about the Indians—indeed somewhat less—than do his contemporaries, the Irishman Ross Cox and the Scotsman Alexander Ross.[14]

The excoriations of the red man that spice the literature of the trade characterized the writings of traders of all backgrounds when they used the pen to indulge their occasional animosities toward Indians—individually, tribally, or universally. Scarcely anyone surpassed the blanket condemnation of the upper Missouri tribes pronounced by Pierre-Antoine Tabeau when he wrote the following:

All that one can say is that, if these barbarians leave no doubt that they are human, intelligent beings, it is because they have the form, the face, and the faculty of speech of human beings. Stupid, superstitious, gluttonous, lewd, vindictive, patient by principle, fierce of temper, cowardly with men of like strength, fearless in assassinations, ungrateful, traitorous, barbarous, cruel, lying, thievish, etc. I add the "and so forth" in fear that these epithets do not wholly comprise their vices and that I may be free to add to them.

In January of 1820 Jacques Porlier of the Wisconsin trade reported a complete disgust with his Indians. Their conduct had been so untoward that Porlier savored the thought of abusing them physically. That apparently would not answer, and so he contented himself with the hope that, while he suffered privation, they would perish of hunger. The journal of Francois-Victor Malhiot, in which he offers all the Indians to the devil for a penny, reveals a similar antipathy. These, of course, represent isolated examples indicating no more than that the Frenchman was quite as capable as anyone else of venting his spleen against the natives.[15]

Annie Heloise Abel, the editor of Tabeau's writings, considered him to be ''race conscious to a degree not usual in a Frenchman.'' This, it seems to me, misses the point. Given the proper circumstances, the Frenchman was fully as ready to work himself into a dudgeon against the Indians as was anyone else. Tabeau underwent a prodigious amount of abuse at the hands of the upper Missouri natives, and he availed himself of the only feasible recourse—damning his tormentors by the written word. Malhiot, operating in the hideousness and depravity of the late Great Lakes trade, registered an outlook quite in accord with conditions around him—''Quelle vie!!! 'Pauvre Malhiot!,' '' he sighed at one juncture. In a moment of sober second thought, while confiding in his superiors in the company, Malhiot anticipated and attempted to dispose of charges of misanthropy which might be made against him. He insisted that he did not feel ''hatred and bad humor.'' Indeed, he called upon the Almighty to preserve him ''from wishing ill to anyone on earth. . . .''[16] Although this plea may resemble the sort of hypocrisy dictated by the necessity of pleasing superiors, North West Company leadership was scarcely the kind to demand benevolence of spirit in its traders. Malhiot's reaction simply revealed the human tendency to lose generosity under trying circumstances.

The significance of such vilifications lies far less in their being confined to the writings of men of a specific origin than it does in their relative infrequency. Traders rarely condemned gratuitously. When Peter Skene Ogden pondered in his journal the advisability of exterminating a part of the Snake nation, he did so against the backdrop of overwhelmingly difficult trade conditions, indeed with the twin specters of starvation and severe Indian harassment near at hand.[17] The plea of extenuating circumstances hardly excuses the sentiments of a Tableau, a Porlier, a Malhiot, or an Ogden; it does, however, make them understandable.

In logical complement to the last point, it needs to be mentioned that traders of Anglo-Saxon background showed quite as much readiness to heap undue praise upon the American natives as did their French counterparts. Because of a solid awareness of frontier realities, men of the trade rather infrequently invoked the heady doctrine of noble savagery. Still, when an English trader indulged his quarrels with the civilized society he had left, he too called upon the "nobility" of the savage to cast a shadow upon civilization. The portrayals of the Indians made at such moments differ markedly from those made by the same men in other contexts, but this stems from the fact that, from the fur trade perspective, the red man had to be dressed up a good deal before he could be used to reproach white culture. Whatever the logical difficulties involved for the trader, none provided better examples of this mechanism than James Adair in his blistering critique of the legal, medical, and military institutions of colonial America, or John Long in his carpings at the parsimony of his more affluent civilized fellows. Though Hoxie Fairchild held that the English view of savagery was "less highly colored and enthusiastic" than that of the French or Spanish, such a rule has dubious accuracy when applied to men in the wilderness. When, for example, Gabriel Franchère sensed the sloth and nastiness of the Columbia River tribes, he grumbled as quickly as any a regret that such a promising land had not earlier fallen the lot of white men.[18]

Most fur-trade descriptions of Indian life stemmed from honest curiosity and sought to enlighten the reader rather than to serve as disputatious tours de force. In their sober and unimpassioned accounts, traders manifested a good deal of sympathetic understanding and, quite often, a willingness to judge the natives by standards other than those of the narrator. Thus, Alexander Ross showed no outrage in discussing the head-flattening practised by the Chinooks, but rather drew an analogy between it and the violence English women worked upon themselves by compression of their waists—"all nations, civilized as well as savage, have their peculiar prejudices.'' Although George Simpson's willingness to extend the benefit of doubt was by no means uniformly abundant, he too reacted generously to the Columbia River custom. It disfigured the young, he readily admitted, ''but as they advance in Life it is not offencive to the Eye   at least was not so to me at first sight and as none but the wretched Slaves have round heads I begin to fall into the Chinook way of thinking that they do not look so well (particularly the Ladies) with round as with Flat Heads.'' Whether a man of Simpson's temperament could indeed ''fall into the Chinook way of thinking'' needs not be answered precisely. He manifested simple tolerance, whatever the case. Cultural relativism, of course, has a fairly recent origin. Still, one could reasonably expect to find something akin to it in the writings of tolerant men of a century or two past. This tolerant perspective does indeed appear in the literature of the fur trade, and, here again, the retreats from the demands of ethnocentrism typify the expressions of one group of men no more than another. Regardless of national derivation, fur traders made at least occasional efforts to explain and to justify ways of doing things that violated the precepts of their own culture.[19]

To the trader the Indian appeared given to cruelty, and none of the natives gained this reputation more fully than some of the Athapascan peoples of the area between Hudson's Bay and the Mackenzie River. The occasional practice of abandoning the weak or the aged represented the most sensational of their reported brutalities. William Wordsworth dramatized such a tragedy in ''Complaint of a Forsaken Indian Woman,'' a heart-rending soliloquy delivered by a dying woman left on a far North trail after her child had been given to another. Detestable and inexcusable as this custom must have seemed to European observers, some traders attempted to alleviate part of the odium attached to such an act. In his narrative of experiences, Thomas Simpson recorded finding the body of a five-year-old Hare girl who had been orphaned and consequently deserted. Such a discovery apparently should have called forth the most wrathful condemnations, but in this context Simpson asked, ''Why should we judge harshly of these poor people?'' For those less capable of generosity, the distant relative of Sir George Simpson quoted a passage from Gibbon telling of things just as dreadful in European history, and bade them ponder it before pronouncing the Indians "a reproach to the human species." Similarly, when Samuel Hearne described the incident which inspired Wordsworth's previously mentioned poetic effort, he demonstrated a remarkable degree of restraint. Though never one to carry a brief for savagery, Hearne explained as well as damned. He pointed out that in the far North the inability to travel was tantamount to a death sentence. A band of Indians who found themselves encumbered with a disabled member faced an age-old ethical problem—should the group sacrifice the weakened individual to secure the well-being of the others? Hearne decided that these people had little choice; survival demanded of them what to outsiders seemed heartless brutality. "If properly considered," he concluded, "it may with justice be ascribed to necessity and self-preservation, rather than the want of humanity and social feeling. . . ." [20]

Although the men in the trade duly noted incidents when the Indian appeared unforgivably indolent, a surprising number of them went on to supply explanations and justifications. And again, such vindications came no more from French traders than from any others. Alexander Ross decided that what he saw as the laziness of the Columbia River natives could be accounted for by the richness of the country, which afforded those tribes little reason to exert themselves. In his comments upon the Crees of the Hudson's Bay area, David Thompson, a Welshman whose generosity of sentiment toward the natives was unexcelled among fur traders, showed an awareness of differing standards of industriousness. The Crees, he pointed out, preferred a six-hour walk over rough terrain to an hour's stint with the white man's pick or ax. To carry the logic of exoneration even further, he noted that "the civilized man has many things to tempt him to an active life, the Indian has none, and is happy sitting still, and smoking his pipe." [21]

When the red man stood accused of reluctance to join physical combat, the trader generally concurred. As an example, Samuel de Champlain once fumed at his seemingly hesitant Huron allies for their failure properly to employ his intricate European military devices, considered them inexcusably lax in taking the initiative against the Iroquois, and gave them the supremely left-handed compliment that the one good thing about their mode of war was their handling of retreats. Still, a good many traders recognized that this apparent lack of valor stemmed not from baseness of character but from a different conception of the meaning of warfare and of conduct proper to it. George Simpson, who rarely seemed to appreciate things other than the Hudson's Bay Company and himself, applauded the mock aspects of Columbia River combat. Failure to rush into sanguinary engagements appeared to him, not craven, but "honorable and manly." David Thompson's strong awareness that Indian values differed from those of the white man removes the apparent derogation from his remark that, "courage is not accounted an essential to the men, any more than chastity to the women. . . ." [22]

Probably no aspect of Indian existence made greater demands upon the understanding of white men among them than their codes of sexual morality. The Frenchman, Pierre Esprit Radisson, exhibited an expected amount of moral censure when he praised a monogamous group of natives for not being "great whoremasters" as, by implication, their polygamous brethren were. Among those who sought to explain rather than condemn, the French seem no more abundant than others. Daniel Harmon, a Vermonter in the employ of the North West Company, viewed with apparent sadness the loose marital connections of some tribes, but quickly added that it made for an advantage often lacking in the civilized system. While persons lived together, they at least did so in harmony. Going beyond this mild vindication, Samuel Hearne made the argument that what was best for one culture was not necessarily best for another. He saw it as only natural, for example, that people of the far North should have a system of plural marriage. Among folk continually on the move the husband and provider simply required more than one helpmate. Hearne went further by excusing what would seem to be a usage more outrageous. He remarked that no stigma should attach to the Chipewyan practice of exchanging wives for a night. It stemmed from respect and friendship among the men, he argued, and served a useful purpose in making one husband responsible for the family of the other in case one should be killed. The fact that Hearne considered most Indian women to be dissolute would seem to enforce rather than negate his tolerance. He took much of the sting from his charge of profligacy by admitting candidly that a matter of perspective was involved. "Indeed it is but reasonable to think," he wrote, "that travellers and interlopers will be always served with the worst commodities, though perhaps they pay the best price for what they have." [23]

To move from attitude to action, one finds little evidence that the supposed intolerance of the Anglo-Saxons prevented them from entering unions with Indian women, or from doing so except with a complete and biologically oriented cynicism. Using the American fur trade as a measure, "the horror of miscegenation" detected by Ruth Benedict in English frontiersmen—though not in others— seems less than compelling. Though there were exceptions, men who spent their time in Indian country generally found consorts there. Bernard DeVoto held that English-speaking traders viewed their tawny wilderness spouses as little more than "foul animals." His use of Daniel Harmon's pondering whether or not to marry an Indian woman, however, fails to convince, for when Harmon eventually returned to his native Vermont, his Indian wife and half-breed children went with him. John Work, though he lived in loyalty with a native woman of the far West, feared for the happiness of an old comrade who had taken a dusky mate and brood eastward. "To join in anything like civilized society with her," he gloomily foretold, "is out of the question." Work spoke, of course, the words of realism, not intolerance.[24]

Regardless of the haphazard nature of many trader-Indian unions, others exhibited elements of constancy and concern. More importantly here, the stereotypical view of the English-speaking trader's relations with native women cannot be accepted at face value, for it is contradicted by too many expressions and actions. Sentiments such as that expressed by Archibald McLeod of the North West Company when he visited an opposition post, are generously scattered in the literature of the trade. McLeod recorded in his diary that his host, James Sutherland, was "of all the Puppies I ever sett eyes on . . . the most nonsensical & dull." However, Sutherland's native wife struck McLeod far differently, and he noted in another entry: ". . . had the *Honor* of playing *Cribbage* with Jeanny, (his wife)." An element of tragedy stemming from misplaced affections appears in a letter from trader John Stuart of the Mackenzie River district to an old comrade. Writing in 1834, with his return to civilization imminent, Stuart bemoaned the fact that "poor unfortunate Mary—of whom, in common with me you always had a high opinion," had entered into an intrigue with "that vile Abenakis, the abominable Anreon." Had she maintained her former good conduct as far as Norway House, he continued, "she most certainly would have become my wife." Evidently, a good many traders of whatever origin looked upon their Indian spouses much as Charles Ross of the Hudson's Bay Company did. When he belatedly informed a sister of his large wilderness family, he noted of the mother of his brood that, "she is not, indeed exactly fitted to shine at the head of a nobleman's table, but she suits the sphere [in which] she has to move much better than any such toy—in short, she is a native of the country, and as to beauty quite as comely as her husband!" [25]

None of this denies that cynicism—stemming from commercial as well as biological considerations—colored many of these relationships; it does question the belief that English-speaking traders were less capable than their French counterparts of sincere regard for women of the wilderness. When men of responsible character took mates under these circumstances, they acted with an approximation of the decorum that would have attended their actions in civilization. The careers of such men as Peter Skene Ogden, Edwin Denig, John Work, David Thompson, William Bent, John McLoughlin, Archibald MacDonald, and John Owen bear this out. Owen, for example, had never bothered to solemnize his union with "Nancy," his Indian wife. However, in 1858 with an epidemic threatening his Rocky Mountain establishment he saw fit to get things in order. "I have been living pleasantly With My old Wife Since the fall of 49," he wrote, "and in case of accident I should feel Much hurt if I had not properly provided for her according to law." [26]

If the difference in attitude between Englishmen and Frenchmen has indeed been overstated, how might the misconception be reasonably explained? First of all, the logic of frontier advance sheds some light on the subject. As Clark Wissler suggested, those who entered a wilderness area first—whether they were French or English—benefited by assuming the easy posture of red man's ally in turning back the inroads of latecomers. Through some of the most engrossing episodes in American development, the French enjoyed the preferential status stemming from prior arrival. A. L. Burt noted that the French moved into the virgin forests more readily than their counterparts to the south because a richer potential of furs lay in front of them and, especially, because of more advantageous geographical position. "The French," he wrote, "were invited into the heart of North America by a magnificent network of highways that was focused in the midst of their settlement." The French, it is commonly assumed, often defeated their English rivals in the race into the interior because they more readily captured the esteem of the natives. Quite possibly, they captured the esteem of the natives because, at critical junctures, they won the race into the interior.[27]

In terms of historiography one needs to recognize the influence of certain major works on frontier history. The widely read books of Francis Parkman and Bernard DeVoto must have done much to propagate this view. Another quite different work that requires mention in this context is Frederick Merk's editing of some of George Simpson's journals and his introductory essay in the same volume. Because of the general excellence and scholarly renown of this work, a reader might assume that Simpson's usually jaundiced attitudes toward the natives exemplified those of most Hudson's Bay men. Actually, Simpson was unusual both in position and in temperament. For example, before considering as typical his carpings at subordinates for their Indian marriages, we must remember that the objects of those criticisms were, like himself, English-speaking Hudson's Bay Company traders. Moreover, *en façon du nord,*

Simpson had, in his early years in the trade, kept his own "bit of brown."[28]

Another relevant historiographical factor stems from the prevalence of a specific literary or historical genre—the Indian-hating "mountain man" narratives of the American far West. While these have probably done much to shape the common conception of frontier attitudes, the world has been spared the reminiscences of their French counterparts, the *voyageurs*. The basic and brutal views of the omnipresent "Jean-Baptiste" rarely got into print, but those of Jim Beckwourth, "Uncle Dick" Wootton, and a good many others from the lowest echelon of the English-speaking fur trade have been dignified by publication. America's lurid interest in its passing frontier in the late years of the nineteenth century spawned a literature—often the work of journalistic amanuenses who knew the public taste—which is not commensurable with the main body of fur-trade sources. The bulk of reliable sources, from the very fact that they were recorded at all, came from men of at least some cerebral attainment, men generally of British, French, Canadian, or American middle-class backgrounds. Because of the comparative advantages of their social origins, they often showed discernment in their writings on the Indians. Their subordinates, whatever their cultural derivations, most likely could not.

Another element which may account for the possible imbalance derives from a modern intellectual point of view. In the 1920's, and to some degree before and after, America's scholarly and intellectual community engaged in a crusade against "puritanism," in a "revolt against the village," and in a fervent renunciation of the Anglo-Saxon racism of the late nineteenth century. Given this atmosphere, it seems understandable that the interpretation of a Francis Parkman, who apparently tagged the Englishman with intolerance, should be accepted and perpetuated. That Parkman may well have been a "racist" himself and thus argued the way he did for the wrong reasons could of course be overlooked. Whatever the reasoning behind it, that interpretation accorded fairly well with the thinking of Americans bent on denying part of their heritage. One scholar has suggested that the influence of Vernon L.

Parrington has helped to prolong a possible misconception regarding attitudes toward the Indian. According to that writer, the Parringtonian animus against New England has been reflected in some major works dealing with frontier outlooks. He felt, for example, that Lucy Hazard, the author of *The Frontier in American Literature,* inherited an anti-New England bias from her teacher, Parrington; and, in turn Albert Keiser incorporated Hazard's viewpoint in his *The Indian in American Literature.*[29] The twentieth-century American may possibly perceive intolerance and bigotry in his Anglo-Saxon forebears because he has been taught to expect it.

The ease with which the traditional interpretation of frontier attitudes can be applied very likely helps account for its acceptance. The idea that the Frenchman was tolerant while the Englishman was intolerant affords a handy method for explaining frontier realities. The cultural origin of the trader offers answers much faster than do some other diverse, amorphous, and rather unmanageable factors which might shed light upon the attitudes of white traders toward their red customers—factors such as the condition of the trade in the time-place setting from which a source comes, the specific tribes with which the author of a source was dealing, the amount of time the trader had spent among Indians generally and among the tribe with whom he was dealing specifically, and, probably most importantly, the personality and outlook of the individual trader himself.

PART 2

THE INDIAN

5. THE NOBLE SAVAGE

IN NARRATING HIS EXPERIENCES IN THE FAR NORTH AS TRADER AND
explorer, Samuel Hearne of the Hudson's Bay Company included a
lengthy treatment of that fascinating animal, the beaver. In doing
so, "honest old Hearne," as a nineteenth-century bibliographer
called him, felt the obligation to temper glowing accounts of the
beaver written by people with inadequate knowledge. According to
him, they greatly overestimated the organizational ability, sagacity,
and ingenuity of this amphibious creature. Because such exaggerations were often so pronounced, Hearne playfully suggested the
existence of an open competition among their perpetrators in devis-
ing falsehoods. According to Hearne, one unnamed author clearly
outdid his fellows by leaving nothing to be desired in his discussion
of beavers except "a vocabulary of their language, a code of their
laws, and a sketch of their religion. . . ." This satiric jibe was a
telling one. It recognized the gratuitous glorification of natural
forms, and it suggested that such efforts were the work of persons
well removed from the supposed virtues of the nature being described.[1]

Because they were versed in the unpleasant ways of the wilderness, fur traders infrequently touched upon the noble savage, that
creature defined by Hoxie Fairchild as "any free and wild being
who draws directly from nature virtues which raise doubts as to the
value of civilization." Proverbially, this virtuous and happy creature has emanated from the imaginations of fireside travelers,
philosophers, and litterateurs. Fairchild's classic work on the subject referred to him as "the creation of a philosopher . . . reacting
from contemporary glorification of culture. . . ." Chauncey
Brewster Tinker located the origin of the convention in an intellec-

tual climate different from that described by Fairchild, but the persons involved in creating the delusion fit the same description. "The 'noble savage,' " according to Tinker, "was the offspring of the rationalism of the Deist philosophers, who, in their attack upon the Christian doctrine of the fall of man, had idealized the child of Nature." And according to A. O. Lovejoy, the cultural primitivist was, by definition, unfamiliar with the people he lauded. Seemingly, traders, with their practical experience in the affairs of the wilderness and its inhabitants, could provide an antidote and a corrosive for the noble savage convention. Having foregone the benefits of civilization—the "land of Cakes" as one trader called it—they should have been disinclined to entertain ideas that compared it invidiously with savagery. To a surprising degree, however, they indulged in the unexpected.[2]

Hoxie Fairchild has written that the philosophers who conjured up noble savages relied upon travelers and explorers for their raw material. This idea, plus the seeming reality that no one should have known the Indian better than the fur trader, causes one to ask to what degree these men supplied grist for the mills of noble savage thinkers. Such theoreticians rarely consulted fur traders. Fairchild mentioned only one trader, James Adair, whose writings lent themselves to the noble savage design. Tinker, in his work of narrower scope, cited none at all. Even Benjamin Bissell's *The American Indian in English Literature of the Eighteenth Century* contains only slight mention of fur-trade evaluations and the way they were woven into more artistic or philosophical treatments of the natives.[3]

Of course, Bissell concerned himself with the eighteenth century, a period in which the only major fur-trade narratives published were those of Joseph Robson in the 1750's, James Adair in the 1770's, Edward Umfreville, Samuel Hearne, and John Long in the 1790's, and Alexander Mackenzie at the turn of the century. However, this does not seem to have been the basic reason for Bissell's failure to utilize such material. The fur traders' considered judgments of wilderness life simply did not coincide with European presuppositions. John Long and James Adair, both of whom seem romantic or fanciful at times, appear in Bissell's study as contributors to the English literary concept of the Indian. The grimly realistic Samuel Hearne appears only once, and the nature of the example is noteworthy and indicative of the general position of the fur trader vis-à-vis the literal, not the noble, savage. Bissell mentioned Wordsworth's citing Hearne as the source of "Complaint of a Forsaken Indian Woman." Hearne presented the incident as sickeningly brutal, though he admitted the possible necessity for such a practice in the subarctic. Wordsworth, on the other hand, passed by the hideousness of the affair and went on to dwell upon the nobility of the sentiments of the unfortunate woman, her amazingly magnanimous understanding, and, especially, her poignant concern for her small child taken from her and given to another. The accurate reportage of a Samuel Hearne could be ignored except as it provided a backdrop for the heroic tragedy of dramatic lyrics.[4] After all, if the fur trader failed to say the proper things about the condition of the natural state, European intellectuals could turn to someone who would—a Baron Louis de Lahontan, a François de Chateaubriand, or a Jonathan Carver.

More directly, it requires no great effort to discover in the fur-trade literature specific and heated denials that the natives were in any way noble. When, for example, Auguste Chouteau felt the necessity of explaining his trade difficulties to the Baron de Carondelet, he pointed directly at the brutishness of savage nature. According to this eminent frontier businessman, "l'homme de la nature" prided himself on his violence, defied "l'ordre et l'harmonie," and, as a society, lived "aux excès de leur barbarie." Writing in the early 1850's, Peter Skene Ogden chided "drawing-room authors" for their misrepresentation of Indian character. He complained that they portrayed the red men as "quiet, peaceable souls, meriting nothing so much as the most delicate attention" from outsiders. Though this experienced Hudson's Bay Company trader recognized "savage virtues," he sought to illustrate the "dark character" of the aborigines and to demonstrate their "natural disposition to war and rapine." Similarly, when Pierre-Antoine Tabeau wrote his narrative of a trading expedition up the Missouri in the year before Lewis and Clark, he left little doubt about the exalted nature of the primitives. Tabeau showed none of Ogden's reservations:

If the Ricara, if the Sioux, is the man of nature so much praised by poets, every poetic license has been taken in painting him; for their pictures make a beautiful contrast to that which I have before me. All that one can say is that, if these barbarians leave no doubt that they are human, intelligent beings, it is because they have the form, the face, and the faculty of speech of human beings.[5]

Others evidenced their disbelief in a somewhat less direct fashion. John McLean, a former Hudson's Bay Company trader, resorted to irony in touching upon the noble savage theme when discussing the Nascopies of Labrador. These people had undergone so little contact with whites that, according to McLean, they could be considered " 'children of nature,' and possessed, of course, of all the virtues ascribed to such. . . ." "Yet I must say," he continued, "that my acquaintance with them disclosed nothing that impressed me with a higher opinion of them than of my own race, corrupted as they are by the arts of civilized life." McLean asserted that only a fear of disgusting his readers kept him from detailing the grosser passions indulged by these "children of nature." In the same vein, James Chambers at Fort Sarpy in Crow country employed evident sarcasm in referring to "Our Noble Crow Warriors" and to the "red 'Sons of Mars.' " Elsewhere in his journal he set down a scurrilous raillery that could hardly be further removed from exoticism or respect for the native race. Apparently unhampered by McLean's Methodist piety or by concern for offending readers, Chambers commented as follows in an entry describing an Indian dance at which "Princess May & her bosom Friend & Maid of Honor 'E 'See 'Tah" were "the observed of all observors":

The princess led the van & made but two or three circles in the yard of the Fort when she placed her divine foot in something of a dark brown substance that emitted an odor like anything but the Otto of roses. May blushed or as good tryed to blush her Lord & Husband was cast down, the Squaws sighed the Bucks laughed & Big Six [a Virginian]

Shame on him, bellowed out May tramped on a green tird, however the miss step broke the Ball thus depriving the Princess of bringing out her powers of fascination before her loving subjects.

Thus, when traders consciously and sincerely discussed the Indian qua Indian, their evaluations generally paralleled Hearne's treatment of the "noble" beaver: they displayed impatience and ridicule in regard to the noble savage concept.[6]

The dichotomy between unmoved realism on the part of fur traders and the contrived glorification by uninitiated intellectuals and artists does not, however, have the clarity one might suspect. After all, the noble savage was a mental construct, and it is not surprising that generally honest, candid, and intelligent men in the fur trade failed to discover him in the flesh. At the same time, it should occasion no greater surprise to find traders demonstrating the tendency toward occasional reserved flirtation with this very concept. Precisely because the noble savage was a mental construct *and* an imaginative device for making a point, the fur trader could, without logical contradiction, utilize the convention if he so desired. To argue that the trader could not ennoble the Indian because his true knowledge and experience stood in direct contradiction, would be to argue that Jonathan Swift in his account of the Houyhnhnms and Michel de Montaigne in his treatment of the Caniballes were, to the best of their ability, expounding truth. Most often the trader wrote of the Indian qua Indian, but not always.

To infer from this that traders saw no real virtues in Indian life is to miss the point. In fact, the traders readily admitted the existence of such virtues, as for example, when they occasionally expressed envy of the free and casual nature of Indian existence. While discussing the serenely pastoral setting of a Sioux camp, the devout Jedediah Smith remarked in his 1822 journal that it would "almost persuade a man to renounce the world, take the lodge and live the careless, Lazy life of an indian." In a similar vein, Thomas Simpson, while traveling between Point Barrow and the mouth of the Mackenzie River, saw Indians and Eskimos enjoying that zest and gusto "which perfect freedom alone can give." Alexander Ross makes the comparison between the civilized and the primitive even more evident with his comment on the apparent happiness of the Columbia River tribes, a state "which civilized men, wearied with care and anxious pursuits, perhaps seldom enjoy." Although these commentators were not guilty of patent flirtation with the noble savage concept (and their remarks appear to have a narrow and precise application), all three men involved themselves in primitivistic assumptions. They compared invidiously the contrived and intricate workings of civilization to the artlessness and simplicity of the natural state. Though none of the three would have admitted it, they substantiated the paradoxical and perhaps playful maxim of Erasmus: " . . . the least unhappy are those who approximate the naïveté of the beasts. . . ." [7]

Although the fur trader now and then portrayed noble savages, his brethren in civilization also occasionally did violence to the trader's generally honest and accurate reportage. For the sake of a philosophical concept, they would by fiat make silk purses out of sows' ears. The description of the Cree chief, Le Sonnant, given in a letter by upper Missouri trader Robert Campbell to his brother in Philadelphia illustrates the point. In this letter, now extant only in the form that it was published in a Philadelphia newspaper, Le Sonnant appeared as a figure of grand proportions. He had eyes set so deep between hawk nose and high cheekbones that no man "even in your *prying* and *starring* city" could tell their color. On the other hand, the chief with only a glance could "peer into your very soul." His head was formed grandly. Even without phrenological training one could see strength of purpose in it, while his physical make-up and carriage attested to his capacity as a leader. [8]

Unfortunately, this flattering description does not fit Le Sonnant. In the same year that Campbell wrote his letter, Carl Bodmer, the Swiss artist accompanying Prince Maximilian, drew that Indian's portrait. Bodmer's Le Sonnant has an aquiline but not a hawk nose. His cheekbones, rather than prominent, are unusually low. His eyes, rather than deep-set, appear prominent on a flat face. His chin is small, and his mouth is loose and has a petulant bearing. The eyes, which were of particular note in the Campbell letter, appeared far different to Bodmer. Along with being prominent rather than deep set, the left one is marred by a noticeable bag beneath it while the right one would be hard pressed to "peer into your very soul" because it is covered by an ophthalmic film so common among Indians. Indeed, Bodmer had difficulty making his subject sit because of the pain. Whether Robert Campbell ordinarily glamorized the Indians is not clear, but it seems justified at least to suspect that his brother or the Philadelphia newspaper edited his letters to increase their appeal to eastern readers. What was probably meant for no more than a passing mention of Le Sonnant became in Philadelphia the glowing account of a very nearly noble savage.*

A similar disparity appears between the two published journals of Jean Baptiste Trudeau. In recording his experiences on the upper Missouri from June, 1794, to March, 1795, Trudeau vilified the natives of the area. His journal covering the remainder of 1795, however, comes to modern readers only by way of a copy of a copy of the original, which document was at one time in the possession of Thomas Jefferson. It has a far different ring. In this latter journal Trudeau divided his eloquence between encomiums on the natural man who observed the laws of "reason, nature and humanity," and disparagement of civilized men who practiced torments of body and

* If Campbell intended to describe an Indian of noble proportions, it is strange that he did not choose one other than Le Sonnant. The Cree, Broken Arm, the Assiniboine, Crazy Bear, and the Crow, Rotten Belly, were often described as fine appearing men who possessed at least some admirable traits of character. All three had occasion to be in the upper Missouri area from which Campbell wrote the above letter.

To satisfy my concern that perhaps I alone considered Bodmer's Le Sonnant an ignoble looking savage, I checked my reactions against those of others. My judgment seemed to be vindicated. George R. Brooks, who edited the recently found private journal of Campbell, referred to the portrait of Le Sonnant as "one of the handsomest and most sensitive in Maximilian's *Atlas.*" I take both descriptives to apply to the aesthetic qualities of the work, not to Le Sonnant. The Campbell journal covering the period from September 21 to December 31, 1833, does not mention Le Sonnant's arrival at Fort William until December 2—two weeks after the date of the letter to his Philadelphia brother. In his journal Campbell did not describe Le Sonnant except to say that "he is certainly the greatest rascal I ever met." George R. Brooks (ed.), "The Private Journal of Robert Campbell," *Missouri Historical Society Bulletin*, XX (October, 1963) and (January, 1964). See part two, pp. 108–9.

soul upon one another by means of "the sword, the gown and the counting house." While people in a civilized state were crazed by a quest for lucre and preference, the savage lived in a condition bordering on that equality "conformable to the dictates of nature" and exhibited such generosity and good will that quarrels, thefts, slander, and cheating never occurred among them.[9]

But not all the noble savages in fur-trade literature were furtively foisted off upon dead or unsuspecting traders. These grim, hardened, and realistic wilderness operators must bear most of the responsibility for the presence in their writings of the symbols of the primitivistic myth. Hoxie Fairchild has written that the noble savage idea, once started, traveled in a circle: literature colored the observations of travelers just as their observations influenced literature.[10] Although this reciprocal effect seems not to have been very compelling where fur men were concerned, the impact of the concept upon traders' writings demands at least passing consideration in explaining why the noble savage reared his exotic head in the pages of fur-trade records. Of course, had all men in the trade been mental and moral degenerates, had they been Mike Finks or even Kit Carsons, this would amount to a meaningless exercise because literary and philosophical conventions would have been lost to them. Such was not the case. The men who recorded their impressions for posterity, for the reading public, or simply for superiors in the trade were men who had, for their time in history, quite good, occasionally excellent, educations. If "literature" colored "observation," there should be some evidence of it in the writings of fur traders.

And, indeed, there is. One element in this influence was an effort to cater to the demands of the reading public. Hoxie Fairchild has written that by 1799 no one considering the publication of travel material could afford to ill use the savages. This generalization needs some qualification where fur men were concerned. For example, Ross Cox, an Astorian who returned to his native Dublin to become a correspondent for a London newspaper, announced in the preface to his narrative that his portrayals of the American Indians would not compare with the "beautiful colouring which the romantic pen of a Chateaubriand has imparted." And Robert Michael Ballantyne, who spent six years as an employee of the Hudson's Bay Company and then went back to Scotland where he wrote over eighty youthful adventure books, seemed unwilling even in the fiction form gratuitously to exalt the savages. In *The Wild Man of the West* his Hawkswing, though a member of a band of heroic trappers, is so voiceless, subdued, and inconspicuous that he hardly measures up to the traditional role of faithful Indian guide, let alone that of noble savage. He never acts as spokesman for virtue or justice, and Ballantyne, though giving him admirable traits, described him quite negatively: " . . . he was not a hero; few savages are." [11]

Nevertheless, the essence of Fairchild's comment seems valid. In spite of Cox's pronouncement at the outset and his conformity with the spirit of it through most of his work, he deals with suspiciously idealized savages later in his work. Of the Flatheads, he wrote: "Their bravery is pre-eminent:—a love of truth they think necessary to a warrior's character. They are too proud to be dishonest, too candid to be cunning." "Their many avocations" left no time for gambling, and the necessity to cooperate precluded quarreling. For a time in the 1830's and 1840's the Flatheads enjoyed a good reputation in the East, probably stemming from their supposed efforts to obtain Christian missionaries for their tribe. In their reminiscences of Rocky Mountain life, Osborne Russell, Zenas Leonard, and Warren Angus Ferris brought their comments on the Flatheads into accord with eastern presuppositions by ascribing bravery, generosity, and friendliness to them. Thus, by indulging this predilection on the part of easterners, men in the fur trade evidenced the basic accuracy of Fairchild's observation.[12]

Even those who apparently had never seen a Flathead showed a perfect willingness to oblige. Though his brief career in the fur trade took him only to the peripheries of Flathead country, Thomas James proclaimed them a "noble race of men . . . the Spartans of Oregon." And James Ohio Pattie's narrative, edited by Timothy Flint at the time that American Christianity was heralding the tawny "Wise Men from the West," went out of its way to mention the Flatheads. Though this tribe did not practice head-flattening, Pattie and Flint understandably assumed that they did, and so pictured them as fine looking creatures except for their "horrid deformity." Finally, one can hardly doubt that the lip-service given the noble savage convention by Isaac Cowie of the late-nineteenth-century trade was dictated by a regard for reading tastes. Late in his volume of recollections, Cowie justified the slaughter of some eighty Assiniboines by a handful of American ranchers armed with repeating rifles. In spite of his approbation of this "signal service," he had seen fit at the opening of his book to invoke the primitivistic mood by describing the Indian of times past in the words of John Dryden:

> Free as the day when nature first made man,
> Ere the base laws of servitude began,
> When wild in woods the noble savage ran.[13]

But many traders, like the European intellectuals who fostered the noble savage notion, employed this fictional creature out of motivation more commendable than that of the Patties and the Cowies. Some of them used the theme in an effort to procure better treatment for the aborigines. Of course, men of religion had often indulged in primitivism to effect that very goal, Bartholomew de Las Casas being a prime example. Fur traders of a religious or humane bent, not surprisingly, did the same thing. John McLean, for example, combined a pique against his former employer, the Hudson's Bay Company, and a strong Methodist piety to make an impassioned appeal in behalf of the American Indians. Earlier in his book, as has been noted, he had left no doubt that the state of nature had little to offer. Still, he called upon the very thing he had earlier denied in making his closing plea for humaneness. With England spending prodigious sums of money and vast amounts of energy in the cause of the benighted Negroes, "can nothing," asked McLean, "be done for the once noble, but now degraded, aborigines of America?" He did not dwell on this former state of nobility because he knew it was a sham. If his primitivism involved untruth, it probably seemed justifiable under the circumstances. McLean must have recognized that a once noble Indian was a more potent argumentative weapon than the barbarians described earlier in the narrative. He used primitivism much as A. O. Lovejoy has argued that Rousseau used it—not as a literal description of an actual condition, but as a disputatious device.[14]

But men of the fur trade went further even than these qualified and somewhat questionable applications of noble savagery. At times they invoked concepts that fit almost perfectly into the primitivistic convention. While ordinarily insisting with vehemence that no Indians in their experience approached nobility, traders tended to harbor a vague presentiment that such a creature could exist somewhere on ahead. A good example appears in the journal of Matthew Cocking on a pioneering trip from York Factory to the Blackfoot country in the early 1770's. "I shall be sorry," he wrote during the course of his journey, "if I do not see the Equestrian Natives [Blackfeet] who are certainly a brave people, & far superior to any tribes that visit our Forts: they have dealings with no Europeans, but live in a state of nature to the S. W. Westerly. . . ." Similarly, the occasionally naïve La Vérendrye carried with him on his way to the Mandans an unrealistically high evaluation of that renowned tribe. Even when seeing and recognizing that this Siouan splinter group did not equal his preconceptions, he seemed incapable of ridding his mind of the flattering prejudices. A philosophical convention could not literally overcome a trader's sense perceptions. However, it could apparently instill in his mind certain muted, paradisiac anticipations that are relevant to the noble savage theme. In a fashion reminiscent of European intellectuals and theorists, these wilderness men of action felt what A. O. Lovejoy called "the charm of the remote and the strange, the craving to imagine, and even to experience, some fashion of life which is at least *different* from the all too familiar visage of existence as it has hitherto presented itself. . . ."[15]

As a corollary and in natural sequence to these romantic expectations, a good deal of evidence indicates that, where trader and Indian were concerned, familiarity bred contempt. Realizations rarely equaled expectations. In practical affairs traders operated on the assumption that the red man's awe and regard for them decreased with time. Probably because it required introspection to recognize the fact, they less often remarked on their own tendency to reciprocate. Nevertheless, the Indian near at hand excited the fur man's wrath and scorn, while the one elsewhere—whether Ross Cox's Flatheads so comfortably removed from the country of the detestable Chinooks, or Matthew Cocking's Blackfeet, or La Vérendrye's Mandans, or the southwesterner Pattie's admirable tribes of the Northwest—conjured up visions of honesty, virtue, and possibly even excellence.

In the average trader this abhorrence of the familiar manifested itself in desires to see the local tribes treated roughly by their enemies. Thus, James Chambers at Fort Sarpy wished his Crows an abundance of ill fortune in their encounters with the Sioux and Blackfeet, and Francis Chardon on the upper Missouri craved the same fate for the surrounding Arikaras and Mandans at the hands of the happily distant Yanktons and Assiniboines. That Chardon's ill will was not, as Bernard DeVoto suggested, indiscriminate, can be shown by his noteworthy desire, expressed to his employer at a trying juncture, "to bid you all adieu for ever—and end my days with the Sioux." However, the best illustration of the working of this mechanism appears in the journal, and in the career, of Rudolph Friederich Kurz. Unlike many of his fellows, Kurz recognized that Aesop's proverb concerning familiarity applied to trader and Indian alike. In describing Edwin Denig, a trader whom he knew quite well, Kurz revealed the following:

Every time a band of Indians annoys Mr. Denig with their begging he flees to me and unburdens his heart by calling them names. At such times he bestows much praise on other Indians who are not here but who get their share of abuse also at some future time. He is always in the best humor with Indians when none are around. . . . Today the red men who were at the fort stood high in his esteem, but since they have shown that his many courtesies only encouraged them to beg, to expect presents, he thinks them good for nothing, not worthy to unloose the shoe laces of Indians who inhabit the eastern domain.

Though the good Indians were ordinarily to the west rather than to the east, the generally realistic Mr. Denig, like many of his fellows, showed a mark of the romantic in condemning the familiar while acclaiming the foreign.[16]

Another element in this complex of primitivistic ideas involves the belief that civilized man soiled the character of the wilderness dweller. The perennial and worrisome conviction that such was indeed the rule has a prominent place in a recent work by Charles L. Sanford. He argues that "human history, converging in the perspective of time on America, is best understood in relation to the pursuit of paradise . . . ," and that "the Edenic myth . . . has been the most powerful and comprehensive organizing force in American culture." As Sanford points out, this conception entailed the blissful assumption that the vices of an overly sophisticated, artificial, and sinful Old World could be exchanged for the faultlessness of simplicity. Psychologically, America represented "a rebirth out of hell," and, unlike Savonarola who could only burn the vanities, sojourners into the wilderness seemingly could escape them. The new society had scarcely been erected in America, however, when the inhabitants experienced the haunting intimation that the corruption of Europe had followed after them.[17]

To some degree the fur traders in the heart of the wilderness recognized the operation of the same mechanism. However, being in contact with the literal primitive, they tended to see themselves in a somewhat different juxtaposition with Europe. Unlike the nonfrontier American who saw himself being seduced by the overcivilization of the Old World, the fur trader seemed to view himself as a part of that vitiating force. As fur traders entertained to some degree Arcadian notions of what lay ahead, so they also felt the misgivings and frustrations in watching the inhabitants of their supposed Eden—the Indians, not themselves—degenerate at the civilized touch. The red man, they insisted, learned only the vices and never the virtues of civilization.

In assessing fur-trade expressions of that idea, one has to face first of all the imponderable problem of whether this degeneration was literally taking place. That question must be left for others. Moreover, one must bear in mind the more demonstrable fact that the virtues-and-vices theme coincided with the best interests of the fur trade. To argue that the advance of civilization entailed the debasement of the natives logically implied the obligation of preserving a primeval state in which Indians perpetuated their virtues, trapped fur-bearing animals, and sold them to traders. This import emerges clearly from a document that Duncan M'Gillivray wrote in an effort to justify the North West Company's dominion over much of the interior of British America. Contact with Christianity and with "civil society" did nothing for the aborigines, he argued; indeed, those so exposed were in the worst condition of any Indians. While they appeared "timid, lazy and wretched," those in the interior were "brave, active & industrious." M'Gillivray's brief sketches of the various tribes—arranged geographically, probably to heighten the drama—described a striking anthropological ascent from east to west. The eastern Algonquians were "insolent, timid & of weak constitutions" while their western relatives to the north of Lake Superior were "more daring, enterprising and industrious." Still farther to the west, the Assiniboines showed even greater excellence by being "bold and intrepid, but in their intercourse with friends, mild and hospitable." This company veteran, using a contrived primitivism, raised the prospect of preserving the red men's nobility and simultaneously (for those of a more practical bent) maintaining several thousand hardy warriors who would protect the empire rather than degenerate into a rabble of debilitated wards of the state.[18]

Because the noble savage was a mental construct, M'Gillivray's reason for invoking it may appear as good as any other. Be that as it may, other traders substantiated the virtues-and-vices facet of primitivism out of honest conviction or, at least, out of a more commendable ulterior motive. As a matter of fact, most fur men seem to have been too candid and unapologetic to have dissembled in an effort to justify their endeavors. Moreover, they intended most of their written expressions only for the eyes of their superiors, an audience that scarcely needed convincing.

The prevalence of the corruption theme in fur-trade literature can be well illustrated by examples from the unquestionably authentic journals of two men whose practical attitudes toward the natives were anything but fawning. In December of 1826 Peter Skene Ogden recorded in his journal his brigade's encounter with some red men whose behavior led Ogden to describe them as "good Indians." At this point he digressed long enough to deplore the fact that they would not remain "good" for very long. "Two years intimacy with the Whites," he wrote, "will make them like all other Indians villains. . . ." Two months later Ogden made the point more precisely. After observing some Indians completely in the "wild state," he noted with sad assurance that "our" influence would soon tame them and thus make them "villains"—"the same is the case with all Indians. . . ." A final illustration comes from the journal of Alexander Henry the younger, a man whose hatred for the natives fairly bristled. Despite his antipathy, however, in the following commentary on some Rocky Mountain peoples he heralded the virtues of noncivilization:

Their morals have not yet been sufficiently debauched and corrupted by an intercourse with people who call themselves Christians, but whose licentious and lecherous manners are far worse than those of the savages. . . . Happy those who have the least connection with us, for most of their present depravity is easily traced to its origin in their intercourse with the whites.

Thus, the fur trader viewed himself, not as the inhabitant of nature's paradise, but as the emissary of the corrupting influence of civilization. Paradoxically, the bulk of the American society considered itself the embodiment of the pristine excellence of nature.[19]

The classic function of a noble savage is, as Hoxie Fairchild has put it, to exhibit "virtues which raise doubts as to the value of civilization." These virtues have been implicit in the fur-trade expressions discussed up to this point. But traders did not always deal in implications and were not always subtle or abstruse. At times they employed the pure use of the noble savage theme by joining the issue directly, by flailing civilization with the cudgel of primitivism, and even by playing an unimaginatively obliging devil's advocate locked in a verbal struggle with a wonderfully rational red man who instructs in the good life. Not all traders, of course, engaged in such antics, and none of them plied the tools of primitivism well enough to conjure up the equal of, say, Baron Lahontan's enviably cerebral, wilderness free-thinker, Adario. However, the significant thing would seem to be, not the quality or the overwhelming quantity of this most straightforward noble savage device, but rather the fact that it appears at all in fur-trade literature.

Sometimes these exercises in primitivism had a selfish, a chauvinistic, or an ethnocentric flavor, with the wisdom of the savage mortifying, not all of civilization, but only the other fellow's. Like ethnocentrics generally, they could applaud their own way only by denigrating the ways of others. Alexander McDonnell, a clerk for the North West Company, demonstrated this tendency when, in a published tract, he recorded what purported to be a speech of a Red River chief. The particulars of the case arouse doubts because McDonnell's eloquent Indian devoted a peculiarly great amount of time to counseling the wisdom of acceding to the supposedly selfless wishes of the North West Company at a time when that concern and Lord Selkirk's ''bad garden-makers'' were struggling for control of the region. James Ohio Pattie used the same device for a slightly different purpose in his portrayal of a remarkably Protestant primitive who exposed and confounded the sophistry of a Catholic priest. Such savages were not only noble, they were obliging as well.[20]

More typically, the fabricators of ideal primitives criticized their own culture. They indulged in cultural self-abnegation rather than the cultural egoism mentioned above. They found the object of their rancor within their own society rather than within someone else's. Furthermore, being civilized men and holding essentially to the values of civilization—''the land of Cakes''—fur traders who utilized the noble savage theme ordinarily channeled the efforts of their aboriginal spokesmen into attacks upon specific institutions or practices. Their attacks were detailed, not wholesale. Like Lovejoy's Rousseau, they reproved civilization; they did not eschew it. Indeed, the burden of their primitivistic message was more nearly social criticism than anthropological regression. Roy Harvey Pearce probably did no more than overstate the case in noting that "at bottom primitivistic thinking in America was always radical." [21]

In *The Quest for Paradise* Charles Sanford demonstrated the anti-intellectual tone of primitivistic thought. Occasionally, a fur trader belittled sophisticated rationality by heralding the intuition of the natural man. David Thompson, for example, himself a product of the Westminster Grey Coat School, conveyed this import in a discussion of the vast, frantic, and seemingly senseless reindeer migrations—movements that entailed huge losses from exhaustion, trampling, drowning, and starvation. Thompson had once attempted to explain this singular phenomenon to some Indians in terms of "Instinct," which he defined as "the free and voluntary actions of an animal for its self preservation." This theory aroused the derision of his tawny listeners, and, in what must have been a patronizing tone, they asked rhetorically if he thought the animals trampled each other, drowned, and died of exhaustion in order to preserve themselves. " 'You white men,' " they taunted, " 'you look like wise men, and talk like fools.' " The migrations, the Indians loftily informed him, were the workings of the reindeer Manito. Thompson seemed unable to parry these thrusts by his red protagonists and terminated the discussion in his narrative by a hurried surrender and a rather apologetic admission of the poverty of learned theories: "I had to give up my doctrine of Instinct, to that of their Manito. I have sometimes thought Instinct, to be a word invented by the learned to cover their ignorance." [22]

But other failings in their fellow men must have appeared far more evident to traders than sophism. For example, they had much more occasion to remark by indirection upon that classic weakness, niggardliness. American Rocky Mountain trader Rufus Sage provided a somewhat extreme illustration in a chapter of his recollections dealing partly with "Nature's nobleman." When Sage's party came upon a pair of Indian ponies, they butchered one and kept the other. Shortly thereafter, they met a band of Arapahoes searching for the selfsame mounts. With hazard in the circumstances, the white spokesman decided that the truth properly and discreetly stated would best appeal to the red sense of justice. After a contrived introduction involving the imminence of starvation, he informed the Indian leader that, "the flesh of the younger one has caused us to bless the Good Spirit. . . ." "My heart is good," the chief replied, but he appeared downcast and went on to indicate that the dead pony had been a favorite of his wife and children. Sensing a highly dangerous impasse, the white leader became very solicitous in seeking ways to make amends. However, the somber red man reassured him with the words, "now my heart blesses the pale faces," and indicated a desire only for a bit of tobacco that the two parties might smoke to friendship. Even the least discerning could hardly have missed the point, but Sage made doubly certain: ". . . where, let me ask, do we find in civilized countries an instance of noble generosity equal to that of the poor savage?" [23]

Of all the fur-trade primitivists, James Adair came nearest to making blanket condemnations of the civilized way. Adair presented Indians "governed by the plain and honest law of nature," a condition making for equality, liberty, and physical soundness. In the late chapters of his work Adair turned his attention to particular blights on civilized society. Where the white man, for example, punished wrong-doers by physical abuse and incarceration, the Indian practiced a gentle rehabilitation. If the culprit had stolen or lied, he received praise for his honesty, and these barbs struck him "so good naturedly and skilfully" that he would die before committing the same offense again. Various institutions fell before the reason and wisdom of the savages who, though they were "unskilfull in making the marks of our ugly lying books, which spoil people's honesty," had on the other hand been "duly taught in the honest volumes of nature." [24]

With the old trader playing the traditional role of devil's advocate, albeit a less effectual and believable one than the reader has a right to expect, the institutions of law, military, and medicine took the brunt of the verbal onslaught. The spokesman for the natural life argued that among "civilized" peoples military titles went to the highest bidders, often "lazy, deformed white men with big bellies" who went about swelling their chests almost as large as their stomachs and speaking sharply to poor folk. Brushing by Adair's feeble insistence upon the "wisdom and justice of our voluminous laws," the natural man demonstrated that the legal system was so complicated and the courts so overrun by men "with cunning heads and strong mouths" that a simple man could not find justice. And medical practitioners dismembered people with far too great abandon. The weight of these evils fell upon the "humble, modest, and poor" whose complaints were drowned out by the "noisy rich." For the simple man the only comfort lay in honesty itself, hardly compensation enough for "a wife crying over helpless children, in a small waste house."[25]

Adair's Indians considered the civilized practice of amputation so heinous that they would have beaten the practitioners of it with knobby poles, revived them, and then cut off their ears and noses with dull knives. The fact that these supposititious wilderness sages did not mention the possibility of a generous and bantering rehabilitation for doctors, as there was for thieves, evidences a real contradiction. Adair, for whom these savages spoke, maintained more consistency in his critique of civilized forms than he did in his contrived championing of the natural life. Indeed, a contrariety between the real and the *ad hoc* savage appears in nearly all such sources. As noted earlier, John McLean portrayed one Indian in his considered description of native life and quite another in his plea for Christian mercy. Edward Umfreville tended to dress up the Indians in those sections of his book which indicted the Hudson's Bay Company, but he straightforwardly exposed the utter viciousness of the red men when he had no argument to make. By the same token, Adair's enlightened aborigines appeared late in his work and bore little resemblance to the barbarous natives he had described at the outset. Though Hoxie Fairchild referred to this trader as the "highly romantic Adair," one finds the Indians depicted early in his book to have been cunning, deceitful, mischievous, dishonest, and, though given to bloody revenge, quite cowardly. The Choctaws, Adair argued, possessed no human attributes "except shape and language."[26]

Thus one must face the question of whether the fur traders

trafficked in authentic noble savages. Were they primitivists, or did they indulge in what A. O. Lovejoy referred to as "supposed primitivism"? Since the noble savage is myth and the clear superiority of civilization over savagery is generally, if not universally, recognized, this involves a knotty problem with some fine distinctions. Quite demonstrably, fur traders at times employed the elements of noble savagery in their writings. The problem hinges upon the question of whether these outward signs truly indicated an inward conviction. Or, was that conviction necessary? Did the fur trader have to maintain the ignorance of believing in the literal existence of noble savages in order to utilize the theme validly? Lovejoy, by calling Rousseau's a "supposed primitivism" because he did not actually believe in the excellence of the natural state, has implied the affirmative.[27]

According to this logic, the trader was capable only of a superficial or artificial form of noble savagery—a tautology, of course. By Lovejoy's definition, the cultural primitivist idealized races or peoples foreign to him, apparently because knowledge would preclude idolizing. Evidently the trader as primitivist was at an overwhelming disadvantage. The scholar or intellectual could convey sincerity, conviction, and consistency by maintaining a semblance of ignorance. He could express his dislike of civilization— also a part of Lovejoy's definition of cultural primitivism—by comparing it invidiously with savagery, and regardless of how much he may have had tongue in cheek, his motivation would go unquestioned. Having seen the savage, the fur trader had dropped from innocence.[28]

Though he probably utilized the noble savage in much the way that the philosopher did, the trader displayed the mark of guilty knowledge, indicating that his noble savage was a contrived device fabricated for an ulterior motive. For example, Edwin Denig once informed Rudolph Kurz that, "I should count myself happy, that, owing to my nearsightedness, I was prevented from entering fully upon the Indian mode of life." Denig apparently assumed that good vision would have destroyed Kurz's cherished notions. Actually, the experienced and intelligent trader had overestimated Kurz's handicap; the young intellectual's powers of observation were not so bad that he still preserved the innocent predilections that he had retained as far west as St. Joseph, Missouri. At that point his ardor for portraying "the romantic mode of life" of the Indian waxed strong. Through the course of his sojourn on the high plains his outlook changed remarkably and came to resemble that of the sympathetic but realistic "Mr. Denig." Near the end of Kurz's stay, he watched Rottenfail's band of Crows ride out of the fort and commented tellingly: "Do but go; the fewer Indians we have in this vicinity the more animals are to be seen. For my studies, beasts of the chase are now more welcome than Indians." While at St. Joseph, with his naïveté unimpaired, Kurz described noble savages and, by common definition, engaged in primitivism. However, when he returned to Switzerland, after a stay in the wilderness had apparently shorn him of his sanguine conviction in primal excellence, Kurz again described noble savages, but engaged in something less than primitivism. Having gained an intimate knowledge of the wilderness, fur traders could only manifest the outward signs of primitivism; they seem to be denied the designation "primitivist." [29]

Whatever the problems of definition, fur traders did utilize the noble savage theme, and they did so essentially to air their grievances—an activity for which they had sound precedent. One suspects, for example, that John Long of the eastern Canadian trade felt personally abused by niggardly treatment, and that he reflected this in his combined carpings at the "parsimonious conduct of those whom providence hath blessed with affluence" and encomiums on the Indians who were free of such "mean sordid sentiments." James Adair seemed quite incapable of maintaining accord with the civilized scheme of things, and so he vented his rancor via noble savages. One of the best illustrations of the workings of this mechanism appears in the writings of Rufus Sage, who portrayed savage excellence in his published narrative of frontier life. The letters Sage wrote to his mother during his sojourn in the mountains reveal a man of fervent religious tendency, of deep and morbid pessimism, who considered himself adrift amidst a sea of enemies.

He despised everything he knew, including himself, and like other dissatisfied souls, he could embrace the foreign for having spiritually forsaken the familiar. Thus, after a year on the fur-trade frontier, he wrote to his mother that, ''the whites in that country are worse than the Indians . . . ,'' and, however just or accurate this observation may have been in its own right, its statement by a person of Sage's outlook is not convincing. A man who could view the crudities and nastiness of savage life and then censure the smokers and chewers among the mountain men for indulging ''their filthy and unnatural taste'' invites an evaluation of inverse bigotry.[30]

Hoxie Fairchild, though chronicling specific declines in the noble savage convention, concluded that the concept was as ''immortal as the phoenix.'' Even excepting what Joseph Hargrave called ''interested people'' who conjured up ''ideal figures'' to serve some selfish design, it is easy to find traces of noble savagery in the modern world. Not even the dominance in the last hundred years of the evolutionary theory has stilled the voices of those who see excellence in the primeval past. For example, Pieter Geyl has lately argued that, of all people, Johan Huizinga, the great Dutch historian, came near approximating this error. Huizinga, he noted, constantly compared the dim present of the 1930's and 1940's with the past—''with an—one would almost say, wilfully—idealized past.'' Commenting on modern literature, the English philosopher C. E. M. Joad wrote in 1948 that ''the refinement of the writer and the elevation of the publication are so regularly proportional to the primitiveness of the subject, that you would almost be justified in supposing that the proper study of intelligent mankind is unintelligent man.'' Had he lived to see it, Joad most likely would have viewed knowingly the appearance of a literary journal entitled *The Noble Savage.* Quite recently, Joseph Wood Krutch pondered the ''chilling implications'' of the contemporary ''infatuation with the primitive.''

The writings of men in the American fur trade indicate that, along with being timeless, the noble savage appears far more universally than one might expect. At times, traders invoked primitive perfection as ''interested people'' and, at other times, like the

Jacksonian Americans discussed by John Ward, they seemed to offer sincere warnings of the evils of overcivilization. In either case, firsthand experience in the crude realities of wilderness existence provided no absolute immunity from that intriguing and perennial passion, the ennobling of the savage.[31]

6. PHYSICAL CHARACTERISTICS

EDWIN DENIG, ONE OF THE MORE THOUGHTFUL TRADERS, ONCE RE-
marked that in the aborigines "physical propensities" predominated over "moral." [1] The prevalence of this assumption, tacit
though it often was, necessitates some consideration of the traders'
impressions of the physical Indian. No great effort will be made
here to expose the blindness, the inaccuracy, or the emotional colora-
tion that occasionally typified these images, though such flaws often
appear self-evident. Just as they did in regard to less palpable red
attributes, traders attempted to make meaningful their observations
of corporeal Indian society via generalization. That they at times
erred in their efforts should cause little surprise. Indeed, probably to
their credit, their depictions of the physical Indian wavered errati-
cally between the universal and the particular. At one moment a
trader would make blanket statements applicable to every native.
Elsewhere he would hesitate, reconsider, except, qualify, and go on
to exhibit a lively awareness of tribal, cultural, environmental, and
individual peculiarities. All people, we are informed, have a desire
to reduce complexity and variety to simplicity and unity. Traders of
course felt that temptation, and patterns emerge from their
writings. However, they also sensed the dangers to fairness and
right reason that were involved.

The trader recognized that the Indian, say, of the Columbia River
was a far different person from the one of the high plains. This
difference manifested itself in terms of physical make-up as well as
in less tangible features. And a key element of that make-up was, of
course, simple attractiveness. Journals kept by these men on trips of
any great distance reveal an awareness of the variations in the
comeliness of the natives almost as surely as they reveal changes in

topography. George Simpson's narrative of his journey around the world evidences this as well as any. Going westward he felt that the Kootenais were much inferior to the Crees, considered the Pend d'Oreilles to be especially handsome, and looked upon the people around Sitka on the upper coast as "the most wretched Indians in appearance that I have ever seen. . . ." [2]

The appreciation of the Indians' appearance varied, but not in a haphazard manner. In regard to those tribes which traders had occasion to mention, a consensus appears, and the transition in Simpson's sentiments largely fitted it. To be sure, in the eyes of the fur men some Indians appeared loathsome, particularly various of the Pacific coast tribes and some of the neighboring inland groups. When Samuel Black remarked that one Pacific coast group had the appearance of "imps staring through human materials," he seems to have expressed the consensus of fur-trade opinion; the traders' aversion toward these Indians can be found in the writings of almost any who beheld them. Men such as David Thompson and the younger Alexander Henry were revolted by the Columbia River tribes after having come overland through the domains of the plains and mountain tribes. Those who came by sea experienced a shock fully as great. Ross Cox, who sailed to the Pacific coast via the Hawaiian Islands, was thoroughly revolted by the natives around Astoria. He later wrote that their odiousness was heightened by contrast with the "lively eyes, handsome features, fine teeth, open countenance, and graceful carriage of the interesting islanders whom we had lately left." [3]

While the appearance of the Pacific coast tribes elicited disgust, that of the plains tribes and some of the Rocky Mountain groups occasioned frequent commendation. The Cheyenne, Arapaho, Nez Perce, Flathead, and Sioux appear often in this connection. George Nidever's assessment of the Arapahoes—"all good looking Indians"—and Henry Boller's reference to the Teton Sioux as "the game cocks of the wilderness, handsome looking, wide-a-wake men," indicate a general tenor. Two Siouan splinter groups—the Mandans and the Crows—received a disproportionate amount of attention for attractiveness. [4]

There is some doubt as to whether the reputation of the Mandans was gained entirely fairly. Possibly, the myth that white, civilized people—probably Welsh—inhabited a part of North America did much to cause prejudgments in favor of this tribe, upon whom this tradition centered for a long time. Moreover, although Indians rarely wore well, the Mandans partially escaped the diminution of respect, even if in a somewhat bizarre fashion. The smallpox that annihilated them at least spared their renown as the most civilized of western tribes. If all sources resembled the writings of the seemingly naïve La Vérendrye, one would be fairly certain of irregular and subjective influences. On seeing the Mandans he denied that they even slightly resembled what had been described to him, yet he went on to describe them in similar terms.[5] But, men whose attitudes seem to have been more firmly anchored in realities also contributed to the notion of the handsome Mandan.

The Crows, on the other hand, owed their fame to nothing but their own qualities. No traditions of lost Europeans added romance to their reputation, nor did they have the benefit of a record of unwavering friendship with the whites as did the Flatheads. To be sure, traders never considered the Crows to be killers; in fact, they were felt to be a uniquely humane group. However, the fur men realized that the Crows were probably unexcelled in thieving, robbing, and begging. Traders must have suspected that booty, more than goods received through barter, made the Crows suffer the white man's presence in Absaroka as quietly as they did. Finally, the Crow notoriety for having a high incidence of sexual aberrations was hardly tailored to make others see the best in them. In spite of all, the Crow warrior, in the traders' estimate, came closest to being the beau ideal of anything offered by aboriginal North America.

Why, precisely, a Crow should be incomparably more pleasing to the eye of a trader than a Clatsop or a Dog-rib is partly a matter of taste and does not lend itself to easy explanation. However, being a part of the plains culture, the Crows and others like them comprised what Robert Stuart called "the affluent." The people of the buffalo country knew privation, certainly; but they would rarely present the spectacle that John Work beheld while leading a fur brigade through California—Indians moving about on hands and knees "gathering & eating different kinds of herbs like the beasts." Admittedly, the fight for sheer survival on the plains often took on tightly contested proportions. However, the ultimate—cannibalism itself—rarely gained the traders' attention—or occasional sympathetic understanding—as it did elsewhere. The Crows, unlike their brethren on the Columbia, did not have "scabby arms, legs, rumps, and bodies, on account of their filthy manner of living, their bad food, and the incessant rain." For all the severity of their element, the high plains Indians enjoyed good fortune. Their relative affluence allowed them to maintain both body and dignity, and they could, if so disposed, show their best side to the white men among them. Looking back on many years in the Missouri River trade, Charles Larpenteur remembered the Crows as being "always well dressed, and extremely rich in horses; so it was really a beautiful sight to see that tribe on the move." [6]

The mention of horses in Larpenteur's comment denotes something more than mere prosperity. The cavalier concept, modified though it may have been, emerges from observations of the plains Indians. David Lavender has argued, reasonably though impressionistically, that the acquisition of the horse worked a transformation in the spirit of the Cheyennes. In them, as by inference in other plains tribes, this windfall exaggerated an already noteworthy *élan*. With the horse, the red men of the plains and Rockies moved into that category of mankind which throughout history has been designated by such terms as "cavalier," "Chevalier," "caballero," and "equerry." [7] Mounted Indians were different from Indians afoot, and white men's reactions reflected the change.

In company with pedestrians from the York Factory area in 1772, Matthew Cocking looked forward with keen anticipation to his meeting with the "Equestrian Natives" (Blackfeet). He expected great things of them, and, significantly, he was not disappointed. To cite another example, Ross Cox, on reaching Celilo Falls during a trip up the Columbia River, came in contact with both mounted and unmounted natives. To him the difference was remarkable: the horsemen appeared clean and well-dressed, acted boldly, though holding themselves manfully aloof. Conversely, the horseless inhabitants of the place went about dirty and nearly naked, conducted themselves with unseemly familiarity, and obviously could not bear a trust. Though the trader rarely deceived himself about the nobility of the red men, he did allow his imagination to be captured, to a degree, by some of the high plains tribes. Thus, Robert Stuart expressed admiration for the boldness, dash, and strategy of the band of Crows who drove off the horses belonging to his returning Astorians. Later in the same day's entry Stuart noted that his party had rations enough for one meal and that they were now relying upon "the inscrutable ways of Providence." The Crow raiders must have appeared grand indeed to have gained praise at that particular juncture.[8]

Finally, a good deal of the plains Indian's appeal probably stemmed from bodily structure. The Cheyennes and Arapahoes were only the tallest of a generally tall people. Robert Stuart described the buffalo hunters as being from five feet eight inches to six feet two inches in height and then invidiously compared the Indians west of the mountains who were "evidently stunted by the badness of their food and the want of proper clothing. . . ."[9] Given an admiration for height, the trader naturally preferred the plains people.

As could only be expected, traders consistently evaluated the red men by white standards of appearance. The Indian who most closely resembled the whites appeared most handsome. To assume the standards of another culture would have been a remarkable psychological feat, and the traders naturally fell short. However, while holding firmly to their own measures of attractiveness, they at times summoned the perspicacity to recognize other tastes in other people. Knowledgeable Samuel Hearne discussed fairly objectively the measure of beauty among the Chipewyans, and admitted that it was appropriate for people in their circumstances. Mattonabbee, his chief guide, had seven wives, most of whom according to Hearne had the proportions of grenadiers. Warming to his subject, he wrote:

Ask a Northern Indian, what is beauty? he will answer a broad flat face, small eyes, high cheekbones, three or four broad black lines a-cross each cheek, a low forehead, a large broad chin, a clumsy hook-nose, a tawny hide, and breasts hanging down to the belt.[10]

This, Hearne argued, demonstrated that there was no absolute standard of loveliness. Hearne's reluctance to adopt Mattonabbee's system of preference should cause no surprise. Mattonabbee, one assumes, would have been as hesitant to accept Hearne's.

Almost without exception the lightest Indian appeared fairest to traders. Indeed, for purposes of disputation these men occasionally bleached the red men. Thus Etienne Veniard de Bourgmont rendered the Omahas white—"the most beautiful tribe" on the continent—in order to stimulate French activities on the Missouri. And, in an effort to end the Hudson's Bay Company monopoly and open its domain to all British endeavors, Joseph Robson magnified the advantages of the far North while referring to the natives as "a white people." Even reliable sources, however, utilized the same standard. A French trader among the Illinois Indians around the turn of the eighteenth century considered them a fine looking group, and remarked that their skin was as close to the color of milk as that of any of the natives. La Vérendrye and David Thompson coupled comments about the light complexion of the Mandans with praise of their appearance, and George Simpson wrote of one tribe that "their looks on the whole are pleasing being more fair and their features more resembling those of the Whites than any other tribe I have seen." Like others, fur traders had little psychological preparation for detecting attractiveness in those who did not in some way resemble themselves.[11]

Beyond preference for certain groups of Indians, the traders almost universally expressed two salient ideas about the appearance of the natives: the women were incomparably more disgusting than the men, and Indian society as a whole was marred by an excessive filthiness. When Alexander Mackenzie remarked of the "contrast between the neat and decent appearance of the men and the nastiness of the women" of a specific northern tribe, he spoke for all traders about all Indians. Even the generally handsome mien of the Crows did not apply to the fair sex, which in fact gained some notoriety for ugliness. Though he considered the Crow men to be "much the finest looking of all the tribes," Edwin Denig suggested that nature had exhausted itself in making them. The women of the tribe had been cheated, and, consequently, "of all the horrid looking objects in the shape of human nature" they were the most so. Denig marveled that Crow men could tolerate Crow women, and, had he been of a waggish bent, he might have hinted at a causal relationship between the hideousness of the females and the rumored prevalence of homosexuality among the males.[12]

At worst, Indian women presented a revolting spectacle. One trader recorded that his party encountered a group of women along the Columbia River who "offered their favors"; but "they were so devoid of temptation, that not one pretended to understand them. . . ." This, of course, represents a sad commentary on Indian charms, recalling the caliber of men in the lower echelons of the trade. Writers of a playful nature could not resist using irony and sarcasm at the expense of the native fair ones. In a letter to his sister, an upper Missouri trader exhibited a common if somewhat grim sense of humor in noting primitive charms. So far in his brief stay two squaws had proposed matrimony—the "Female Bear" and a Mandan woman "rejoicing in the euphonious name of the 'Bob-tail Cow' [I can't help thinking of the cows in the swill stables of New York with their tails rotted off]." With feigned punctilio, Samuel Black regularly referred to Indian women as "ladies." His mock gallantry reached almost ludicrous heights when, in writing of some women crawling about, pulling and devouring roots, he remarked that "without disparagement to the Thecannie Ladies they have no small resemblance to the Bears when surprised at the same occupation. . . ."[13]

At best, of course, these women appeared quite tolerable, and a glance at fur-trade genealogies dispels any notion that the attitudes expressed above were all-encompassing. Playful and peculiar Samuel Black employed his usual hyperbole in referring to the women of one tribe as the "Thloadenni Sylvan Nymphs," but in the same entry he slipped into a more earnest tone when he noted their "timerous kind of under side look that says much without intending it." Indeed, the women of some tribes had widespread reputations for attractiveness, especially those of the related Cree and Ojibway nations; and a disproportionate number of traders' wives and consorts came from the Lake Superior–Lake Winnipeg area. Duncan Cameron felt that some of them would have been "real beauties" but for the darkness of their skin. Along with fine features and excellent teeth, Cameron credited them with "pretty black eyes, which they know very well how to humour in a languishing and engaging manner. . . ." Cameron's fellow North West Company man, Peter Grant, ignored pigmentation and insisted that these women rivaled the charm of "more civilized and accomplished *belles.*" [14]

Although the Crees and Ojibways seemed naturally the fairest, the traders knew that the repulsiveness of Indian women stemmed largely from their never-ending drudgery and, in many cases, virtual slavery, and this consideration mitigated their bad impression. David Thompson, a man who always sought explanations, felt that ugliness was, like other of the drawbacks of savagery, a matter of circumstances. When considering the often-remarked tendency of Indian women to age quickly, he explained that "like the labouring classes the softness of youth soon passes away." In their natural situation Indian women seemed unengaging in comparison to their mates and nauseating by white standards, but traders recognized that a good scrubbing and an easier existence made them tolerable. Charles Ross must have spoken for many men in the profession when, in informing his sister of a previously unmentioned Indian wife, he wrote: ". . . she is a native of the country, and as to beauty quite as comely as her husband!" [15]

On one occasion in 1836 the Mandan women turned out in force to work a general cleanup of the village. Their trader, Francis Chardon, readily detected the singularity of the event. "Miracles," he noted with heavy sarcasm, "will happen some times." That traders should have been appalled by the dirtiness of savage life seems only natural. Nearly all of them remarked on it and examples of their disgust are legion. The statement by an early English trader on Hudson's Bay that the Indians lived "much like ye Irish" gives eloquent testimony to their bad impressions. As with beauty, though, tribes differed in degree, and once again certain of the Pacific coast groups received the greatest censure. When Alexander Mackenzie credited the Cree women with being the "most comely" on the continent, he explicitly contrasted them with those of tribes having "less cleaned habits." Joseph M'Gillivray described a people fitting Mackenzie's unelaborated and unenviable qualifications when he wrote of the Carriers of New Caledonia. This Hudson's Bay man, whose squeamishness had been destroyed by twenty-five years in the trade, wrote that none equaled the Carriers in filth and nastiness. Then he went on to expand on the subject by writing:

Excremental filth, is round and in their Cabins contaminating the pure air of Heaven—they are charged with Lice and Fleas, which they eat with the greatest avidity—their persons so loathesome from accumulation of dirt, that it exceeds credibility . . . the Women . . . when disposed to appear in full Gala . . . put an additional smear of Salmon Oil on their Hair—which is most offensive—Powdered over with the down of Birds—painted with Charcoal and Red Ochre . . . and when this Brute . . . approaches the Fire Side—the Stench is most intolerable, it is perfectly sickening—a deadly faintness seizes you—and you must open the doors to admit fresh air.[16]

A few traders rationalized the Indian's lack of cleanliness. With a generosity tinged with practicality, they admitted that an incrustation of filth helped protect the Indian from the elements and from insects. David Thompson entered the lists on the side of tolerance by occasionally mentioning that the red men were as clean as could be expected—"without soap." [17] Though the trader was generally fearful of the effect that civilization would have upon the savage, he apparently felt that a bar of soap would work an improvement.

Pierre-Antoine Tabeau once admitted that as recompense for manifest undesirable traits the upper Missouri tribes possessed advantages in physical abilities, being active, well-built, and durable. Traders generally saw more to admire in the red man's bodily capacities than in his appearance. However, the consensus of opinion revealed a far more circumscribed approval than one might imagine. In an evident reservation, traders failed to ascribe constitutional soundness to those least appreciated tribes of the very far West. Colin Robertson of the Hudson's Bay Company referred to the Beaver Indians of the upper reaches of the Peace River as being delicate of constitution and generally short-lived. He and George Simpson, who made a remarkably similar evaluation of the Beavers, made a connection between the physical condition of this tribe and their immoderate use of liquor, but both felt that alcohol only worsened a natural debility. Similarly, American mountain man Zenas Leonard remarked on the ''very delicate and feeble'' nature of the Merced River Indians of California and suggested that their acorn diet might account for their weakness.[18]

As the far West tribes were exceptions to the rule of general physical well-being, so they contradicted the more precise principle that the Indian had great endurance but little strength. Traders seem to have given them credit for neither. Samuel Black in his 1824 Rocky Mountain journal remarked of the Sekanis that ''few of them are capable of strong exertion, for after climbing a Mountain or two & passing but a very few miles in a Valley they are at their utmost efforts & come back to their Tents with feverish limbs & when any unusual exertion requires some days to recruit. . . .'' To some degree, of course, the Indians could have earned their reputation for debility because they were unwilling to exert themselves to the extent that traders desired. Black implied as much when he mentioned breaking camp an hour and a half after sunrise, a time of day that seemed too early for the constitution of his Sekanis, ''particularly when Employed by us.'' While Alexander Mackenzie was on his pioneering venture along the river which came to bear his name, he noted disgustedly that his Indians were complaining of fatigue. The red men of the party may have been less impressed with the need for haste than was Mackenzie, for the next day's entry shows that the stop was made on the previous night at 10:00 P.M. and that the party was again under way at 2:15 A.M. Be this as it may, the far West tribes gained a reputation for feebleness.[19]

Excepting these groups, Indians generally had a reputation for endurance bordering on the proverbial. Edwin Denig and David Thompson, two of the most perceptive observers of the aborigines, insisted that in tests of endurance the Indian would easily excel the white, but would be no match for him in sheer strength. Relying upon his thorough knowledge of the Assiniboines, Denig cited some extraordinary feats of running—Indians tiring out the best of horses in the course of a two-day race, and one native's covering 190 miles in two days and a night. The plains Indians, according to Denig, achieved these amazing results by traveling twelve to fifteen miles at a "short trot," resting briefly, and continuing on. "Upon the whole," he wrote, "the European would stand much more hard work in every way, but the Indian would be his superior in active exercise, abstemiousness, and loss of sleep." In contrasting the red man's endurance with the white man's strength, Denig struck upon a principle with which nearly all fur-trade expressions agree.[20]

In the trader's estimate the red man's ability to withstand adversity went beyond overcoming fatigue while afoot. Most sensationally, their physical resiliency manifested itself in a stoical conduct under torture. Though they dwelt on this theme far less than did fictional portrayers of savage life, traders did mention it occasionally. However, this phenomenon will be treated in a different context. Torments designed by nature rather than by man afforded the best opportunity for the Indian to demonstrate his fiber for the fur men. Traders generally conceded, for example, that the natives defied the rigors of cold weather better than the whites among them. James Clyman recorded seeing Crow warriors riding all day on the high plains in the dead of winter, bare from the waist up; and Jacob Fowler witnessed Cheyenne children frolicking naked in the snow and ice in temperatures that would kill a white child in a half hour. Once again, David Thompson went beyond awe to attempt explanation: ". . . the natural heat of their bodies is greater than ours, probably from living wholly on animal food."[21]

Physical injury itself presented less danger to the red man than to his white brother. James Isham of the Hudson's Bay Company felt that Indians had tremendous healing power and an "incrediable strong constitution." Seeing Indians leave the post evidently injured beyond repair only to return in a few months completely well, or seeing them race naked from their sweating huts into an ice-cold river led him to believe that "nought can hurt them." In demonstration of the idea that Indians could recover from "apparently mortal" wounds, Edwin Denig, himself a doctor's son, cited the impressive example of an Assiniboine who had been set upon by three Blackfeet near Fort Union. When the attackers fired, one ball broke the Assiniboine's thigh, another shattered the opposite tibia, and the third pierced the man through the abdomen and came out near the spinal column. After closing in for kill and coup, one of the Blackfeet ran a knife around the victim's crown and partially lifted the scalp. Annoyed that the man still struggled, another ran a lance a foot down into the chest cavity, entering it near the collarbone and pushing it down along the inside of the ribs. Before aid could reach him the hapless Assiniboine had extracted the lance and was flailing at his tormentors who, as a final gesture, stabbed the man with knives "several more" times in the body. After being brought back to the fort, solely for burial, the man recovered. Despite the hideous nature of his wounds, the Indian revived without any care whatsoever and did so in spite of the fact that in the hot weather his wounds turned purple and showed every indication of being gangrenous.[22]

In his *History of the Dividing Line,* William Byrd, a man of some experience in Indian trade, wrote that like our "Woodsmen" the native was a glutton; but he held up better in spare times. The idea of the red man's ability to withstand privation became widespread, and it complements the concept of his durability. Samuel Hearne recalled that the Chipewyans not only bore hunger well but they did so in a rare good humor. He mentioned some who, after three or four days without food, were "as merry and jocose . . . as if they had voluntarily imposed it on themselves; and would ask each other in the plainest terms, and in the merriest mood, if they had any inclination for an intrigue with a strange woman?" A corollary of the same belief held that the Indian could take sustenance that would have repelled or sickened a needy white man. While traveling with some Gros Ventres in the arid region west of their Missouri

River villages, Alexander Henry the younger came upon a pond which, though it seemed a godsend at first glance, was "a mere [absolute] poison to the taste and smell." Notwithstanding the vile condition of the water, the Indians drank heartily. "These savage brutes," according to the awed trader, "can drink stinking, stagnant water with as good stomach as if it were spruce beer." [23]

Dissenting voices were occasionally raised in regard to these various aspects of hardiness. Pierre-Antoine Tabeau suspected that the Arikaras, whom he saw playing a form of hockey on the Missouri River ice in sub-zero weather without benefit of clothes, were guilty of affectation. Samuel Black denied that the Indians of New Caledonia—here again, some of those much-maligned western groups—were in any way impervious to the cold; and Charles Mackenzie insisted that natives manifested their vaunted fortitude in the face of pain only when the injuries resulted from combat. One form of their durability, however, never aroused doubt—the toughness of the Indian woman before and after childbirth. She might go about "blind drunk, tumbling among stumps and stones a few days previous to . . . delivery," or perform the "painful drudgeries of her station an hour after, with her first tender infant on her back." Whichever it was, the Indian woman made the trader certain that, as Duncan Cameron put it, "Divine Providence" had bestowed upon her a physical make-up suitable for her miserable life.[24]

Though agreement was not unanimous, the trader generally admitted the Indian's bodily capacity to survive the harshness of the wilderness. However, in regard to the skills, partly physical and partly mental, which could make survival something more than mere existence, he showed less certainty, less willingness to rate the Indian highly. The popular, modern image of the red man as infallible hunter, exquisite woodsman, and superb tracker and guide did not always occur to the man who knew him best. Occasionally, a trader credited the savage with superior physical senses. Edwin Denig, for example, wrote that the Indians of the upper Missouri had sight that was "truly astonishing," and that they possessed similar excellence in their awareness of location. As an example of the latter ability, he mentioned that an Indian could shoot twenty or thirty arrows a hundred yards or so in several directions into snow or tall grass, and with no difficulty he would be able to pick up every one. A white man, on the other hand, would be hard pressed to find any. Similarly, the younger Alexander Henry, though never one to exaggerate the natives' virtues or accomplishments, testified to the Ojibways' "astonishing" know-how in tracking big game. "The bend of a leaf or blade of grass" sufficed in setting these canny red men onto an animal's trail. However, the notable thing about such observations lies not in their prevalence but in their paucity. With Indian toughness, there were doubts and exceptions; with Indian capabilities, these were even greater.[25]

A first and rather moderate step in altering the picture of the Indian as a superman of the wilderness was taken by men such as Warren Ferris who insisted that the Indian had no *innate* qualifications making him superior in outdoor attainments. The white man, he felt, could with proper attention perform the same feats; and to bear out this point, he held that the experienced Rocky Mountain trappers equaled their red confreres.[26]

For all the popular insistence that an Indian was practically incapable of becoming lost, fur traders had surprisingly frequent guide problems. Of course, even when Indians were thoroughly friendly, various things could account for their seeming incompetence—fear of enemies ahead, concern for families behind, or plain misunderstanding. However, it appears that simple inadequacy entered in also. Thus, the Moose Fort journal of January 26, 1784, noted the return of two men from an unsuccessful hunting and fishing trip. Among less decisive misfortunes, the Indian who acted as guide "has not yet carried them to the Lake where they expected to have caught fish, but on the contrary has frequently lost his road." In the winter of 1766 while traveling south of Mackinac, John Porteous called particular attention to the directional failures of some Indians encountered by his party. Following a most expressive *nota bene,* Porteous commented thus: ". . . we pick up a parcel of Indians yesterday afternoon in the bay that had lost their way.'' And while struggling with the practical consequences of faulty guidance, Simon Fraser passionately wrote his man off as ''a damned blockhead.'' [27]

And peculiar though it may seem for traders to have gainsaid the Indian's renown as hunter, they often did precisely that. John Long, an Englishman with an obvious fondness for the aborigines, conceded that ''the Virginians'' equaled them in every way in this pursuit, and such men as John McLoughlin, Joseph M'Gillivray, John Rae, and George Simpson openly disparaged the tawny Nimrods. Samuel Black went so far as to analyze the shortcomings of the Sekani huntsmen. Their tendency to miss game, he noted, came not so much from lack of practice or from faulty weapons, as it did from ''their own perturbation & precipitation   sometimes leveling from the muzzle [while] forgeting the Breach.'' Thus, unless very close to their target, they fired high. At other times, however, this accurate, if not syntactical, description of what today would be called ''buck fever,'' failed to satisfy Black. In writing of the Beaver Indians, he noted that ''this missing business,'' coming as it did after ample practice and causing people to starve amidst plenty, was an enigma beyond solution. The ultimate in Indian ineffectualness appears in a journal of Simon Fraser. Watching his red hunters returning empty-handed to draw their rations, he grumbled in what must have been embarrassed disgust that ''instead of feeding us we have been obliged to provide for them. . . .'' [28]

Certain considerations bear noting, however, in regard to these uninspiring commentaries on Indian huntsmen. First, by way of qualification, the criticism of native hunters does not always make clear whether the fault-finding arose from failure to take animals important in the trade or from inability to take animals of any kind. George Simpson wrote of New Caledonia that, ''In respect to Fur Bearing Animals, we know that the Natives are Wretched Hunters. . . .'' What kind of hunters they may have been otherwise, if hunters at all, Simpson did not specify. Elsewhere, he referred to some Mackenzie River Indians as being both ''miserable Beaver Hunters'' and ''wretched bad   large animal hunters.'' Here, the meaning is clear. These people could neither benefit the company in the most obvious way nor could they even help supply the people in the trade with necessities, for their inability to take game kept them continually flirting with hunger.[29]

Second, by way of specification, the tribes whose hunting know-how left most to be desired were those to whom virtue or ability of any kind was least often ascribed. With the exception of John Long's, all of the foregoing doubts and qualifications of the Indians' talent afield applied either to far West tribes or to groups closely akin to them. Some of the coast tribes, of course, made no pretense of hunting, and many of the river peoples relied primarily upon fish. Still, many of them, like their eastern fellows, lived by the chase. When a trader did criticize the performance in this capacity of tribes farther to the east, he generally laid their shortcomings to an excess of independence rather than a shortage of skill. Thus, an early upper Missouri trader, in listing the drawbacks for trade in that area, pointed out that the Indians of the region were indifferent beaver hunters. They ignored the fur animals to take buffalo, an animal that attracted them more because the hunt was brief, active, and exciting. And the buffalo provided the very necessities which eliminated any dependence upon the trader with his demands to bring in beaver. A trader at Big Stone Lake in Minnesota expressed these misgivings in the heat of the moment, castigating his Sioux charges for not doing as he wished. Let them hear of buffalo within a hundred miles, he fumed, and "traps are abandoned, and promises disregarded."[30]

This complaint suggests a final point worth mention. An almost universal fur-trade assumption held that the Indian, in whatever sphere, followed a proper course of action, not because of its propriety, but because of necessity. Thus, he failed to make good hunts until urgency prodded him. Though this theme will be treated much more fully later, a warning against giving credit from American Fur Company management—men of long practical experience in the trade—to their man in southern Missouri illustrates the working of the principle. Without goods on faith the natives must bring furs to satisfy their needs and desires—"and that is the only way to make them Hunt."[31]

The Indian was also reproached as a fighter. Without going into his qualifications as a "soldier" or a warrior, it is well to point out that, for a man whose chief attributes were supposedly physical, the Indian was taken very lightly by the trader when it came to individual or near-individual contests. Experienced men of the trade such as Alexander Henry the younger, Charles Chaboillez, John Work, and Peter Skene Ogden mentioned incidents wherein they had administered drubbings to natives. And even staid George Simpson remarked on the excellent effect wrought upon refractory savages by a white fist on the nose—"or, as it is technically termed, by a muzzler." The Indian, expert though he may have been with lance or bow, was completely taken aback by such a move, wrote Sir George, and even the "ferocious" Blackfeet reacted by clasping the battered nose with one hand and throwing the other hand over the mouth in a gesture of amazement. Samuel Hearne, after the successful termination of a brawl involving pilfered brandy, also attested to the efficacy of a "little old English Play" in handling recalcitrant red men. "English Play" probably seemed strange and awesome to the Indian, who evidently possessed and acted upon a far different code of conflict. Moreover, the trader was unlikely, perhaps unable, to chronicle a set-to that ended adversely. However, the trader commonly scorned the Indian's ability in close physical contact.[32]

The Indian, then, as a physical specimen did not seem as impressive in the eyes of the trader as one might expect. The fur man generally considered the savage to be amazingly durable; but he was hesitant and doubtful regarding attributes further removed from this rudimentary quality. Occasionally, however, the red man's efforts in an area of more refined bodily activity did impress his white observers. Various men of the trade recorded their wonder at the Indians' feats at sleight-of-hand. Some of these performances impressed the traders so much that they were certain only of their skepticism in confirming the dextrous and denying the occult. But the actions of the "jongleurs," along with that of the ballplayers and riders, were only exceptions to the consensus that the Indian was physically unenviable except for his endurance and his tenacity of life. Some men went so far as to place the Indian in general, rather than specific, physical inferiority to the white man. In the first of his frontier narratives Alexander Ross, no enemy of the Indian, wrote that:

In the wide field of gymnastic exercise, few Indians—I might say none— have been found to cope with civilized man. In all trials of walking, of running, of fatigue, feats of agility, and famine, even in the Indian's own country, he has to yield the palm of victory to the white man. In the trials of the hot bath alone the savage excels.

Though his remark may have been more prophetic than analytic, George Simpson, after mentioning his party's being passed by Indian canoemen on the Columbia River, predicted that, "in the long run, however, savages stand no chance against whites, being inferior alike in steadiness, and perseverance, and strength." As a whole, the fur trade would have disagreed with this evaluation in particulars rather than in substance.[33]

7. THE FORCE OF SELF-INTEREST

WHEN EDWARD UMFREVILLE FOUND HIMSELF STYMIED BY GUIDE TROUbles during a 1784 canoe trip through the country north of Lake Superior, he concluded that "Indians will be Indians to the last of the chapter."[1] Reiterations of the disgust, resignation, and certainty of that remark abound in fur-trade literature. When an exploratory canoe trip seemed about to go to smash, when things went awry generally, or, indeed, when fortune smiled openly, the trader relied upon the shorthand of an essential Indian nature. The trader, whether in adversity or prosperity, knew that at bottom the Indian would be an Indian still. He did not carry this conviction to the haughtiness of believing that he could reliably predict the actions of his tawny charges. Indeed, he felt that their nature—a very human nature—precluded that. His claim was less pretentious, more negative. At the least, however, the trader's belief in an Indian ethos that he had fathomed to some degree allowed him to prepare psychologically. After the fact, almost nothing the red man did surprised the trader. What was the grain in the aboriginal make-up that supposedly ran so true?

To clear the way, it should be recalled that traders appeared earlier in this study as men who sagely recognized the manifest diversities within the Indian way of life. Though a contradiction seems evident, no turn-about is intended. To be sure, traders saw variety within Indian society, but they also saw a substantial unity; they were certain that a native genius existed. They never abandoned their vivid recognition that a Pai-ute was a much different fellow from a Crow or that an Atnah little resembled an Assiniboine; but they did indicate that certain themes transcended individual, tribal, or even cultural divisions. To hold such seemingly incompatible ideas may seem deceitful, but modern students of culture face a parallel dilemma. In order to confound the stereotypes of the ill informed, they proclaim the infinite idiosyncracy of humankind. On the other hand their quest for meaningful generalizations leads them to delineate "basic personality structures," "national characters," and "patterns of culture." Geoffrey Gorer, a practitioner of one such form, circumvented the problem at least to his own satisfaction by noting that "the concept of national character in no way denies the variations of individual personality. . . ."[2] Of course, I do not mean to imply that the often random jottings of fur traders approach the level of the sophisticated formulations of modern anthropologists. However, the quandary posed by the unwillingness of variety to consort with unity looms large in both cases. The purport of Gorer's statement can well apply to fur-trade thinking.

Popular tradition provides a somewhat contradictory account of one notable aspect of the American Indian's character—his selflessness. On the one hand, it pictures the red man as completely openhanded, indiscriminately bestowing a traditional Indian welcome with all of its vaunted amenities—some of which were embarrassingly basic. On the other hand, it has coined the phrase "Indian-giver"—he whose gift carries the obligation or expectation of commensurate return. A check of two standard compilations of proverbial usages indicates that the American aborigine has survived more as a symbol of venality than of generosity. Should any doubts linger as to the justice of this reputation, one finds none other than James Fenimore Cooper listed as the most prominent source of the "Indian-giver" convention. Nevertheless, the supposed magnanimity of the red man is well known if not proverbial. Popular culture almost unfailingly portrays the Indian in this way, and scholarly sources lend support to the idea of savage liberality. The anthropologist, Clark Wissler, wrote of an institutionalized "law of hospitality" among red men, and recently Howard Peckham described the Indian as being "so indifferent to wealth that his extreme generosity shamed the white man."[3]

Fur-trade sentiments, quite naturally, showed no absolute accord on this point. After all, a great diversity of cultural groups and physical conditions confronted the fur man : from the trade-oriented upper Pacific coast tribes to the Great Basin groups who lived, almost literally, from hand to mouth ; to the fortunately situated tribes of the buffalo plains ; and on to others in still different circumstances. Moreover, conditions of the fur trade underwent vast changes from the moment that the first and awe-inspiring *coureur de bois* pushed his way into a tribe, through the period when separate and conflicting concerns importuned, cajoled, and threatened the native for his pelts, to the time when monopolies held harsh and close control over the trade of the wilderness.

Even allowing for these variations in circumstances, however, a surprisingly uniform attitude toward Indian selflessness emerges. Far from being ashamed before the savages' supposedly inspiring munificence, the trader instead was exasperated, often enraged, at the opposite attributes manifested in his swarthy customers. Perhaps he could not be impressed by the Indian's generosity because he knew the Indian too well, so well, in fact, that the trader felt he had fathomed the motivation behind the Indian's displays of altruism, and thus could discriminate between the apparent and the real. Or again, perhaps he placed an unfortunate and unjustified misconstruction upon the red man's acts and misread policy for prodigality. He was unmoved, regardless. A central contention of this study holds that the more the trader saw of the Indian the greater were his misgivings. As the fur trade was an economic form, the trader's awareness of Indian attributes having economic overtones was perhaps keener than it was of other features. Knowing the economic Indian best, he tended to appreciate him least. Whatever the reasoning, the quintessence and dominating force of Indian character, by the trader's telling, was self-interest. In one of his youthful fiction tales, ex-trader Robert Michael Ballantyne presented two Rocky Mountain trappers in a discussion of Indian motivation. The two had more than academic interest in the subject because they sought a plan to free the rest of their party, recently captured by the savages. The dialect-speaking "Bounce" favored moving in directly and swiftly to effect the escape. He insisted that " 'savages always invariably thinks o' number one, before they thinks on nothin' else.

Now, as men judge themselves so they judge others—that's a fact, as all feelosophy has proclaimed, an' all experience has pruven.' "
" 'Wot then?' " Logic indicated that the native captors imagined the remainder of the party to be in full flight from hazard, as they would be were circumstances reversed. Thus, the craven selfishness of Indian character would afford "Bounce" and "Gibault" the element of surprise.[4]

Of course, Indian generosity is too all-pervading a theme not to have had some manifestations in the fur-trade literature. However, these sources do not always hold up under close scrutiny. In the case of William Johnston, a brother-in-law of Henry Rowe Schoolcraft who engaged in the nineteenth-century trade in Wisconsin and Minnesota, interested partisanship appears evident. In letters to his sister, this young man, a half-breed with an evident pride in his native ancestry, damned the traders as a group while praising the selfless character of the Indians or, at least, of those as yet undefiled by white contact.[5]

Johnston's, of course, was an unusual case, but panegyrics on native liberality appeared often in materials of qualified or questionable reliability, in which the author emphasized the niggardliness of white society by stressing the altruism of savagery. Since John Long seems never to have attained the prominence and well-being which he felt he deserved, he sprinkled his narrative with carpings at his more fortunate and, as he would have us believe, more mercenary contemporaries. His work nicely typifies that kind which lauded savagery only in denigrating civilization. He managed to compact this duality in the following comparison:

Notwithstanding the cruelty of Savages, they possess virtues which do honour to human nature, and exhibit instances of generosity and kindness which the most philanthropic soul cannot exceed. They are ignorant of those mean sordid sentiments which disgrace many more enlightened, and more wealthy; and from the knowledge I have of their disposition, I am sure they would blush at the parsimonious conduct of those whom Providence hath blessed with affluence.[6]

Savage generosity not only shamed civilized selfishness, but the red man also came close, in this case, to being called as witness against his more refined brother.

Regrettably, at least part of the argument in regard to the attitudes of people such as Johnston and Long has to be *ad hominem*. A final demonstration that Indian generosity was used as a polemical device can be made largely from internal inconsistency. In his journal entry for January 18, 1852, Rudolph Kurz denied that Indians ever showed generosity to whites and severely qualified the liberality they showed each other. Yet, on February 1 in a lengthy and elaborate essay Kurz argued against the Judaic theory of Indian origins by comparing the "thrifty, calculating" nature of the Jew and the "liberality" of the American aborigine.[7] Whether the young intellectual wandered into this contradiction while in the passion of disquisition, or whether this particular entry, long and involved as it is, was one which he revised and lengthened after his return to Switzerland—a place comfortably removed from the unflattering realities of savagery—Kurz's affirmation of Indian selflessness appears thoroughly contrived.

Fur-trade materials of unquestioned reliability do occasionally mention Indian generosity, but, when the trader spoke of this feature of the savage make-up, he did so in cold specifics, not in impressively glowing generalities. Recalling a visit to a Blackfoot camp, Charles Larpenteur recognized their hospitable behavior, writing that he "could not have been better treated. . . ." Larpenteur, however, inferred no principle from this experience; indeed his work is notably lacking in generalizations of any sort. Men as hard-bitten as Duncan M'Gillivray and Alexander Henry the younger, at specific times, ascribed a commendable altruism to certain bands who had given them a good welcome. Here again, however, one need not look for elaboration on this theme. When men such as Henry and M'Gillivray generalized about Indian nature, they dwelt upon aspects other than the admirable or the virtuous.[8]

In regard to openhandedness, as with other properties of the red men, the fur traders distinguished by tribe and by individual. Alexander Mackenzie's narrative of his pioneering trip across the continent clearly shows this tendency to discriminate. He praised the Crees as generous and hospitable, but labeled the neighboring Chipewyans as selfish and inordinately aware of their own interests.

David Thompson made a similar evaluation of the Crees when he wrote concerning them : "Those acts that pass between man and man for generous charity and kind compassion in civilized society, are no more than what is every day practised by these Savages. . . ." To still the surmise that this might represent a blanket appraisal, however, we need only to look at Thompson's day-by-day journals while he was among other Indians. Regarding the peoples of the Pacific region Thompson expressed far different feelings.[9]

Generosity was also an individual matter. When Alexander Ross recounted the kindness with which a Snake chief treated a lost and nearly frozen trapper, he did not warm to the subject by dwelling fondly upon such attributes within the Indian character. Rather, he concluded simply that, "the pleasing and moreover the friendly conduct of Ama-Ketsa toward him [the trapper] was a strong proof of that chief's good will towards our people." [10] To Ross the incident was gratifying and significant, but its consequence sprang from the friendly involvement of an important personage, not from its typifying the actions of the red race. He viewed it as an individual act and no more. As so often occurred in white observations of the Indians, a commendable particularity elicited no inclination to generalize.

Even when the trader credited the Indian with generosity he often qualified his admission by insisting that the trait appeared in a circumscribed form. George Simpson, for example, hinted at the ritualistic rather than the heartfelt quality of Indian benevolence. He pointed out that, among certain tribes, even the enemy was well treated if he could gain the chief's lodge unperceived. In other circumstances, however, these same Indians, according to Simpson, showed a vicious treachery. William Hardisty considered the hospitality of the Loucheux to be a matter of custom alone, and he held that a visitor, though well received at first, soon encountered their natural selfishness and, consequently, received miserly treatment. Edwin Denig maintained that the Indians of the upper Missouri area had unjustly gained a reputation for "pure hospitality" simply because necessity and selfish enjoyment led them to entertain a great deal.[11]

Some writers considered the Indian to be liberal only with specific items, generally the most basic nutritive requirements. Thus, Samuel de Champlain wrote that the Indians showed a good deal of charity toward one another with respect to food, but otherwise they were highly avaricious. By the same token, when Rudolph Kurz read self-interest into the apparent sincerity of the native gift-giving, he excepted gifts of meat, which he felt were given without regard to recompense. William Hardisty commented that the Loucheux showed a degree of generosity with regard to food, although their natural character was selfish. Lest the import of the latter comment should evade his readers, he added parenthetically " (But where will you find an Indian who is not?)." [12]

Finally, the red man faced the charge that his assistance and hospitality extended only to those within a specific category—be it band, tribe, or Indian society itself. From his experience among the Chipewyans, Samuel Hearne strongly affirmed this state of affairs. He wrote that he had never seen a people "that possessed so little humanity, or that could view the distresses of their fellow-creatures with so little feeling and unconcern." "Though they seem to have a great affection for their wives and children," he continued, "yet they will laugh at and ridicule the distress of every other person who is not immediately related to them." On one occasion Hearne upbraided the party with which he was traveling for their treatment of a helpless and destitute band that they encountered. Hearne's Indians, as soon as they became certain of the others' inability to resist, pillaged them and ravished several of their women, even though the strangers were Chipewyans also. In answer to his remonstrances, the trader received a clear intimation that, had his own sister been there, she would have suffered the same fate. [13]

Another qualification placed upon the generosity of the aborigines, and one which seems nearly to negate it, held that eventual selfish gain motivated the Indian. Here, the trader displayed general accord with the later, popular concept of the "Indian-giver." The entire chronological scope of the fur trade and almost every geographical area provide confirmation for the cynical nature of savage liberality. In the second decade of the seventeenth century Champlain stated that, "They give nothing for nothing. . . ." One hundred years later William Byrd of Virginia refused a proffered gift, "knowing that an Indian present, like that of a Nun, is a Liberality put out to Interest, and a Bribe plac'd to the greatest Advantage. . . ." [14] And at the end of the fur-trade era, men such as Edwin Denig and Rudolph Kurz made similar remarks. In this there was agreement.

To the trader this obnoxious feature of the Indian character appeared in various forms. To cite an example of one variation on a theme, the savages often readily offered a trader physical assistance in his travails. The trader would soon learn, however, as did Peter Skene Ogden on one occasion, that, having performed the task they so obligingly offered to do, they "took good care to make very extravagant demands for their services. . . ." Quite naturally, once the source of wealth had dried up, the cooperation ceased. This practice extended to the point where fur men sometimes surmised that the Indians had been instrumental in creating the need for such help. In one of his narratives Alexander Ross recounted an instance wherein his large canoe capsized in the Columbia River, and only the efforts of the Chinook boatmen saved the vessel from destruction and the men aboard from death. Looking back on the incident, the old trader could not help but suspect that "the sordid rascals had upset us wilfully, in order to claim the merit of having saved us, and therewith double recompense for their trip." Unlike Ross, the botanist David Douglas, whose frequent travels and various friendships with men in the trade seemed to mold his thinking much in their pattern, did not go away grumbling about having been duped. Instead, he frustrated a similar, albeit somewhat less sensational, plan. While he ate in an Indian camp, one of his hosts pilfered Douglas' knife. At first, the botanist offered a reward for its return; but, feeling that he would have to go beyond the value of the knife on this tack, he started a search and soon found the missing article on one of the "knaves." "When detected," wrote Douglas, "he claimed the premium, but as he did not give it on the first application, I paid him, and paid him so well, with my fists that he will, I daresay, not forget the *Man of Grass* for some days to come.'' [15]

At other times traders came to the realization that more pleasurable manifestations of generosity had strings attached. Pierre-Antoine Tabeau found that he could not afford to attend the feasts to which he was invited, for each meal he ate caused him to owe fifty, by the Arikara conception of reciprocity. While traveling by company steamboat on the Northwest coast George Simpson had a similar experience involving the amenities. An Indian chief aboard the boat offered Simpson his wife, with, as the Governor put it, ''more generosity than justice,'' for the man had designs on an English woman traveling on the boat. From the native perspective it appeared that a proper regard for Simpson's wants was the procedure best devised to forward his project. This self-interested approach could apply to much broader areas as well, even to trading and trapping rights within a tribal domain. The pattern described by Tabeau, Simpson, and others appears in an 1831 letter from ex-trader William Gordon to Secretary of War Lewis Cass in which he pictured the Crows as thoroughgoing thieves, but gave them credit for never killing white men. ''This they frankly explain,'' wrote Gordon, ''by telling us if they killed, we would not come back & they would lose the chance of stealing from us.'' The informal guarantee of physical safety for the one side entailed, tit for tat, a license to plunder for the other.[16]

Though he felt that the red extorters used other and more vicious kinds of economic skulduggery only against the whites, the trader apparently considered ''Indian-giving'' to be a common feature of intraracial, as well as interracial, affairs. Rudolph Kurz and Edwin Denig agreed that an Indian would victimize an Indian only slightly less readily than he would victimize a white. Whether it was a desire for material goods or the need of aid and friendship, there had always to be an interested motive behind Indian generosity. Denig, for one, seemed close to understanding the basis for such self-interestedness when he pointed out that, in an existence as tenuous as the Indian's, a show of generosity was a highly necessary thing.

One could not afford any more enemies than nature had already provided:

The sharing of the meat with each other in times of scarcity is no mark of liberality, or done from any other principle than the foregoing remarks present. It is a loan, or obligation, laid upon the person, to be repaid when their situations become reversed, or whenever the claimant thinks proper to remind him of it, which sooner or later he is sure to do in some way.[17]

Though the Indian may have exasperated his trader by what the latter saw as the mildly extortionate practice of "Indian-giving," he angered the fur man far more by exhibiting another facet of his supposedly self-interested nature. Probably no comment about the red race appears more commonly, and with fewer contradictions or reservations, than that the Indian was a perfect ingrate. A Minnesota trader exhibited a customary amount of vehemence in exposing the knavery of a local aborigine: "He has acted," the fur man informed his superior, *"as every indian will*   ungratefully and with deception. . . ." Men as varied in time, place, circumstance, and outlook as Pierre Esprit Radisson, Matthew Cocking, Thomas Fitzpatrick, Daniel Lamont, and John McLean, to mention only a few, remarked of the Indian's unwillingness or inability to express thanks. Thomas Simpson stated the traders' case quite well in describing an influenza outbreak around Fort Chipewyan in the 1830's. During the epidemic the Indians suffered greatly, but those who managed to get to the fort received such good treatment that few of them died. Indeed, they enjoyed such kind and effective care that "even the cold heart of the red man warmed into gratitude, and his lips uttered the unwonted accents of thanks."[18]

Such kindness might not always be welcome, however. "Fearing future reflections," William Miles at York Factory hesitated to give medical aid to an Indian boy whose arm had been shot off. Regardless of help extended, Miles knew that trouble would ensue if the youngster died. It speaks well for the humanity, and the courage, of the men at the post that, after being importuned, they cared for the lad—successfully, happy to say. Still, their anxiety that they might incur the wrath of ungrateful red men shows clearly in their posture at the outset, turning over to the natives "Lint & Turlington" with which to dress the wound themselves. To give, and then to receive no appreciative acknowledgment rankled the trader; to give, and to receive injury in return—ingratitude compounded—enraged him. No other shortcoming elicited from the fur man such heady and wrathful execrations of the red race as this did. In central Oregon in the fall of 1826, supposedly friendly Indians set the prairies ablaze around the camp of Peter Skene Ogden's brigade. After chronicling a "most providential escape," Ogden went on to reason that "villany for kindness" is "Indian gratitude." It seems largely to have been the same trait that threw George Simpson into his colossal dudgeon against the Chipewyans. After describing their character as disgraceful to human nature, Simpson argued that

. . . such Wretches are only fit to inhabit the inhospitable clime they live in and no one who has had an opportunity of knowing them will commiserate their situation: had they the most remote sense of gratitude, they could not do otherwise than idolize their protectors, and bliss the Day that the Honble. Hudsons Bay Compy. entered among them, but to that virtue their hearts are inaccessible and if the Country did not still abound with valuable Furs it would not be dealing too harshly to leave them to their fate. . . .[19]

There might be several reasons for the Indian's reputation as an ingrate. Quite possibly, they failed to demonstrate the observable display of thankfulness familiar to the white man because many Indians suppressed their emotions before strangers. Again, much of what the trader considered to be commendable generosity may have appeared to the aborigine as no more than a matter of course. David Thompson maintained that acts of "generous charity and kind compassion" passed among at least some of the savages as "acts of common duty,"[20] and, if this is correct, the traders' benevolence might pass unheralded. There are, however, matters both paradoxical and contradictory involved here—paradoxical because the Indian appears boorish for being so urbane, contradictory because this line of reasoning runs counter to that contained in the bulk of fur-trade literature.

If, in retrospect, this highly nonchalant acceptance of benevolence helped explain the Indians' seeming lack of thankfulness, it did little at the time to assuage the traders' disapprobation. To a man on the scene it probably bore out the darkest estimate of the natives' ingratitude. The fur man easily recognized that Indians accepted altruism in a blasé manner—so much so that once a favor, a kindness, or a hand-out was tendered, it could be discontinued only at the expense of amicable relations. A letter written by John Thomas of the Hudson's Bay Company reproving a subordinate for making unauthorized gifts to the Indians bears this out nicely. Though he ordered an end to further extensions of such prodigality, the trader instructed his inferior to continue the same gifts to the same Indians at the same time, for a withdrawal would alienate them. Comparably, Kenneth McKenzie of the Upper Missouri Outfit complained to an Indian agent that the red men did not discriminate between the government and the American Fur Company. Because McKenzie had at times been present when a government agent made distributions, the Indians expected the same whenever he returned to the Fort Union area. Suffering under the "odium of keeping back their presents," the "King of the Missouri" complained indignantly that "indiscriminate distribution of presents" militated against good relations. The red man, he insisted, quickly "claims as a right what was intended as a boon." Finally, Rudolph Kurz, the sometimes depicter of noble savages, gave a hypothetical illustration of this aspect of Indian nature that speaks for the fur trade generally:

. . . if one presented an Indian with a gift every day in the year—this morning, a horse; tomorrow, a gun; the day after tomorrow, a blanket; the next day, a knife; and so on until the last day in the year—and then might forget or simply neglect to give him anything at all on the 365th day, he [the Indian] would be all the more angry on account of the omission.[21]

Some traders traced the Indians' ungratefulness to a failure of comprehension and placed little emphasis on their having become so accustomed to openhandedness that they became careless in acknowledging it. Joseph Rolette of the American Fur Company, for example, advised against buying out an independent Minnesota trader because it would be difficult to collect the red debts owed him. Indians, he pointed out to Ramsay Crooks, never "pay well" anyone but the individual who gave them their credits. In describing the vexing task of a trader among the Arikaras, Pierre-Antoine Tabeau ascribed much of Indian ingratitude to their inability to understand the meaning of the fur trade. In this regard, Tabeau began from the principle that, "stupidity . . . far from detracting from malice renders it more unruly. . . ." The Arikaras had become habituated to receiving handouts, and so they looked upon the traders as "beneficent spirits" who, because they had the wherewithal, should supply all the native wants. By this gross misconception, Indians viewed merchandise brought up the river, not as company property, but as Indian property. Moreover, any delay in distribution attendant upon such base considerations as prices or quality of furs evidenced an improperly selfish design on the part of the trader. One of the more intelligent men of the tribe asked Tabeau, " 'Why do you wish to make all this powder and these balls since you do not hunt? Of what use are all these knives to you? Is not one enough with which to cut your meat?' " But, these were rhetorical questions, and the Indian went on to tell the trader: " 'It is only your wicked heart that prevents you from giving them to us. Do you not see that the village has none?' " [22]

Some men went beyond Tabeau, however, by charging that the Indian's ignorance was more reprehensible than a simple unawareness of economic forms. They accused the savage of being psychologically incapable of understanding altruism, an idea which received conditional or muted statement from various quarters. Duncan Cameron played lightly on the theme when he wrote of the inhabitants of the Nipigon country, "Being themselves unacquainted with honor and honesty, they are very distrustful of us. . . ." However, it was Edwin Denig, with all his sympathy for the Indian, who clarified and elaborated this state of affairs at greatest length. At one point he explained the Crow Indians' fear of paper, writing, and pictures by arguing that they saw these things as partaking of supernatural powers. The Crows, if they had such objects and skills, would utilize them to pursue evil ways, and they could not help feeling that the white man intended them for the same function. To have the power to work evil and not to use it was inconceivable to the Crow mind. In his other lengthy treatment of the plains tribes—material written in accordance with a governmental form devised by Henry Rowe Schoolcraft—Denig made even stronger statements of this point. Shortly after opening the section "Intellectual Capacity and Character" by stating his preference for the savage over the "ignorant white," Denig wrote:

On subjects in which their actual experience and observations are at fault, even if supported with good arguments, they are suspicious and incredulous. They listen, doubt, but say little. On all such topics their minds receive a bias from their superstitions and lack of appreciation of motive. They can not conceive of any efforts made through motives of charity, benevolence, or pity, nor realize any other disinterested action, even if it be for their benefit, because all they do is in expectation of reward, and being destitute of the above principles of actions are disposed to attribute interested views to everyone else.[23]

On one occasion Samuel Hearne quoted a Chipewyan leader as saying that his people had " 'nothing to do but consult their own interest, inclinations, and passions and to pass through this world with as much ease and contentment as possible, without any hopes of reward, or painful fear of punishment, in the next.' " By such commentaries, the Indian emerged as a rank hedonist and materialist, and traders rarely failed to brand him precisely so. Operating upon this conviction, they never thought of dealing with natives without lavish material manifestations of good will. The wheels of diplomacy always required a greasing in the form of largesse. During the War of 1812, Robert Dickson operating in the Mackinac area received a vote of confidence in regard to his munificence in dealing with the red men. His superiors in Montreal—William M'Gillivray and James Gill among others—recognized that his activities, which apparently went beyond the strictly commercial, demanded it. "For gaining any point with them . . . ," they concluded, "it is indispensable, to make them presents. . . ." Only a few years earlier, in an attempt to reach the mountain tribes via the upper Missouri villages, Francois-Antoine Larocque found himself stymied by the Gros Ventres. He reasoned that he could call the leaders to a meeting and appeal formally for passage; but to do so "without making presents would be worth no more than addressing the words to a heap of stones."[24]

On the cruder levels of the trade the same held true. Duncan Cameron of the North West Company recalled that on one occasion he arrived at a Hudson's Bay Company post and promptly set about luring away some of their Indians. He invited two of the best ones to his tent saying that he wished to make them a present—"as I well knew that an Indian is very little influenced by words unless those words are accompanied by something more substantial." No amount of wisdom could move an Indian, according to Jean Baptiste Trudeau, unless that wisdom manifested itself in material form.[25]

Things less mundane in nature also bore a price tag. After watching some new converts to Catholicism finance a drinking party with their recently awarded, civilized garb and hearing them discuss the possibility of returning for another baptism and more clothes, Conrad Weiser decided that even religion was meaningless unless afforded generous material support. And the remarks of a late seventeenth-century Illinois trader anticipate the eventual debasement of America's aborigines:

They would prostitute their daughters or sisters a thousand times for a pair of stockings or other trifle. I have got men to agree a hundred times that their fathers, their brothers, and their children were worse than dogs, because they hoped I would give them a little red paint or a five-*sol* knife.[26]

Edwin Denig again elaborated most fully on the ultimate, logical conclusion of self-interestedness. In his discussion of native warfare, for instance, he made practical suggestions based on the idea that "There is always an opening to the heart of an Indian through his love of gain," and added matter-of-factly, "most chiefs, soldiers, and heads of families are open to bribes." Finally, in comments referring specifically to the Assiniboine but, by inference, to all of Indian society, the Fort Union trader wrote:

They appear to look upon every person as a source from which benefit is to be derived, [and] care but little for individuals or principles if some gain is realized. This runs through the whole course of their operations. . . . It is more or less the great motive of all savage nations. It forms the basis of all their transactions. . . .[27]

In the eyes of the trader the Indian not only possessed crass and venal inclinations, he also applied them practically in the market place. If fur traders ever heard the story of the sale of Manhattan, their incredulity must have vied strongly with their jealousy. Strange as it may seem, traders almost universally gave the Indian credit, or condemnation, for proficiency as a bargainer. Daniel Lamont of the Upper Missouri Outfit tacitly conveyed this impression in a letter of instruction to Emillien Primeau on the White River. Lamont informed his subordinate that he had sent some lances, which had been costly to obtain. "To make a profit" they should sell for two robes. "Make the trial," he continued, "and, if you find the Indians will not buy them at that price, let them have them for one." The evidence indicates, not that the fur men unmercifully hoodwinked the innocent and trusting primitives, but almost the reverse. The traders often expressed themselves, sometimes even petulantly, as being put upon by the canny red men. For example, after recounting his economic maltreatment at the hands of the Poncas, a disgruntled Jean Baptiste Trudeau explained (in language hardly suited to an exploiter) how the Indians justified their conduct. Other tribes, the Poncas loftily informed Trudeau, treated him even worse than they did; thus he should not complain of relatively minor skulduggery.[28]

One can, of course, consider the source of evidence, such as John Rae's testimony before the 1857 Parliamentary committee on the Hudson's Bay Company. When a committee member asked him directly, "Were they [the Indians] shrewd in their dealings?," the former trader and explorer answered, "Perfectly shrewd." Here,

Rae was testifying in behalf of a trade empire fighting for its life, and his words must be considered in that light. Contrarily, Joseph Robson in a patent effort to destroy the monopoly of the Hudson's Bay Company reported that the Indians parted with their furs on such "amazing low terms, as will scarcely be credited" by outsiders.[29] However, the majority of fur-trade sources do not involve such polemics. Nor were they written to please. Rather, they came from hardened, candid, and unapologetic men of affairs who, most likely, did not give much concern to what people thousands of miles away thought of their methods. In such writings one would except some explicit instances of colossal economic legerdemain practised at the red man's expense and, perhaps, an occasional self-satisfied chortling at deceptions well-wrought. Examples of this, however, appear only infrequently.

Strange as it may seem, traders far more commonly nursed a feeling of being abused. At first glance, Francois Chouteau's 1830 letter appears to evidence the Indians' helplessness in matters of trade. He mentioned an instance wherein the Kansas bought merchandise "sans savoir les prix ni la quantité, comme une bande d'animaux Brute." Indeed, "ces monstre de kans ne pouvent resister quand il voient le butin si [?] bon ou mauvais." However, it was someone else's goods that the monsters purchased so ignorantly. And, in spite of his every effort, they had indeed been able to resist the sight of Chouteau's merchandise. With none of Chouteau's artfulness, a Fort Miamis trader informed his employer that business with the natives in his quarter would be poor—"for I will not give my goods away for nothing." In his usual tone of light cynicism and self-pity, Alexis Bailly soliloquized on the misconceptions of those who indulged in "speculative philanthropy." It was very well, he noted, for others to provide the benighted savages with food, clothes, and other necessities; but "for my part they have so often cheated me that I cannot even get my own. . . ." George Simpson matched Bailly in his jaundiced view of the natives, but, unlike the French-Canadian, he combined it with a supreme confidence in his own abilities and those of civilized men generally. Still, he occasionally paid the red men grudging tributes for their awareness of the factitious intricacies of the trade. In one context, he wrote that the Indians of the Vancouver area, having lost their ability to use force, resorted to various ruses, a favorite being to stretch the tails of land otters and pass them off as the more valuable sea variety. According to Sir George, "these artists of the north-west could dye a horse with any jockey in the civilized world. . . ." Though he is a somewhat peripheral figure for purposes of this study, mountain man "Uncle Dick" Wootton must have expressed the misgivings of much of the trade when he commented as follows: "I don't know whether or not the Indian has descended from the Jew, but I know he has some of the same instincts in trade." [30]

High trade policy reflected these assessments of the red man's commercial acumen. Robert Stuart, at the time agent for the American Fur Company, emphasized the necessity of ordering the trade goods early, in order that they might be "particularly manufactured, *according to advice.*" Recently, the company traders had suffered the handicap of inferior blue stroud and second-rate blankets, and he insisted that such material would not answer. The goods must be of particular size and quality—for example, the borders on the stroud and blankets must not be of mixed colors but of solid blue, and a deep, rich blue at that. Recognition of these demands and preferences, he concluded, though it might be of little moment "in dealing with Whites," was "all important with the savage." [31] Evidently, some sources have overstated the ease of doing business with the aborigines.

One of the precise, Indian techniques of the market place, traders insisted, was that of invoking pity. By their telling, fur men usually dealt in an atmosphere charged by fervent pleas for compassion. Many of them reacted to this as did Charles Chaboillez, a man who reportedly kept a journal enshrouded by "a vast business-like calm." When charity-seeking natives begged a keg to compensate for, or perhaps to nullify, their "Pityful" condition, he brusquely informed them to "go & work the Beaver" before coming for handouts. And Simon M'Gillivray, accused of being heartless by an Indian whose tale of outrageous fortune failed to elicit largesse, confided in his journal that, "I thank him very much for the compliment.'' Many traders grumbled about the natives' conduct in trade affairs, but James Isham took the trouble to record facsimiles of trader-Indian discourses. The following evidences the blending of the emotional and the practical that so often enraged the trader:

. . . we Livd. hard last winter and in want. The powder being short measure and bad, I say! —tell your Servants to fill the measure and not to put their finger's within the Brim, take pity of us, take pity of us, I say! —we come Long way to See you, french sends for us but we will not here [hear], we Love the English, give us good . . . black tobacco, moist & hard twisted, Let us see itt before op'n'd, —take pity of us, take pity of us I say! [32]

Whether or not this practice enhanced the red man's mercenary effectiveness eludes ready answer. However, the frequent recording of it does indicate that, to the trader, the Indian had something more than a rudimentary grasp of what transpired when buyer and seller came together.

Bernard DeVoto's comment that there was no problem ''which fire-water could not solve'' represents a stock view of fur-trade realities. But this is somewhat less than true. Even the ultimate commercial weapon had drawbacks. Overlooking for now the trepidations the fur men felt when dealing with drunken Indians, it should be noted that liquor or the promise of liquor did not always serve its fundamental purpose. It did not unfailingly circumvent what the trader saw in his red customer as a deeply ingrained awareness of self-interest. Around 1670 John Lederer, in reciting the difficulties in bargaining with the savages, admitted that liquor might put them in ''an humour of giving you ten times the value of your commodity. . . .'' However, should they become aware of the trader's design, they would assume an even more obstinate and demanding posture, liquor or no. More than two hundred years later a trader among the Arikaras pointed out the uselessness of liquor in the trade with that tribe because they would not drink unless paid to do so. In the ultimate of venality, they insisted that, since they would provide the entertainment, the observer should not only provide the liquor but pay to watch as well. Indeed, several groups—including the Crows, the Chipewyans and various of the Pacific coast tribes—abstained from liquor until long after the traders came among them.[33] Traders often used the word ''debauch'' to describe a facet of their activities but they used it in its now obsolete sense—to seduce from an allegiance. Where competition prevailed, they almost universally resorted to blandishments, money, liquor, or other expedients to lure Indians—or whites—from previous loyalties. Their use of the word did not connote debasement, though the popular conception of their affairs probably hastened the obsolescence of the word as they meant it.*

The fur trader, then, accused the Indian of having an overweening interest in self. But that seemed to be the very feature which most typified the actions and outlook of the accuser. For all his insistence that the natives were niggardly, ungrateful, and materialistic, we cannot help but wonder. Surely, at the very least, the pot called the kettle black. Was it comforting, we can ask, for these men to see in their economic victims the same reprehensible traits that were apparent in themselves? Or has the scoundrelly role of the men in the trade been overstated? Have Kenneth McKenzie's still, and George Simpson's opposition to Indian schools, and fur-trade recipes for Indian grog drawn too much attention at the expense of less sensational, more realistic, often judicious and even just, day-by-day approaches to contact with people of a primitive culture?

Many of these men were very sympathetic to the savages; all of their commentaries could scarcely have been nothing more than rationalizations for brutal exploitation. Edwin Denig, the most intelligent and thorough exponent of the doctrine of Indian self-interestedness, never gratuitously denigrated the red man. He understood the Indian, acknowledged what seemed to be limited virtues, and often attempted to explain his shortcomings. Like the great majority of the traders, he had a native wife. Indeed, it

* When, for example, Robert Campbell found that one of his employees was acting as a spy for opposition trader, Kenneth McKenzie, he noted that McKenzie had, via promises and forty dollars in cash, ''debauched him.'' George R. Brooks (ed.), ''The Private Journal of Robert Campbell,'' *Missouri Historical Society Bulletin*, XX (January, 1964), 115.

appears that he may have suffered a voluntarily imposed ostracism for the contumely connected with bringing his tawny spouse back to civilization.

The only tenable position is the middle ground; the concept of the self-interested Indian provides commentary both on the trader and on the Indian. Robert Campbell of the upper Missouri trade understood that egoism and selfishness were not confined to the red race or the white race—they were parts of the human circumstance:

I could make some handsome compliments to myself on recommending sobriety, when I had no spirits to sell; and very strongly deprecating the use of "fire water" by our friends the "red skins." The advice was certainly good, be the motive as it may. Indeed such is the world, with all its attempts to dissemble. Self interest predominates; and the only difference in its exercise, in savage and civilized life, is that in the former we acknowledge, in the latter you conceal your motives.[34]

Self-interest—the prime moving force in the Indian ethos—represents no more than the central core of a complex of attributes seen by traders in the primitives around them. Time and again they called attention to such traits as dishonesty, lack of principle, treachery, fickleness, hypocrisy, affectation, exaggeration, and so on in descending importance toward the peripheries. But traders did more than list the flaws in the Indian's grossly perverse make-up. Tacitly, they sorted, arranged, and categorized. One can note in the illustrative listing above a descent in ethical gravity, one might say, from cardinal to venial. Traders systematized; but they did not do so precisely in terms of ethical principles. Their order of outrageousness of native qualities only roughly corresponds to that of the moralist. The disparity stems from differing criteria. As argued in an earlier chapter, the Indian had two possible claims to the fur man's esteem—he lent himself to economic designs, or he kept himself happily absent. By the same token, those attributes of his manifestly unsavory character appearing least reprehensible and eliciting readiest acceptance were those which did not handicap trade relations, or which least frequently impinged upon the trader's awareness.

8. A LACK OF PRINCIPLES

THE RED MAN STOOD ACCUSED OF POSSESSING A CHARACTER OUTRA-
geously bereft of guides to right conduct. Because the trader saw
self-interest as the basic Indian motivation, he felt that the red
man's actions did not readily or spontaneously follow a righteous
course. Only force or fear made the savage act properly. At the
outset of North American settlement, Captain John Smith judged
the aborigines to be "inconstant in everie thing, but what feare
constraineth them to keepe . . . ," and fur-trade opinion of the
next 250 years repeatedly endorsed his view. Indeed, Indian misconduct against the fur trade almost without exception elicited just
such an analysis. When George Simpson wrote of some of his red
charges that they were "solely prevented from committing the most
atrocious crimes by a fear of the consequences . . . ," he expressed
both a stock interpretation of Indian conduct and the equivalent of a
policy statement by the most powerful fur-trading organization.[1]

Having analyzed the conduct of their tawny customers in this
way, traders went on to outline a method of operation based upon
the alleged realities of Indian nature and designed to hold those
realities in check. Nothing, perhaps, comments more tellingly on the
trader's conception of the Indian than the superabundance of
testimonials to the efficacy, indeed to the necessity, of meting out
swift and severe retribution for Indian wrong-doings—ruling with a
"rod of iron" as George Simpson called it.

This outlook permeated every level of the trade. As a policy-
maker, Simpson, for example, ceaselessly reiterated the theme both
in appraising business for superiors and in exhorting better efforts
from inferiors. Traders in the field, the men conducting day-by-day
affairs at the point of contact between red and white cultures,

supported the doctrine fully as much, and, where possible, gave it practical application. The views of two prominent Hudson's Bay Company traders, John Work and Peter Skene Ogden, typify these sentiments. After finding some of his horses wounded by arrows, Work emphatically discounted any course other than severe treatment as a basis for rapport with the savages. At another point, when thefts became insupportable, he stated the sinister conviction that he would have to destroy one or two Indian villages in order to acquaint the natives with the standards of decorum demanded by Hudson's Bay traders. While facing starvation and suffering harassment by the Modocs in southwestern Oregon in the winter of 1827, Ogden put his consistent belief into brutally stark terms: "I am of opinion that if on first discovering a strange Tribe a dozen of them were shot, it would be the means of preserving many lives. . . ." Later, in his recollections of fur-trade life, Ogden (apparently if not really) toned down the ardor of his conviction—perhaps for general consumption or possibly because he was then removed from the specter of starvation—and discussed the less startling necessity of treating the Indians with "the greatest severity" from the outset.[2]

Obviously, this theory could not always be fulfilled. In that event, however, other traders felt no compunctions in sharply criticizing their fellows for lack of determination, and they complained bitterly of the ill effects wrought by nonobservance of a basic tenet. In January of 1814 an expedition comprised of North West Company men and recently dispossessed Astorians set out from Fort George (formerly Astoria) on what was ostensibly a venture to recover stolen goods and to chastise the pillagers. Though the party included some experienced and hardened men (Alexander Henry the younger for one), it achieved little. When the irresolute punishers encountered the red pirates of the Columbia, they limited themselves to a feigning action and a storm of verbal abuse. Elliott Coues, who knew the methods commonly employed by North West traders, considered it an "inexplicable . . . fiasco." Moreover, the writings of some of the principles do little to destroy Coues's evaluation. Gabriel Franchère, a leading member of the party, seemed apologetic and unconvincing in ascribing the abortion to the fact that humanity had taken precedence over vengeance. And considering the source, Alexander Henry's day-by-day account, though detailed, seems strangely subdued.[3]

On the other hand, Alexander Ross, who did not accompany the vengeance-seekers, castigated them for their failure. For the expedition to return without achieving its purposes, he insisted, compounded tenfold the pernicious nature of the situation. Ross, himself no brute, saw fit to describe the effort as "inglorious," and did not hesitate to say that the participants had brought disgrace upon themselves. Similarly, when Alexander McLeod prepared to lead a comparable expedition against the Umpquas for pillaging and murdering most of Jedediah Smith's party, Doctor John McLoughlin urged him to inflict stern punishment upon the evil-doers. Though Smith and his men were Americans and, in a fashion, interlopers in the Oregon country, McLoughlin argued that Smith's goods must be recovered and his men avenged or no one would be safe. Fifteen years later McLoughlin still looked upon McLeod's expedition with regret, for it had terminated mildly rather than severely. A good deal of suffering, he felt, had sprung from this lack of resolution on the part of white men. With like logic, Joshua Pilcher, the moving force of the Missouri Fur Company, unsparingly reproached Colonel Henry Leavenworth who commanded an ineffectual punitive campaign against the Arikaras in 1823. In an open letter to Leavenworth published in the St. Louis *Missouri Republican*, Pilcher accused the Colonel of both imbecility and culpability. Going from personal shortcomings to an analysis of the situation, Pilcher, who had been on the scene as Leavenworth's subordinate, based his charges upon the firm realities of Indian nature. "I am well aware," he conceded, "that humanity and philanthropy are mighty shields for you . . . ," being compelling arguments among those ignorant of the "disposition and character of Indians." Old hands like himself, he indicated, knew better. The Arikaras "know no law," and thus necessity demanded a chastisement "which would strike terror to the hearts of these remorseless monsters of the wilderness. . . ." Whatever the circumstances,

Indian wrong-doings demanded harsh and immediate punishment.[4]

The theory of sternness had obvious corollaries. The good trader, for example, made it a rule always to maintain a bold front, studiously suppressing feelings of trepidation. In his recollections John McLean gave a dramatic example of the validity of this principle, recounting an incident when an Iroquois confronted one of McLean's acquaintances with a loaded weapon and an intent to kill. Immediately upon seeing the red man's purpose, the trader bared his chest, glared fiercely at the assassin, and exclaimed, " 'Fire, you black dog! What! did you imagine you had sent for an old woman?' " According to McLean, this boldness, based on a thorough knowledge of Indian character, saved the man's life. Had he shown fear, the Indian would have killed him. As it was, the angry Iroquois lost composure, and command of the situation slipped away from him. The trader's "undaunted attitude . . . staggered the resolution of the savage." Soon the weapon wavered in the Indian's hand. A moment later he threw it on the ground, telling his intended victim to leave.[5]

Though McLean managed to recall a striking illustration, this theme ordinarily gained expression in the context of simple advice. In 1796 James Mackay wrote instructions to the novice, John Evans, who was preparing for an expedition to the Pacific via the headwaters of the Missouri. The veteran trader counseled the young man on how to maintain good relations with the natives. In a central part of this advice, Mackay warned him: "Appear always on guard and never be fearful or timid, for the savages are not generally bold, but will act in a manner to make you afraid of them. If, however, they see that you are courageous and venturesome they will soon yield to your wishes." Yet another ramification of the same conviction held, logically but quite futilely, that Indian debts should be demanded and collected with rigor and care. Instructing a subordinate on how to get the Delawares and Kickapoos to pay, Pierre Menard pointed out with sound businesslike reasoning the hazards of forbearance—"it will make a great difference against the Interest of all the Traiders and against ther standing and reputation. . . ." In a letter to a less experienced colleague, Charles W. Borup twice emphasized the necessity of treating the Indians fairly. Evidently, the intelligent Dane meant fairness to be interpreted with just rigidity, for he counseled his fellow trader not to "give way to them one iota," but rather to "let them understand that they must pay for what they get. . . ." By way of exhortation Ramsay Crooks advised Green Bay trader John Lawe to be more "wide awake"; because Lawe felt that others would act honorably as he did, he erred in being "easy and unsuspecting." Consequently, Crooks noted, the people around the bay took advantage of their trader, and unless corrected "they will root you out of house and home. . . ." Finally, though treated elsewhere in this study, the urgency of carrying one's self with aloofness and dignity while among the savages comprises an element of this over-all position.[6]

Almost universally, traders believed that acting contrary to these tenets invited disaster. To lose the respect of the Indians could prove fatal. In preparing for his second try to reach the northern ocean, Samuel Hearne decided to take only Indians, excluding Europeans. On his first attempt in 1769, he had taken two white men, but "the Indians knowing them to be common men, used them so indifferently, particularly in scarce times, that I was under some apprehension of their being starved to death. . . ." To remain aloof and to nurture an appearance of importance did more than feed egotistical self-esteem. As Peter Fidler recorded during a winter spent with a roving band of far North Indians,

 . . . it is an invariable custom with all Indians & none more so than these I am with that the more an European does of work with them the worse he is respected by them & [he] gets generally the worst victuals & frequently but little of it when he complys to do every thing they bid him whereas if he stiffly refuses from the first . . . they will be very kind to him & will give him a larger allowance of provisions than had he listened to every request. . . .[7]

Familiarity generated contempt and caused short rations as well.

When James Chambers wrote in the Fort Sarpy journal that Robert Meldrum was having trouble clearing the post of Indians for the night—"the Old Man stormed   the Indians laughed and made sport of him''—he expressed the stock opinion that the red man almost without exception interpreted forbearance as timidity. ''The Indians,'' Chambers continued, ''have never troubled me, in fact take the Crows in the right way & they are good people but to coax & pay a Crow to go out of the Fort will not answer.'' To ''take'' them in the right way implied something far removed from Meldrum's indulgence. When Daniel Duluth had two Indians executed by breaking their skulls, he appealed to the same premise. Although it was a grim business, their apparent implication in the deaths of two of Duluth's party demanded it. A display of benevolence, however praiseworthy, would have been lost on the natives, and they would have become even more vicious, supposing that the French feared them. The Indians, it was repeatedly argued, could not comprehend actions based on humanity or generosity. Such actions indicated to them weakness or cowardice, and they immediately pressed what they saw as an advantage. Evidences of this outlook are legion, and almost every trader who gave any consideration to the bases of Indian actions noted the uselessness of observing benevolent niceties in relations with people who could not understand them—people who, as Charles Larpenteur put it, felt that might makes right. And occasional mention indicates that traders apparently considered the red men as quick to impose upon the permissiveness of other Indians as that of whites. Thus Chambers wrote of Bears Head, a Crow chief, that he was ''a good easy man & lets his people do as they please and the consequence is that the Bucks are raping the Squaws in broad day light in every corner. . . .'' What could one expect, he must have mused, of people without principles? [8]

In its turn, dishonesty appeared to comprise one of the more noteworthy elements of the red man's unprincipled nature. The vast majority of traders would have agreed with James Isham's observation that Indians refuted the proverb, '' 'what all say's is true.' '' With Indians, profession bore little relation to reality. Though the Indian may live in tradition as a symbol of probity, traders saw him quite differently. Such a blemish, real or imagined, would make itself felt in trade policy. Continually, the Indian's falseness led to

counseling of subordinates by superiors, to reassurances of employers by employees, and to individual self-fortification through misanthropic reflections and forebodings. The effective trader refused
to trust the Indian. Though certainly not unforeseen by his superior,
a Minnesota trader's assurance that "I have long known what value
to set upon Indian promises" must have comforted his superior. A
more generous mental posture would make itself felt—if not with
the Indians, then certainly with one's fellows and employers. When
the Sauk and Fox tribes belatedly made arrangements for clearing
some debts, Ramsay Crooks expressed gratification. He wrote that it
would palliate some of the bad business that the recently deceased
Russell Farnham—"one of the best meaning of men"—had done
with those tribes "by reason of his always unlimited confidence in
their honesty and industry. . . ." [9]

Indians manifested dishonesty in ways other than false promises.
Traders considered them liars generally and at times implied that
they avoided truth out of congenital fault or imponderable perversity. Traveling across the Dakota prairies toward a Missouri River
establishment, the young New Yorker, Ferdinand Van Ostrand,
chanced upon a band of natives and asked of conditions ahead. Much
snow, he was informed. But he found, certainly not to his surprise,
that such was not the case—"Lied—as usual." Similarly, the Indian
appears in fur-trade literature as having an amazing penchant for
exaggeration. This, of course, could take various forms, but the red
man's real forte seemed to be the embroidering of bad news to the
point of what Bernard Ross called "truly horrific proportions."
Although the tendency to draw the doleful long bow appears to have
been widespread, Indians of the far North were counted the real
masters of the form. Bernard Ross, for example, had often seen "the
murdered restored to life and the starved to death jolly and fat."
Thomas Simpson went from the particular to the general in regard
to exaggerated ill tidings:

It is a general rule among the traders, not to believe the *first* story of an
Indian. He will tell you on arriving, that there are no deer, and afterwards
acknowledge them to be numerous: that he has been starving, when he has
been living in abundance: that certain individuals are dead; yet, after he

has smoked his pipe and eaten his fill, ask him what is the matter with these same persons, and he will describe some trifling ailments. . . .[10]

For the trader, traits of this sort had an unfathomable element about them. But other manifestations of Indian deceitfulness were more readily explained—and in terms nicely in keeping with the dominant force of Indian nature. Dishonesty, like other failings, represented a ramification of aboriginal self-interest. Alexis Bailly complained to a government Indian agent that the current administration of the wilderness left "too much for Indian Honesty." Specifically, Indians took credits from him but, once their hunts were finished, they overlooked their obligations and traded elsewhere—"My Creditors (as they are called) . . . practice fraud with something like systems. . . ." Peter Pond found a way to play upon this Indian failing by using cheap baubles to entice fur-laden red men. The natives, he argued, came to his post to filch his studiously unguarded "things for the finger," and then stayed to do their serious trading as well. But Pond's sagacity did not always prevail over native inclinations. Indeed, via his intriguing orthography, he conveyed much of the import of Bailly's later complaint and damning judgment:

When you Mete them in Spring as Know them Personeley   ask for your Pay and thay will Speake in thare One [own] Language   if thay Speake at all   Which is not to be understood or [in] Other ways thay Will Look Sulkey and Make you no answer and you loes your Debt.[11]

Looking "Sulkey" and making you no answer involved a passive approach. The Indians of Samuel Hearne's experience used more initiative and imagination: they disguised themselves or changed their names in order to avoid paying a debt. However, Edwin Denig recorded the last word in deceitfulness. When all his tricks and ruses proved futile before a white man's adamant insistence upon his just due, the encumbered primitive would haughtily assert that the trader had no business trusting him with a debt in the first place.

Indians also bore an unenviable reputation for backbiting and slander, and Samuel Hearne paid high tribute to Mattonabbee by noting that he was the only Indian Hearne had ever seen, save one, who did not treat his neighbors in that way. Here again, motivation appeared evident to the traders. Indians welcomed any chance to prejudice their fellows in the eyes of luxury-bearing white men. When Jean Baptiste Trudeau decided to leave the Missouri and go to the Poncas on the Niobrara, the Omahas warned him against it. His party would be abused, pillaged, or perhaps murdered, the Omahas helpfully advised, because the Poncas were an uncivilized people—Trudeau rendered it, "n'est point humanisé." But Trudeau recognized this as nonsense; the Omahas wished to keep traders away from the Poncas so that they could continue to buy furs from their more provincial Siouan brothers at a pittance and sell them at a premium in the Missouri River trade. A similar situation led Pierre Esprit Radisson to conclude that "envy reigns everywhere amongst poor barbarous wild people, as at courts." [12]

Devious ways more subtle and delicate also appealed to the Indian. Unless the trader misread him, the native approached virtuosity in his use of emotional pretensions. In defense, fur men often armed themselves with a thorny exterior of ill tempered prejudgment. Indian affectation ran so rampant, for instance, that cordial overtures were sometimes considered *ipso facto* evidence of disaffection. For example, the reverential appearance of his Iroquois trappers set loose premonitions of sinful reality in the mind of Alexander Ross. Their singing of hymns one evening after encampment conjured up no benign sentiments in this devout fur-trade veteran. Instead, he immediately doubled the watch. In a similarly common vein, Thomas Fitzpatrick told in a government report that he made it a principle "to double the guard and become more vigilant . . . whenever I found them very officious and professing great friendship. . . ." [13]

Native histrionics went beyond friendship, flattery, and the like. By the traders' telling, they dissembled masterfully in other ways as well. References to their shamming illness as an excuse for poor hunts or as a means of avoiding other obligations are legion. Suspicion of Indian sickness became so ingrained in traders that it took little more than mention of it to raise their ire. Nearly all claims of indisposition, short of smallpox, met disbelief. In a somewhat ludicrous, though fairly typical instance of this, "Charlie the chief," who was accompanying John Work's brigade in Nez Perce country, apparently took cramps while swimming and had to be helped out of the water. Laid out on the bank, "Charlie" requested two or three "drams" to ease him over the rigors of his affliction. At this point Work's concern vanished, to be replaced by skepticism—his journal implies clearly that the Indian had feigned his seizure; and Charlie, he noted, "is undoubtedly an artful knave." [14]

A whole complex of Indian shortcomings stemmed from dishonesty. Fickleness, for example, appeared to the trader as a universal in the character of the red primitives. When a Fort William employee stole the prized wife of another, trader Robert Campbell noted derisively that "this proves the instability of the dear angels." And the masculine counterparts of "dear angels" appeared no better. Far from the emotionally stalwart, principled men of unwavering hatreds and allegiances, Indians seemed to be the very embodiment of inconstancy. In their treatments of the much maligned tribes of the Pacific coastal areas, traders occasionally read into the aboriginal nature an acute emotional or psychological unsteadiness. More often, however, they described simple caprice or whimsicality. Unlike the straightforward primitive of our popular culture, openly manifesting and steadfastly maintaining his likes and dislikes, the fur traders' Indian alarmed the white man by his unpredictability. Thus, Alexander Henry the younger revealed apprehension in the following remarks on the people of the plains:

. . . [they] are much given to gusts of passion; a mere trifle irritates them and makes a great commotion, which a stranger would suppose must end in bloodshed. But the matter is soon adjusted, and their passion quickly subsides. They are fickle and changeable; no confidence can be placed in them; the most trifling circumstance will change their minds. [15]

On a level far less mystifying to their white observers, the Indian seemed to operate in an inconstant fashion as a matter of policy, as a matter of interest. Robert Campbell described this tendency in recounting the termination of an interview with a chief, who left vowing everlasting friendship—"which being interpreted; means, as long as I had wine and goods to give, and he had robes and beaver to trade." Whichever it was, whimsy or policy, traders placed little reliance upon the natives. Most would have agreed with the analysis of the problem, if not with the solution, offered by Francis Chardon. "It is impossible to Know Friend or Enemie," he wrote, "however I consider them all the latter, as an Indian is soon turned, like the wind, from one side to the other." Chardon had a patent streak of misanthropy, but many others of less caustic temperament subscribed to views not far removed. Indian declarations of amity almost without exception evoked sneers of mockery and disbelief. Moreover, though one would expect discretion to have dictated a careful weighing of hostile postures, traders often took them just as lightly. "Ambiguous words and certain glances" might have sinister import, according to Pierre-Antoine Tabeau, but direct threats were to be scorned. In the chidingly sarcastic tone so prevalent in fur-trade literature, Ferdinand Van Ostrand recounted an episode that revealed a customary disdain for red menaces: "One of my Ree [Arikara] friends in consequence of a slight unpleasantness in the store this morning informed me that he would close my fashionable and brilliant career today—but he has failed to carry out the pleasant programme. I have lost confidence in that Indian's word." However stated, traders made it a rule not to depend on Indian professions.[16]

From caprice and undependability it was only a step to treachery, and the Indians achieved notoriety among the fur men for this trait. Although often inclined to give the natives benefit of doubt, Alexander Ross set down an intense but nonetheless characteristic indictment of them in his discussion of the *Tonquin* massacre. "Perfidy is the system of savages," he wrote, and "treachery and cunning are the instruments of their power. . . ." To a large degree, however, traders seemed psychologically, if not always physically, able to cope with red treachery. Most of them probably assumed a stance similar to that of the younger Alexander Henry, who maintained a vigorous mistrust of the Indian under any circumstances. If foul play materialized, it came at least as no surprise. Traders accepted perfidious designs as a matter of course, and coolly made allowances for them. As one scholar has written of Charles Chaboillez, the North West Company man who preceded Henry by a year in the Pembina region, "he was a veteran . . . nothing surprised or fazed him. . . ." [17]

The Indian's nonobservance of the tenets of upright living manifested itself to the trader in ways which less decisively influenced the trade, in ways more personal than social or economic. Because the trader knew the Indian well, he fully recognized these failings but the fur men reacted far differently to personal inadequacies than to those which appeared in socioeconomic relations.

With almost complete accord, fur-trade sentiment judged the Indian to be indolent. The length and frequency with which traders remarked on this defect become almost burdensome, although some expressions of it do have the merit of unintended drollery. Thus, James Adair referred to the red men as "great enemies to profuse sweating," and insisted that an Indian hurried, " 'only when the devil is at his arse.' " This attribute so strongly impressed traders that David Thompson, never one to be unkind in his evaluations of Indians, used it as salient evidence to demonstrate his thesis that the industrious Eskimos were racially separate from the other American aborigines. And James Mackay refused to believe that the mounds of the Ohio Valley could be the works of "beings so excessive indolent & lazy as the present Indians of America who would rather starve a week than work a day." [18]

Laziness, of course, evidenced itself in improvidence. With the possible exception of the Chipewyans, traders considered the natives notably unconcerned with what the future had in store. Rather than the canny primitive, always maintaining command of his position in nature's scheme, the Indian appears in fur-trade literature as one whose congenital thriftlessness left him buffeted by every exigency of the wilderness. In fact, his sufferings and his starvation often seemed to stem directly from improvidence. Charles W. Borup gave a typical expression of this state of affairs in a letter to his superior, Ramsay Crooks. The company must hasten a supply of ammunition to a particular post, he wrote, "for as usual the improvident Indians have neglected to supply themselves. . . ." [19]

Thriftlessness found its most obvious expression in Indian gluttony. The native's capacity for food impressed traders so mightily that they considered it a more prodigious feat than any achieved through the chase or the raiding party. They stood in awe of the red man's ability to eat. Before recording the astounding particulars, Pierre-Antoine Tabeau reasoned that in gluttony the Indian experienced his foremost happiness. Consequently, it comprised the object of greatest interest and monopolized all conversation. As did nearly every other trader, Edwin Denig set out to inform civilization of the Indians' "incredible" gastronomical achievements, but he gave it up as futile. No one who did not know Indians, he concluded, could grasp even an approach to the truth—"it can not be realized." This, like improvidence itself, caused the red man hardship; he would not rest, according to the traders, until all was gone.[20]

Traders saw the Indian as loafer, wastrel, and glutton. They considered these qualities interesting, noteworthy, remarkable, and sometimes unfortunate, but not necessarily or always reprehensible. For all their abundant awareness, traders seldom attached any great amount of odium to these shortcomings, which largely affected the Indians, not the traders. Being at one remove from the sphere which most concerned the fur men, these traits appeared less evident and important. The Indian exhibited these characteristics primarily in his own affairs and only incidentally in the market place, the arena in which he came under the traders' severest judgments.

Had these alleged failures been completely confined to areas divorced from the traders' central interests, they would probably have excited little or no disapproval. In many fur-trade situations, however, the lives of the Indian and the trader were inextricably bound together. Where the Indian was expected to harvest furs, his indolence hindered the trade. In the Hudson's Bay domain, where the company succored Indians in times of privation, improvidence and gluttony could result in disaster for white and red alike. John Rae, himself an exquisite hunter and outdoorsman, expressed complete disgust at the ineptness, laziness, and improvidence of the company's far North Indians. They refused to do even the simplest and easiest food-procuring tasks unless threatened by a cessation of rations. Most aggravating of all, the company received—as thanks for humanity, patience, and forbearance—unending censure from "would-be-philanthropists" who were completely ignorant of wilderness realities.[21]

The Indian's improvidence became actively malign in what the trader saw as an utter disregard for the natural abundance of the wilderness. This point has attracted a fair amount of controversy, but with some few exceptions fur traders agreed that the Indian was a wastrel and a spoiler. He overkilled, it was held, whenever he could, taking only tongues and marrow bones while leaving the carcasses for the carrion-eaters. Some men argued that the Indian possessed an innate passion for taking life. In their frontier narratives Samuel Hearne and Thomas Simpson insisted that an Indian could not pass even a bird's nest without destroying the eggs or killing the young. Pointing out the difficulties of eventually transforming America's natives into graziers, Alexander Ross commented that they look upon animals "with more of a butcher's than a herdsman's eye." Occasionally, a trader became incensed at the Indians' seemingly useless slaughter and suggested that, for this wantonness, the perpetrators deserved whatever fate had in store for them. After recording how Hudson's Bay natives killed scores of reindeer, took only the tongues and let the rest wash out with the tide, James Isham anticipated and applauded the opinion of a higher tribunal: "I think itt's no wonder that godalmighty shou'd fix his Judgemen't upon these Vile Reaches [wretches], and occation their being starvd and in want of food, when they make such havock of what the Lord sent them plenty of. . . ."[22]

When the Indian's improvidence impinged more closely upon the workings of the fur trade, it took on censurable proportions. No one detected God's wrath descending upon the Indian for manifesting simple indolence, or for gorging himself and wasting supplies already taken. However, the tendency to overkill—whether it involved caribou in the far North, buffalo on the plains, or the exasperating reluctance to discriminate properly between male and female beaver—struck too close to the trader's awareness to be indulgently overlooked. It affected both his chances for survival and his economic success in the wilderness. God as well as man might well direct his attentions to such a failure.

Just as the trader devised an interpretation of the Indian's unprincipled conduct in socioeconomic relations and then went on to prescribe a course of action best suited to circumvent that conduct, so he at least partially constructed a theory of Indian action on these more personal levels. In regard to the latter, however, the trader rarely assumed such positive or indignant tones. He arrived at a less precise answer to a less evident problem.

Fur traders operated from the assumption, implicitly or explicitly stated, that the Indian pursued a properly industrious and provident course only when pressed by wants, just as he had followed a righteous course in his dealings with others only when pressed by force or fear. Right principles, in either case, were lost to him. Francis Chardon at the Mandan post stated the theme succinctly when he noted in his journal: ''—Hunger makes the Wolf move—Mandans all out after buffaloe. . . .'' An opportunity to elaborate on this belief presented itself to Samuel Black in New Caledonia in the summer of 1824. Some Carriers who had agreed to assist him in reaching a neighboring tribe began to stall. Black informed these ''plegmatic sheepish looking Gentlemen'' that their best interests would be much enhanced by carrying out their agreement, but to no effect. The crux of the matter was that his Indians stood in no real need of anything; to Black, this explained the situation completely, for once these people had their ''Wantages,'' they cared nothing about the future and refused to move.[23]

If the Indian, whose basic needs were notably small, could be induced to act diligently only when faced with keenly felt needs, then the trader had to create some wants, had to make the Indian feel hard-pressed more often. Such needs would take the place of ordinary principles of right and assiduous conduct. First of all, the trader lured the red man into heightened activity with the products of a more advanced technology. These, however, failed to answer every purpose. Not all Indians saw the necessity of obtaining knives, cloth, beads, or firearms. The argument that quick-drying woolens would prevent many of the respiratory ailments induced by soggy skin clothes involved the kind of reasoning supposedly unavailable to the red man. To the plains hunters the white man's cumbersome, muzzle-loading weapon held no great fascination, for the rapid-firing bow and arrows were a more effective buffalo-killer. Consequently, some Indians went to no great pains to procure European goods. Edwin Denig noted that the Assiniboines, for example, unlike the Crows and Blackfeet, showed little desire for such things; and George Simpson made a similar comment about the Beavers, a tribe which he considered rather admirable in other respects.[24]

Elsewhere Simpson shed light on the procedure to be followed with reluctant peoples such as the Assiniboines and the Beavers. In a hypothetical statement of Indian thinking, he had the red man say: " 'It is not for your Cloth and Blankets that we undergo all this labor and fatigue . . . but it is the prospect of a Drink in the Spring . . . that carries us through the Winter and induces us to work so hard.' " Here, Simpson put the "philosophy of rum" in a deluxe fashion—making the Indian himself admit that, at bottom, spirits alone made him toil. Straightforward assertions of this proposition appear frequently throughout the fur-trade literature. For many traders it must have provided a conscience-stilling rationalization for spreading havoc and misery by the keg. However, to assume that the "philosophy of rum" was specious justification and no more would overburden the righteous indignation of the modern perspective. Even the young and idealistic Rudolph Kurz gave respectful and rather convincing expression to this seemingly execrable theme before taking exception to it. At the beginning of his remarks, Kurz aired the views of his superior, "Mr. Denig." According to Denig (via Kurz) liquor brought only one ill effect, which was more than offset by advantages: it precipitated a slight rise in the number of killings. But the Indian was abundantly prepared, psychologically, for bloodshed. Consequently, this should be viewed from the perspective of the Indian, who would take it in stride, not from that of the white, who might be appalled. On the credit side, liquor caused Indians to act far more reliably and industriously: they worked harder, hunted more effectively, dressed better, and lived more prosperously. Kurz made no attempt to refute these arguments, and indeed, he admitted that they were "doubtless very true." Instead, he called upon things more cogent to him than the immediate welfare of the aborigine—such things as the unconscionable profits of trade involving liquor and a rather hazy and not entirely relevant indictment of the trader for opposing civilization. In short, even the romantic gave more than tacit agreement to the basic assumption of the "philosophy of rum." [25]

A modern world of more sanguine views may look askance at the traders' operating theories and the reading of Indian character from which their methods were adduced. Of course, fur-trade sources readily lend themselves to rigorous subjective examination, and under such scrutiny they might well reveal varying sinister and ulterior motivations. However, in fairness it should be noted that fur-trade ideas on how best to get along with the red man stemmed also—perhaps even basically—from convictions honestly held. To infer that the doctrine of harsh punishment, for example, thinly veiled authoritarian personalities or desires to shed native blood, or to infer that the conscious posture of aloofness represented no more than snobbishness and intolerance, though easily done, would be unjust. Given the proposition that the Indian lacked a system of principles, it naturally devolved upon the trader to obviate what, in his mind, could readily become rampant anarchy. In an age far less permissive than the present, this complex of attitudes probably represented a fair approximation of what the same men believed in regard to justice and social concord in civilization as well as in savagery.

Moreover, the trader explained as well as indicted. The fur-trade consensus held that those Indian actions that could be reasonably explained at all, arose largely from concern with self. Yet these men showed at least a limited awareness of other ways of resolving the untoward conduct of their red customers. Deviousness and dishonesty, for example, admitted of varying interpretations. In pondering the fickle nature of the red man Alexander Ross struck upon an explanation reminiscent of now-discredited theories of anthropology—primitive behavior was childish. ''It would appear,'' he wrote in one of his narratives, ''that the Indian is in some respect a mere child, irritated and pleased with a trifle.'' A less thoughtful, but certainly realistic, explanation of the same phenomenon appears in a journal kept by Matthew Cocking. This Hudson's Bay Company trader had the colossal task of luring the Indians of the western interior down to the bay posts past the ''Pedlars''—men such as the Frobishers, Alexander Henry the elder, Peter Pond, and Peter Pangman, all of whom were later instrumental in forming the opposing North West and XY companies. Though nearly at wit's end and totally exasperated by Indians and their ill kept promises, Cocking had to concede that liquor was a factor in explaining Indian fickleness. The red man simply could not pass Grand Portage or The Pas if the ''Pedlars'' were there with alcohol, and, once in his cups, he sold his furs to any bidder.[26]

One would expect to find these men occasionally, or perhaps often, explaining the inaccuracy of Indian information (or even dishonesty itself) in terms of misunderstandings and failures of communication between peoples of vastly different cultures. Some instances do appear. For example, although Philip Turnor showed skepticism about an Indian's description of Great Slave Lake, he did not ascribe the questionable information to deception. Rather, he felt that the difficulties arose from the fact that his interpreters left much to be desired. In a demonstration both of generosity and of understanding, Peter Skene Ogden left off bemoaning the inaccuracy of native accounts of the fur potential of southern Idaho to describe briefly the reason for such misintelligence. Though he believed implicitly in Indian dishonesty and selfishness, Ogden did not rely upon these ready-made answers. Instead he wrote that the Indians lacked proper comprehension of what the trader sought, for they

. . . can form no Idea of a Country abounding in Beaver   a small stream with six Lodges appears to them inexaustable, and it is not with an intention of deceiving that they represent their Country rich, as it is their interest to see us amongst them, but [it is rather] to be attributed to their Ignorance in not knowing better.[27]

They did not often utilize such obvious means of explanation, but traders recognized that cultural idiosyncrasies, at least to some degree, accounted for the red man's seeming propensity for lying. Reasoning in a mechanistic vein, James Adair wondered if the head-flattening practised by the southeastern tribes did not cause their "fickle, wild, and cruel tempers." In a somewhat more sophisticated tone, Alexander Ross commented significantly: "When an Indian in his metaphorical mode of expression tells you anything, you are not to suppose that you understand him, or that he literally speaks the truth." Matters of temperament had significance, also; and observers of the far North tribes hinted that their morose and pessimistic outlook helped account for their preposterous exaggerations of ill tidings. Occasionally, a trader hit upon the idea that a differing set of values explained the Indian's failure to emphasize simple honesty. In treating an incident pointing up the occasionally mentioned tendency of Indians to protect articles left in their trust, but to steal with abandon any and everything else, Robert Campbell advised: " 'Trust to their honour and you [your goods] are safe: trust to their honesty and they will steal the hair off your head.' " [28]

To the trader certain forms of etiquette loomed even larger as bases for Indian falseness. The people of some tribes, for instance, showed a marked reluctance to answer direct questions. This unwillingness appeared primarily when a man was asked his name, but it applied to other things as well. Quite often a direct question elicited from the red man both evasiveness and outright misinformation. This native tendency gained the quite perceptive attention of Alexander Ross in one of his narratives of frontier experience. At one point he recalled how certain kinds of information could be obtained from the red man only by indirect questioning. Bluntly to ask an Indian his name was to have him hesitate; to ask his age was to invite equivocation. In support of his position Ross recounted an incident wherein an acquaintance asked a Snake chief the population of his tribe. The man received no answer, only the return question—why did he wish to know? After being informed that "the great white chief" desired this knowledge, the Indian remarked, " 'Oh! oh! tell him then . . . that we are as numerous as the stars.' " [29] A less extreme metaphor could well have induced temporary belief, followed by eventual skepticism, rather than the implicit understanding and acceptance of a cultural trait.

Ironically, the Indian's almost proverbial politeness in verbal intercourse seemed to play a large part in fostering distrust in the minds of white observers. The red man had a reputation for hearing out the views of any speaker, however objectionable. The white man, accustomed to airing his dissent as it came to mind, misconstrued this courtesy, interpreting it as agreement with the speaker. Later, when the Indian acted in a contrary fashion, he was maligned for his seeming falseness. This feature of Indian etiquette could cause misunderstanding with traders, but in relations with missionaries it bred tragic disillusionment. In the twilight of his career, Alexander Ross drew upon his knowledge of Indian ways to acquaint the Christian world with the pitfalls involved in dealing with the red man. He warned especially that one must be careful in accepting Indian appearances,

> . . . for nothing is more deceptive than the character and demeanour of a savage in the presence of his spiritual instructor. Indifference is mistaken for modesty, cunning for diffidence, and the savage habit of hanging down his head and looking at the ground when spoken to on religious matters, is taken for reverence. . . . An Indian never appears more pliable and devout than when he is meditating your destruction.[30]

One step beyond this misleading, and sometimes treacherous, politeness was the practice of negotiating situations by consenting to whatever the white man said. Philip Turnor felt that overwillingness to assent compounded his problems with interpreters, for even when baffled by an unfamiliar dialect, the Indian, when asked, would say he understood. Often the native in an effort to be gracious simply concocted information calculated to please the white man. Thus, David Thompson considered it futile to ask the Crees about their religious beliefs for, "they will give the answer best adapted to avoid other questions, and please the enquirer.'' Even when asked something about which he was completely ignorant the Indian rose to the occasion by giving judiciously informative, though completely fabricated, answers. After remarking that of all the Indian's flaws ''false information'' was the worst, James Isham insisted in his unique style that when questioned, ''they will answer to what I Desir'd, at the same time neither her'd see, or new any thing of the matter. . . .''[31]

After invoking God's anger against the Indians for their senseless slaughter of game, Isham appended the thought that, ''their ignorance may perhap's Justifie them something. . . .'' The unprincipled actions of the Indian in trade relations struck the trader as malign, perverse, and inexcusable. In the case of dishonesty and some of its ramifications, traders made efforts (often hesitant, to be sure) to fathom in terms other than selfishness or innate waywardness. With more personal traits—such as indolence, improvidence, or immorality—traders went even further to devise defenses or extenuations for the red man. Hudson's Bay man Dugald Mactavish, for example, transformed what could easily have been a censure for thriftlessness into a preface to understanding by describing the Indians' seemingly peculiar outlook on life:

They lead a curious life, one day they are in the midst of plenty, the next they are starving—they have no care about them—when they have any thing to eat, they continue at it until it is finished altho' they have no immediate prospect of getting any thing more for a Month to come[.] Let an Indian come to the Fort starving, even eating his Moccasins as is often the Case, make him drunk, give him a couple pounds of Flour, and a little grease for his supper, and he will be the happiest man alive—he will neither think of what has past, or what has yet to come before him—he drives all care aside, and even when he comes to himself again, he leaves the Fort as happy and as contented, as if he was sure of abundance before him. . . .[32]

Various men explained Indian faults as being natural and unavoidable results of the savage mode of life. Alexander Ross and the New Englander, Daniel Harmon, ascribed the sloth of the Pacific coast tribes to the fact that subsistence was easily gained. Turning this formula on its head, Edwin Denig argued that the ''apathy of disposition'' of the Assiniboines sprang from too frequent encounters with hardship. In attempting to explain the native's appalling tendency to overkill game, Samuel Hearne suggested that, being wanderers, they considered anything encountered to be a windfall of which the greatest advantage should be taken. Whatever the case, the blame lay elsewhere than with the Indian. Although these and other men were at times hindered by Indian shortcomings which in white cultural context would have drawn severe moral stricture, they saw fit to record such traits primarily and to damn them only secondarily.[33]

To those many traders of Scotch, English, or American middle-class background, such things as sloth and wastefulness must have involved real moral implications; but, then as now, dissoluteness probably violated their moral sensibilities even more. Interestingly, the trader spoke of the Indian's dissoluteness in extenuating terms as frequently as he treated indolence or thriftlessness in that way. Here again, as the Indians' faults increased in distance from the fur man's *awareness* and from his *central interests,* the blame decreased even where the flaw became more serious. Even after discounting the debauchees, whose numerical prominence in the trade has been overdone, the Indian's lack of ''morals'' did surprisingly little to incense or outrage the trader.

Disregarding the anthropological realities of the matter, the trader saw the Indian as subscribing to a far different moral code, a code apparently much less restrictive than that of white society. In manuscripts prepared for publication, traders quite often eased over these realities by generalizing, while avoiding any demonstrative specifics. In his essay on the Arikaras, Edwin Denig explained that, because the blunt realities could not ''for certain reasons be explained here,'' he would limit himself to hinting at ''what might be shown were the barrier of decency withdrawn.'' In day-by-day accounts, however, traders did not concern themselves overmuch about delicacy. Fur-trade sources frequently describe incidents such as that recorded by Pierre-Antoine Tabeau in which a Sioux and a trader came to an agreement over the favors of the Indian's pretty young wife. The man's "well-beloved" seemed reluctant at first, according to Tabeau, but soon material considerations assumed their proper significance and she recognized that "knives with green handles were not common; that the vermillion was a beautiful red; that the tobacco—in short, well, what else?" The bargain was struck, the young woman entered, and the husband firmly held the door.[34]

Though the trader repeatedly had occasion to record what to him must have been serious moral lapses, he rarely passed judgment. In a paragraph on "Ludness" James Isham remarked that "Maidens are Very rare to be found at 13 or 14 Years . . . ," and then added "fine Ladies &c." Mild and inferential as that afterthought of disapproval may seem, few traders went beyond it. Alexander Henry the younger, whose sympathy for the aborigines was closely circumscribed, showed a wondrous restraint in recording the amorously intended but unconsummated midnight visit of some Mandan women to the lodge where he and his men lay. He noted that their "kind offers" met refusal, and concluded noncommitally that "they retired very much displeased, and muttering something we could not understand." Elsewhere Henry said that "Chastity does not seem to be a virtue among the Crees . . . ," an idea that he certainly could have stated in a more damning way. And the occasionally wrathful George Simpson relied upon similarly generous understatement in noting that "the Chipewyan fair ones are not celebrated for their continence. . . ."[35]

Some men attempted openly to qualify or to excuse such actions. The always understanding David Thompson, after having been shocked by the blatant lasciviousness of the Mandans, commented by way of mitigation that the whites who had preceded him to the Missouri villages were not "examples of chastity." Duncan Cameron, a less fastidious individual, at least implied an extenuation in noting that the natives of the Nipigon country exhibited sexual looseness primarily when influenced by liquor. Even in the climate of complete degradation of the late plains trade, James Chambers at Fort Sarpy avoided moralizing or pontificating and instead utilized the gentler tools of irony, sarcasm, and feigned outrage in chronicling an instance of debauchery. His entry of January 21, 1855, opens:

My pen refuses to write what is to come   Oh the ways of the wicked world, thou Vile Seducer man could you not of spared 'Her. Oh Frailty thy name is Women   What   shall I utter those damning words   the Princess has fallen aye fallen   the Seducers tongue was too much for her. . . .

Editor Anne McDonnell's deletion of obscenity cuts short Chambers' soliloquy at this point, but it seems apparent that the Princess incurred no stigma for having fallen. In fact, the same "Princess" apparently fell often during Chambers' stay at Sarpy.[36]

Thus, the trader showed a noteworthy degree of tolerance for Indian traits and actions which seemingly should have aroused his disgust. He bore no love for the Indian, but he willingly excused or overlooked what seemed to him mere peccadilloes. However, his tolerance was both circumscribed and selective. When narrowly moral predilections were affronted, the trader showed a surprisingly enlightened readiness to record without judging. What he saw as the red man's manifest indolence, improvidence, gluttony, or lasciviousness elicited little moral outrage. As a general rule, however, the excusable flaws in Indian nature were those which had little or no impact on the economics of trader-Indian relations, or those whose manifestations could be avoided. If they failed to meet these conditions, they excited wrath rather than understanding. For example, the market place sorely tried and often defeated native honesty. Consequently, traders railed against the innate falseness of the red race. But dishonesty could occur elsewhere, and when it did fur men toned down their indictments. They made hesitant but telling admissions that some of the red man's deceitfulness was a matter of appearance rather than reality and that the circumstances were extenuating rather than damning. The distinction appears with significant clarity in Edward Umfreville's remarks on the Crees. In matters of trade he put them down as more given to fraud than any other tribe in his experience. But shortly thereafter, when describing their actions outside his vocational sphere, he spoke of "instances of honesty and fidelity . . . which would do honour to a people governed by the wisest laws. . . ."[37] In turn, the Indian's alleged self-interestedness, which was almost unfailingly present, naturally vexed the trader because it impinged upon his awareness in the two worst possible ways—economically and continually. Thus, selfishness was universally noted and condemned. Perhaps, being men of an essentially business pursuit, traders were incapable of seeing, reluctant to admit, or loath to countenance economic conceptions differing from the ones they harbored. Regardless of the fur-trade perspective, however, the Indian's nature appeared singularly unappealing, being based on self-interest and shot through with moral and ethical grossness.

9. A DIGNIFIED BEARING

IN AFFAIRS OF TRADE THE NATIVES IMPRESSED TRADERS AS BEING AC-
tively perverse. In areas of personal actions and of noneconomic
social relations the Indians seemed quite unprincipled, though not
entirely blameworthy. Judgments of traits largely devoid of meaning in trader-Indian relations were still more kindly. Where the
trader knew the Indians well, he had very little good to say about
them. Where he had less reason and occasion to know them, he came
closer to crediting them with what Peter Skene Ogden referred to as
"the fine qualities attributed to them in recent publications." [1] Of
course, the trader knew his customers well enough to avoid becoming
maudlin over any aspect of their make-up. Moreover, in regard to
features appearing most praiseworthy, individual traders made
serious qualifications and reservations, or simply disagreed. These
considerations notwithstanding, most traders saw the Indians as
possessing a dignity of bearing and action which bordered, if in no
other way than by comparison with their manifold objectionable
features, on the enviable.

Of course, this sentiment, though pervasive, was not universal.
Often, for example, the red man's mien, whatever it was, engendered
in the mind of the trader a corrosive distrust. As indicated earlier,
traders operated from the ungenerous conviction that the native was
a poseur whose air probably screened artful knavery. On a less
sinister and suspicious level, they frequently subjected the simple
primitive to a bantering and sarcasm that left little room for
appreciation. With tongue well in cheek young Henry Boller made
reference to " 'the lords of the forest and prairie' "—who "lounge
about the Fort, keeping near the kitchen. . . ." Chief Four Bears,
he noted in gentle mockery, thinks more of himself than does anyone

else, "and pays his visits with great dignity, wrapped in a painted robe, generally about meal time. . . ." Where dignity was concerned, portrayal often gave way to parody. Finally, though it may be a triviality, one can hardly help wondering about the impact of such unengaging sobriquets as "le Merde d'Ours," "Le Merde d'Eturgeon," and others even more grossly awesome. Surely, such names, though perfectly proper among Indians, seem ill designed to engender veneration in white minds yet untaught what Eric Goldman has depicted as the modern mood of the humorlessly "unraised eyebrow." Indeed, Indian usages such as these must often have titillated the puckishness of an earthy breed of men not yet wedded to doggedly constructive thoughts. Nevertheless, in spite of the attractions that a burlesque must have had for men in a grim, monotonous, and occasionally perilous calling, they treated the savage bearing more nearly with approbation than with irony.[2]

Traders occasionally commented on the Indians' fine physical carriage. In his discussion of the high plains tribes, David Thompson wrote that in walking the Indian appeared to glide over the ground while his white brother swayed clumsily from side to side and swung his arms "as if to saw a passage through the air." This comparison, Thompson wrote in evident admiration of the Indian, had quite often vexed him. However, in making this comment on red stateliness Thompson placed himself in a minority. As a rule traders interpreted such deportment quite differently. In the first place the physical Indian did not impress the trader. Moreover, what a few men like Thompson saw as a commendably aristocratic carriage struck many others as simply an element of the red man's almost ludicrous foppery. Traders saw nothing exalted about being a dandy, and most of them considered the Indian just that—an "exquisite," Henry H. Sibley called him. Indeed, when Edwin Denig called Indian men "the most consummately vain fops in existence," he spoke for the great majority of his fellow traders. The red man had to demonstrate his true dignity in ways more subtle than physical presence.[3]

In a television production which impressionistically chronicled the opening of the trans-Mississippi West, Hollywood actor Gary

Cooper concluded the treatment of the Indian wars by reciting a part of Chief Joseph's memorable speech of surrender. At the end of his outstanding but tragic retreat, the vanquished Joseph spoke for his people as follows:

I am tired of fighting. Our chiefs are all killed. Looking Glass is dead. Too-hul-hul-sote is dead. The old men are all dead. It is the young men who say yes or no. . . . It is cold and we have no blankets, no food. The little children are freezing to death. I want to have time to look for my children and see how many of them I can find. Maybe I shall find them among the dead. Hear me! My chiefs, I am tired; my heart is sick and sad. From where the sun now stands, I will fight no more, forever.[4]

In using his words, the popular medium took no poetic license. Scholarly works show an equal willingness to conclude discussion of the red men's struggles with Joseph's poignant words. In *The Growth of the American Republic,* for instance, Samuel Eliot Morison and Henry Steele Commager dutifully invoke the pathos of the defeated Nez Perce leader before hurrying on to more impelling themes in industrial America; and in his notable study of social and intellectual history, Merle Curti includes Joseph's speech of capitulation in his remarks on "The Indian in American Thought." In addition to serving as a more sophisticated and less condescending substitute for such traditional Indian contributions as popcorn, squash, and sunflower seeds, Joseph's oration perhaps has replaced the now suspect speech of Logan as the prime evidence of the Indian's primitive eloquence. The Indian survives in tradition as a moving and powerful speaker, and to some degree this reputation for oratorical ability accords with attitudes expressed by fur traders.

In 1811 Henry Brevoort, a member of a prominent New York family, passed a brief sojourn at Mackinac in the employ of his relative John Jacob Astor before going on to the less rigorous atmosphere of Paris. While engaged in his wilderness duties Brevoort wrote a few letters to his friend Washington Irving in which he related his discovery of a pair of noble Indian orators. In a letter of June 28 he expressed considerable enthusiasm concerning two "genuine Indian orations," which he had sent to be published in the press "of either party." Seemingly enraptured by his find, Brevoort insisted that one of the speeches had been delivered with such "graceful elocution" that "Ogilvy himself might have been instructed in attitudes." Some two weeks later he again wrote Irving, to inquire about the publication of the speeches and to inform him that one of the two orators, a man of great dignity, was leading a deputation to Washington. With a tinge of regret he added that he would have given the eloquent Indian a letter of introduction to Irving had New York been on the delegation's itinerary. Though the primitive was always best admired from afar, one can hardly help sharing Brevoort's disappointment over the opportunity denied Irving's circle.[5]

Brevoort's lack of extended experience in the trade perhaps accounts for his effusive praise of Indian oratorical abilities. Most traders struck a medium between Brevoort's unqualified enthusiasm and such disparaging commentaries as Captain John Smith's description of an Indian welcoming speech—"Which they do with such vehemency and so great passions, that they sweate till they drop; and are so out of breath that they can scarce speake. So that a man would take them to be exceeding angry or starke mad"—or William Hardisty's similar picture of Loucheux speakers who went without inhaling until they literally gasped, and then closed their tirades on an "infernal screech, which is particularly disagreeable to a white man's ears."[6]

A sufficient number of traders expressed respect for the Indian's oratorical ability to indicate that as a group they were at least mildly impressed. Here again, the more extreme statements acclaiming Indian oratory appear in sources which border on the peripheries of authenticity. However, hardened traders with little inclination toward gratuitous fawning often admitted the red man's forensic capability. Thus, shortly before writing a self-warning never to trust Indians, Simon Fraser remarked that the Yakimas appeared to be good orators, having an "extremely handsome" manner of delivery. Similarly, Duncan Cameron credited the inhabitants of the Nipigon country with possessing in a high degree "the talent of natural eloquence." More than a century earlier, John

Lederer favorably compared the efforts of the upper Virginia natives with those of "men of Civil education and Literature." [7]

Other men cited practical demonstrations of the high quality of Indian oratory. When Charles Larpenteur faced death in a largely hostile Indian camp, a "good old friend" spoke in his behalf, and spoke so eloquently that the murderous design fell through. Under quite different circumstances, Nicola, chief of the Okanogans, delivered a brief speech that became a part of Hudson's Bay Company tradition. When that singular personality Samuel Black was murdered by a young Indian whose uncle's sickness and death had been superstitiously laid at Black's door, Nicola spoke Black's eulogy to an assembly of traders and Indians gathered to pay respects and to keep the affair from spreading. One of the traders on the ground, Archibald McKinley, recorded the old leader's words, and concluded in evaluation: "Never shall I forget it; it was the grandest speech I ever heard." Of course, Larpenteur may have been incapable of a discerning view. Perhaps any speech working a man's salvation would sound inspired, in retrospect if not at the moment. And a closer scrutiny might suggest that the power of Nicola's tribute stemmed as much from fear of further curtailment of an already meager ammunition supply as from Black's passing. Or, perhaps, emotion eroded critical powers when an Indian spoke the last words for a much loved companion. (Only George Simpson, whose nemesis Black had been in the turbulent days at Ile-á-la-Crosse twenty years earlier when different companies demanded their loyalties, seemed unable to develop a fondness for the peculiar and redoubtable Samuel Black.) Whatever the cause, experienced traders generalized and particularized about the Indian's eloquent oratory.[8]

The emphasis upon oratory differed according to tribal or cultural areas. This may account for dissenting opinions such as those of John Smith and William Hardisty. Fur-trade records at least tacitly bear out the existence of such variations. The Algonquians of the Great Lakes area, for instance, must have placed a great emphasis upon these formalities and, apparently, considered them an integral part of any trading session. Accounts written by George

Croghan, Robert Rogers, and Sir William Johnson mention an amazing amount of speech-making, far more than apparently attended affairs of trade elsewhere.[9]

A student of nineteenth-century literary portrayals of the Indian has defined three basic ways in which writers presented the red man. One of these, drawing largely upon the popularity of the King Philip tradition, pictured the Indian as a freedom-loving and statesmanlike patriot.[10] Here, of course, the Indian's reputed forensic capability had a comfortable context. This scholar listed Henry Brevoort's friend, Washington Irving, as the most prominent proponent and popularizer of this genre. Thus, one can visualize Irving's friend at Mackinac eagerly eavesdropping on Indian conversations, however trivial, hoping to detect the gleam of genius that the man of letters felt was there.

Just as with other aspects of cultural primitivism, a few individual traders tended to substantiate this glorified picture of the American primitive. Robert Campbell's letters to his Philadelphia brother, which in places sound suspiciously unlike the expressions of an experienced trader, offer a case in point. Commenting on a Shoshoni chief's speech on his tribe's relations with the Crows, Campbell told his brother that the man's efforts would have shamed some of civilization's orators. Campbell admired both the chief's style and his import, for every sentence showed "evidence of deep policy, and consummate political skill." The Indian's reputation for statesmanlike and selflessly patriotic oratory invited comparison with the Greek and Roman greats of the past, and occasionally a fur man obliged. For example, in one of his less reasonable moments Ross Cox wrote that in his estimation the speech of a young Walla Walla pushed the efforts of the ancients into insignificance. In a comparison only slightly less detractive from Greek and Roman fame, Hudson's Bay Company chaplain, John West, effusively praised the eloquence of a Chippewa whose people had been asked to move from their traditional homeland.[11]

These three instances present the Indian's eloquence as an element of his patriotic fervor. Cox's young Walla Walla, for instance, concluded a chronicling of his tribe's previous political and military disasters with the portentous pronouncement: ". . . we are *now a nation!*"—surely an illusory grandiloquence on the part of someone. In addition, these comments all appeared in the early nineteenth century, a period affording a nationalistic perspective, however inappropriate, from which to view the actions of primitives. As so many have noted so well, the traveler's prejudices went with him. Thus, Ross Cox may have used the Walla Walla as an obliging vehicle for his own sentiments. Moreover, these three illustrations fail to rise completely above suspicion or reservation as fur-trade sources. Campbell's letters have a ring of noble savagery that would have come far more readily from an eastern editor than from a St. Louis fur trader. Writing in Ireland years after the incidents described, Cox tended to portray his Indians in extremes of good and bad; while West, the chaplain, may have seen things in the Indians that were lost to members of the company engaged in more mundane pursuits.

Moreover, traders generally heard orations that bore little resemblance to the statesmanlike addresses mentioned by Campbell or Cox. Such speeches prefaced trading sessions and were designed by the natives to put the white man in a properly charitable and pitying frame of mind. Apparently, Indians considered trading sessions worthy of maximum oratorical effort. Since they entered into these affairs ceremoniously, their formal speeches cannot be compared to the uninspired and occasionally quarrelsome discourse attendant upon white economic parleys. Of course, bickering and haggling abounded. However, such things came after the lofty and benevolent ideal spelled out in the opening ritual had degenerated into the workaday reality of buyer facing seller. In his Mackinac journal Robert Rogers abstracted many of these introductory speeches and in them the verb "beg" and the nouns "charity" and "pity" recur with striking frequency. Rogers saw fit to record rather than analyze or generalize, but Edwin Denig in his lengthy essay on the northern plains tribes examined Indian oratory closely. At the outset Denig noted a remarkable disparity between the hundreds of genuine Indian orations he had heard and those devised by writers of fiction. The "figures and tropes" employed by authors did not exist, and the famed use of metaphor appeared only occasionally. More fundamentally, in accord with that widely held interpretation of Indian action, of which he was the most persuasive proponent, Denig argued that nothing appeared in an Indian speech unless it tended "to gain their object . . . and Indians seldom speak [orate] otherwise." [12]

In this discussion the Fort Union trader included two speeches which he had previously recorded. He inserted them with what was probably a pretense of reluctance and apology, saying that they in no way rivaled the achievement of the "celebrated Logan" and adding that they would be a woeful disappointment to "novel writers and romantic authors of Indian tales." The first, a speech by chief Crazy Bear to his wrongfully dissatisfied followers, aroused Denig's respect. The other, a far more typical effort, served as a preliminary to a trading session and abounded in patent begging and flattery designed to inspire liberality. So that its purpose would not elude those who read his essay, Denig generously sprinkled the text of the speech with footnotes, indicating such realities as: "A blanket is wanted"; "Hint for a chief's coat"; "Medal or gorget"; "Hint for a general present of ammunition . . ." ". . . tobacco is not only wanted but plenty of it." In spite of such reservations, like most other traders Denig had a certain degree of admiration for Indian orations. He admitted, for example, that native speakers achieved a degree of eloquence in their brevity, bold assertions, and pointed questions.[13]

To a large degree, Denig's reaction to these two speeches represented general fur-trade attitudes, which ranged from admiration to disgust, depending upon the situation. In spite of Blackfoot raiders Crazy Bear of the Assiniboines had gone to the 1837 Fort Laramie conference, only to return to a skeptical and abusive people. Later, when the chief stood triumphantly before a "smiling pile" of United States government largesse and orally vindicated his efforts in behalf of those who had derided him, Denig expressed respect. On the other hand, when "Le Chef du Tonnerre" shamelessly flattered and begged the Fort Union trader—"your name is in the clouds; your father was a chief; you will be greater than he. . . . Let me feel something soft over my shoulders''—he registered disgust.[14] As with the traders' over-all evaluation of their red customers, where they had most opportunity to observe, they had least inclination to admire. Perhaps regrettably, a performance such as that of Crazy Bear could pass unknown or unnoted, while that of a ''Le Chef du Tonnerre'' became the norm as an everyday trade reality. Thus, traders recognized the Indian's oratorical potentiality, but the reality of his most common performances marred the record.

In an area far more general, traders credited the Indian with a dignified comportment. In situations that would have brought visibly emotional reactions from others, the aborigine maintained a stoic mien. There were, of course, a great many exceptions to this rule. Earlier it has been noted that in some circumstances and especially among some tribes the Indian often appeared given to passion. In matters not involving trade, however, fur men generally saw the natives as admirably disinclined toward emotional displays.

As one evidence of this, traders verified the Indians' reputation for taciturnity. Peter Grant's comment that the Chippewas were ''grave and serious, even in their amusements they speak little but always to the purpose,'' is typical of fur-trade attitudes. Not all cultures, of course, maintained this reserve. The Dinnaens seemed to have been a far more loquacious set; but when traders encountered such groups, they made it evident that their garrulity was exceptional. Thus Daniel Harmon spoke of the Carriers of New Caledonia as being ''unusually talkative.'' And when Alexander Mackenzie came in contact with the Chipewyans on his famous exploratory venture he showed surprise at their lack of ''cold reserve,'' an Indian trait to which he had become accustomed.[15]

More centrally, the Indian showed an enviable resignation in the face of adversity. Hardened traders such as Edwin Denig, Samuel Hearne, Charles Larpenteur, and Peter Skene Ogden readily attested to the Indian's ability to bear hardship without complaint. When pressed directly for an assessment of the Indian, John Porteous noted that his greatest social virtue was patience. Ogden made the most dramatic statement of this virtue in his journal of

1826. While working the barren regions of southeastern Oregon, he became acquainted with the privations suffered by the Snakes of the area, and after dwelling upon depressing particulars, the Hudson's Bay man went on to moralize:

. . . miserable unfortunate creatures to what sufferings and cruel privations are you not doom'd to endure but the almighty has so ordained it What an example is this for us, when we are as at present for instance without Beaver and reduced to one meal a day how loudly and grievi-ously do we complain, but in truth how unjustly and without cause when I consider the Snakes suffrings compared to . . . ours many a day do they pass without food and still without a complaint or murmer. . . .[16]

The Indian openly manifested few of the ordinary emotions; for example, he showed little indication of amusement. Using mirth as a means of comparison, John McLean recalled that the Eskimo "when his risibility is excited" laughed "with right good will," while the Indian's rigid features never betrayed his feelings. In anger, the Indian remained calm, and sentiments of joy, love, and sympathy worked no surface manifestations. The trader most often connected the concept (and the term) of stoicism with the red man's repres-sion of sorrow. During the strife which eventuated in the merger of the Hudson's Bay and North West companies, a North West Company man at Fort William sadly watched some of his comrades being unceremoniously loaded into opposition boats to be taken away as captives. He admitted unashamedly that the sight brought tears to his eyes, and, should anyone doubt the pathos of the moment, he added the *ne plus ultra:* "I saw what perhaps few have ever seen,—I saw *an Indian weep!*" Because this comment appeared in one of the numerous polemics stemming from the controversy, the literal fact of an Indian's having wept at the humiliating departure of North West traders admits of grave doubts. Nevertheless, the account embodied a widely held view of Indian aplomb. More typically, however, traders considered the loss of a child as the situation best suited to try a person's stoicism. Wilderness dwellers knew death as an omnipresent reality, and traders had frequent occasions to comment on the Indian's deportment at such times.

Samuel Black's statement on the death of a child among the Carriers, a tribe generally credited with little dignity or stoicism, typifies traders' conclusions: ". . . the Father tho anxious in the sickness of the child, sits now like a true Philosopher unmoved. . . ." [17]

Knowing the Indian well, the trader expressed more qualifications and reservations about his stoic nature than did the casual observer. And he perhaps had the better understanding. Although the Indian's reputation made him appear almost unhumanly averse to, or (like a brute) incapable of showing emotion, the trader insisted that such was not the case. Instead, he felt that the Indian consciously strove to achieve an unmoved deportment. When James Adair, as something of a practical joke, engaged some Indians in an impromptu horse race which eventuated in their being scratched and torn by briars, he did not suggest that the Indians were unconcerned. They suppressed their disgruntlement, but only because their pride demanded such restraint. By the same token, traders insisted that the natives experienced the full range of emotions but that in front of others, especially strangers, they were loath to express them. Even the much heralded reticence fell away when the Indian was with close friends or was discussing lively subjects. George Simpson, for example, wrote that "notwithstanding the taciturnity of savages among whites, they are, when by themselves, the most loquacious of mortals, apparently regarding idle gossip as one of the grand objects of life." Edwin Denig concurred by noting that the natives' seeming predisposition to taciturnity was not at all impregnable—"as when obscene subjects are introduced this faculty is laid aside. . . ." According to Denig, the Indian had potent emotions, but unlike the white man, he betrayed them in slight, almost unobservable ways. The experienced trader, he wrote, could evaluate the Indians' moods by "their ways, their eye, countenance, smile, and every movement" as surely as one could judge the feelings of a civilized person in a violent burst of passion.[18]

Since traders considered sorrowful situations the most valid tests of stoicism, they expressed themselves most fully in regard to the Indians' lack, or suppression, of emotion in this context. This, however, raised a semantic problem, and traders hesitated somewhat in applying the term "stoical" to the Indians' reactions at the loss of loved ones. Their indecision sprang from uncertainty as to the meaning of the word. Did it connote absence of emotion or suppression of emotion? They insisted that the Indian felt the pain of loss as much as the white man, and, thus, if stoicism meant lack of emotion, the term did not apply. Thus Thomas Simpson, on his way from Red River settlement to the Athabasca, passed a deserted camp near which were several graves. With evident irony Simpson referred to the graves as "simple, but affecting memorials of the 'stoics of the wood,' the men without a tear." By implication, the true stoic would have left the dead lay, unburied and untended. In a similar discussion David Thompson explained that among the Algonquian people the women gave themselves up fully to grief but "the men sorrow in silence, and when the sad pang of recollection becomes too strong to be borne, retire into the forest to give free vent to their grief." Peter Skene Ogden witnessed such a situation on the shores of Lake Superior when he came upon a man and two small children weeping at the grave of a recently deceased mother. Ogden, too, stumbled over the word, "stoic." The father, he noted, was "in the indulgence of that grief which, stoic though he is supposed by hasty and ill-informed observers to be, is no less characteristic of the American savage, than of the civilized European." [19]

Though a semantic problem beset him, the trader did not hesitate to generalize regarding Indian actions in woeful circumstances. The red man fell heir to the same trials of soul as the white man, and he comported himself admirably. Thus, any difference lay in the way in which the Indian visibly responded to tribulations. The matured opinion of Rudolph Kurz expresses this well, though his overtones are probably more positive than most traders could have accepted. The sight of Crees uproariously amused by the few garbled words of Mr. Denig's parrot moved the young intellectual to generalize. He noted the mistaken belief that Indians were invariably "stoical," pointed out the gay aspects of their social life, and then got to the nub of the problem:

That an esteemed brave respects himself and guards against doing injury to his own dignity by unbecoming behavior . . . I think is perfectly proper. That is neither stoicism nor the assumption of an official mein, but simply shows respect for his own worth, his inherent dignity, his noble pride.[20]

When Samuel Black made the previously cited remark about the bereaved Carrier who bore up like "a true Philosopher," he recorded a quite different conduct on the part of the man's wife. Indeed, evidence of the traders' admiration of the exterior lack of emotion among Indian men emerges from the frequently stated criticisms and suspicions directed at the opposite features in Indian women, who protested their grief too much. When a woman at Fort George on the Saskatchewan lost a young son, Duncan M'Gillivray appended to his remarks on her manifest grief the unkind qualification that an Indian's showers of tears could be turned on or off at will. Similarly, overt expressions of sorrow on the part of the Illinois women did little to convince the Sieur de Liette, an early trader among them. In a thoroughly caustic vein, he commented that their grief, like that of their civilized sisters, was for themselves, not their departed mates. In an account of the cremation of a far West Indian, Peter Skene Ogden cast doubt upon the genuineness of the widow's bereavement; speaking of her sorrow he added the ungenerous aside, "feigned or real."[21]

The ritualized grieving patterns of native women repelled the traders. Although masculine abstention from such displays may have been fully as much dictated by cultural patterns, it appeared to the traders to be more self-imposed and certainly more admirable. Indeed, when a sorrowing Indian sought liquor to destroy his inhibitions, and thus to give full and open vent to his sorrows, traders became openly critical. Alexander Henry the younger complained that the whites had caused the Indian to ignore their traditional stoicism and to clamor for liquor to drown their sorrow. Others like John McLean and Alexander Mackenzie wrote regretfully that Indian men never registered grief unless influenced by liquor.[22]

The Indian, then, appeared admirably taciturn and stoical; but, again, as with all other traits, the bases of judgment which gained him this high rating were those comfortably removed both from the traders' everyday experience and from the mechanics of the trade. For instance, Charles Larpenteur's previously cited commentary on the Indian's uncomplaining nature had a telling reservation. When they spoke to a white man, he remarked, Indians had a multitude of complaints. Though Samuel Hearne also firmly attested to the absence of grumbling during hardships, he made almost precisely the same qualification. When he was alone with Indians on an arctic trail and the destruction of some previously cached goods threatened their very survival, they did not bemoan the loss at all but only "put the best foot foremost." In the post, however, in matters of trade, they acted quite differently. When dealing with their trader they filled their stories with "plenty of sighs, groans, and tears, sometimes affecting to be lame, and even blind, in order to excite pity. Indeed, I know of no people that have more command of their passions on such occasions. . . ." In fact, Hearne averred that he had seen a woman who, in such a situation, had one side of her face "bathed in tears" while the other showed a "significant smile."[23]

Finally, some few traders saw much of the Indian's unemotional demeanor as hinging upon the alleged basis of all Indian actions, self-interest. Edwin Denig, in spite of his mild admiration for the Indian's stoical bent, maintained consistently that self-interest was one of a group of explanations for the red man's stoicism. They rarely committed themselves verbally or emotionally because, he argued, they were always suspicious and circumspect with their fellows who might be trying to take advantage of them.[24] The fact that Denig relied only partially upon this, his favorite thesis, indicates a general fur-trade reluctance to gainsay this element of the red man's dignity.

The most thrilling manifestation of the Indian's stoicism consisted in his allegedly exquisite conduct under torture. It has received more attention from literary writers than has any other aspect of the red man's ability to endure. The best of the poetic treatments of the theme centered on the "son of Alknomock" who worked anguish on his properly sensitive captors by hurling at them, in nice couplets, the defiance of his death song:

> Begin, ye tormenters: your threats are in vain:
> For the son of Alknomock can never complain.

Not surprisingly, parallels do appear in Indian trade literature, though not at all with the frequency one might expect. In his recollections of days in the mountains, Zenas Leonard told of the hideous torments the Crows had practised on some captured Blackfeet. The victims followed the conventional code, and, in spite of the devilish efforts of their captors, none murmured a word of complaint or sigh of protest. Similar accounts follow a well defined form. Often, the sufferers in such tales did the fabled "son of Alknomock" one better. They not only humiliated their punishers by refusing to cry out in anguish; they insulted and taunted them as well. Indeed, as James Adair implied, contrived discourtesy occupied such a prominent place in the protocol of torture situations that even escape itself took second rank to it. Thus, a young Catawba, while being led to his final agonies in a Seneca camp, broke loose, outran his enemies to a nearby river, and swam across. Though time was decisive and the tangled refuge of his element lay beckoning before him, "his heart did not allow him to leave abruptly. . . ." And so "he first turned his backside toward them and slapped it with his hand . . . ," shouted a war cry, and then raced away. Though hardly dignified, it does have a cavalier overtone. Most captives, of course, had no opportunity to show such a full command of the proprieties and had to make do with less flourish. While Flatheads tormented a captured Blackfoot, the unfortunate red man, according to Ross Cox, reviled his enemies by saying that they did not know their business. When Flatheads fell into the hands of his tribe, he arrogantly informed them, they were made to cry aloud like little children. With his scalp, one eye, and all fingernails torn away, and his body hideously burned by heated gun barrels, the Blackfoot managed his final insult: " 'It was I,' he addressed the chief, 'that made your wife a prisoner last fall;—we put out her eyes;—we tore out her tongue; we treated her like a dog. Forty of our young warriors. . . .' " At this point the chief cut short the man's revelations with a rifle ball.[25]

One suspects that fur-trade narrators such as Cox and Leonard (especially the former) did not overburden themselves with fears of exceeding the bounds of absolute fact. After all, they wrote long after the incidents described and quite conceivably had learned how civilization felt that a tortured Indian should act. Cox's more fastidious readers may have been taken aback by the seeming contradiction between the Blackfoot's own heroic fortitude and his bestial treatment of the chief's wife. However, this could be resolved by interpreting that final disclosure as no more than an outrageous fabrication designed to shorten useless suffering. Such a reading would have the added benefit of preserving mental serenity by keeping heroes and villains clearly identifiable. Few, if any, day-by-day chroniclers related such feats of valor.

The fur-trade consensus granted that the Indian bore up amazingly well under hardship, even torture. But traders saw this as a different kind of courage (if courage at all), for bravery did not enter significantly into the trader's conception of Indian dignity. The Indian, it was held, possessed a closely circumscribed type of valor, and the trader saw no contradiction in crediting him with amazing fortitude under torment and at the same time considering him generally a coward. James Adair, apparently a friend of the Indian and a man who chronicled some classic incidents of the Indian's conduct under torture, generalized on the red man's nature at the outset of his book by saying that it was "timorous." Wherever one looks, he will find essentially the same sentiment. By way of illustration, James Mackay of the Missouri River trade remarked caustically on the "dastardly spirit" of the red race; Martin McLeod in the Minnesota area saw his Indians as being "miserably timid"; and according to Bartholomew Berthold, the Mahas "have been, are, and will be forever cowards."[26]

Seemingly, traders translated their belief in Indian timidity into practical action. Performance apparently matched profession when an enraged John Stuart sought out the Indian who had been stealing the affections of his consort. Though the red man was well armed, the trader encountered little difficulty in subduing him—"like most Indians he is blustering in words, . . ." but "like all Indians also, he shrank into himself when he saw the danger was evident. . . ." Charles Chaboillez must have operated from the same principle in his handling of problems at the Pembina post. For example, when Laganash became troublesome during a drinking bout, Chaboillez "gave him a good Beating. . . ." Subsequently, the resentful Indian fired his gun at the fort, and Chaboillez, carrying his own weapon, went out to take the quarrel to the red man's ground. Laganash, however, wanted none of it, and "beg'd to be excused. . . ." Later in the winter, the Robe Noir shot four of the post's dogs after having brooded over the "pityful" circumstances imposed upon his people by the traders. Chaboillez responded precisely as before. He went directly to the disgruntled native—"(luckyly his knife went only true my Coat)"—and administered "a good Beating." By and large, the specter of Indian hostility weighed far less heavily upon traders than one might suppose. When Jean Baptiste DuBay, for example, composed a detailed letter for Ramsay Crooks arguing the necessity of his having a better weapon, he made no mention of possible dangers from red men of his Wisconsin region. His present weapon had proved inadequate, not because menacing Indians failed properly to respect it, but because its bore was too small to bring down "beneson" unless he scored a heart-shot. The same disparaging assumption may have led Mouse River trader Peter Garrioch to parody the defenseless condition of his party. In his customary manner of effusive grandiloquence Garrioch noted that one of the imposing foursome possessed something in the "form and shape of a gun" but it lacked all the "qualities and principles" thereof. Another "had also a gun, *by name*, but O, it was ridiculous to the last degree." It would, he was certain, have killed a mouse at a foot, but beyond that he would not venture. Though Garrioch considered it "exceedingly Providential" that these weapons did not have to be put to the test, the fact that they were in the condition described serves as an indirect commentary on the pusillanimity of potential molesters.[27]

William Byrd of Westover, while pondering the question of why Indians, who usually "behaved like Cowards," could comport themselves so well in the face of torment, supplied an answer to this seeming paradox. They had, he decided, a "Passive Valour."[28] Though the term itself seems not to have appeared elsewhere in fur-trade literature, it quite adequately conveys the traders' view of this element of Indian nature.

When John Stuart went to chastise "the abominable Anreon" and when Charles Chaboillez ventured out to batter Laganash and Robe Noir, they found comparatively obliging foes. Apparently sensing that their physical well-being was only mildly threatened, such red men took their drubbings with rare resignation, or, from the trader's perspective, out of faintheartedness. Because the red man's valor was passive, he had to be facing death to manifest it. Where one finds a fur trader speaking of savage courage (and they often did), it is almost certain to be in particular and well-defined contexts—Indians outnumbered and struggling for tribal existence, or physically cornered and fighting for personal existence. On the rare occasion when the younger Alexander Henry complimented a tribe for bravery it was the Sarcees, a splinter group located in the no-man's-land between Dinnaens and Algonquians and continually pressed for survival. By the same token, Peter Skene Ogden lauded the outnumbered and harassed Flatheads for their intrepidity in staving off the southwestward-bound Blackfoot confederation. These men only suggested the rule of passive valor, but Peter Grant in his discussion of the Chippewa defined it almost precisely. Ideal warriors, he wrote, struck the enemy unprepared and mastered the techniques of evading pursuit. "Should they, however, be discovered and obliged to fight a regular battle, they generally behave with great bravery, seldom asking or giving quarter." Similarly, Edwin Denig recorded that when the Assiniboines were forced to fight they did so fiercely, indeed, with "almost unequalled desperation." Though his comment contains something of a tautology, the choice of words is revealing. In given circumstances, he argued, Indians could fight with "desperation." In fact, by fur-trade logic, with "desperation" was the *only* way they could fight. True mettle would at times demand the active qualities of initiative and volition in meeting hazards. But the Indian's "courage" was "passive" and so he fought only out of "desperation." [29]

In physical conflict, resignation born of hopelessness, as Denig intimated, could eventuate in rash heroics, which, though not self-willed, appeared rather admirable. Outside the sphere of combat, however, it often led to an enervating fatalism which not only seemed craven but probably aggravated the difficulties as well. Traders often argued that an Indian injured in the chase or wounded on the warpath bore up amazingly well. If, however, they fell victim to a disease or received an injury in commonplace circumstances, they became abject and pitiable figures. Thomas Simpson noted that, in spite of noteworthy fortitude under some conditions, "the least sickness makes them say, 'I am going to die!'" In the winter of 1781 and 1782 William Walker at Hudson's House had occasion to comment on Indian comportment in the face of devastation by a smallpox epidemic. Fear, he wrote, rendered them apathetic. When one was struck down, those around him lost heart and failed even to provide for themselves, thus through loss of strength making themselves readier victims. Worse yet, they made no effort to nurse or restore those who had contracted the disease: "These Natives are such a Dastardly kind of people, that if any of their Relations should be bad with this disorder, they think they need not look for any Recovery, they just throw them away, and so the poor Soul perishes. . . ." By the traders' telling, resignation could lead to base fatalism, as well as to a mildly enviable reckless valor.[30]

Obviously, red man and white held differing concepts of the purpose of physical combat and of the anticipated and respectable approach to it. In a recent anthropological work on the North American Indians, Harold E. Driver pointed out that the game-like quality of Indian warfare—the premium placed upon striking an enemy, even harmlessly, and then withdrawing with body intact and honor aggrandized—has been overdone. Nevertheless, he conceded that this outlook, often termed the "coup" concept, constituted a prominent aspect of Indian warfare. A cultural peculiarity such as this failed, of course, to impress all traders. Thus, when William Laidlaw regretfully informed a fellow in the trade that the Sioux, after killing only twenty Arikaras, had lost resoluteness and were trying to arrange peace, he concluded impatiently and emphatically, "so much for Indian Warfare—." To illustrate the red man's "great aversion to going to the 'Spirit Land' before his allotted time," Henry Boller told of an unexpected encounter between a small party of Assiniboines and another of Sioux. Although they nourished mutual and traditional hatreds and both groups were prowling in quest of human prey, they struck no blows. The equality of sides, three on each, completely disconcerted both parties, and an embarrassing stalemate ensued, brought on by a mutual unwillingness to contest a force of like size. "What was to be done?" the trader asked rhetorically. "Fight it out like the Hosalii & Curialii of olden times? Far from it—!" Instead, swallowing enmity, they smoked sociably, stripped, exchanged clothes, hesitated ill at ease, cut off their hair, exchanged it, smoked again, and then rode in opposite directions. The story, according to Boller, was "as true as it is ridiculous." To traders, this alleged native aversion to striking a force of equal strength took on especially odious proportions. When James Mackay made his reference to their "dastardly spirit," he did so in the context of vilifications of war parties which skulked about an enemy's camp, murdered an old woman or two, and then withdrew in exultation. Yukon trader, Alexander Murray, in a discussion of Kutchin military operations imparted his disgust in an admirably succinct fashion by appending to the word, "guerriers," the parenthetical afterthought "(meurtriers)."[31]

Regardless of these unflattering commentaries, traders showed a surprising willingness to describe dispassionately rather than to criticize the idiosyncrasies of the red man's code. George Simpson, whose appreciation for things Indian was closely circumscribed, applauded the mock warfare of the Columbia River tribes for being "more honorable and manly" than the vendettas of eastern Indians.

Simpson's recognition of strange standards of valor betokens a widespread tendency to give the savage benefit of doubt. Traders considered the red man's courage a limited thing, but they took the sting from their remarks by pointing out that the native subscribed to a different set of values. They extended to the Indian the dignity of courage, not in accordance with their own, seemingly more demanding criteria, but in accordance with the Indian's. David Thompson put it bluntly but not unkindly in noting that "courage is not accounted an essential to the men, any more than chastity to the women. . . ." Others avoided the apparent, if unreal, condescension of Thompson's evaluation by describing a native code that fully countenanced withdrawal in the face of death. The Indian, it was argued, did not uselessly sacrifice himself or his fellows. Though he would go to every "hardship and fatigue" to indulge his innate vindictiveness, "yet he seldom endangers his own safety by rushing headlong into danger." Instead, according to the usually censorious Duncan M'Gillivray, the Indian bides his time "with the most astonishing patience, and if he cannot attack without risking his own life he restrains his resentment 'till another occasion." By the same token, the raiding party that killed two of the enemy while losing none itself appeared successful, while the one that struck down thirty but lost ten seemed a colossal disaster. Such a code impressed some as despicably craven. But others—including such ready critics as Tabeau, Simpson, and M'Gillivray—seemed to recognize that the lines separating valor, discretion, and cowardice were often indistinct. Given this concession, the Indian did not come off badly. The red man possessed only a circumscribed kind of courage. But the trader did recognize elements of dignity in the Indian's composure, his manful resignation, and his "passive valour" in the face of torture and death.[32]

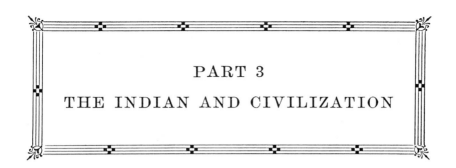

PART 3
THE INDIAN AND CIVILIZATION

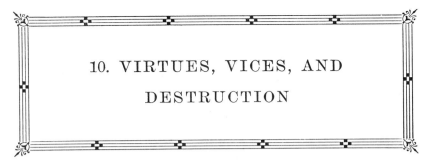

10. VIRTUES, VICES, AND DESTRUCTION

EARLY IN 1832 A SMALL DELEGATION OF UPPER MISSOURI INDIANS VISited Washington, D.C. The group included a plains Ojibwa, a Yanktonai Sioux, and the notable plains Cree leader, Broken Arm. However, an Assiniboine delegate, the Light, became the feature attraction of the tour. While on the trip East this young Indian caught the eye of frontier artist George Catlin, who painted a striking portrait of him. During his stay in Washington the Light enjoyed great popularity, overshadowing the rest of the delegation, even the handsome and dignified Broken Arm. His carriage, his spotless skin clothes, his friendliness, and, if Catlin did not err too much on the side of generosity, his handsome features fascinated the ladies of the city. Moreover, the primitive visitor strongly impressed President Andrew Jackson.[1]

But, if the Light stirred eastern imaginations in Baltimore, Philadelphia, New York, and at the Capitol, civilization had an even greater impact on him. Tradition holds that the mutual admirers, the President and the young Assiniboine, exchanged names and suits of clothes. Though history makes no mention of Jackson's using either gift, the Light went home in full military regalia and, for the remainder of his short life, was known as "Jackson." Moreover, the Assiniboine went beyond such personal marks of civilization. He tried to impress upon his less fortunate fellows how wonderful the white man's land really was. But his tales, true though they were, did not find ready listeners. Indians of the Fort Union area considered him a confirmed liar and derided him for it. Finally, in a feud stemming from his caning a disbeliever—a method of settling points of honor which he had observed at a Washington social gathering—the Light fell the victim of a fellow red man. He had survived only about a year after his tour in civilization.[2]

Broken Arm, on the other hand, remained prominent among his people for many years. He returned to the wilderness with no stories about the magnificence of white society. Instead, he lied unashamedly, telling his people that the whites were few in number, pitiful, and obviously inferior to the Crees.[3]

The story of the Light and of Broken Arm possesses the qualities of a parable and a prophecy. On the one hand stands the Indian who sought for and achieved a degree of mutual respect between himself and civilization, but who, however ill advisedly, attempted to copy the ways of the white man and even to impose them upon his people. As a result he was destroyed. On the other hand there is the Indian who made no compromise, and who lived out his life in primitive respect and prosperity.

When the Light ascended the Missouri on his way home, George Catlin was his fellow passenger aboard the steamboat. Again the artist painted the Assiniboine, but this time he did a comparative study—before and after the taint of civilization. In one panel Catlin portrayed the young Indian standing proudly and handsomely in native dress; in the other he presented "Jackson," a ludicrous figure in an ill worn uniform, tottering in stiff leather boots while whiskey bottles protruded from his back pockets. Since Catlin had great affection for the primitives, his disgust at the transformation causes little surprise. Others had the same feelings, however. In his memoirs, Charles Larpenteur, who came to the upper Missouri in the year preceding the Light's death, recorded his impressions of that ill fated Assiniboine:

All the manners and other good things which he brought from Washington, to show his people what an advance he had made in civilization, was a white towel, which he used to wipe his face and hands, and a house-bell, which he tied to the door of his lodge. His people said that all he got from the whites was a gift of gab. . . . [After his death] a requisition for Indian skulls was made by some physicians from St. Louis. His head was cut off and sent down in a sack with many others. Which of them came out first is hard to tell; but I don't think his did.[4]

In his unique expression of civilization's deleterious effect upon the Indian, Larpenteur voiced the opinion of the majority of traders.

Fur-trade opinion held that the few admirable qualities the red man possessed were inherent in the wilderness circumstances. Tampering with these circumstances robbed the Indian of his happiness. In a discussion of the two kinds of Indians of the Hudson's Bay area, Samuel Hearne elaborated this idea. Some Indians ignored the company's desires and followed an effortless life tending the deer pounds. Others, however, craved the products of civilization and thus spent their winters in a hard and dangerous pursuit of skins and furs. Trapping exhibited the much-approved virtue of industry, but it did not bring happiness. Those indolent ones who followed the deer stayed content while their more ambitious fellows exposed themselves to misery in their search for pelts, only to achieve a few meaningless trivialities which further whetted their appetites. While discussing the fact that the red man's happiness vanished the moment he took up the white man's ways, Alexander Ross concluded, in what was probably as much definition as it was simile, that, ''like a wild animal in a cage, his lustre is gone.'' [5]

Like a wild animal also, the Indian did not readily lend himself to transformation. With some notable exceptions such as Edwin Denig, traders doubted that the red man had undergone much basic change in outlook as a result of early white contacts. Here, of course, one can ask whether fur traders conceived of themselves as emissaries of civilization or as temporary sojourners in the wilderness. As an example, one can find remarks such as that of the apparently cultured Norwegian, W. F. Wentzel, explaining to his correspondent, Roderic McKenzie, that he had failed to write to McKenzie's son because, ''I am an Indian, he is a Christian. . . .'' [6] Whether or not Wentzel's remark was facetious, most traders, as maintained elsewhere in this study, saw themselves in a different light.

Traders, whatever their self-conception, generally believed that the Indian, though he had assumed some superficial and unsavory attributes, remained at heart an Indian. William Byrd of Westover, a participant in the Virginia trade, pointed out the remarkable lack of real effect that the whites had exerted. Even those young Indians educated at William and Mary reverted to savagery as soon as they were released. Writing from an upper Missouri post, Henry Boller informed his sister that ''Mr. M'Bride's squaw'' had attacked that gentleman with a butcher knife. In Indian fashion, Boller wrote, the young woman had broodingly indulged an unfounded jealousy '' 'till her Indian blood was up,'' and then she went for a knife. Having been frustrated in her attempt and having received a thrashing for it, she openly sought death. Though Boller had elsewhere spoken of the woman as ''like a sister to me,'' he saw the futility of trying to change her. For seven years she had been Mr. M'Bride's only wife and had been exceptionally well treated. Her spouse thought so highly of her that he had hoped to take her ''below'' and fit her into white society. ''But it was no use,'' the young Pennsylvanian concluded, ''an Indian would be an Indian still.'' In recording his experiences on the Pacific slope, Peter Skene Ogden dwelt upon the same theme. He commented that Indians whom traders had taught to wear European clothes and to comport themselves in something approximating a civilized manner were only rendered more dangerous by the ''specious mask.'' ''Their modern virtues,'' he wrote in emphasizing the incongruity, ''become them about as well as these garments, and are just as consistent with their real character.'' Robert Michael Ballantyne, a Hudson's Bay trader turned adventure writer, expressed himself on the subject through a dialect-speaking Rocky Mountain trapper: '' 'This is wot it comes to. Savages is savages all the wurld over, and they always wos savages, an' they always will be savages, an' they can't be nothin' else.' '' [7]

Some traders detected a process of mutual degradation under way where civilization touched savagery. Though this theme has its widest expression in editors' introductions, it does appear occasionally in the text of a thoughtful trader. Proponents of the idea assumed the deleterious effect upon the Indian and then spent most time discussing what might be called anthropological retrogression. Like the resolution of the reformed drunkard fallen into bad company, the civilized man's veneer of refinement quickly fell away in an unrestrained and undisciplined atmosphere. According to these men, civilization required preventive maintenance, for by implication it was a delicate thing. Charles MacKenzie believed that it was much easier to barbarize a civilized man than to civilize an Indian. Arriving at the logical conclusion to this reasoning, a Minnesota trader reluctantly explained the white man's backsliding in the wilderness by the theory that human beings had a natural tendency toward savagery "as the normal condition of the human race." But such comments are infrequent. Indeed, truly civilized men who went into the wilderness seem to have done an admirable job of maintaining their civilization.[8]

Far more commonly the trader discussed the red man's descent in much simpler terms, terms which recur so often in fur-trade literature that they approximate a cliché. The trader used the theme of "virtues and vices" to express the red man's corruption at civilization's touch. The Indian, it was held, quickly learned the white man's vices but was unwilling or unable to assume his virtues. Even under religious tutelage, Alexis Bailly commented typically, "they have acquired, the vices of Civilization without any of its morals & are sunk to the lowest degradation. . . ." Beyond this, the trader expressed the idea, sometimes explicitly, sometimes tacitly, that the red man held fast to his own failings while neglecting and losing his primitive merits. This latter point seems to have been a corollary. Often it went unstated, probably because the Indian appeared to have so few virtues of his own that their loss was unimportant or undetectable. Here one suspects that traders who were loath to give the Indian credit for anything could for the purposes of argument invoke savage virtues when belaboring the virtues-and-vices theme. Thus James McKenzie, who detested Indians, at least implied that they possessed some good qualities when in the native state. While discussing the Indians who were in steady contact with civilized influences at the Red River settlements, Thomas Simpson gave a more typical expression of this attitude. He conveyed most of the elements of the formula when he wrote of the Indians that, "while they lose the haughty independence of savage life, they acquire at once all the bad qualities of the white man, but are slow, indeed, in imitating his industry and his virtues." [9]

The half-breed became a focal point of interest to those discussing the interaction between civilization and savagery. Many traders, especially those who compiled memoirs or narratives, had a great deal to say about mixed bloods, but their opinions will be used here only for a specific purpose. Though their ideas were often contradictory—perhaps because of emotional involvement—traders pictured the half-breed as a compound of white and red evils. Thus fur-trade veteran Alexander Fisher counseled his fatherless nephew on the ways of the wilderness world. Adopting a paternal tone, the elder Fisher recommended a general outlook informed by positive thinking—"try it before you say you cannot do it." In terms of specifics, the young man should avoid native women: "Permit me . . . to observe to you that you must not in any account get yourself entangled with the Squaws, for if you do, you are a lost man, you will get a family and of a Spurious kind, that you will regret as long as you live. . . ." More precisely, James McKenzie wrote of the Labrador half-breeds: ". . . in them we find concentrated all the vices of the whites and Nascapees, without one of their virtuous qualities." "This heterogenous and most wretched species," McKenzie continued, were "neither one thing nor the other, neither Nascapees nor whites, but, like the mule between the horse and the ass, a spurious breed. . . ." The half-breed, then, embodied a practical unfolding of the theme of virtues and vices.[10]

However, traders distinguished among half-breeds much as they did among tribes. Some men insisted by way of a somewhat bizarre chauvinism that half-breeds of one nationality surpassed those of another. Thus, George Simpson and John McLean considered French half-breeds to be contemptible rogues in comparison to those with English blood in their veins.[11]

Traders also differentiated between male and female mixed bloods. Though these distinctions were rarely offered explicitly, the sentiment appeared in veiled form whenever fur men faced the problems of finding a niche in society for their half-breed children. Of course, some traders did not worry about such niceties, but many did. The following letter of John Askin suggests that populating the wilderness with unclaimed half-breed children, for all its frequency, may have affronted fur-trade sensibilities far more than is generally supposed. Writing from Mackinac, Askin reminded a departed acquaintance that backwoods life provided only humble entertainment,

. . . while you at London could have all your wants & wishes Supplied, as well as your wanton wishes. ———— Apropos now we are on the Subject, there is a Boy here who was sold to the Ottawas, that every body but yourself says is yours, he suffered much poor child with them, I have at length been able to get him from them on promise of giving an Indian Woman Slave in his Stead—he's at your service if you want him, if not I shall take good care of him untill he is able to earn his Bread without Assistance————

Indeed, one is led to believe that the biologically oriented cynicism of traders' relations with Indian women has been somewhat overdone. Ross Cox, a man who occasionally dramatized, wrote that sterile women were prized by men in the trade because the traders were reluctant to father half-breed children. However accurate this may have been, traders often made conspicuous and extraordinary efforts to prepare such offspring for substantial adulthood, and indeed, the heartbreak and tragedy attendant upon such attempts became bywords of the fur trade. These men did not need the "marginal man" concept to understand the difficulty and futility of trying to place such children in white society.[12]

When Alexander Fisher beseeched his young relative to forego ties with Indian women, he asked too much. However good the advice, he had not taken it himself, nor did his nephew. Most likely, he had suggested the ideal. Nevertheless, he showed no hesitance to accommodate himself with reality, however tragic and tawdry it might become. Thus in 1832 he requested more information about his nephew's wilderness brood and urged the young father to ascertain the rates of tuition at the Red River schools. In the following spring the uncle expressed grave concern. Henry Fisher had taken a different wife, and that was clearly a foolish move. Henry's family had reached an adequate size, "and with your old wife perhaps she would have given you no more." Though his fears of increase proved unfounded, the elder Fisher was forced to wage a verbal campaign to prevent his nephew from running off to seek his fortune elsewhere—with the American Fur Company on the upper Missouri, with a brother at Prairie du Chien, or as a farmer in lower Canada. Henry must stay, the uncle argued, and meet the responsibilities of wife and family. By 1839 the nephew began to receive the returns on his mixed-blood progeny. His eldest son, while at Mr. Pritchard's School in Ft. Garry, "manifested every disposition without coming to open violence, to get out of it as soon as he could—." In 1840 the Fishers reaped the full harvest of disenchantment. The half-breed children provided the heartbreak for which they seemed designed. Keep a strict eye on daughter Betsy, Uncle Alexander urged, and get her married if possible. "Very unpleasant reports" had reached him concerning the actions of the girl as well as the fact that she had been able to gull her father. In the tawdry drama there was a nemesis—the girl's mother whom Henry had long since discarded. According to the elder Fisher, she was spreading in the Red River settlements the story of her unmarried daughter's pregnancy, "and it is well known, that she held the Door while a certain person was crashing" Betsy's sister. After this indelicate revelation Alexander attempted to write of other things. But the compulsion to persist proved too great and soon he was bemoaning the fact that his nephew's son, Alexander, had "turned out to be a very bad subject," having been near imprisonment only shortly before. "Time," he concluded resignedly, "will only tell." [13]

The seemingly inevitable transformation in a father's outlook from hopeful pride to frustrated disillusionment is typified by the correspondence of Chief Trader Archibald MacDonald in regard to his son by Princess Sunday, daughter of the renowned Chinook, Comcomely. In April of 1836 he wrote to a retired trader in the East that sons must have proper guidance because "all the wealth of Rupert's land will not make a *half-breed* either a good parson, a shining burger or an able physician, if left to his own discretion while young." MacDonald obviously did not intend to fall into such an error. He was sending the boy to the Red River settlement for education. Then, if his retired friend, who was a banker in Ontario, would agree, the lad would go on to him for practical training. "Bear in mind he is of a particular race . . . ," he cautioned his old acquaintance, but then he went on to suggest hopefully, and perhaps playfully also, that a kinsman of Comcomely might have a great future.[14]

Apparently such was not to be. After the boy's stay at Red River, MacDonald wrote to his friend, who would have charge of the young half-breed: "So far good; still I cannot divest myself of *certain indescribable fears. . . .*" A year later in a prologue to disenchantment, he prepared himself for failure by writing that although the wilderness was not the place for such young men, "how many have done well out of it." His remark of eleven months later—"I am truly at a loss what to say . . ."—speaks for itself. By 1842, after the elapse of six years, the cycle had been completed. The trader had found his son a position in Indian country. On March 30 of that year, he instructed the young man's patron in Ontario as follows: "For God's sake don't lose sight of my son, until he is fairly embarked in that concern which I believe is the most suitable for every mother's son of them, bad as it has proved to many." [15]

The case of Betsy notwithstanding, mixed-blood daughters seem never to have posed as difficult problems as their masculine counterparts. Considering women's passive role in society, such girls often had to do little more than be properly feminine. In short, far less was expected of them than of their half-breed brothers, both by fur-trade fathers and by the environment into which they hoped to move. One can readily see this contrast in attitudes in the writings of Alexander Ross, himself the head of a mixed-blood family. In a general discussion of these people he referred to them as indolent, thoughtless, improvident, sullen, and licentious. "They alternately associate with the whites and Indians," he wrote, "and thus become fatally enlightened. They form a composition of all the bad qualities of both." When discussing only the women of this stock, however, he showed a far different attitude. He complimented their fairness, delicacy of form, "their light yet nimble movements, and the penetrating expression of the 'bright black eye. . . .'" He concluded that all this made them "objects of no ordinary interest." In a world that expected little more than femininity from the weaker sex, these constituted weighty qualifications. Moreover, for the half-breed male to have taken a white spouse would have been to violate the sexual prerogatives of the dominant half of the dominant race. The half-breed woman suffered less handicap in this regard. Mundane realities thus probably played a large part in making half-breed sons appear incorrigible while daughters aroused fewer fears. Whatever the case, the half-breed represented living testimony to the deleterious impact of civilization upon savagery.[16]

Traders, although reluctant to specify what evils the aborigines were learning from civilization, occasionally asserted that the red men were becoming more prone to lie, to steal, or to cheat. This, of course, involved a contradiction, for traders had portrayed the Indians as being perfect adepts at those activities in their own right. To hold that whites debased the Indians' honesty or concern for property rights was to offer a sad commentary on the virtue of the whites. Civilization, then, rather than perfecting the Indians' old vices, must have been providing them with some new ones. John McLean mentioned such a fault when he discussed the efforts to Christianize the Indians around Norway House: they had learned just enough to enable them to swear.[17] This foible may have disturbed McLean's Methodist piety, but most traders centered their attention on another white innovation, alcohol. Though they did not always state it explicitly, traders believed that liquor was the symbol of the red men's fall at the touch of civilization.

That a great many Indians had a craving for liquor and that drinking led to almost unspeakable depravity requires little arguing. Statements regarding the Indian's passion for liquor occur equally in the writings of those who sympathized with the natives and those who despised them. Of the latter, Alexander Henry the younger wrote concerning the Salteurs that "love of liquor is their ruling passion," and Richard Marten of the Hudson's Bay Company complained that, "Brandy, Brandy, Brandy is the constant cry of these miserably debauched wretches. . . ." On the other hand, a man as kindly and understanding as David Thompson recorded virtually the same thing, and a similarly sympathetic John

McLean held that to "grog drinking . . . no earthly bliss can be compared in the Indian's estimation. . . ." The debauchery that attended such a craving appears throughout fur-trade literature, perhaps most vividly in the journals of the younger Alexander Henry.[18]

Why, if the Indian had so few virtues in the first place, did liquor have such a noticeably deleterious effect? Surely, by the traders' own testimony, alcohol could not have been undermining a wilderness idyll. Why then should Alexander Mackenzie show great regret for the ill effects of liquor in precisely the same context in which he pointed to such prevalent, indigenous vices as incest and bestiality? Drunkenness would seem to have been mild and almost innocuous in comparison. Young Rudolph Kurz, operating under the naïveté of frontier inexperience, supplied a reasonable enough answer to this seeming paradox in attitudes. At St. Joseph on his way up the Missouri he observed some of the local tribes and recorded his good impression of their "dignified manner." He had to qualify this somewhat, however, for when intoxicated the Otoes, Foxes, and Iowas appeared far different. Kurz's insistence that an Indian in such a condition was no worse than a "drunken American" did little to gainsay his judgment of Indians. Seemingly, the white man, even a "drunken American," had other virtues. To the men of the fur trade, however, the Indian had little more than a dignified bearing to recommend him. Liquor did so much to abase the Indian in the trader's eyes because it deprived him of the only virtues with which he had been credited.[19]

In drinking sessions the modicum of serenity and aloofness of native life gave way to an ugly familiarity such as that described by Duncan M'Gillivray: "Men, Women and children, promiscuously mingle together and join in one diabolical clamour of singing, crying, fighting &c and to such excess do they indulge their love of drinking that all regard to decency or decorum is forgotten. . . ." The strictly maintained reticence fell away, as M'Gillivray put it, "in proportion to the quantity of Rum they have swallowed." The often remarked discretion in the face of danger disappeared to be replaced by a rowdy bellicosity. Only alcohol, Samuel Hearne noted in exasperation, could raise an Indian's courage. Even stoicism, so important in holding what little of the trader's respect the red man enjoyed, vanished before spirits. ''All in good crying trim,'' kindly John McLean muttered of a particular band, ''that is, intoxicated.'' Even the younger Alexander Henry, whose impatience with things Indian was colossal, expressed regret that liquor weakened the ''ancient customs'' and allowed the Indians to manifest an abject, shameful, and drunken sorrow.[20]

Various traders generalized even further about the changes in Indian behavior wrought by alcohol. While being hounded for rum by the friends of a deceased member of his exploring party, Alexander Mackenzie made a telling comment on the Indian and alcohol. Of the matter at hand he noted that it was ''extreme degradation'' for an Indian to weep when sober. However, in a more comprehensive vein he added that ''a state of intoxication sanctions all irregularities.'' By this formula, alcohol acted in a dual role in effecting the debasement of the Indian: as active agent and as face-saving justification, both cause and excuse. For some, the workings of such a psychological device only evidenced further the perversity of the aborigines. Thus, Francois-Victor Malhiot recorded a hectic night with drunken Indians who became unbearably quarrelsome, followed by a morning in which the night's misconduct was all laid to drink. The apologies and self-justifications did little to relieve Malhiot's anger, however, and he closed his account by calling their appeals ''the usual excuses of such black dogs!'' With less passion and more understanding, Duncan Cameron noted that intoxication served as a valid exoneration for sexual misbehavior by Indian women. Indeed,

. . . the crimes, murders, folies they committ when inebriate are entirely attributed to liquor, so that, when mischieviously inclined, they feign to be drunk, expecting that no one will lay their crimes to their account when in that state. If you find fault with an Indian for any thing he has done when the least in liquor, his answer will invariably be that he remembers nothing about it. . . .[21]

The traders held that such manifestations of the Indian's dignity as reticence and stoicism were consciously self-imposed, not inherent. Had these been innate characteristics, liquor could have altered the Indian's behavior only while he was intoxicated. Because such features were consciously maintained, however, liquor had both the obvious direct effect *and* a more subtle and insidious tendency to destroy the will to maintain such postures. Alcohol became both a means and an excuse to abandon those culturally prescribed inhibitions that the trader regarded as dignified and admirable. Traders did not intimate that the red man's besotted conduct was unique, that his actions differed in kind from those of a white man similarly indisposed. Intoxication had such an adverse effect only because it undermined those few features of Indian character which maintained a tenuous hold on the fur man's respect. Liquor destroyed what was to the trader the Indian's only enviable feature, his dignity of bearing.

Drunkenness and debauchery have remained as stigmas upon the fur trade, and perhaps quite justifiably so. Still, a reservation of sorts needs to be entered. Liquor and its attendant evils were not universals of the trade. The Crows, for example, abstained from alcohol almost completely. Charles Larpenteur wrote that in 1833 the Crows were not drinking and that they did not begin until years later. As late as the 1850's, with the fur trade practically a thing of the past, Edwin Denig remarked that this tribe would not touch liquor. The Crows, it should be remembered, were not so isolated that one fur-trade concern could beneficently administer monopoly and withhold alcohol; they lived in an area that frequently had competition. Moreover, the Chipewyans also had a reputation for abstinence, and men such as Ross Cox and Gabriel Franchère attested to the same disinclination among the Pacific coast and Columbia River tribes.[22]

A few years after Cox's and Franchère's experience on the Columbia, George Simpson wrote that these Indians had at last succumbed to the lure of alcohol, though they had formerly held in contempt anyone who used it.[23] By the same token, no one has suggested that Crow abstinence is a contemporary phenomenon, though it did to a large degree survive the fur-trade era. The Indian, then, did not immediately fall victim to liquor. The classically lurid accounts of the ravages of fur-trade liquor came from men operating among the Algonquian peoples in an area bounded by the Ohio River, the hundredth meridian, and Hudson's Bay. This vast area, roughly conterminous with the Great Lakes watershed, had been open to the trade longer perhaps than any other region discussed in fur-trade literature. One could conclude that in this area the liquor-laden trader had had more time to play upon the red man's unfortunate weakness and, thus, to defile him.

On the other hand, one might reason that it was less the active agency and conscious policy of the trader than it was the force of circumstances which besotted the Indian. In 1832 when Kenneth McKenzie felt the pinch of government liquor policy on the upper Missouri he peevishly complained to a colleague that he was neither able nor willing "to bear the onus of debarring my old friends of their dearest comfort. . . ." The "King of the Missouri" could hardly have been less convincing. But he argued more tellingly that he would lose trade to his competitors if he did not have spirits. Although the plea of contingent necessity might on occasion have been put to hypocritical use, its logical, if not ethical, soundness can hardly be gainsaid. A dry Fort Union may not have seen, as McKenzie put it, an Indian "in a twelvemonth." The same reasoning led Ramsay Crooks to insist upon the American Fur Company's use of alcohol in spite of its effects upon the "Natives who are its victims." At other times, when "this abominable traffic" could effectually be prevented, Crooks appeared vehement in denying its use to his traders. Similarly, at the time that Louisiana Territory came into American hands, Pierre Chouteau of St. Louis presumed to advise Secretary of War Henry Dearborn. During the Spanish regime, he pointed out, liquor sales had been closely circumscribed, and it would behoove the United States to adopt a like policy. To be sure, a dry trade held a good deal of attraction for fur men. After a description of the drunken orgies which surpassed "civilized belief," David Lavender concluded that "out of self-interest, if nothing else, responsible traders deplored the horror." [24] Though Lavender's comment referred to the Great Plains trade, it has general applicability. And, most assuredly, the questionable curb of self-interest was preferable to none at all.

As time passed the forests became barren of furs, and the Indian became dependent upon civilized products, ill suited for wilderness pursuits, and pauperized. Perhaps the hopelessness of his situation as much as an innate proclivity or the unconscionable designs of others turned the Indian to alcohol. Duncan Cameron, never one for apologies or evasions, implied as much when he wrote the following explanation of native drunkenness:

It is not from absolute sensuality, nor for the sole pleasure of drinking, that the flavour of liquor creates such an irresistable craving for more; they merely seek in their orgies a state of oblivion, of stupefaction, and a kind of cessation of existence, which constitutes their greatest enjoyment. I have often seen them, when they could get no more liquor, boil tobacco and drink the juice of it to keep themselves in a state of intoxication.

Duncan M'Gillivray's application of this principle to a particular instance is hardly pleasing to contemplate but it renders the compulsion of oblivion comprehensible. At his Saskatchewan River post in March of 1795 an Indian woman lost a child to disease. With the pretense of making a sacrifice to the uneasy spirit of a previously deceased husband, the aggrieved woman secured a small keg. Having obtained the liquor, however, her true intent appeared:

She very deliberately conveyed a pot of it to her mouth; fixed her eyes on the roof of the House in an extacy and emptied it to the Bottom: —She returned again to the charge without loss of time, and soon lost remembrance of the death of her son in a fit of drunken clamour.

For Indian society generally, the longing for the solace of the keg may well have become increasingly intense.[25]

The trader's conviction that the Indian withered at the white man's touch may represent a simple reflection of reality. They recorded what to them was—and what indeed may have been—literal fact. Logic, of course, does not preclude the possibility that what someone says about something can be true, that the object really possesses the qualities which the mind of the describer attributes to it. When the trader talked about the Indian, he certainly did more than reflect himself. But in his moments of greatest objectivity the trader more nearly interests the anthropologist and the historical student of Indian culture. For the purposes of this study, attitudes and impressions loom larger than reality. When the trader discussed the corruption of the Indian, he at least tacitly revealed himself as well as the red man, civilization as well as savagery.

Beyond the logical possibility that the trader no more than recorded what really was occurring, his remarks on civilization's ill effects upon the natives may well have reflected disingenuity. Conceivably, humanitarian instincts could have impelled him to use what influence he had to secure the Indian better treatment. Civilization, he might have felt, need only be alerted to the ruin of the aborigines. A portrayal done in properly sensational and gloomy colors might effect that end. Certainly, fur-trade literature provides illustrations of such an approach, John McLean's recollections being a prime example. On the other hand, the trader might have utilized such arguments in the selfish interests of the trade. Dramatically to impress white society with the decay of the primitives could help to stem the civilized advance, thus perpetuating the fur trade and, coincidentally, the red man. Apparent examples of this device occur also, most notably in the writings of fur-trade administrators.

In addition to these most evident and most appealingly mechanistic explanations, one encounters a complex of sentiments and ideas involving the respective merits of civilized and natural forms. These, too, influenced traders' reactions to the natives. In the past few years several scholars have sought to describe the degree to which primitivistic assumptions, or their opposite numbers, have informed the thinking of the American community. They have pondered the question of how America conceived of itself vis-à-vis the wilderness and its inhabitants. Unlike the possibility mentioned above—the traders' impersonally recording the realities of the crude life—the Americans portrayed by these scholars operated subjectively. They consciously and studiously sought self-definition.

By theorizing about the wilderness before them, or about the civilization behind them, they attempted to come to a better realization of what they themselves were. Moreover, their cerebrations in this regard provided a rationale and a policy on which to base a seemingly inevitable physical expansion westward.

American thinking on these matters could, it would seem, have fixed upon any spot, ranging from the archetype, primitivism, to its opposite, progress. Probably, individuals took positions from one end of the spectrum to the other. But intellectual historians dealing with the subject have been concerned, however validly, with the totality of American sentiments and with confining that totality to a particular sector of the range. Though their interpretations have not encompassed the entire scope from primitivism to progress, these historians have differed markedly in their assessments of how the American viewed nature and the child of nature.

In a work published in 1944 Arthur Ekirch argued the prevalence and influence of the concept of progress in pre-Civil War United States. In the book he gave little attention to the wilderness or its dwellers. The thinking of Ekirch's Americans had no place in it for misgivings about the red man's fate or for soul-searching and hesitance stemming from the possibility that primitive existence might possess praiseworthy or superior features. With a few exceptions, such as an aristocratic James Fenimore Cooper and a doubt-ridden Herman Melville, "the American made the idea of progress both a law of history and the will of a benign Providence." The frontier and free land, far from instilling in the popular mind an admiration for the crude virtues, made this nation "peculiarly susceptible to a belief in so dynamic an idea as that of progress." This "dynamic" and "ruthless" doctrine lent "a comforting aura of historic inevitability and of righteous respectability" to the ultimate extinction of the American natives. Though the merciful sensibilities of a few were outraged, most Americans fastened their attention on "the advantages to the white man which would result from the displacement of the noble savage. . . ." Here Ekirch used "noble savage" as no more than an ironic synonym for Indian.

However, this choice of terms could have been misleading, for, by his reading, the American mind came close to the antithesis of primitivism with its tendency to resort to noble savagery.[26]

Nine years later Roy Harvey Pearce developed this theme much more fully in *The Savages of America: A Study of the Indian and the Idea of Civilization.* Ekirch had been only incidentally concerned with the Indian; Pearce devoted a book to him. For both men the concept of progress predominated in American thinking and, of course, tailored the impression that the native made upon the American mind. Pearce employed different terminology, but in general outline his "Idea of Civilization" closely approximates Ekirch's "Idea of Progress." According to Pearce, for example, when the American came into the presence of the red man and felt problems arising, he worked out a solution "as an element in an idea of progress"—"the grand Christian, civilized Idea of Progress." Pearce ascribed the origin of this American belief to the Scottish moral and common-sense school rather than to the French *philosophes* as had Ekirch, but the upshot was the same. After a brief and futile flirtation with the hope of lifting the Indian with them, Pearce's Americans fell back upon the doctrine of savagism. By this formula the red man appeared at the bottom of a unilinear scale along which the white man was well advanced. "The savage would be understood as one who had not and somehow could not progress into the civilized, who would inevitably be destroyed by the civilized. . . ." Via the theory of savagism, the Indian provided a reverse mirror image of what the white man was and at the same time a worrisome and portentous model of what he could become if he did not progress. "What Indians signified was not what they were, but what Americans should not be. Americans were only talking to themselves about themselves. But they succeeded in convincing themselves that they were right, divinely right. Only with such conviction—cruel, illogical, and self-indulgent as it was—could they move on." The Indian became a mere obstacle and, willy-nilly, by the concept of savagism, "the zero of human society." [27]

Where Ekirch had all but ignored primitivism by describing its opposite number, Pearce joined the issue directly by arguing that such an outlook had no chance in the American climate. Of course, the nation did not go unmoved by the destiny of the red man. "Concern for the Indian's sad fate," Pearce noted, "was as deep and as honest as certainty of his inevitable destruction." The author's seemingly incongruous combinations of descriptives convey the mood—for example, the "tragic and triumphant" meaning of progress, and feelings of "pity and censure." There was sadness, but no doubts and no soul-searching. To be sure, the new society had inherited from European culture a full-blown "primitivistic mode." "The trick for Americans was to preserve the mode in the face of primitive actuality. The trick soon became merely humorous or it simply failed." Some, like Benjamin Franklin, made a game of noble savagery; others of a more earnest bent, like Michel de Crèvecœur, fabricated exalted aborigines; the Quaker, William Bartram, indulged in self-delusions; Philip Freneau resorted to the intricate and unlikely device of an Indian at twice remove *dreaming* of primitive perfection; and John Robinson could only manifest in an incoherent fashion his own neuroses. The facts prevailed. "The forces which informed the idea of savagism at one and the same time destroyed the idea of the noble savage and made isolated radicals of those who would believe in it." American thinking was pervaded by "an antiprimitivistic assumption so deeply certain as not to need developing." [28]

On the continuum between primitivism and progress, Ekirch and Pearce placed the American mood near the latter point. This interpretation has not gone unquestioned. In *Virgin Land*, his classic study of the meaning of the West, Henry Nash Smith portrayed an American nation much less convinced of the inferiority of natural forms. He by no means argued a construction diametrically opposed to that of Pearce and Ekirch. He did, however, ease the locus of American thinking to a position more nearly equidistant between the two extremes. Smith spent much time, for example, on such things as the "refined hostility to progress" infecting men like Parkman. However, in the face of the exhilarating physical tasks confronting young America, these attitudes could not carry the day.

Indeed, as the nineteenth century wore on, they fell more and more into disuse. Ultimately, according to Smith, the rout became complete. ". . . The static ideas of virtue and happiness and peace drawn from the bosom of the virgin wilderness . . . proved quite irrelevant for a society committed to the ideas of civilization and progress, and to an industrial revolution." But the positive tone of the last statement, so reminiscent of Arthur Ekirch, fails to convince fully. After all, Smith never resolved such contradictions in the nation's sentiments as that involving "Daniel Boone: Empire Builder or Philosopher of Primitivism?" Most notably, Smith's concluding chapter, in which he bemoaned the pernicious influence of the Turner hypothesis, would seem to be grounded upon the vitality, not the impotence, of a residue of notions affirming the beneficence of nature. He pictured "the bankruptcy of primitivism" and "the dying theory of cultural primitivism." But in quarreling with the Turner tradition—"a system which revolved about a half-mystical conception of nature"—Smith in part substantiated the viability of those very suppositions.[29]

In a work dealing with the symbolic significance of Andrew Jackson, John Ward demonstrated more precisely the paradoxes noted by Smith in America's attitudes toward nature and civilization. What emerges is an American outlook milder still in regard to natural forms than that portrayed by Smith. Jacksonian America, Ward argued, felt a dual attraction—or, perhaps better, repulsion. Poised between the physical wilderness of nature ahead and the societal wilderness of Europe behind, the new nation held a middle ground attitudinally as well as geographically. Americans insisted that the good life struck a balance between civilization and savagery. They plotted man's search for felicity not on a unilinear scale oriented away from nature but on a curve, the optimum point of which was equally removed from both extremes. In a more positive vein, the romantic conceptions of the time indicated that man derived moral, intellectual, and physical sustenance from nature. Nature possessed dynamic attributes and to turn one's back on it was to debilitate one's self. By emphasizing the American mood's concern with balance—or, perhaps, its ambivalence—Ward placed that mood approximately at the mid-point between espousal of nature and espousal of civilization.[30]

Finally, though he specifically disclaimed the intention, Charles Sanford in a 1961 publication seemed at times to move early American thinking even further toward primitivism. He insists that *The Quest for Paradise* involves ''the intellectual tradition to which both the 'philosophers of primitivism' and the 'trailblazers of progress' have subscribed.'' Nevertheless, his treatment of the American mood until well into the nineteenth century appears more nearly in accord with, and in description of, the ''philosophers of primitivism.'' Agreeing with Pearce, Sanford reasoned that contact with the red man helped America achieve identity. However, that contact also ''begot an idealized view of human nature, which since the Declaration of Independence and until quite recently has dominated an optimistic American world outlook. [Though stifled] until the struggle for empire had terminated . . . this last development grew out of a cult of nature. . . .'' Natural simplicity, Sanford wrote, need not be a focal point of the paradisiac myth. ''Paradise'' can assume various guises—''power, ease, sexuality . . . worldly riches.'' It is no more than an ''assertion in behalf of all the fancied goods of life in a world which must remain forever restrictive and imperfect, therefore evil.'' But by Sanford's telling the potentially vast array of alternatives seems absent through much of American history. Indeed, however coincidentally, the synonymity of paradise and nature obtrudes. For example, the author noted the anxiety over the supposed invasion of the new continent by ''urban European civilization'' with its attendant sophisticated vices. This worrisome unfolding manifested itself in the rise of towns and in the burgeoning of a southern aristocracy. ''By the process of symbolic transference . . . , the polarization of America and Europe, paradise and hell, nature and civilization became internalized.'' Sanford's limiting the contrapuntal relationships to these three would seem to have significance. The associations of America, paradise, and *nature*, juxtaposed against Europe, hell, and *civilization* come near to being equations, equations which would seem to bear out the existence of a strong primitivistic bent in

nascent America. According to Sanford, "the Edenic myth
. . . has been the most powerful and comprehensive organizing force in American culture." Apparently, through much of our
history it took the form of primitivism.[31]

It may be a questionably meaningful exercise to consider fur-
trade attitudes in the light of these interpretations. Traders, of
course, operated within the wilderness and possessed a thorough
knowledge of it and its inhabitants. By definition, the Americans
described by Ekirch, Pearce, Smith, and Sanford did not. Nevertheless, like their eastern brethren, traders were civilized men, often
studiously so. If America took a stand on the respective merits of
nature and civilization, these knowledgeable frontiersmen—operating where, as Leslie Fiedler put it, "the Noble Savage . . .
confronted Original Sin"[32]—should have made worthwhile, if
unheeded, contributions to the discourse.

Evidence of the Pearce and Ekirch point of view exists in the fur-
trade literature. For example, fur traders, like Pearce's Thomas
Hart Benton, occasionally put "the burden of extinction on a
civilized God, not on civilized men." James Mackay, a shadowy
figure of the Missouri trade, illustrates the invocation of a divine
sanction for progress. "It seems," he wrote, "that the Almighty has
decreed the total extinction of the whole race. . . ." According to
him, the positions of white man and red were analogous to those of
Israelite and Canaanite, and God's favor appeared evident—" 'By
little & little I will drive them out from before thee until thou be
increased & inherit the land. . . .' " Moreover, traders at times
combined their forecasts of Indian extinction with an exuberant
condescension that would have gained the envy of the most militant
prophets of progress. "When a superior race," George Simpson
once wrote, "without fraud or violence, plants its thousands where
an inferior race could hardly maintain its hundreds, nothing but the
mere mawkishness of sentimentality could attempt to avert or retard
the change. . . ." In his treatment of Henry Rowe Schoolcraft,
Pearce has that student of Indian culture tacitly concluding that the
red man, as savage, was "so abhorrent as to be abolished from human
history. . . . If pity will do no good, then little but censure is left."

If this was indeed Schoolcraft's sentiment, a statement by Thomas Fitzpatrick could have led him to it. In correspondence with the scholar, the famed mountain man wrote:

Let the civilized man, if possible, divest himself of all partiality and prejudice, and view the Indian impartially, just as he finds him, without attempting to cast imputations on anything but the right cause, which is their own innate proneness to evil, and it will be found that that very innate principle of wickedness and depravity, is the greatest cause of hastening them off to destruction; I believe, moreover, that all the aid from the wealthiest governments of Europe, united with that of the United States, could not redeem or save a tithe of these people, inasmuch as I consider them a doomed race, and they must fulfill their destiny.[33]

Despite the vehemence of such statements, the Simpsons, Mackays, and Fitzpatricks occupied an atypical position in fur-trade thinking. The great majority would have been repelled by the harsh historicism in the outlook portrayed by Pearce and Ekirch. Without arguing their sensitivity, these frontier operators seemed disinclined to stomach the strident and brutal implications of a view that identified history and progress. Irvin Wyllie has argued that in the late nineteenth century, men harboring the misanthropic notions of social Darwinism were more readily found in intellectual than in business circles. By the same token, if Pearce's assessment of American attitudes is correct, its severe inferences fit much more easily the thinking of the enlightened easterner than that of the intelligent but straightforwardly practical man of affairs of the wilderness. To be sure, most of the latter anticipated an unhappy future for the natives, but in doing so they extended "pity" and withheld "censure." Thus aged Montana trader Alexander Culbertson noted compassionately that the seemingly doomed Piegans were mercifully spared the knowledge of their fate and so could go through the remainder of their days in the bliss of ignorance. And Peter Skene Ogden, a man whose equilibrium had often been sorely tested by the aborigines, considered the outrages worked upon them and regretfully welcomed the euthanasia of extinction. "It is almost the only consolation remaining to the philanthropist under these circumstances," he wrote, "that, ere long, the race must become extinct." [34]

But traders evidenced inclinations more telling than the above-mentioned failure openly to deny natural merits. Some applauded the simple life. In one of his mordant jottings Alexis Bailly reviled the fickle world in which "prosperity makes friends and poverty drives them away. . . ." "Return to your farm," he soliloquized, "and . . . live the life of a philosopher   despise the world and its allurements   it is the only means of finding contentment. . . ." In a commonplace composition reminiscent of Polonius, trader Hugh Heward portrayed "Paternus" sagely directing his son toward "Simplicity of Life." And after advising a sister to substitute "Calisthenic exercises" for attendance at hot, lengthy parties, young Henry Boller congratulated himself on escaping the city, its social functions, and (his especial abhorrence) railroads. "I feel strongly inclined," he added, "to continue keeping out of their way." There is also the possibility that the virtues-and-vices motif itself partakes of primitivism. Percy G. Adams has suggested that the debasing of unsophisticated life was the kind of thing that primitivistically prejudiced travelers often depicted. Thus when Edward Umfreville referred to Indians as being "enervated and debased" by "commerce with Europeans," we are free to infer at least that he was toying with a romantic conviction. [35]

Finally and most importantly, as maintained in a previous chapter, traders occasionally dealt in noble savages. Whether the compulsion stemmed from conviction, altruism, or selfishness, the fact remains that these hardened men spoke of natural virtues. Like Charles Sanford's exiles from sin, they sensed the decay of primal goodness. The Indian did indeed lose his "lustre"; and that they regretted. Like John Ward's insurgent democrats, they at least tacitly counseled balance rather than rampant flight from nature. Their allegiance went to civilization—"the land of Cakes." But, however inevitable civilization's ultimate mission, traders could not help suffering some misgivings. At the outset of a long career in the Minnesota trade, Martin McLeod pondered the condition of the Red Lake natives. For a moment he envied "these simple but happy

people." "Yet upon reflection," he conceded, "they appear miserable . . . ," and it would be admirable to try to civilize them. Then,
as quickly, the doubts returned—"perhaps, they would not be so
happy. . . ." After all, McLeod concluded:

> If ignorance is bliss
> 'tis folly to be wise.[36]

Like Henry Nash Smith's America puzzling over the proper description of Daniel Boone—"Empire Builder or Philosopher of
Primitivism"—fur traders felt the ambivalent pull of both the
progressive and the primitive.

11. AN UNCERTAIN DESTINY

IN 1857, JOHN ARTHUR ROEBUCK OF THE PARLIAMENTARY COMMITTEE
on the Hudson's Bay Company asked former trader John Rae: "Has
it not been found by experience that the red man is opposed to that
kind of life which we call civilized life?" "Exactly so," Rae
answered, "there is no doubt about it." "And wherever the
civilized man comes," Roebuck continued, "the.red man disappears?" "Yes," Rae agreed, "that is the result, generally speaking." However leading Roebuck's queries and however great Rae's
inclination to make his answers suit company interests, the ex-trader
spoke for most men in that calling. With similar certainty, John
Owen noted of some Rocky Mountain Indians in the 1850's that
"they are Indians & Indians they will Ever remain   To Christianize, Civilize, & Educate the Indian is a farce long Since
Exploded." Despite their belief that civilization blighted and ultimately destroyed the American native, however, traders considered
possible methods of fitting the Indian into the white man's order.
Though they would have agreed with Rae and Owen, most traders
added enough qualifications, reservations, and simple hopes to take
the bite off the unhappy fate they foresaw for the aborigines.
Consistency often deserted them when they reached the concluding
chapter of a frontier narrative wherein form demanded forecasts
for the Indian's future. The ideals of improvement and preservation
clashed openly with the apparent realities of the red man's nature.
There seemed no way of resolving civilization's deleterious effect
upon the natives and the manifest historical necessity of allowing
the white man's way to work its will. The hopelessness and inevitability of the final outcome appeared abundantly evident, but traders
generally avoided outright statements of the obvious.[1]

The honest realism of Rae and Owen most often gave way to an equivocal posture indicating both the futility and the desirability of attempting to civilize the Indian. In considering such possibilities Charles Larpenteur wrote typically that ''from what I have seen, and knowing him as I do, I would say it cannot be done; yet there is nothing like trying.'' [2] It would be to the white man's credit to attempt the impossible. An anthropological lost cause, like a military one, had some fascination.

With civilization as with other things, traders distinguished among Indians. Some, they felt, had a better chance of conversion than did others. Various means of differentiation occurred to fur-trade observers. Among others, Kit Carson dwelt upon the obvious necessity of concentrating efforts upon the younger generation while allowing older Indians to die unreconstructed. John Long stated explicitly the often implied rule that Indian women were more easily transformable than Indian men.[3]

More importantly, traders used the tenuous criterion of tribal diversity. Edwin Denig seemed to harbor no hopes that civilization could ever transform the innately perverse Arikaras. The Assiniboines, he felt, accepted the white man's ways slowly, but he explained this by what might be called their ingrained conservatism. In contrast, however, the Crows and Blackfeet, according to the Fort Union trader, quickly recognized the utility of civilized goods and methods and endeavored to obtain and use them. In making these distinctions, Denig dealt with peoples of different stocks—Caddoan, Siouan and Algonquian. Differing propensities for civilization appeared also among groups more closely related. After concluding that the American native in general was unsuited to civilized ways, Thomas Simpson conceded in a footnote that ''marked distinctions'' did indeed exist among tribes in that respect. As an illustration, he used the disparity between the readily converted Swampy Crees and their close relatives, the ''proud'' Saulteaux. Alexander Ross substantiated this appraisal in his discussion of the notable meeting ground for civilization and savagery, the Red River settlements. The Indians involved were largely Crees and almost exclusively Algonquians, but of this apparently homogeneous group only the Swampies, according to Ross, exhibited any real inclination for civilization.[4]

When Thomas Simpson referred to the Saulteaux as being intransigent savages, he touched upon an idea that quite often appeared, either explicitly or implicitly, when traders discussed the possibility of civilizing the red man. To the trader the most easily civilized Indian appeared the least admirable. Here the thinking of the fur men resembled the outlook described by Bernard DeVoto as belonging to Jason Lee and, by implication, to missionaries generally. According to DeVoto, Lee failed to stop as intended among the Flatheads and Nez Perces because he had no desire to work among tribes who were still Indians in every sense of the word and who had the many faults and the few virtues attendant thereto. Instead, Lee sought Indians who had felt the impact of civilization, who had become to some limited degree white men. According to DeVoto, Lee turned his back on the raw primitiveness of the valley of Ham's Fork because it provided the setting in which the Indian could survive. The trader and the red man viewed that locale as ''a celestial place''; the easterner, Jason Lee, considered it repulsive, and so he set out to find a field where the identical processes of degradation and civilization had been at work on the aborigines. The missionary found what he sought farther west, where the Indians had become white men—''about as much as was possible, which is to say they were degenerate, debauched, diseased, despairing, and about to die.''[5]

To the missionary such people appeared the proper objects of Christian activity, and, similarly, to the trader they were proper objects of the civilizing process. Time and again, when traders named tribes suited for civilization they chose those of the Pacific slopes and coast. These people, of course, consistently occupied the bottom strata of the traders' scale of preference. Although they embodied least of the characteristics that seemed admirable to the fur men, they were consistently nominated for transformation into civilized beings. Although atypical in his merely mild disgust with the Columbia River peoples, Gabriel Franchère's statement of their potentialities speaks for the majority of knowledgeable traders who went beyond the Rockies. In his narrative he wrote that,

In spite of the vices that may be laid to the charge of the natives of the Columbia, I regard them as nearer to a state of civilization than any of the tribes who dwell east of the Rocky Mountains. They did not appear to me so attached to their customs that they would not easily adopt those of civilized nations: they would dress themselves willingly in European mode, if they had the means.

That the traders simply considered the Pacific tribes to be higher on an anthropological scale than other Indians seems reasonable, but there is little if any explicit evidence for it. Franchère's phrase, "nearer to a state of civilization," could imply this; but he evidently saw these people as being more socially malleable rather than more advanced. Thomas Simpson stated it quite simply—they were "more pliant and tractable" than other natives. In his reference to the miserably deprived and almost beast-like Snakes of southeastern Oregon, Peter Skene Ogden left no doubt. Their proximity to civilization did not cause him to recommend them to missionary efforts. Instead, they deserved attention because men of the cloth "could twist them in any form they pleased." [6]

If Bernard DeVoto was correct, the enthusiast, Jason Lee, must have welcomed the sight of the degraded wretches of the Willamette whom he could make into "herdsmen, users of soap, tee-totalers, hymn-singers, monogamists, and newspaper-readers. . . ." Apparently, when men of similarly fervid outlook engaged in the fur trade, they had similar reactions. Jedediah Smith, for example, would have agreed wholeheartedly with Jason Lee's desire to find some un-Indian-like Indians. The sequence of some of Smith's remarks on the natives of the Sacramento Valley appears significant, and a bit appalling. In one paragraph the Bible-toting mountain man pointed to these people as the Indians most likely to respond to "Civilizing and Christianizing." In the next paragraph he recorded that "a great many" of these prospective Christians "appear to be the lowest intermediate link between man and the Brute creation." [7]

The average trader did not react with Smith's unique enthusiasm. That a broken and besotted Chinook or a brute-like Digger was more civilizable than a Flathead or a Cheyenne appeared to the fur man as no mark of excellence. Men of religion might eagerly accept the seeming reality that the Indian had to be shattered and degraded before a wonderful transformation could be worked, but to the trader this "truth" was far less palatable. Even David Thompson could not extol such an unfolding. Thompson seems never to have wandered from righteousness after the day in his youth when the devil visited him on the Saskatchewan. This "puritan," as his most recent editor called him, admired and defended the Indians of the plains and northern forests; but he despaired of their ever being Christianized. For the natives of the Columbia he had nothing but contempt; yet, he felt, they would be converted. "No doubt," he wrote, "a few years hence will find them cultivating the ground, and under the instruction of Missionaries." One wonders if Thompson ever suspected the workings of perversity in a mechanism that dictated the transformation only of the least admirable natives.[8]

Obviously, the Indian who had undergone what Jason Lee saw as preparation for civilization could hardly have appeared inviting to any but the zealot. The idea that the most civilizable Indian was least admirable sprang from the basic notions that traders harbored in regard to the natives. With an overtone of primitivism, they believed that Indians at the farthest remove from white men were the best. Civilization blighted the red man, and thus stigma rather than merit went with a desertion of savagery. The Indian who fell most quickly appeared the weakest and the least worthy.

According to the trader, Indian virtues inhered in Indian circumstances and therefore disappeared when conditions changed. Most obviously, this held true of civilization's effect upon the red man. However, causes other than the tide of white advance could upset the tenuous existence of native goodness. Edwin Denig, for example, concluded that the Arikaras were degraded because enemies had confined them to river villages, and they had consequently lost their war spirit. Their sedentary and agricultural life precluded a properly Indian approach to conflict and, of course, to life itself.

This settling down did not enhance the Arikaras; it debased them. According to Denig, "Indians to be Indians must have war." Thus, when an Indian for whatever cause deviated from his natural way of life, when he became something else—a farmer for example—he degenerated into that most shockingly dissolute and perverse being, an Arikara. Among the Arikaras, turned as they were from properly Indian pursuits, the young men had nothing of import to do, had no hierarchy of honors to mount, and so they spent their time in "circumventing the young women." Similarly, the older men, "thrown upon their own resources . . . seduce each other's wives." [9] Needless to say, Denig could not have ascribed such a state of affairs to white plowmen. The phrase "Indians to be Indians" indicates clearly that the red men did not react to the influences of agrarian confinement as did white men. The Indian was truly something apart, a being *sui generis*.

Robert Stuart noted approximately the same pernicious effect upon the Indians who gathered at the falls of the Columbia River to live at their leisure upon fish. Stuart considered this unnatural and called the Indians "worthless dogs" who sought to indulge "sloth without fear of starvation." The Astorian concluded that the fishing places "like our great cities may with propriety be called the School of Villainy or the Head Quarters of vitiated principles." [10] Perhaps Stuart, a product of rural Scotland, gave vent to his own predilections about the good life and expressed a dominant impulse toward agrarianism. Beyond imposing his own ideas of ruralism and primitivism upon the people of the wilderness, he indicated that for the Indian there was but one existence, and to deviate from it was to lose virtue. Stuart, it should be recalled, rated the nomads of the high plains, a people well removed from agrarianism, far above the sedentary and agricultural tribes of the transmontane region. He denounced the Indians of the falls not because they had wandered away from a *pastoral* or *agrarian* life, but rather because they had departed from what he considered a properly *Indian* existence. He did not identify the effects of "great cities" upon white people and the effects of "noted Fishing Places" upon red people; he simply drew an analogy between the two. Both violated the natural order.

Stuart's implication emerges clearly: the Indian was meant to be a wanderer and huntsman. A red man removed from his natural setting, by outside agency or by inclination, became a bastardized being.

Despite the seeming hopelessness involved in this reasoning, traders did express themselves as to the most efficacious ways of taming the American aborigine. There was, as Larpenteur put it, nothing like trying. Though seldom impressed favorably by the Indian, the trader nevertheless felt a compulsion to offer suggestions for avoiding his extinction.

In their recommendations, traders often revealed themselves as being more culturally tolerant than the society from which they came. They seem to have been less bent upon destroying the Indian's way so that he might more easily be molded in the white man's image. For example, many humane people within civilization urged that the Indian have the private property system imposed upon him. Fur traders seem never to have entertained such a notion. Rudolph Kurz went to the extreme in objecting to the fact that the Indian was damned for not accepting a pattern of life that was no more than a sham based on the dollar. Though traders rarely went that far, they did evidence a marked readiness to accommodate themselves to alien circumstances and to tolerate, if not accept, strange ways of doing things. Writing from Fort Garry in 1823, Donald Mackenzie gave this prescription for maintaining rapport with the heterogeneous society of the Red River settlements:

. . . with the Priests, we will hold discussions from the era of that directing old prototype . . . ever mindful of giving no kind of umbrage to their dearly beloved bigotry . . . ; with the Scotch and Irish, let us scour up our rusty Erse, and loudly extol that prince of old Fingal; with the French and the Swiss we will be frenchified, et vive la bagatelle; with the Canadians we can pass their voyages over again; with the Brules [métis] listen to their feats against the Sioux, and with the Indians you know, we shall be Indians still.[11]

Mackenzie's formula hardly equaled Polonius' advice to Laertes, as one writer suggested, but it did reflect tolerant good judgment.

Traders offered two positive proposals for transforming the Indian. The first and by far the less frequent stemmed from the assumption that trade was the natural instrument of civilization. By this conception the white man should expose the Indian to the greatest possible degree of trade activities. As the Indian participated, he would naturally assume a civilized conduct. Of the handful of men who counseled this approach, George Simpson had the greatest influence. However, Thomas Fitzpatrick, a mountain man turned Indian agent, expressed the theme most clearly and consistently. Trade, Fitzpatrick argued, would

. . . accustom them imperceptibly to those modes of life which can alone secure them from the miseries of penury. Trade is the only civilizer of the Indian. It has been the precursor of all civilization heretofore, and it will be of all hereafter. It teaches the value of other things besides the spoils of the chase and offers to him other pursuits and excitement than those of war.[12]

But Simpson and Fitzpatrick spoke for few traders. Alexander Ross expressed a far more typical view of the impact of trade when he wrote of the Indians: "They require but little, and the more they get of our manufacture the more unhappy will they be, as the possession of one article naturally creates a desire for another, so that they are never satisfied." [13] The vast preponderance of positive proposals for civilizing the Indian dealt with the necessity of turning him to agriculture. The Indian, by this view, could never learn another mode of existence as long as he continued to wander. He had to cease being a nomad for civilization to work its effect, and agriculture was the obvious sedentary pursuit for wilderness people. Occasionally, a trader in the warmer climates struck upon the perennial panacea of silk culture, while farther to the north traders advised less exotic agrarian pursuits. Whatever the form, the essence remained the same. The farm held out the only real hope for turning the Indian from his primitive ways.

Both of these positions, of course, have an element of paradox about them. The concept of trade runs counter to the strongly held belief that the Indian withered at the white man's touch. Considering their general toleration, if not liking, for the Indians, traders seemingly would not counsel subjecting the red race to contacts that would debase and destroy it. The contradiction begins to disappear when one focuses his attention upon the sources of the trade-as-civilizer concept. When Alexis Bailly of the Minnesota trade urged the establishment of a new government agency one hundred miles south of Fort Snelling, he used three arguments. First, and probably most compelling, the Indians of his area refused properly to recognize their obligations to Alexis Bailly—the present system, he noted, left "too much for Indian Honesty." Thereafter, he spoke of the mitigating effect that agents and traders would have upon the immensely bad relations between the Sioux and the Sac and Fox. And, though it hardly convinces modern readers, Bailly argued that putting traders among the natives gave them "an insight in agriculture   Softens their Manners & prepares them for Civilization." Men such as Bailly occasionally hinted in a rather left-handed fashion at this possibility for transforming the Indian, but only two men strongly and consistently advised it—Thomas Fitzpatrick and George Simpson. Both men held views which explain their maintaining a position that clashes with the general fur-trade consensus. Although not entirely consistent in it, both made unhurried, thoughtful, and mature expositions of the idea that Indians would soon cease to exist. Thus, considering the Indians doomed, these men could logically be unconcerned with their welfare. Other objectives could take precedence. When Fitzpatrick argued that there should be made "such modifications in the 'intercourse laws' as will invite the residence of traders amongst them, and *open the whole Indian territory to settlement*," one suspects that he had considerations in view other than, as he put it, "the improvement of the Indians." [14]

Fitzpatrick may have been loath to see the working out of the Indians' fate, and he may have felt reluctant to recommend a course of action that cynically took this fate into account. One rests assured, however, that George Simpson, whose sensibilities seem rarely to have extended to things beyond his person and the Hudson's Bay Company, suffered little mental anguish. Simpson once argued that Christian conversion would increase the Indians' consumption of trade goods and so ultimately benefit the company. The same reasoning held that the more dependent upon the trade the natives became, the better consumers they would be.[15] Feeling as he did about the imminence of the Indians' extinction and about the welfare of the Hudson's Bay Company, Simpson could reasonably have felt that the red men should be good consumers while they lasted. Thus, to advise the spread of trade among the Indians was only to operate in terms of the realities.

Similarly, the belief of those who advised turning the Indian to agriculture collided with the idea that the Indian's goodness, such as it was, inhered in a peculiar existence. Indeed, for all that traders argued the desirability of agriculture, they were aware that their insistence was paradoxical. Kit Carson, an especially vociferous proponent of farm life for the natives, unintentionally admitted the futility of such a plan when he urged the government to place troops over the tribes and force them to till the earth. Others conveyed their misgivings more openly. Thomas Simpson, for example, prefaced an argument questioning the possibility of turning the far North peoples to pastoral pursuits with the satiric but significant words, "It had, I understand, been sagely proposed by certain theorists. . . ." Even Alexander Ross ultimately despaired. He maintained a good deal of honest concern for the red men's future throughout his long fur-trade career, and in the first of his narratives he advocated agriculture as the means of civilizing the natives. In the last of his three books, however, he intimated that such a plan sprang from idle dreams. On the basis of knowledge of the experiments at Red River, he conceded that it was a terribly difficult task, "almost a hopeless one, to accustom the children of the wilderness to the use of the hoe, the spade, or the plough. . . ."[16]

The fur men's quandary becomes even more evident when it is recalled that they often scorned those Indians who engaged in sedentary rather than nomadic pursuits. Those who advised agriculture must certainly have seen the dilemma involved in proposals that would have had the Crows, the Sioux, or the Crees follow in the footsteps of the Arikaras or the Chinooks.

Actually, traders had little to offer in the way of positive proposals. In light of their general pessimism about the perpetuation of Indian society and their ambivalence in regard to the virtues and vices of primitive life, not to mention their own economic interests, they could hardly have had many suggestions that were worth while. The idea of trade as a civilizer was not widely accepted and was probably adopted with cynical fatalism by those who did express it. The farm as a hope for Indian perpetuation and civilization had a natural attractiveness, but traders could not maintain this position with anything resembling heartfelt consistency or conviction. Positive proposals simply did not accord with the traders' general fatalism in regard to the Indian. Even the most obvious and direct solution to the problem of the Indian and civilization—amalgamation—merited only extremely rare mention in fur-trade literature. Edwin Denig, father of a mixed-blood family, felt that it would be the logical answer, "if it were not for the popular prejudice. . . ." Aside from the odium of miscegenation, this answer fell short because it created half-breeds, the very epitomes of the debasing effect of white contact. Alexander Ross, whose book *The Red River Settlement* has more to say about this problem than any other one source, made the point nicely in his recommendations for the perpetuation of the red race. "Amalgamation deteriorates us," he wrote, "without improving them," and so he advised the placement of Indians fifty miles from whites. Among other advantages, there would be no intermingling and, thus, the natives "might still retain something of their native spirit and independence. . . ." [17]

Faced by such perplexities, traders turned to proposals that were negative rather than positive in nature, proposals which had the easier function of recommending what should not, rather than what should be done. The attitudes of traders toward Christianity as the implement of civilization demonstrates the negative nature of their approach to transforming the natives. These men were generally skeptical about the effect that religious tutelage would have. Indeed, they counseled its postponement until the Indians were more civilized, but they had few suggestions for achieving that civilized state.

Of course, it is not difficult to find sources which openly recommended the hasty conversion of the aborigines. In nearly all cases, however, factors obtrude which make these recommendations at best questionable. When the influential George Simpson, for example, assured his superiors of the success of the Christian efforts at Red River in the face of general opinion to the contrary, one suspects that his expression may have been influenced by the dictates of company policy. Business considerations probably demanded occasional lip-service to the aspiration of Christianizing the Indians. But traders could also arrive at that position through honest misunderstandings of Indian nature. Simpson here again seems to be a case in point. Like others, the Governor at times apparently mistook the red man's respectful and reverential treatment of all things religious and his materialistic desire for "good medicine" for an honest and reasoned desire for Christianity. Generally, the Indian showed tolerance and respect for the beliefs of others. Indeed, he had no qualms about accepting novel doctrines if they produced results. The men who knew the Indian best understood this blend of theological openmindedness and opportunism, but others did not. The less reliable the source, the less likely it is to show awareness of this reality. Thus, in the questionable recollections of Isaac Rose, the reader finds the Sioux listening with reverent awe to a sermon by Samuel Parker while, by contrast, the mountain men showed disinterest, even sarcasm and levity. According to Rose, the Indians' sober and engrossed attitude demonstrated their desire "to become acquainted with the mystery of the 'Unknown God.' " [18]

Far more typically, Peter Skene Ogden in his book on wilderness life related a didactic story regarding the Indian and Christianity. He told of a missionary's calling together his flock of tawny "communicants" for Sunday services. During the solemnities a young Indian obviously in the final stages of tuberculosis collapsed and expired. Before anyone could intervene, the brother of the deceased leaped up and cut off the head of an old woman who, he suspected, had caused his brother's death by occult means. The veteran brigade leader commented that such things occurred frequently among "these supposed converts to the merciful precepts of

Christianity.'' * Similar accounts appear with such prevalence in fur-trade literature as to take on the proportions of a genre. Even Robert Michael Ballantyne, whose youthful adventure stories provided excellent vehicles for moralizing, showed a slight but unseemly indecision. In one of his novels he staged a verbal encounter between an artist and a fur trader as to whether anything could alter "savage nature.'' The artist maintained the affirmative, insisting that Christianity had such power; the trader, though his "natural disposition was kind, hearty, and peaceable,'' held that all was futile. Though the outcome would seem to have been foregone and though the artist did get somewhat the better of his opposition, the argument really comes to no conclusion. Instead, it simply ends, and it does so with peculiarly unsatisfying prematurity. Earlier in the same work when Ballantyne had his characters debating the good life—civilization or savagery—he extricated them and himself from an impasse by having a flock of ducks explode into flight, thus disturbing the pastoral discourse. Perhaps the compulsion properly to inform young minds precluded such a contrived device where Christianity was concerned.[19]

Many traders clearly conveyed the hopelessness of Christian indoctrination for the red men; and at face value that is what Peter Skene Ogden did in the illustration above. In essence, however, he argued not for the abandonment of such efforts but for a realistic caution and moderation, for an awareness of the difficulties involved, and for a delay in full-scale exertions to bring the Indians under the sway of the white man's religion. He cited the sanguinary incident, he explained, "to show how mistaken are the views of those benevolent enthusiasts, who are prone to exaggerate the most distant

* [Peter Skene Ogden], *Traits of American Indian Life & Character By a Fur Trader* (modern ed.; San Francisco, Calif., 1933), pp. 84–85. Ogden noted in this context that, for their belief in sorcery, the Indians were "less to be ridiculed and blamed than our own countrymen of a past generation, whose infatuated belief in the worst horrors of witchcraft led them into excesses ten times more horrible than this unprovoked murder. And surely when these deeds come eventually to be judged at that tribunal where we must all appear, the irregular impulse of the savage breast will plead for extenuation far more efficaciously than the systematic barbarities of those blind credulists . . .'' (p. 85).

shadow of success into the fullest confirmation of all the most sanguine hopes that may be entertained by their supporters.''[20]

In a day when the word ''enthusiasm'' carried the weight of stricture, Ogden may have been severe, but, according to general fur-trade opinion, civilized people operated from a gross misconception about the impact of Christianity upon the aborigines. This fallacy held that the Indian sincerely welcomed the white man's religion and that it quickly and beneficently transformed him. In the first of his published works Alexander Ross effectively described the forwarding of this fond but unfounded belief:

The pious and charitable world contribute with a liberal hand; the missionary is sent out to the wilderness to instruct and convert the heathen . . . the young and the old are catechised, baptism is administered and the sacrament of the Lord's Supper follows. . . . But this is not all: the missionary's journal goes home, more labourers are required for the vineyard, periodicals circulate the marvellous success, and all the world, except those on the spot, believe the report. . . . These reports are no sooner laid before the public, than a pious interest is again excited. . . . Other missionaries are sent forth, who to prove their own zeal and success, heighten if possible the colouring of the former picture, by the addition of still more marvellous reports. . . . Yet the picture is delusive: the savage is still a savage. . . .

According to Thomas Fitzpatrick, reports such as those described by Ross were not only wrong, they were detrimental as well. No single thing except the extreme forbearance shown the Indians did more to prejudice their real welfare than the ''erroneous opinion . . . that nothing but the introduction of Christianity was wanting to make them happy and prosperous.''[21]

In the context of condolences sent to a comrade who had lost a child, a grim John Work pointed to the solace of true, heartfelt religion. By contrast, he mentioned the ''professional religion'' which was being brought into the Columbia River area. It reeked of ostentation, he grumbled, it was too ''puritannical,'' and, most importantly, it seemed to be doing little good—cases of ''venery'' being as frequent as ever. When Martin McLeod took umbrage at what he considered a gratuitous slur on traders passed by a missionary, he went even further and openly called religion to account. By whose reading of Christianity were men of the cloth authorized to defame the traders before their Indians? "Was it," McLeod asked with evident sarcasm, "to instill such charitable views [that] Missionaries have been sent among them and is it to teach them 'Peace and good will to all men' [?]" McLeod, who read the Bible for its historical content, appears singular in taking the quarrel to religion. Many traders, however, suspected and intimated that religion had an adverse effect upon the natives. Not only the popular misconception about its impact, but the institution itself was either harmful or of questionable value.[22]

McLeod's contemporary in the Minnesota trade, Alexis Bailly, noted in one of his acerbic, random jottings that "Religious societies have done no good in this country." And indeed, judging from affairs at Green Bay, they only hastened red degradation. If the consequence of civilized contact was bad, it could hardly be expected that the effect of one of its major institutions would be otherwise. In an early letter George Simpson broached the subject with the misanthropic observation that Christian training did little beyond filling "the pockets and bellies of some hungry missionaries and schoolmasters and rearing the Indians in habits of indolence." To justify this testy remark he relied upon the ever-present formula for illuminating the effects of white contact upon the natives—Bailly saw Indians acquiring "the vices of Civilization without any of its morals." "They not only pick up the vices of the Whites upon which they improve," Simpson wrote, "but retain those of the Indian in their utmost extent." Simpson, of course, expressed himself far differently later in his career, but his early analysis would have found favor with many. Even Alexander Ross, a devout man with great sympathy for the aborigines, seemed to conclude in the last of his fur-trade narratives that Christianity's effect upon the Indians was less than salutary. In a discussion of the endeavors of the Red River missionaries, Ross, who worked with the Swampy Crees, chronicled the deterioration in condition of the Swampies from "docile and teachable" to "saucy, tricky and dishonest."[23]

In addition to the noneffect or ill effect of Christianity, experienced traders harbored another conviction that dampened their enthusiasm for converting the Indians. Being creatures of self-interest, the natives often approached religion in a thoroughly pragmatic fashion. According to traders, they considered the missionary's bestowal of Christian blessings as tantamount to success in field and battle. When given the acid test and found lacking, Christianity lost its attraction and the missionary appeared as an impotent herald of a meaningless creed. The Indians then eschewed Christianity and reverted to their traditional beliefs. To compound their distrust, traders often suspected that the natives cynically maintained a reverential appearance in the hope of material rewards. A trader at Churchill, for example, complained that conversion gave the Indians ample justification to ''trifle away their time in singing & preaching'' when they should have been providing for impoverished families. Alexander Ross wrote of this failing with regretful understanding:

When a savage is offered at once food and truth, —both or neither, —he is at least as ready as civilized men, whether laity or clergy, have often been, to take the one for the sake of the other; in fact, he is strongly tempted to consider what he calls "praying" as something that makes the pot boil.[24]

To be sure, traders did not universally ascribe the Indians' religious practices to a materialistically motivated effort to enlist the forces of nature or the supernatural for their own ends. Indeed, some traders respected the spiritual aspects of native life. Because he consistently and convincingly maintained the self-serving nature of Indian actions, Edwin Denig serves as a good illustration. He, like others, attested to the opportunistic way in which Indians received the white man's faith. He recognized, however, that the Indian's observation of his *own* religion was ethically praiseworthy. As a matter of preference, Denig chose the native over the ignorant white, and part of his reason lay in Indian ''superstitions and religion.'' In these, he insisted, one could find a

. . . grand chain of thought, having for its conclusion the existence of a Supreme Power, much more satisfactory and sublime in the aggregate than the mixture of bigotry, infidelity, enthusiasm, and profanity observed in the actions and language of the lower class of Christians.

Warming to his subject, Denig compared the Indian to the only lower-class Christian at hand—the *engagee*. The Indian emerged far superior. The red man, according to the Fort Union trader,

> . . . reverences his unknown God in his way. Though the principle be fear and the object Creation, it leads to reliance and resignation when his own resources fail, whereas the whites spoken of vent their displeasure for the most trifling grievances and accidents in eternal curses on the Great Disposer, the Virgin Mary, and all other holy persons and objects they deem worthy of their execration.

Coming from a man who interpreted Indian actions in terms of self-interestedness, this represents no small praise. The clause, "though the principle be fear and the object Creation," indicates that Denig had not abandoned his favorite thesis. He candidly admitted, however, that Indian religion had exalted and praiseworthy aspects. Here as elsewhere, traders apparently saw civilization debasing the Indian. The crass and venal aspects of the red man's approach to religion came out, not so much when he observed his own forms as when he gave in to the lure of the white man's way.[25]

The upshot of all such reservations about the desirability and possibility of Christian conversion was that the Indian had to be civilized before he could be Christianized. Alexander Ross spoke for traders generally when he argued that temporal and spiritual enlightenment should be united. Indeed, the former should take precedence. To the missionary's insistence that the holy word could not wait, Ross replied, " 'To everything there is a season. . . .' " This argument, of course, contains some faulty logic because traders lacked any positive proposals for civilizing the aborigines and in many cases despaired of its ever being done. The inconsistency comes out boldly in the memoirs of Charles Larpenteur. In light of his argument that the Indian would cease to exist, his advice to postpone religion and education seems a patent *non sequitur*. If George Simpson were making this argument, one could rightfully suspect an ulterior motive in the form of economic consideration. Considering the more typical expressions of such men as Larpenteur, Alexander Ross, Edwin Denig, or Peter Skene Ogden, however, the suspicion seems unjustified. They wrote in the twilight of personal careers and of the fur-trade era, and apparently stood to lose little, whatever the fate of the trade. Moreover, they exhibited a good deal of honest sympathy for the Indians. When filling out the governmental form devised by Henry Rowe Schoolcraft, Denig made a revealing comment on his motivation and, quite likely, that of many of his fellows in the trade. On the form he saw the following caveat, which apparently was not meant for his perusal: " 'In all questions where the interests of the tribes clash with those of the persons whom you may consult, there is much caution required.' " Denig conceded that the interests of traders were opposed to innovations; indeed, innovations would ruin the trade. Nevertheless, he wrote, "we prefer placing things in their proper light, aiming at general good, and thus without further comment the whole is left in the hands of those for whom it is intended." Thus, the defective reasoning of a Charles Larpenteur may have sprung not so much from pursuance of self-interest as from a clash between ideals proposed by others and what to traders seemed the realities.[26]

Finally, fur traders showed their basically negative attitude in their occasional proposals that the Indian had to be civilized away from civilization. After Kit Carson became a government Indian agent, he counseled this approach. He did not argue for the perpetuation of islands of savagery, but did insist that the natives should be transformed in isolation. Prostitution, drunkenness, and other vices had not yet blighted the Indians with whom he dealt, and thus his proposal represented an uneasy peace between civilization's demands upon the wilderness and the fur-trade consensus that civilization would destroy the Indian. "Humanity, as well as our desire to benefit the Indian race," he wrote, "demands that they be removed as far as practicable from the settlements." [27]

While Carson and others maintained this hedged and inconsistent position, some traders gloried in a more pleasing prospect. They did not plead with civilization to allow the primitives the temporal and physical range in which to conform to the sweep of progress.

Instead, they foretold that Indians, at least some of them, would find a haven. On a trip northward from the Missouri to the Mouse River, Henry Boller sensed so strongly the "barrenness and desolation" of the countryside that he doubted that civilization could advance into it. Similarly, Robert Stuart in 1841 anticipated Daniel Webster on the imminent close of slavery's expansion as it approached the plains. The "endless naked waste" stretching to the Rockies would effectually thwart the westward course of American society, thus guaranteeing a future for at least part of the red race. David Thompson dwelt on the theme even more fully. Although he accepted the apparent reality that wherever the white man touched the Indian, the Indian was doomed, Thompson, with not always reliable foresight, predicted that some regions would be left untouched. From his knowledge of what is now North Dakota, Thompson reasoned that "these great Plains appear to be given by Providence to the Red Men for ever, as the wilds and sands of Africa are given to the Arabians." He took a similar view of the vastness of northern Canada, another area which, he supposed, would be left undefiled. The "Supreme Being," Thompson maintained, had given this expanse, like the Great Plains, "to the Deer, and other wild animals; and to the Red Man forever, here, as his fathers of many centuries past have done, he may roam, free as the wind. . . ."[28]

The basic sentiment, if not the consistent overt expression, of fur-trade attitudes toward the Indian appears here in Thompson's forecast. One need do no violence to his logic to infer a certain kinship between "the Deer," the "other wild animals," and the "Red Man." Given a respite from the sweep of progress, they could go on existing. The Indian was not meant to live as the white man did. With resignation and regret Thompson, a pious man, noted that the Indians who continued to exist beyond the reach of the white man could never, by the nature of their circumstances, be imbued with the "sacred truths of Christianity." Indeed, civilized life itself was denied them.[29]

Civilization, in the traders' view, ran against the grain of Indian nature. Indeed, the Indian in many cases remained convinced that his existence was superior to that of the white man. Comments appear frequently in the literature of the trade in regard to the natives' tendency to look down upon the whites. In a typical case Charles MacKenzie presented Missouri River Indians arguing that, " 'White people do not know how to live, they leave their houses in small parties, they risk their lives on the great waters, among strange nations, who will take them for enemies. What is the use of beaver? Do they make gunpowder of them? Do they preserve them from sickness? Do they serve them beyond the grave?' " When told that some Indians cooperated by exerting themselves in search of furs, they retorted tersely: " 'We are no Slaves!' " [30]

Traders viewed tolerantly the red man's claim to superiority. Evidently they recognized elements of truth in the primitive's criticism of the white man's ways. Traders knew that their own lives were filled with drudgery, hardship, and danger. Peter Skene Ogden must have spoken for many when he complained that "a Porter in London is a King in comparison with me. . . ." Most of them could probably have sympathized if not agreed with the words of the not yet famous Sitting Bull, whose observations on civilization and savagery Charles Larpenteur recorded. In his statement the Hunkpapa Sioux conveyed what the trader considered to be the solitary Indian virtue of dignity, and what he saw as the utter hopelessness of the red man's position vis-à-vis civilization. After urging his fellows to withdraw to the ways of their ancestors, the young Indian leader declared: " 'I don't want to have anything to do with people who make one carry water on the shoulders and haul manure. . . . The whites may get me at last, but I will have good times till then. You are fools to make yourselves slaves to a piece of fat bacon, some hard-tack, and a little sugar and coffee.' " Larpenteur ended his memoirs with the recalcitrant Sioux's defiant and prophetic statement. It served well as the finale of a book; it could serve equally well as the epitaph for a people and as the motif of fur-trade attitudes toward them. [31]

NOTES

INTRODUCTION

1. Fred A. Crane, "The Noble Savage in America, 1815–1860: Concepts of the Indian, with Special Reference to the Writers of the Northeast" (Ph.D. dissertation, Yale University, 1952), p. 382.

2. Daniel Boorstin, "Editor's Preface" in William T. Hagan, *American Indians* (Chicago, 1961), p. vii.

3. Bernard DeVoto, "Joseph Kinsey Howard" in Joseph Kinsey Howard, *Strange Empire: A Narrative of the Northwest* (New York, 1952), pp. 8–9.

4. Howard Peckham, "Indian Relations in the United States" in John Francis McDermott (ed.), *Research Opportunities in American Cultural History* (Lexington, Ky., 1961), p. 32.

5. Henry H. Sibley Papers (MSS in the Minnesota Historical Society, St. Paul), Incidents of Indian Warfare.

6. John C. Ewers (ed.), Edwin Thompson Denig's *Five Indian Tribes of the Upper Missouri: Sioux, Arickaras, Assiniboines, Crees, Crows* (Norman, Okla., 1961), pp. xxx-xxxi.

CHAPTER 1

1. Francis Paul Prucha, *American Indian Policy in the Formative Years: The Indian Trade and Intercourse Acts 1790–1834* (Cambridge, Mass., 1962), pp. 71–73.

2. James McKay [*sic*] to John Evans, Jan. 28, 1796, in A. P. Nasitir (ed.), *Before Lewis and Clark: Documents Illustrating the History of the Missouri 1785–1804* (St. Louis, Mo., 1952), II, 412.

3. J. N. B. Hewitt (ed.), "Journal of Rudolph Friederich Kurz . . . ," trans. Myrtis Jarrell, *Bureau of American Ethnology Bulletin*, CXV (1937), 205; Anne McDonnell (ed.), "Original Journal of James H. Chambers, Fort Sarpy," *Contributions to the Historical Society of Montana*, X (1940), 115–16.

4. Lewis H. Garrard, *Wah-To-Yah and The Taos Trail . . .* (Norman, Okla., 1955), pp. 88–89; cited in LeRoy R. Hafen and W. J. Ghent,

Broken Hand: The Life Story of Thomas Fitzpatrick, Chief of the Mountain Men (Denver, Colo., 1931), p. 225; cited in introduction to James F. Kenney (ed.), *The Founding of Churchill: Being the Journal of Captain James Knight* . . . (Toronto, Ont., 1932), pp. 69–71.

5. Frederick Jackson Turner, *The Frontier in American History* (New York, 1920), p. 4; Louis B. Wright, *Culture on the Moving Frontier* (Bloomington, Ind., 1955), p. 11; W. F. Wentzel to Roderic McKenzie, April 30, 1811, in L. R. Masson, *Les bourgeois de la Compagnie du Nord-Ouest, recits de voyages, lettres et rapports inédits relatifs au nord-ouest Canadien* . . . (New York, 1960), I, 108; William G. and George W. Ewing Papers (MSS in the Indiana State Library, Indianapolis), *On the Indian Trade* By a Backwoodsman (Washington, D.C., February, 1821), twelve-page pamphlet; Theodore C. Blegen (ed.), *The Unfinished Autobiography of Henry Hastings Sibley Together with a Selection of Hitherto Unpublished Letters from the Thirties* (Minneapolis, Minn., 1932), p. 15.

6. Documents Historiques années 1818–1866 (MSS in the Archdiocesan Archives, Archbishop's Residence, St. Boniface, Manitoba), Alexander Fisher to Henry Fisher, March 15, 1832; Alexander Fisher to Henry Fisher, March 15, 1833; Alexander Fisher to Henry Fisher, March 15, 1837; American Fur Company Papers (MSS in the New York Historical Society Library, microfilm copy in the Missouri Historical Society, St. Louis), Charles W. Borup to Ramsay Crooks, May 20, 1840.

7. William Edgar Papers (MSS in the New York Public Library, photocopy in the Burton Historical Collection, Detroit Public Library, Detroit), Fr. Hambach to Edgar, Nov. 2, 1766; Grace Lee Nute (ed.), "The Diary of Martin McLeod," *Minnesota Historical Bulletin,* IV (1921–22), 422–23.

8. Nute (ed.), "Diary of McLeod," pp. 361, 366, 423–29; Martin McLeod Papers (MSS in the Minnesota Historical Society, St. Paul), McLeod's memorandum book of 1841, 1842, and 1843.

9. American Fur Company Papers, Ramsay Crooks to the editor of the *Catholic Herald,* Philadelphia, March 30, 1839; Henry H. Sibley to Ramsay Crooks, Jan. 10, 1840; Annie Heloise Abel (ed.), *Chardon's Journal at Fort Clark 1834–1839* . . . (Pierre, S.D., 1932), p. 51. See Laurence Sterne, *A Sentimental Journey Through France and Italy* (chapter titled "The Passport   The Hotel at Paris"); John Askin Papers (MSS in the Burton Historical Collection, Detroit Public Library, Detroit), diary, history notes, and essays of Hugh Heward.

10. Frederick Merk (ed.), *Fur Trade and Empire: George Simpson's Journal.* . . . (Cambridge, Mass., 1931), p. xix; E. E. Rich (ed.), *Journal of Occurrences in the Athabasca Department By George Simpson, 1820 and 1821, And Report* (Toronto, Ont., 1938), p. 122.

11. Douglas McKay, "Men of the Old Fur Trade: Peter Skene Ogden," *The Beaver: A Magazine of the North*, Outfit 269 (June, 1938), no. 1, pp. 7–9.

12. Peter Garrioch Collection (MSS in the Public Archives of Manitoba, Winnipeg), Peter Garrioch's Journal of a Trip from Red River Settlement to St. Peter's Minn., and on to Prairie du Chien, 1837–1838 (edited typescript by George H. Gunn); Hewitt (ed.), "Journal of Kurz," pp. 166–67, 180.

13. McDonnell (ed.), "Journal of Chambers," pp. 100, 101, 102–3.

14. Edgar Papers, William Maxwell to Edgar, May 26, 1772.

15. Robert Stuart to Mary (his daughter), March 25, 1848, in Helen Stuart Mackay-Smith Marlatt (ed.), *Stuart Letters of Robert and Elizabeth Sullivan Stuart and their Children 1819–1864, With an Undated Letter Prior to July 21, 1813* (n.p., 1961), I, 60; Garrioch Collection, Peter Garrioch Diary, 1843-47.

16. Rich (ed.), *Journal of Occurrences in the Athabasca Department*, p. 356.

17. Hugh MacLennan, "By Canoe to Empire," *American Heritage*, XII (October, 1961), 99; Malcolm McLeod (ed.), *Peace River. A Canoe Voyage from Hudson's Bay to Pacific, by the Late Sir George Simpson in 1828 Journal of the late Chief Factor, Archibald McDonald, who accompanied him* (Ottawa, Ont., 1872), p. 16; George Bryce, *The Remarkable History of the Hudson's Bay Company . . .* (London, 1902), p. 280; in the concluding paragraph of a biographical work, Arthur S. Morton pictured the Governor as "a man of feeling, whose words seldom revealed him." However, according to Morton, "his deeds did." *Sir George Simpson, Overseas Governor of the Hudson's Bay Company: A Pen Picture of a Man of Action* (Portland, Ore., 1944), p. 273. The import of this closing observation is not entirely borne out by the pages which precede it.

18. See Milo Milton Quaife (ed.), Charles Larpenteur's *Forty Years a Fur Trader on the Upper Missouri* (Chicago, 1933), pp. 156–57, 170–71. Of course, beyond the probability that he was a teetotaler, Larpenteur's motivation in making such accusations, as well as his accuracy, is difficult to ascertain; R. M. Patterson, "Introduction" in E. E. Rich (ed.), *A Journal of A Voyage from Rocky Mountain Portage in Peace River to the Sources of Finlays Branch and North West Ward in Summer 1824 (By Samuel Black)* (London, 1955), pp. xix, xliii.

19. American Fur Company Papers, Robert Stuart to Ramsay Crooks, Jan. 25, 1824; John C. Ewers (ed.), Edwin Thompson Denig's *Five Indian Tribes of the Upper Missouri: Sioux, Arickaras, Assiniboines, Crees, Crows* (Norman, Okla., 1961), p. xxxi; Edward Umfreville, *The*

Present State of Hudson's Bay. Containing a Full Description of that Settlement, and the Adjacent Country; and Likewise of the Fur Trade . . . (London, 1790), p. 176; Askin Papers, John Askin Diary 1774–75; Ewing Papers, W. G. Ewing to Hon. Wm. C. Linton [?], April 2, 1833, Letterbook 1830–37.

20. American Fur Company Papers, Robert Stuart to John Lawe, Nov. 7, 1824; McLeod Papers, McLeod to Rev. Mr. Potter, missionary, Sept. 25, 1849. This document evidently is a rough draft.

21. Meridel Le Suer, "The First Farmers' Revolt," *Mainstream,* XV (March, 1962), 21–26; [Peter Skene Ogden], *Traits of American Indian Life & Character By A Fur Trader* (modern ed.; San Francisco, Calif., 1933), p. 3.

22. John Porteous Papers (MSS in the Burton Historical Collection, Detroit Public Library, Detroit), John Porteous to James Porteous, n.d. [1762]; William Woodbridge Papers (MSS in the Burton Historical Collection, Detroit Public Library, Detroit), Robert Stuart to Woodbridge, Feb. 26, 1841; Robert Stuart to Woodbridge, June 3, 1841; Robert Stuart to Woodbridge, June 29, 1841.

23. T. C. Elliott (ed.), "Letter of Donald Mackenzie to Wilson Price Hunt" (July 30, 1822), *Oregon Historical Quarterly,* XLIII (September, 1942), 197; W. S. Wallace (ed.), John McLean's *Notes of a Twenty-five Years' Service in the Hudson's Bay Territory* (Toronto, Ont., 1932), p. xxvii; Isaac Cowie, *The Company of Adventurers: A Narrative of Seven Years in the Service of the Hudson's Bay Company During 1867–1874 on the Great Buffalo Plains* (Toronto, Ont., 1913), pp. 227–30; Roderic McKenzie Papers (MSS in the Masson Papers, McGill University, Montreal, photocopy in the Minnesota Historical Society, St. Paul), printed circular.

24. Dousman Papers (MSS in the Ayer Collection, Newberry Library, Chicago), George Davenport to O. N. Bostwick, Sept. 9, 1824; "The Diary of Hugh Faries" in Charles M. Gates (ed.), *Five Fur Traders of the Northwest: Being the Narrative of Peter Pond and the Diaries of John McDonell, Archibald N. McLeod, Hugh Faries and Thomas Connor* (Minneapolis, Minn., 1933), p. 200; Abel (ed.), *Chardon's Journal,* p. 60.

25. Alexander Mackenzie, *Voyages from Montreal on the River St. Laurence* [sic], *through the Continent of North-America, to the Frozen and Pacific Oceans* . . . (3rd American ed.; New York, 1803), p. viii; Percy G. Adams, *Travelers and Travel Liars, 1660–1800* (Los Angeles, Calif., 1962), pp. 228–29; [Ogden], *Traits of American Indian Life,* p. 91.

26. Elliott Coues (ed.), *New Light on the Early History of the Greater Northwest: The Manuscript Journals of Alexander Henry and of David Thompson* (New York, 1897), II, 749; J. B. Tyrrell (ed.), *David*

Thompson's Narrative of his Explorations in Western America 1784–1813 (Toronto, Ont., 1916), p. 507; Philip Ashton Rollins (ed.), *The Discovery of the Oregon Trail: Robert Stuart's Narratives of His Overland Trip Eastward From Astoria in 1812–13.* . . . (New York, 1935), p. 15; Ross Cox, *The Columbia River; or, Scenes and Adventures During a Residence of Six Years on the Western Side of the Rocky Mountains* . . . (3rd ed.; London, 1832), I, 102–3.

27. Alexander Ross, *Adventures of the First Settlers on the Oregon or Columbia River: Being a Narrative of the Expedition Fitted out by John Jacob Astor* . . . (London, 1849), p. 91; J. V. Huntington (trans. and ed.), Gabriel Franchère's *Narrative of a Voyage to the Northwest Coast of America in the Years 1811, 1812, 1813, and 1814 or the First American Settlement on the Pacific* (New York, 1854), p. 243.

28. Adams, *Travelers and Travel Liars* (see especially chapter VIII); John Dunn, *The Oregon Territory, and the British North American Fur Trade. With an Account of the Habits and Customs of the Principal Native Tribes on the Northern Continent* (Philadelphia, 1845); Umfreville, *The Present State of Hudson's Bay,* pp. 63–64. Compare this with E. E. Rich (ed.), *James Isham's Observations on Hudson's Bay, 1743 and Notes and Observations on a Book Entitled "A Voyage to Hudsons Bay in the Dobbs Galley, 1749"* (Toronto, Ont., 1949), pp. 85–86. An astounding case of coincidence could also account for the similarity, as could the possibility that trader-Indian discussions were amazingly typed and restricted.

29. Alexander Henry, *Travels and Adventures in Canada and The Indian Territories between the Years 1760 and 1776* (New York, 1809), p. 97; Milo Milton Quaife (ed.), Alexander Henry's *Travels and Adventures* (Chicago, 1921), p. xii; Reuben Gold Thwaites (ed.), John Long's *Voyages and Travels of an Indian Interpreter and Trader* . . . (Cleveland, Ohio, 1904), pp. 198, 199; R. W. G. Vail, *The Voice of the Old Frontier* (Philadelphia, 1949), p. 365.

30. John C. Ewers (ed.), *Adventures of Zenas Leonard Fur Trader* (Norman, Okla., 1959), p. 37.

31. William Goetzmann, "The Mountain Man as Jacksonian Man," *American Quarterly,* XV (Fall, 1963), 402–15.

CHAPTER 2

1. Fur Trade Collection (MSS in the Public Archives of Manitoba, Winnipeg), Journal of Occurrences at Fort William, Dec. 2, 1830, to June 4, 1831.

2. Henry H. Sibley Papers (MSS in the Minnesota Historical Society, St. Paul), William Aitkin to Sibley, January, 1837; Dorothy O. Johansen

(ed.), *Robert Newell's Memoranda: Travles in the Teritory of Missourie; Travle to the Kayuse War; together with A Report on the Indians South of the Columbia River* (Portland, Ore., 1959), p. 6.

3. George Simpson, *Narrative of a Journey Round the World During the Years 1841 and 1842* (London, 1847), II, 433.

4. James McKenzie, "The King's Posts and Journal of a Canoe Jaunt through the King's Domains, 1808" in L. R. Masson, *Les bourgeois de la Compagnie du Nord-Ouest, recits de voyages, lettres et rapports inédits relatifs au nord-ouest Canadien. . . .* (New York, 1960), II, 411.

5. Duncan Cameron, "The Nipigon Country, 1804—With Extracts from His Journal" in Masson, *Les bourgeois*, II, 242; Thomas Simpson, *Narrative of the Discoveries on the North Coast of America; Effected by the Officers of the Hudson's Bay Company During the Years 1836–39* (London, 1843), p. 347; J. B. Tyrrell (ed.), *David Thompson's Narrative of his Explorations in Western America, 1784–1813* (Toronto, Ont., 1916), p. 22; W. S. Wallace (ed.), *John McLean's Notes of a Twenty-five Years' Service in the Hudson's Bay Territory* (Toronto, Ont., 1932), pp. 266–67.

6. "Memoir Accompanying Pond's Map in the British Museum" in Gordon Charles Davidson, *The North West Company* (Berkeley, Calif., 1918), pp. 259–66; Roderic McKenzie Papers (MSS in Series M., Public Archives of Canada, Ottawa; photocopy in the Minnesota Historical Society, St. Paul), Roderic McKenzie, Some Account of the Northwest company containing analogy of nations ancient and modern.

7. Clark Collection (MSS in the Missouri Historical Society, St. Louis), James Mackay, Notes on Indian Tribes.

8. *Ibid.*

9. Henry R. Schoolcraft, *Historical and Statistical Information Respecting the History, Condition and Prospects of the Indian Tribes of the United States . . .* (Philadelphia, 1851–57), I, 261–62.

10. James Adair, *The History of the American Indians; Particularly Those Nations adjoining to the Mississippi, East and West Florida, Georgia, South and North Carolina, and Virginia . . .* (London, 1775), pp. 5, 307–8.

11. J. B. Tyrrell (ed.), *Journals of Samuel Hearne and Philip Turnor* (Toronto, Ont., 1934), p. 458.

12. Rufus Sage, *Rocky Mountain Life; or, Startling Scenes and Perilous Adventures in the Far West* (Boston, 1880), p. 230. Sage's work was first published in 1846 under a somewhat less lurid title; Tyrrell (ed.), *David Thompson's Narrative*, p. 80.

13. Simpson, *Narrative of a Journey Round the World*, I, 251–52.

14. Abert Papers (MSS in the Missouri Historical Society, St. Louis), Thomas Fitzpatrick to Lieut. J. W. Abbert [Abert], Feb. 5, 1846; Bernard

R. Ross, William L. Hardisty, and Strachan Jones, "Notes on the Tinneh or Chepewyan Indians of British and Russian America," *Smithsonian Institution Annual Report* (1866), p. 315.

15. Philip Ashton Rollins (ed.), *The Discovery of the Oregon Trail: Robert Stuart's Narratives of His Overland Trip Eastward From Astoria in 1812–13. . . .* (New York, 1935), p. 12.

16. T. C. Elliott (ed.), "Journal of David Thompson," part one, *Oregon Historical Society Quarterly*, XV (March, 1914), 52–61.

17. Kenneth Spaulding (ed.), Alexander Ross's *The Fur Hunters of the Far West* (Norman, Okla., 1956), p. 166; Ross Cox, *The Columbia River; or, Scenes and Adventures During a Residence of Six Years on the Western Side of the Rocky Mountains . . .* (3rd ed.; London, 1832), I, 122–23; II, 118; J. V. Huntington (trans. and ed.), Gabriel Franchère's *Narrative of a Voyage to the Northwest Coast of America in the Years 1811, 1812, 1813 and 1814 or the First American Settlement on the Pacific* (New York, 1854), p. 268; Arthur T. Adams (ed.), *The Explorations of Pierre Esprit Radisson* (Minneapolis, Minn., 1961), p. 144.

18. J. N. B. Hewitt (ed.), Edwin Thompson Denig's "Indian Tribes of the Upper Missouri," *Bureau of American Ethnology Forty-sixth Annual Report* (1928–29), p. 406; Tyrrell (ed.), *David Thompson's Narrative*, pp. 345–46; Bernard DeVoto, *The Course of Empire* (Boston, 1952), p. 247; Peter Pond, "Narrative" in Charles M. Gates (ed.), *Five Fur Traders of the Northwest: Being the Narrative of Peter Pond and the Diaries of John McDonell, Archibald N. McLeod, Hugh Faries and Thomas Connor* (Minneapolis, Minn., 1933), p. 58; Rollins (ed.), *Robert Stuart's Narratives*, p. 12; Alexander Ross, *Adventures of the First Settlers on the Oregon or Columbia River: Being a Narrative of the Expedition Fitted out by John Jacob Astor . . .* (London, 1849), p. 223.

19. Cited in E. E. Rich (ed.), *James Isham's Observations on Hudson's Bay, 1743 and Notes and Observations on a Book Entitled "A Voyage to Hudsons Bay in the Dobbs Galley, 1749"* (Toronto, Ont., 1949), p. xl; Wallace (ed.), McLean's *Notes,* p. 135.

20. Frederick Merk (ed.), *Fur Trade and Empire: George Simpson's Journal . . .* (Cambridge, Mass., 1931), xxxi–xxxiv.

21. Stella M. Drumm (ed.), John C. Luttig's *Journal of a Fur-Trading Expedition on the Upper Missouri 1812–1813* (St. Louis, Mo., 1920), pp. 85–86; Annie Heloise Abel (ed.), *Chardon's Journal at Fort Clark 1834–1839 . . .* (Pierre, S.D., 1932), p. 97; Elliott Coues (ed.), *New Light on the Early History of the Greater Northwest: The Manuscript Journals of Alexander Henry and of David Thompson* (New York, 1897), I, 238–39, 243.

22. James McKenzie, "Extracts from his Journal, 1799–1800" in

Masson, *Les bourgeois,* II, 381; Abel (ed.), *Chardon's Journal,* p. 7; William Edgar Papers (MSS in the Burton Historical Collection, Detroit Public Library, Detroit), Isaac Todd to Edgar, June 20, 1770; Francois-Victor Malhiot "Journal du Fort Kamanaitiquoya a la Rivière Montréal, 1804–1805" in Masson, *Les bourgeois,* I, 254.

23. Masson, *Les bourgeois,* I, 225; Henry H. Sibley Papers (MSS in the Minnesota Historical Society, St. Paul), Grand Portage Letter Book and Account Book 1823–24.

24. T. C. Elliott (ed.), "Journal of Peter Skene Ogden; Snake Expedition, 1827–1828," *Oregon Historical Society Quarterly,* XI (December, 1910), 370.

25. John Thomas to William Bolland, Aug. 3, 1785; John Thomas to Edward Jarvis, Aug. 9, 1785, in E. E. Rich (ed.), *Moose Fort Journals, 1783–85* (London, 1954), pp. 316, 318.

26. G. P. deT. Glazebrook, "Introduction," in *ibid.,* p. xiv.

27. Edward Jarvis to John Thomas, June 27, 1784, in *ibid.,* p. 208; Fur Trade Collection (MSS in the Public Archives of Manitoba, Winnipeg), Journal of Transactions and Occurrences at Fort William, Dec. 23, 1838, to Jan. 30, 1840.

28. John Lawe Papers (MSS in the Chicago Historical Society, Chicago), Lawe to Major Brevoort, Sept. 17, 1828; Wallace (ed.), *McLean's Notes,* p. 64; J. L. Lewes to James Hargrave, April 1, 1843, in G. P. deT. Glazebrook (ed.), *The Hargrave Correspondence, 1821–1843* (Toronto, Ont., 1938), p. 430; K. G. Davies (ed.), *Peter Skene Ogden's Snake Country Journal, 1826–27* (London, 1961), p. 102; Anne McDonnell (ed.), "Original Journal of James H. Chambers, Fort Sarpy," *Contributions to the Historical Society of Montana,* X (1940), 100.

29. Sibley Papers, Ramsay Crooks to Sibley, Oct. 13, 1837; Lawe Papers, Ramsay Crooks to Lawe, Feb. 6, 1835; Pierre Menard Papers (MSS in the Illinois Historical Survey of the University of Illinois, Urbana), Menard to E. K. Kane, Dec. 8, 1830.

CHAPTER 3

1. [Peter Skene Ogden], *Traits of American Indian Life & Character By a Fur Trader* (modern ed.; San Francisco, Calif., 1933), p. 38.

2. [Duncan M'Gillivray], "Some Account of the Trade Carried on by the North West Company," Dominion of Canada, *Report of the Public Archives for the Year 1928,* p. 68; Arthur S. Morton (ed.), *The Journal of Duncan M'Gillivray of the North West Company at Fort George on the Saskatchewan, 1794–5* (Toronto, Ont., 1929), p. 53; Edward Umfreville, *The Present State of Hudson's Bay. Containing a Full Description of that Settlement, and the Adjacent Country; and Likewise of the Fur Trade. . . .* (London, 1790), pp. 198–99.

3. Chouteau Collections (MSS in the Missouri Historical Society, St. Louis), Daniel Lamont to Pierre Chouteau, Jr., Dec. 30, 1830, Fort Tecumseh and Fort Pierre Letterbook.

4. Elliott Coues (ed.), *New Light on the Early History of the Greater Northwest: The Manuscript Journals of Alexander Henry and of David Thompson* (New York, 1897), II, 512; John McDonell, "Some Account of the Red River (about 1797)—With Extracts from his Journal 1793-1795" in L. R. Masson, *Les bourgeois de la Compagnie du Nord-Ouest, recits de voyages, lettres et rapports inédits relatifs au nord-ouest Canadien . . .* (New York, 1960), I, 108.

5. George Simpson to Andrew Colvile, May 20, 1822, in Frederick Merk (ed.), *Fur Trade and Empire: George Simpson's Journal . . .* (Cambridge, Mass., 1931), p. 179; Alexander Henry, *Travels and Adventures in Canada and The Indian Territories between the Years 1760 and 1776* (New York, 1809), pp. 299-312; Morton (ed.), *Journal of M'Gillivray*, p. 31.

6. Ross Cox, *The Columbia River; or, Scenes and Adventures During A Residence of Six Years on the Western Side of the Rocky Mountains . . .* (3rd ed.; London, 1832), II, 121-22, 127.

7. John C. Ewers (ed.), Edwin Thompson Denig's *Five Indian Tribes of the Upper Missouri: Sioux, Arickaras, Assiniboines, Crees, Crows* (Norman, Okla., 1961), pp. 52-53.

8. E. E. Rich (ed.), *Journal of Occurrences in the Athabasca Department By George Simpson, 1820 and 1821, And Report* (Toronto, Ont., 1938), p. 376; E. E. Rich (ed.), *Part of Dispatch From George Simpson Esq* Governor of Ruperts Land to the Governor & Committee of the Hudson's Bay Company London . . .* (Toronto, Ont., 1947), pp. 7-8.

9. Merk (ed.), *Fur Trade and Empire*, pp. xxxi-xxxiii; Rich (ed.), *Journal of Occurrences in the Athabasca Department*, p. 371; Rich (ed.), *Part of Dispatch From George Simpson*, p. 8.

10. Ewers (ed.), Denig's *Five Indian Tribes*, p. 23.

11. W. S. Wallace (ed.), John McLean's *Notes of a Twenty-five Years' Service in the Hudson's Bay Territory* (Toronto, Ont., 1932), p. 119; *Report of the Select Committee on the Hudson's Bay Company* (London, 1857), p. 58; Peter Garrioch Collection (MSS in the Public Archives of Manitoba, Winnipeg), Peter Garrioch Diary.

12. Josiah Mooso, *The Life and Travels of Josiah Mooso: A Life on the Frontier among Indians and Spaniards, not seeing the Face of a White Woman for Fifteen Years* (Winfield, Kan., 1888), pp. 97-105.

13. Rich (ed.), *Part of Dispatch From George Simpson*, p. 64; Umfreville, *Present State of Hudson's Bay*, pp. 209-11.

14. Annie Heloise Abel (ed.), "Trudeau's Description of the Upper Missouri," *Mississippi Valley Historical Review*, VIII (June–September, 1921), 177; Chouteau Collections, Daniel Lamont to Pierre Chouteau, Jr.,

Dec. 30, 1830; William Laidlaw to David Mitchell, Nov. 27, 1831; William Laidlaw to Kenneth McKenzie, Feb. 15, 1832, Fort Tecumseh and Fort Pierre Letter Book; Henry A. Boller Papers (MSS in the North Dakota Historical Society, Bismarck), "A pretty Nest of Birds!" [undated correspondence or miscellany]; Henry A. Boller to H. J. Boller, Feb. 5, 1860.

15. Lawrence J. Burpee (ed.), "Journal of a Journey Performed by Anthony Hendry, To Explore the Country Inland . . . , A.D. 1754–1755," *Proceedings and Transactions of the Royal Society of Canada* (third series), vol. I (1907), section 2, pp. 338, 351; Lawrence J. Burpee (ed.), "Journal of Matthew Cocking, from York Factory to the Blackfeet Country, 1772–73," *Proceedings and Transactions of the Royal Society of Canada* (third series), vol. II (1908), section 2, pp. 110–11; Pierre Menard Collection (MSS in the Illinois State Historical Library, Springfield), Menard to ———[?], April 21, 1810; Kaskaskia Papers (MSS in the Missouri Historical Society, St. Louis), Pierre Menard to A. Langlois, Oct. 7, 1809.

16. *Report of the Select Committee,* p. 105; Documents Historiques années 1818–1866 (MSS in the Archdiocesan Archives, Archbishop's Residence, St. Boniface, Manitoba), Geo Simpson to the Right Rev[d] the Bishop of Juliopolis, April 18, 1837.

17. Henry Drummond Dee (ed.), "The Journal of John Work, 1835: Being an Account of His Voyage Northward . . . in the Brig *Lama,* January–October, 1835," *British Columbia Historical Quarterly,* VIII (April, 1944) (July, 1944) (October, 1944), IX (January, 1945) (April, 1945).

18. [Ogden], *Traits of American Indian Life,* p. 12; St. Louis *Missouri Republican,* June 7, 1827.

19. Meriwether Lewis Anderson Collection (MSS in the Missouri Historical Society, St. Louis), Reuben Lewis to Meriwether Lewis, April 21, 1810.

20. [Ogden], *Traits of American Indian Life,* pp. 13–14.

21. J. B. Tyrrell (ed.), *David Thompson's Narrative of his Explorations in Western America, 1784–1813* (Toronto, Ont., 1916), p. 355; Isaac Cowie, *The Company of Adventurers: A Narrative of Seven Years in the Service of the Hudson's Bay Company During 1867–1874 on the Great Buffalo Plains* (Toronto, Ont., 1913), p. 230.

22. Hudson's Bay Company Papers (MSS in Beaver House, London; photocopy in Minnesota Historical Society, St. Paul), Lac Pluie report of 1822–23; Documents Historiques, Wm. J. Christie to Henry Fisher, March 16, 1853; Fur Trade Collection (MSS in the Public Archives of Manitoba, Winnipeg), Journal of Occurrences at Fort William, July 17, 1829, to June 29, 1830; William G. and George W. Ewing Papers (MSS in the Indiana State Library, Indianapolis), Jas. Avaline to G. W. Ewing, Dec. 31, 1831.

23. Ayer Collection (MSS in the Newberry Library, Chicago), Simpson's River Expedition, 1833 (transcript of Simon M'Gillivray journal), Laut

Transcripts II; Morton (ed.), *Journal of Duncan M'Gillivray,* pp. 75–76; Anne McDonnell (ed.), "Original Journal of James H. Chambers, Fort Sarpy," *Contributions to the Historical Society of Montana,* X (1940), 158.

24. H. P. Biggar *et al.* (ed.), *The Works of Samuel De Champlain* (Toronto, Ont., 1922–36), VI, 20–22; Francois-Victor Malhiot, "Journal du Fort Kamanaitiquoya a la Rivière Montréal, 1804–1805" in Masson, *Les bourgeois,* I, 253; Duncan Cameron, "The Nipigon Country, 1804—With Extracts from His Journal" in *ibid.,* II, 270.

25. Thomas Fitzpatrick, "Report" in *Report of the Commissioner of Indian Affairs* (1851), p. 334; John McLoughlin to the Governor, Deputy Governor, *etc.,* July 6, 1827, in E. E. Rich (ed.), *The Letters of John McLoughlin From Fort Vancouver to the Governor and Committee: First Series, 1825–38* (Toronto, Ont., 1941), pp. 47–48; J. N. B. Hewitt (ed.), "Journal of Rudolph Friederich Kurz . . . ," trans. Myrtis Jarrell, *Bureau of American Ethnology Bulletin,* CXV (1937), 3, 204, 269.

26. William Edgar Papers (MSS in the Burton Historical Collection, Detroit Public Library, Detroit), Fred. Hambach to Edgar, July 5, 1763; Edward Jarvis to John Thomas, Aug. 24, 1784, in E. E. Rich (ed.), *Moose Fort Journals 1783–85* (London, 1954), p. 326; Boller Papers, Boller to [his mother], July, 1858.

27. Kenneth A. Spaulding (ed.), Alexander Ross's *The Fur Hunters of the Far West* (Norman, Okla., 1956), p. 155; Alexander Ross, *Adventures of the First Settlers on the Oregon or Columbia River: Being a Narrative of the Expedition Fitted out by John Jacob Astor . . .* (London, 1849), pp. 110–11; Hewitt (ed.), "Journal of Kurz," p. 268; cited in Richard Glover, "Introduction" in E. E. Rich (ed.), *Cumberland House Journals and Inland Journals 1775–82: Second Series, 1779–82* (London, 1952), p. xxv.

28. Annie Heloise Abel (ed.), *Chardon's Journal at Fort Clark 1834–1839 . . .* (Pierre, S.D., 1932), p. 78; Garrioch Collection, Peter Garrioch Diary, 1843–47.

29. Grace Lee Nute (ed.), "The Diary of Martin McLeod," *Minnesota Historical Bulletin,* IV (1921–22), 422; Documents Historiques, William L. Hardisty to His Lordship Alexander Taché, Bishop of St. Boniface, Nov. 24, 1864; Martin McLeod Papers (MSS in the Minnesota Historical Society, St. Paul); Cuthbert Cumming to James Hargrave, March 1, 1831, in G. P. deT. Glazebrook (ed.), *The Hargrave Correspondence, 1821–1843* (Toronto, Ont., 1938), pp. 66–67.

30. Frederick Jackson Turner, *The Frontier in American History* (New York, 1920), p. 37; Richard Glover (ed.), *David Thompson's Narrative, 1784–1813*) Toronto, Ont., 1962), p. 43. Glover feels that a new editing of Thompson's narrative is justified for several reasons: J. B. Tyrrell's was published in 1916; the "hagiographical myth" that has enshrouded Thomp-

son's memory needs some questioning; another chapter has come to light—in which the cited incident is related. Elsewhere in this study Tyrrell's edition is used; Nute (ed.), "Diary of McLeod," p. 438; Alexis Bailly Papers (MSS in the Minnesota Historical Society, St. Paul), personal memorandum book and miscellaneous accounts, 1823–26.

31. Abel (ed.), *Chardon's Journal,* pp. 55, 58; Pierre Menard Collection, Francois Chouteau to [Pierre Menard], March 31, 1829.

32. Menard Family Collection (MSS in the Illinois State Historical Library, Springfield), L. Vallé to Pierre H. Lorimier, July 25, 1821; American Fur Company Papers (MSS in the Chicago Historical Society, Chicago), R. Stuart to Jean B. Beaubien, Aug. 24, 1826 (typescript of original).

33. James Adair, *The History of the American Indians; Particularly Those Nations adjoining to the Mississippi, East and West Florida, Georgia, South and North Carolina, and Virginia* . . . (London, 1775), p. 224.

CHAPTER 4

1. Francis Parkman, *The Conspiracy of Pontiac* (Everyman's Library ed.; New York, 1908), I, 54–57.

2. A. L. Kroeber, *Cultural and Natural Areas of Native North America* (Berkeley, Calif., 1939), p. 92; Ruth Benedict, *Patterns of Culture* (Boston, 1934), p. 11.

3. Paul C. Phillips, *The Fur Trade* (Norman, Okla., 1961); Hiram Martin Chittenden, *The American Fur Trade of the Far West* (Stanford, Calif., 1954), II, 847 and *passim;* E. E. Rich, *The History of the Hudson's Bay Company 1670–1870* (London, 1958). See, especially, his chapter XLI, "Life and Trade by the Bay"; Bernard DeVoto, *The Course of Empire* (Boston, 1952), p. 87.

4. R. Douglas and J. N. Wallace (eds. and trans.), *Twenty Years of York Factory 1694–1714: Jérémie's Account of Hudson Strait and Bay* (Ottawa, Ont., 1926), pp. 32, 38–39; La Vérendrye to Beauharnois, May 21, 1733, in Lawrence J. Burpee (ed.), *Journals and Letters of Pierre Gaultier de Varennes de la Vérendrye and his Sons* . . . (Toronto, Ont., 1927), p. 98.

5. Joseph Robson, *An Account of Six Years' Residence in Hudson's Bay, From 1733 to 1736, and 1744 to 1747* . . . (London, 1752), pp. 48, 53–54; Edward Umfreville, *The Present State of Hudson's Bay. Containing a Full Description of that Settlement, and the Adjacent Country; and Likewise of the Fur Trade* . . . (London, 1790), pp. 210–14.

6. J. B. Tyrrell (ed.), *Journals of Samuel Hearne and Philip Turnor* (Toronto, Ont., 1934), p. 362; Stanley Vestal, *Kit Carson, The Happy Warrior of the Old West: A Biography* (New York, 1928), p. 228. The Nordic racism that appears in this work needs to be taken into consideration also;

Milo Milton Quaife (ed.), Charles Larpenteur's *Forty Years a Fur Trader on the Upper Missouri* (Chicago, 1933), pp. 139–41.

7. James McKenzie, "The King's Posts and Journal of a Canoe Jaunt Through the King's Domains 1808" in L. R. Masson, *Les bourgeois de la Compagnie du Nord-Ouest, recits de voyages, lettres et rapports inédits relatifs au nord-ouest Canadien* . . . (New York, 1960), II, 419–20.

8. See John C. Ewers (ed.), Edwin Thompson Denig's *Five Indian Tribes of the Upper Missouri: Sioux, Arickaras, Assiniboines, Crees, Crows* (Norman, Okla., 1961), and J. N. B. Hewitt (ed.), Edwin Thompson Denig's "Indian Tribes of the Upper Missouri," *Bureau of American Ethnology Forty-sixth Annual Report* (1928–29); H. P. Biggar *et al.* (ed.), *The Works of Samuel De Champlain* (Toronto, Ont., 1922–36), III, 52; Burpee (ed.), *Journals and Letters of La Vérendrye*, pp. 148–49.

9. John McLoughlin to the Governor, Deputy Governor, *etc.*, July 6, 1827, in E. E. Rich (ed.), *The Letters of John McLoughlin From Fort Vancouver to the Governor and Committee: First Series, 1825–38* (Toronto, Ont., 1941), p. 48; Annie Heloise Abel (ed.), *Tabeau's Narrative of Loisel's Expedition to the Upper Missouri*, trans. Rose Abel Wright (Norman, Okla., 1939), pp. 153–54; Daniel Greysolon DuLuth to ———, April 12, 1684, in *Collections of the State Historical Society of Wisconsin*, XVI, 114–25; St. Louis *Missouri Republican*, Oct. 15, 1823.

10. Mrs. H. T. Beauregard (ed. and trans.), "Journal of Jean Baptiste Trudeau among the Arikara Indians in 1795," *Collections of the Missouri Historical Society*, IV (1912), 33; Duncan Cameron, "The Nipigon Country, 1804—With Extracts from His Journal" in Masson, *Les bourgeois*, II, 273; "Memoir on La Salle's Discoveries, By Tonty, 1678–1690" in Louise Phelps Kellogg (ed.), *Early Narratives of the Northwest, 1634–1699* (New York, 1917), p. 300.

11. Doane Robinson (ed.), "Fort Tecumseh and Fort Pierre Journal and Letter Books," *South Dakota Historical Collections*, IX (1918).

12. [Peter Skene Ogden], *Traits of American Indian Life & Character By A Fur Trader* (modern ed.; San Francisco, Calif., 1933), p. 3.

13. DeVoto, *Course of Empire*, p. 161.

14. James Adair, *The History of the American Indians; Particularly Those Nations adjoining to the Mississippi, East and West Florida, Georgia, South and North Carolina, and Virginia* . . . (London, 1775); J. B. Tyrrell (ed.), *David Thompson's Narrative of his Explorations in Western America 1784–1813* (Toronto, Ont., 1916); Ewers (ed.), Denig's *Five Indian Tribes;* Hewitt (ed.), Denig's "Indian Tribes of the Upper Missouri"; Samuel Hearne, *A Journey From Prince of Wales's Fort in Hudson's Bay, to the Northern Ocean. Undertaken by Order of the Hudson's Bay Company* . . . (London, 1795); E. E. Rich (ed.), *James Isham's Observations on*

Hudson's Bay, 1743 and Notes and Observations on a Book Entitled "A Voyage to Hudsons Bay in the Dobbs Galley, 1749" (Toronto, Ont., 1949) ; Alexander Ross, *Adventures of the First Settlers on the Oregon or Columbia River: Being a Narrative of the Expedition Fitted out by John Jacob Astor* . . . (London, 1849) ; Kenneth A. Spaulding (ed.), Alexander Ross's *The Fur Hunters of the Far West* (Norman, Okla., 1956) ; Alexander Ross, *The Red River Settlement: Its Rise, Progress, and Present State. With Some Account of the Native Races and Its General History, to the Present Day* (London, 1856) ; J. V. Huntington (ed. and trans.), Gabriel Franchère's *Narrative of a Voyage to the Northwest Coast of America in the Years 1811, 1812, 1813, and 1814 or the First American Settlement on the Pacific* (New York, 1854) ; Ross Cox, *The Columbia River; or, Scenes and Adventures During A Residence of Six Years on the Western Side of the Rocky Mountains* . . . (3rd ed.; London, 1832).

15. Abel (ed.), *Tabeau's Narrative*, p. 172; Jq. Porlier to L. Grignon, Jan. 25, 1820, in *Collections of the State Historical Society of Wisconsin*, XX, 153–54.

16. Abel (ed.), *Tabeau's Narrative*, p. 12; Malhiot, "Journal," pp. 225, 241.

17. K. G. Davies (ed.), *Peter Skene Ogden's Snake Country Journal, 1826–27* (London, 1961), pp. 49–75. See also T. C. Elliott (ed.), "Journal of Peter Skene Ogden; Snake Expedition, 1827–1828," *Oregon Historical Society Quarterly,* XI (1910), 369–70.

18. Adair, *The History of the American Indians*, pp. 429–38; Reuben Gold Thwaites (ed.), John Long's *Voyages and Travels of an Indian Interpreter and Trader* . . . (Cleveland, Ohio, 1904), p. 157; Hoxie Neale Fairchild, *The Noble Savage: A Study in Romantic Naturalism* (New York, 1928), p. 12; Huntington (ed. and trans.), Franchère's *Narrative of a Voyage*, p. 110.

19. Ross, *Adventures of the First Settlers*, p. 100; Frederick Merk (ed.), *Fur Trade and Empire: George Simpson's Journal* (Cambridge, Mass., 1931), p. 96.

20. Thomas Simpson, *Narrative of the Discoveries on the North Coast of America: Effected by the Officers of the Hudson's Bay Company During the Years 1836–39* (London, 1843), pp. 187–88; Hearne, *A Journey From Prince of Wales's Fort*, pp. 202–3.

21. Ross, *Adventures of the First Settlers*, pp. 236–37; Tyrrell (ed.), *David Thompson's Narrative*, p. 80.

22. Biggar *et al.* (ed.), *The Works of Samuel De Champlain*, III, 66–78; Merk (ed.), *Fur Trade and Empire*, pp. 97–98; Tyrrell (ed.), *David Thompson's Narrative*, p. 93.

23. Arthur T. Adams (ed.), *The Explorations of Pierre Esprit Radis-*

son (Minneapolis, Minn., 1961), p. 147; Daniel W. Harmon, *A Journal of Voyages and Travels in the Interior of North America* . . . (modern ed.; New York, 1922), p. 58; Hearne, *A Journey From Prince of Wales's Fort,* pp. 124–25, 128–29.

24. Ruth Benedict, *Race: Science and Politics* (New York, 1940), p. 167; DeVoto, *Course of Empire,* p. 256; John Work to Edward Ermatinger, Feb. 15, 1837, in "Old Letters from Hudson Bay Company Officials and Employes [*sic*] from 1829 to 1840," fourth part, *Washington Historical Quarterly,* II (October, 1908), 259.

25. "The Diary of A. N. McLeod" in Charles M. Gates (ed.), *Five Fur Traders of the Northwest: Being the Narrative of Peter Pond and the Diaries of John McDonell, Archibald N. McLeod, Hugh Faries and Thomas Connor* (Minneapolis, Minn., 1933), pp. 133, 139; "Journals and Correspondence of John McLeod, Senior, Chief Trader, Hudson's Bay Company, who was one of the Earliest Pioneers in the Oregon Territory, from 1812 to 1844" (MSS copied from the originals in the Dominion Government Archives by R. E. Gosnell; unpublished typescript in the Library of Congress), John Stuart to John McLeod, March 2, 1834, pp. 185–86; Charles Ross to Mrs. Joseph MacDonald, April 24, 1843, in "Five Letters of Charles Ross, 1842–44," *British Columbia Historical Quarterly,* VII (April, 1943), 107.

26. Seymour Dunbar and Paul C. Phillips (ed.), *The Journals and Letters of Major John Owen Pioneer of the Northwest, 1850–1871* . . . (New York, 1927), I, 188.

27. Clark Wissler, *Indians of the United States: Four Centuries of Their History and Culture* (Garden City, N.Y., 1954), p. 74; A. L. Burt, "If Turner Had Looked at Canada, Australia, and New Zealand When He Wrote about the West" in Walker D. Wyman and Clifton B. Kroeber (ed.), *The Frontier in Perspective* (Madison, Wis., 1957), p. 62.

28. Merk (ed.), *Fur Trade and Empire,* pp. 57–58; see E. E. Rich (ed.), *Journal of Occurrences in the Athabasca Department By George Simpson, 1820 and 1821, And Report* (Toronto, Ont., 1938), pp. 23, 88.

29. Fred A Crane, "The Noble Savage in America, 1815–1860: Concepts of the Indian, with Special Reference to the Writers of the Northeast" (Ph.D. dissertation, Yale University, 1952), pp. 18–19.

CHAPTER 5

1. Thomas W. Field, *An Essay towards an Indian Bibliography* . . . (New York, 1873), p. 164; Samuel Hearne, *A Journey From Prince of Wales's Fort in Hudson's Bay, to the Northern Ocean. Undertaken by Order of the Hudson's Bay Company* . . . (London, 1795), p. 231.

2. Hoxie Neale Fairchild, *The Noble Savage: A Study in Romantic Naturalism* (New York, 1928), pp. 2, 22; Chauncey Brewster Tinker,

Nature's Simple Plan: A Phase of Radical Thought in the Mid-Eighteenth Century (Princeton, N.J., 1922), pp. 88–89; Arthur O. Lovejoy and George Boas, *Primitivism and Related Ideas in Antiquity* (Baltimore, Md., 1935), p. 8; "Journals and Correspondence of John McLeod, Senior, Chief Trader, Hudson's Bay Company, who was one of the Earliest Pioneers in the Oregon Territory, from 1812 to 1844" (MSS copied from the originals in the Dominion Government Archives by R. E. Gosnell; unpublished typescript in the Library of Congress), John M. McLeod to John McLeod, March 16, 1833, p. 177.

3. Fairchild, *The Noble Savage,* pp. 97–120; Benjamin Bissell, *The American Indian in English Literature of the Nineteenth Century* (Yale Studies in English, Vol. LXVIII [New Haven, Conn., 1925]).

4. Bissell, *The American Indian,* p. 189; Hearne, *A Journey From Prince of Wales's Fort,* pp. 202–3.

5. Chouteau Collections (MSS in the Missouri Historical Society, St. Louis), Auguste Chouteau to Baron de Carondelet, April 18, 1797; [Peter Skene Ogden], *Traits of American Indian Life & Character By A Fur Trader* (modern ed.; San Francisco, Calif., 1933), pp. 1–3; Annie Heloise Abel (ed.), *Tabeau's Narrative of Loisel's Expedition to the Upper Missouri,* trans. Rose Abel Wright (Norman, Okla., 1939), p. 172.

6. W. S. Wallace (ed.), John McLean's *Notes of a Twenty-five Years' Service in the Hudson's Bay Territory* (Toronto, Ont., 1932), p. 259; Anne McDonnell (ed.), "Original Journal of James H. Chambers, Fort Sarpy," *Contributions to the Historical Society of Montana,* X (1940), 101–2, 106–7.

7. Maurice S. Sullivan (ed.), *The Travels of Jedediah Smith: A Documentary Outline Including the Journal of the Great American Pathfinder* (Santa Ana, Calif., 1934), p. 5; Thomas Simpson, *Narrative of the Discoveries on the North Coast of America; Effected by the Officers of the Hudson's Bay Company During the Years 1836–39* (London, 1843), pp. 179–80; Alexander Ross, *Adventures of the First Settlers on the Oregon or Columbia River: Being a Narrative of the Expedition Fitted out by John Jacob Astor* . . . (London, 1849), p. 94; Desiderius Erasmus, *The Praise of Folly,* trans. Leonard F. Dean (Chicago, 1946), pp. 73–74.

8. Robert Campbell to Hugh Campbell, Nov. 16, 1833, in Charles Eberstadt (ed.), *The Rocky Mountain Letters of Robert Campbell* (n.p., 1955), pp. 14–16.

9. "Journal of Jean Baptiste Truteau on the Upper Missouri, 'Première Partie,' June 7, 1794–March 26, 1795," *American Historical Review,* XIX (January, 1914), 311–33; Mrs. H. T. Beauregard (ed. and trans.), "Journal of Jean Baptiste Trudeau among the Arikara Indians in 1795," *Missouri Historical Society Collections,* IV (1912), 26–30.

10. Fairchild, *The Noble Savage*, p. 429.

11. *Ibid.*, p. 119; Ross Cox, *The Columbia River; or, Scenes and Adventures During a Residence of Six Years on the Western Side of the Rocky Mountains* . . . (3rd ed.; London, 1832), I, vi; Robert Michael Ballantyne, *The Wild Man of the West. A Tale of the Rocky Mountains* (Philadelphia, n.d.), p. 47.

12. Cox, *The Columbia River*, II, 140–41; Osborne Russell, *Journal of a Trapper; or, Nine Years in the Rocky Mountains 1834–1843* . . . (2nd ed.; Boise, Ida., 1921), p. 38; John C. Ewers (ed.), *Adventures of Zenas Leonard Fur Trader* (Norman, Okla., 1959), pp. 33–34; Paul C. Phillips (ed.), Warren Angus Ferris' *Life in the Rocky Mountains: A Diary of Wanderings* . . . (Denver, Colo., 1940), p. 88.

13. Walter B. Douglas (ed.), Thomas James's *Three Years Among the Indians and Mexicans* (St. Louis, Mo., 1916), p. 53; Timothy Flint (ed.), *The Personal Narrative of James O. Pattie, of Kentucky, During an Expedition from St. Louis* . . . (Cincinnati, Ohio, 1833), p. 100; Isaac Cowie, *The Company of Adventurers: A Narrative of Seven Years in the Service of the Hudson's Bay Company During 1867–1874 on the Great Buffalo Plains* (Toronto, Ont., 1913), pp. 28, 451–53. Cowie slightly misquoted this passage from Dryden's *Conquest of Granada*, part I, act I, scene 1.

14. Wallace (ed.), *McLean's Notes*, p. 355; A. O. Lovejoy, "The Supposed Primitivism of Rousseau's *Discourse on Inequality*," *Modern Philology*, XXI (1923), 165–86.

15. Lawrence J. Burpee (ed.), "Journal of Matthew Cocking, from York Factory to the Blackfeet Country, 1772–73," *Proceedings and Transactions of the Royal Society of Canada* (third series), vol. II (1908), section 2, p. 110; Lawrence J. Burpee (ed.), *Journals and Letters of Pierre Gaultier de Varennes de la Vérendrye and His Sons* . . . (Toronto, Ont., 1927), pp. 316–43; Lovejoy and Boas, *Primitivism and Related Ideas in Antiquity*, p. 8.

16. McDonnell (ed.), "Journal of Chambers," p. 100; Annie Heloise Abel (ed.), *Chardon's Journal at Fort Clark, 1834–1839* . . . (Pierre, S.D., 1932), pp. 34, 45; Bernard DeVoto, *Across the Wide Missouri* (Boston, 1947), pp. 242–43; Chouteau Collections, F. A. Chardon to Pierre Chouteau, Jr., May 18, 1835; J. N. B. Hewitt (ed.), "Journal of Rudolph Friederich Kurz . . . ," trans. Myrtis Jarrell, *Bureau of American Ethnology Bulletin*, CXV (1937), 204.

17. Charles L. Sanford, *The Quest for Paradise: Europe and the American Moral Imagination* (Urbana, Ill., 1961), pp. vi, 3, 94.

18. [Duncan M'Gillivray], "Some Account of the Trade Carried on by the North West Company," Dominion of Canada, *Report of the Public Archives for the Year 1928*, pp. 63–67. His treatment of the Blackfeet does

not fit the pattern I have described. However, their recalcitrance probably precluded their ennoblement.

19. K. G. Davies (ed.), *Peter Skene Ogden's Snake Country Journal, 1826–27* (London, 1961), pp. 35, 68; Elliott Coues (ed.), *New Light on the Early History of the Greater Northwest: The Manuscript Journals of Alexander Henry and of David Thompson* (New York, 1897), II, 710–11.

20. Alexander McDonnell, *Narrative of Transactions in the Red River Country from the Commencement of the Operations of the Earl of Selkirk, till the Summer of the Year 1816 . . .* (London, 1819), pp. 7, 71; Flint (ed.), *Personal Narrative of James O. Pattie,* pp. 79–80.

21. Roy Harvey Pearce, *The Savages of America: A Study of the Indian and the Idea of Civilization* (Baltimore, Md., 1953), p. 146.

22. Sanford, *The Quest for Paradise.* See, for example, pp. 62–63; J. B. Tyrrell (ed.), *David Thompson's Narrative of his Explorations in Western America, 1784–1813* (Toronto, Ont., 1916), pp. 101–2.

23. Rufus Sage, *Rocky Mountain Life; or, Startling Scenes and Perilous Adventures in the Far West* (Boston, 1880), p. 314.

24. James Adair, *The History of the American Indians; Particularly Those Nations adjoining to the Mississippi, East and West Florida, Georgia, South and North Carolina, and Virginia . . .* (London, 1775), pp. 378–79, 429–30, 434.

25. *Ibid.,* pp. 431–38.

26. *Ibid.,* pp. 4–5, 285, 438; Edward Umfreville, *The Present State of Hudson's Bay. Containing a Full Description of that Settlement, and the Adjacent Country; and Likewise of the Fur Trade* (London, 1790). Compare, for example, his remarks on pages 29 and 36 with those on pages 103 and 199; Fairchild, *The Noble Savage,* p. 98.

27. In "The Noble Savage in America, 1815–1860: Concepts of the Indian, with Special Reference to the Writers of the Northeast" (Ph.D. dissertation, Yale University, 1952), pp. 376–78, Fred A. Crane suggested that Lovejoy's definition was overly rigorous. He argued that Lovejoy overemphasized conviction in the literal reality of primal excellence as a touchstone of primitivism. Crane felt that primitivism more nearly involved values "imagined" to exist in simple circumstances.

28. Lovejoy and Boas, *Primitivism and Related Ideas in Antiquity,* pp. 7–8.

29. Hewitt (ed.), "Journal of Kurz," pp. 205, 269.

30. Reuben Gold Thwaites (ed.), John Long's *Voyages and Travels of an Indian Interpreter and Trader . . .* (Cleveland, Ohio, 1904), p. 157; Rufus Sage to Mrs. J. Sage, July 20, 1842, in LeRoy R. and Ann W. Hafen (ed.), *Rufus B. Sage: His Letters and Papers 1836–1847 with an annotated reprint of his "Scenes in the Rocky Mountains and in Oregon, California,*

New Mexico, Texas, and the Grand Prairies" (Glendale, Calif., 1956), I, 90; Sage, *Rocky Mountain Life,* p. 197.

31. Fairchild, *The Noble Savage,* p. 364; Joseph James Hargrave, *Red River* (Montreal, Quebec, 1871), pp. 410–11; Pieter Geyl, "Huizinga as Accuser of His Age," *History and Theory: Studies in the Philosophy of History,* II (1963), 236; C. E. M. Joad, *Decadence: A Philosophical Inquiry* (London, 1948), p. 293; Joseph Wood Krutch, "The Infatuation with the Primitive," *Saturday Review,* XLV (Sept. 29, 1962), 14; John Ward, *Andrew Jackson: Symbol for an Age* (New York, 1955).

CHAPTER 6

1. J. N. B. Hewitt (ed.), Edwin Thompson Denig's "Indian Tribes of the Upper Missouri," *Bureau of American Ethnology Forty-sixth Annual Report* (1928–29), p. 595.

2. George Simpson, *Narrative of a Journey Round the World During the Years 1841 and 1842* (London, 1847), I, 128, 142, 226.

3. E. E. Rich (ed.), *A Journal of A Voyage from Rocky Mountain Portage in Peace River to the Sources of Finlays Branch and North West Ward in Summer 1824 (By Samuel Black)* (London, 1955), p. 51; Ross Cox, *The Columbia River; or, Scenes and Adventures During A Residence of Six Years on the Western Side of the Rocky Mountains . . .* (3rd ed.; London, 1832), I, 102.

4. William Henry Ellison (ed.), *The Life and Adventures of George Nidever, 1802–1883* (Berkeley, Calif., 1937), p. 14; Henry A. Boller Papers (MSS in the North Dakota Historical Society, Bismarck), Journal of a Trip to, and Residence in, the Indian Country. Commenced Saturday, May 22ᵈ 1858.

5. Lawrence J. Burpee (ed.), *Journals and Letters of Pierre Gaultier de Varennes de la Vérendrye and his Sons . . .* (Toronto, Ont., 1927), pp. 316–43.

6. Philip Ashton Rollins (ed.), *The Discovery of the Oregon Trail: Robert Stuart's Narratives of His Overland Trip Eastward From Astoria in 1812–13 . . .* (New York, 1935), p. 12; Alice Bay Maloney (ed.), *Fur Brigade to the Bonaventura, John Work's California Expedition, 1832– 1833 for the Hudson's Bay Company* (San Francisco, Calif., 1945), p. 33; Elliott Coues (ed.), *New Light on the Early History of the Greater Northwest: The Manuscript Journals of Alexander Henry and of David Thompson* (New York, 1897), II, 819–20; Milo Milton Quaife (ed.), Charles Larpenteur's *Forty Years a Fur Trader on the Upper Missouri* (Chicago, 1933), pp. 36–37.

7. David Lavender, *Bent's Fort* (Dolphin paperback; Garden City, N.Y., 1954), p. 123.

8. Lawrence J. Burpee (ed.), "Journal of Matthew Cocking, from York Factory to the Blackfeet Country, 1772–73," *Proceedings and Transactions of the Royal Society of Canada* (third series), vol. II (1908), section 2, p. 110; Cox, *The Columbia River,* I, 122–23; Rollins (ed.), *Robert Stuart's Narratives,* pp. 134–35.

9. Rollins (ed.), *Robert Stuart's Narratives,* p. 12.

10. Samuel Hearne, *A Journey From Prince of Wales's Fort in Hudson's Bay, to the Northern Ocean. Undertaken by Order of the Hudson's Bay Company* . . . (London, 1795), pp. 88–89.

11. Marcel Giraud (ed.), "Etienne Veniard DeBourgmont's 'Exact Description of Louisiana,'" trans. Mrs. Max W. Myers, *Missouri Historical Society Bulletin,* XV (October, 1958), 16–17; Joseph Robson, *An Account of Six Years Residence in Hudson's-Bay, From 1733 to 1736, and 1744 to 1747* . . . (London, 1752), p. 48; "Memoir of DeGannes Concerning the Illinois Country" in Theodore C. Pease and Raymond C. Werner (ed.), *The French Foundations 1680–1693* (Springfield, Ill., 1934), pp. 327–28; Burpee (ed.), *Journals and Letters of La Vérendrye,* p. 340; J. B. Tyrrell (ed.), *David Thompson's Narrative of his Explorations in Western America 1784–1813* (Toronto, Ont., 1916), pp. 233–34; Frederick Merk (ed.), *Fur Trade and Empire: George Simpson's Journal* . . . (Cambridge, Mass., 1931), p. 96.

12. Alexander Mackenzie, *Voyages From Montreal on the River St. Laurence [sic], through the Continent of North-America, to the Frozen and Pacific Oceans* . . . (3rd American ed.; New York, 1803), p. 209; John C. Ewers (ed.), Edwin Thompson Denig's *Five Indian Tribes of the Upper Missouri: Sioux, Arickaras, Assiniboines, Crees, Crows* (Norman, Okla., 1961), pp. 154–55.

13. Tyrrell (ed.), *David Thompson's Narrative,* p. 499; Boller Papers, Boller to Annie (his sister), July, 1858; Rich (ed.), *Samuel Black's Journal,* p. 33.

14. Rich (ed.), *Samuel Black's Journal,* p. 120; Duncan Cameron, "The Nipigon Country, 1804—With Extracts from His Journal" in L. R. Masson, *Les bourgeois de la Compagnie du Nord-Ouest, recits de voyages, lettres et rapports inédits relatifs au nord-ouest Canadien.* . . . (New York, 1960), II, 247; Peter Grant, "The Sauteux Indians, about 1804" in *ibid.,* II, 315.

15. Tyrrell (ed.), *David Thompson's Narrative,* p. 80; Charles Ross to Mrs. Joseph MacDonald, April 24, 1843, in "Five Letters of Charles Ross, 1842–44," *British Columbia Historical Quarterly,* VII (April, 1943), 107.

16. Annie Heloise Abel (ed.), *Chardon's Journal at Fort Clark 1834–1839* . . . (Pierre, S.D., 1932), p. 85; "Extract of Mr. Thomas Gorst's Journall in the Voyage to Hudsons Bay begun the 31th day of May 1670" in Grace Lee Nute, *Caesars of the Wilderness: Médard Chouart, Sieur des*

Groseilliers and Pierre Esprit Radisson, 1618–1710 (New York, 1943), pp. 287–88; Mackenzie, *Voyages From Montreal,* p. 85; "Report of Fort Alexandria Western Caledonia Columbia River District Outfit 1827 P. Joseph McGillivray Chief Trader H. B. Co." in E. E. Rich (ed.), *Part of Dispatch From George Simpson Esqr Governor of Ruperts Land to the Governor & Committee of the Hudson's Bay Company London . . .* (Toronto, Ont., 1947), p. 204.

17. Tyrrell (ed.), *David Thompson's Narrative,* pp. 19, 488.

18. Annie Heloise Abel (ed.), *Tabeau's Narrative of Loisel's Expedition to the Upper Missouri,* trans. Rose Abel Wright (Norman, Okla., 1939), p. 173; E. E. Rich (ed.), *Colin Robertson's Correspondence Book, September 1817 to September 1822* (Toronto, Ont., 1939), p. 111; E. E. Rich (ed.), *Journal of Occurrences in the Athabasca Department By George Simpson, 1820 and 1821, And Report* (Toronto, Ont., 1938), p. 388; John C. Ewers (ed.), *Adventures of Zenas Leonard Fur Trader* (Norman, Okla., 1959), pp. 87–88.

19. Rich (ed.), *Samuel Black's Journal,* pp. 35, 91; Mackenzie, *Voyages From Montreal,* p. 133.

20. Hewitt (ed.), Denig's "Indian Tribes of the Upper Missouri," p. 529; Tyrrell (ed.), *David Thompson's Narrative,* pp. 80, 129.

21. Charles L. Camp (ed.), *James Clyman American Frontiersman 1792–1881: The Adventures of a Trapper and Covered Wagon Emigrant as Told in his Own Reminiscences and Diaries* (Portland, Ore., 1960), p. 21; Elliott Coues (ed.), *The Journal of Jacob Fowler . . .* (New York, 1898), pp. 53–57; Tyrrell (ed.), *David Thompson's Narrative,* p. 80.

22. E. E. Rich (ed.), *James Isham's Observations on Hudson's Bay, 1743 and Notes and Observations on a Book Entitled "A Voyage to Hudsons Bay in the Dobbs Galley, 1749"* (Toronto, Ont., 1949), pp. 96–97; Hewitt (ed.), Denig's "Indian Tribes of the Upper Missouri," pp. 429–30.

23. John Spencer Bassett (ed.), *The Writings of "Colonel William Byrd of Westover in Virginia Esqr."* (New York, 1901), p. 144; Hearne, *A Journey From Prince of Wales's Fort,* p. 70; Coues (ed.), *New Light,* I, 371.

24. Abel (ed.), *Tabeau's Narrative,* pp. 174–75; Rich (ed.), *Samuel Black's Journal,* p. 100; Charles MacKenzie, "The Mississouri Indians, A Narrative of Four Trading Expeditions to the Mississouri, 1804–1805–1806" in Masson, *Les bourgeois,* I, 372; Cameron, "The Nipigon Country," pp. 256–57; John McDonnell, "Some Account of the Red River (about 1797)—With Extracts from his Journal 1793–1795" in Masson, *Les bourgeois,* I, 287.

25. Hewitt (ed.), "Indian Tribes of the Upper Missouri," pp. 527–28; Coues (ed.), *New Light,* II, 449–50.

26. Paul C. Phillips (ed.), Warren Angus Ferris' *Life in the Rocky Mountains: A Diary of Wanderings* . . . (Denver, Colo., 1940), p. 302.

27. E. E. Rich (ed.), *Moose Fort Journals, 1783–85* (London, 1954), p. 28; John Porteous Papers (MSS in the Burton Historical Collection, Detroit Public Library, Detroit), John Porteous Journal, March 15, 1765, to May 27, 1766; "First Journal of Simon Fraser from April 12th to July 18th 1806," Dominion of Canada, *Report of the Public Archives for the Year 1929,* p. 145.

28. Reuben Gold Thwaites (ed.), John Long's *Voyages and Travels of an Indian Interpreter and Trader* . . . (Cleveland, Ohio, 1904), p. 72; E. E. Rich (ed.), *The Letters of John McLoughlin From Fort Vancouver to the Governor and Committee: First Series, 1825–38* (Toronto, Ont., 1941), p. 15; "Fort Alexandria Report," p. 203; John Rae to the Governor-in-chief, Governor, *etc.,* April 17, 1851, in E. E. Rich (ed.), *John Rae's Correspondence with the Hudson's Bay Company on Arctic Exploration, 1844–1855* (London, 1953), p. 156; Rich (ed.), *Journal of Occurrences in the Athabasca Department,* pp. 381, 395; Rich (ed.), *Samuel Black's Journal,* pp. 35, 131; "Journal of Simon Fraser," p. 145.

29. Merk (ed.), *Fur Trade and Empire,* p. 74; Rich (ed.), *Journal of Occurrences in the Athabasca Department,* p. 395.

30. Abel (ed.), *Tabeau's Narrative,* pp. 162–63; Henry H. Sibley Papers (MSS in the Minnesota Historical Society, St. Paul), Martin McLeod to Sibley, July 10, 1845.

31. Menard Family Collection (MSS in the Illinois State Historical Library, Springfield), Menard & Vallé to Peter H. Lorimier, June 7, 1821.

32. Coues (ed.), *New Light,* II, 578; Harold Hickerson (ed.), "Journal of Charles Jean Baptiste Chaboillez, 1797–1798," *Ethnohistory* (Summer, 1959), p. 293, and (Fall, 1959), p. 384; T. C. Elliott (ed.), "Journal of John Work, June–October, 1825," *Washington Historical Quarterly,* V (October, 1914), 270; E. E. Rich (ed.), *Peter Skene Ogden's Snake Country Journals, 1824–25 and 1825–26* (London, 1950), pp. 157–58; Simpson, *Narrative of a Journey Round the World,* I, 240; J. B. Tyrrell (ed.), *Journals of Samuel Hearne and Philip Turnor* (Toronto, Ont., 1934), pp. 171–72.

33. See, for example, Abel (ed.), *Tabeau's Narrative,* pp. 188–89; Hearne, *A Journey From Prince of Wales's Fort,* pp. 193–220; Cameron, "The Nipigon Country," pp. 264–65; Clark Collection (MSS in the Missouri Historical Society, St. Louis), James Mackay, Notes on Indian Tribes. These men generally saw their way through Indian magic but were impressed nonetheless. For unappreciative skepticism see John Porteous Papers (MSS in the Burton Historical Collection, Detroit Public Library, Detroit), John Porteous to James Porteous, n.d. [1762]; Alexander Ross,

Adventures of the First Settlers on the Oregon or Columbia River: Being a Narrative of the Expedition Fitted out by John Jacob Astor . . . (London, 1849), p. 312; Simpson, *Narrative of a Journey Round the World,* I, 159–60.

CHAPTER 7

1. R. Douglas (ed.), *Nipigon to Winnipeg: A Canoe Voyage through Western Ontario By Edward Umfreville* . . . (Ottawa, Ont., 1929), p. 17.

2. Geoffrey Gorer, *The American People: A Study in National Character* (New York, 1948), p. 16.

3. Archer Taylor and Bartlett Jere Whiting, *A Dictionary of American Proverbs and Proverbial Phrases, 1820–1880* (Cambridge, Mass., 1958), p. 199; Burton Stevenson, *The Home Book of Proverbs* (New York, 1948), p. 1236; Clark Wissler, *Indians of the United States: Four Centuries of their History and Culture* (Garden City, N.Y., 1954), pp. 255–56; Howard Peckham, "Indian Relations in the United States" in John Francis McDermott (ed.), *Research Opportunities in American Cultural History* (Lexington, Ky., 1961), p. 31.

4. Robert Michael Ballantyne, *The Wild Man of the West. A Tale of the Rocky Mountains* (Philadelphia, n.d.), pp. 154–55.

5. J. Sharpless Fox (ed.), "Letters on the Fur Trade 1833 By William Johnston," *Michigan Pioneer and Historical Collections,* XXXVII (1909–10), 154, 171, 182, 194–95.

6. Reuben Gold Thwaites (ed.), John Long's *Voyages and Travels of an Indian Interpreter and Trader* . . . (Cleveland, 1904), p. 157.

7. J. N. B. Hewitt (ed.), "Journal of Rudolph Friederich Kurz . . . ," trans. Myrtis Jarrell, *Bureau of American Ethnology Bulletin,* CXV (1937), 269–70, 285.

8. Milo Milton Quaife (ed.), Charles Larpenteur's *Forty Years a Fur Trader on the Upper Missouri* (Chicago, 1933), pp. 237–38; Arthur S. Morton (ed.), *The Journal of Duncan M'Gillivray of the North West Company at Fort George on the Saskatchewan, 1794–5* (Toronto, Ont., 1929), pp. 42–43; Elliott Coues (ed.), *New Light on the Early History of the Greater Northwest: The Manuscript Journals of Alexander Henry and of David Thompson* (New York, 1897), II, 520.

9. Alexander Mackenzie, *Voyages From Montreal on the River St. Laurence* [sic], *through the Continent of North-America, to the Frozen and Pacific Oceans* (3rd American ed.; New York, 1803), pp. 85–86, 102–7; J. B. Tyrrell (ed.), *David Thompson's Narrative of his Explorations in Western America, 1784–1813* (Toronto, Ont., 1916), p. 81; T. C. Elliott (ed.), "Journal of David Thompson," *Oregon Historical Society Quarterly,* XV (June, 1914), 109.

10. Kenneth A. Spaulding (ed.), Alexander Ross's *The Fur Hunters of the Far West* (Norman, Okla., 1956), pp. 174–75.

11. George Simpson, *Narrative of a Journey Round the World During the Years 1841 and 1842* (London, 1847), pp. 191–92; Bernard R. Ross, William L. Hardisty, and Strachan Jones, "Notes on the Tinneh or Chepewyan Indians of British and Russian America," *Smithsonian Institution Annual Report* (1866), pp. 313–15. This citation is to Hardisty's contribution; J. N. B. Hewitt (ed.), Edwin Thompson Denig's "Indian Tribes of the Upper Missouri," *Bureau of American Ethnology Forty-sixth Annual Report* (1928–29), pp. 513–15.

12. H. P. Biggar *et al.* (ed.), *The Works of Samuel De Champlain* (Toronto, Ont., 1922–36), III, 52–53; Hewitt (ed.), "Journal of Kurz," p. 269; Ross, Hardisty, and Jones, "Notes on the Tinneh," p. 314.

13. Samuel Hearne, *A Journey From Prince of Wales's Fort in Hudson's Bay, to the Northern Ocean. Undertaken by Order of the Hudson's Bay Company* . . . (London, 1795), pp. 51, 285.

14. Biggar *et al.* (ed.), *Works of Champlain*, III, 52; John Spencer Bassett (ed.), *The Writings of "Colonel William Byrd of Westover in Virginia Esqr."* (New York, 1901), pp. 102–3.

15. E. E. Rich (ed.), *Peter Skene Ogden's Snake Country Journals, 1824–25 and 1825–26* (London, 1950), p. 204; Alexander Ross, *Adventures of the First Settlers on the Oregon or Columbia River: Being a Narrative of the Expedition Fitted out by John Jacob Astor* . . . (London, 1849), pp. 66–67; David Douglas, *Journal Kept By* . . . *During His Travels in North America* . . . (New York, 1959), pp. 198–99.

16. Annie Heloise Abel (ed.), *Tabeau's Narrative of Loisel's Expedition to the Upper Missouri,* trans. Rose Abel Wright (Norman, Okla., 1939), pp. 144–45, 207–8; Simpson, *Narrative of a Journey Round the World,* I, 186–87; William Gordon to Lewis Cass, Oct. 3, 1831, in U.S. 22nd Cong., 1st sess., S. Exec. Doc. 90, pp. 28–29.

17. Hewitt (ed.), Denig's "Indian Tribes of the Upper Missouri," p. 515.

18. Henry H. Sibley Papers (MSS in the Minnesota Historical Society, St. Paul), Mártin McLeod to Sibley, Feb. 25, 1848; Thomas Simpson, *Narrative of the Discoveries on the North Coast of America; Effected by the Officers of the Hudson's Bay Company During the Years 1836–39* (London, 1843), pp. 67–68.

19. Fur Trade Collection (MSS in the Public Archives of Manitoba, Winnipeg), Journal of Occurrences at York Factory kept by Robert Miles, 1829; K. G. Davies (ed.), *Peter Skene Ogden's Snake Country Journal, 1826–27* (London, 1961), pp. 9–10; E. E. Rich (ed.), *Journal of Occurrences in the Athabasca Department By George Simpson, 1820 and 1821, And Report* (Toronto, Ont., 1938), p. 376.

20. Tyrrell (ed.), *David Thompson's Narrative*, p. 81.

21. John Thomas to P. Turnor, Oct. 9, 1783, in E. E. Rich (ed.), *Moose Fort Journal, 1783–85* (London, 1954), pp. 156–57; Chouteau Collections (MSS in the Missouri Historical Society, St. Louis), Kenneth McKenzie to Major Fulkerson, Dec. 10, 1835, Fort Union Letterbook; Hewitt (ed.), "Journal of Kurz," pp. 154–55.

22. American Fur Company Papers (MSS in the New York Historical Society Library; microfilm copy in the Missouri Historical Society, St. Louis), Joseph Rolette to Ramsay Crooks, Jan. 20, 1835; Abel (ed.), *Tabeau's Narrative*, pp. 134–35.

23. Duncan Cameron, "The Nipigon Country, 1804—With Extracts from His Journal" in L. R. Masson, *Les bourgeois de la Compagnie du Nord-Ouest, recits de voyages, lettres et rapports inédits relatifs au nord-ouest Canadien . . .* (New York, 1960), II, 249; John C. Ewers (ed.), Edwin Thompson Denig's *Five Indian Tribes of the Upper Missouri: Sioux, Arickaras, Assiniboines, Crees, Crows* (Norman, Okla., 1961), p. 171; Hewitt (ed.), Denig's "Indian Tribes of the Upper Missouri," p. 595.

24. Hearne, *A Journey From Prince of Wales's Fort,* p. 345; Robert Dickson Papers (MSS in the Minnesota Historical Society, St. Paul), Proceedings and Report of a Confidential Board, assembled at Montreal on the 8th day of January, 1813 (photocopy); Ruth Hazlitt (ed. and trans.), "The Journal of Francois Antoine Larocque from the Assiniboine River to the Yellowstone—1805," *Historical Reprints: Sources of Northwest History,* no. 20 (State University of Montana), p. 8.

25. Cameron, "The Nipigon Country," p. 273; Mrs. H. T. Beauregard (ed. and trans.), "Journal of Jean Baptiste Trudeau among the Arikara Indians in 1795," *Missouri Historical Society Collections,* IV (1912), 43.

26. William Beauchamp (ed.), *The Life of Conrad Weiser As it Relates to His Services as Official Interpreter Between New York and Pennsylvania and as Envoy Between Philadelphia and the Onondaga Councils* (Syracuse, N.Y., 1925), p. 80; "Memoir of DeGannes Concerning the Illinois Country" in Theodore C. Pease and Raymond C. Werner (ed.), *The French Foundations, 1680–1693* (Springfield, Ill., 1934), p. 328.

27. Hewitt (ed.), Denig's "Indian Tribes of the Upper Missouri," p. 470; Ewers (ed.), Denig's *Five Indian Tribes,* pp. 70–71.

28. Chouteau Collections, Daniel Lamont to Emillien Primeau, Nov. 26, 1830, Fort Tecumseh and Fort Pierre Letter Book; "Journal of Jean Baptiste Truteau on the Upper Missouri, 'Première Partie,' June 7, 1794–March 26, 1795," *American Historical Review,* XIX (January, 1914), 332.

29. *Report of the Select Committee on the Hudson's Bay Company* (London, 1857), p. 37; Joseph Robson, *An Account of Six Years Residence in Hudson's-Bay, From 1733 to 1736, and 1744 to 1747 . . .* (London, 1752), p. iii.

30. Menard Collection (MSS in the Illinois State Historical Library, Springfield), Francois Chouteau to chèr oncle [Pierre Menard], July 15, 1830; John Askin Papers (MSS in the Burton Historical Collection, Detroit Public Library, Detroit), John Anderson to Askin, March 19, 1798; Alexis Bailly Papers (MSS in the Minnesota Historical Society, St. Paul), Personal memorandum book and miscellaneous accounts, 1823; Simpson, *Narrative of a Journey Round the World,* I, 188; Howard Louis Conard, *"Uncle Dick" Wootton The Pioneer Frontiersman of the Rocky Mountain Region . . .* (Chicago, 1890), p. 110.

31. American Fur Company Papers, Robert Stuart to William B. Astor, October, 1823, Robert Stuart's Letter Books 1823–30.

32. Harold Hickerson (ed.), "Journal of Charles Jean Baptiste Chaboillez, 1797–1798," *Ethnohistory* (Summer, 1959), pp. 267, 291; Ayer Collection (MSS in the Newberry Library, Chicago), Simon M'Gillivray's Journal of Occurrences at Fort Simpson (Laut Transcripts, XII); E. E. Rich (ed.), *James Isham's Observations on Hudson's Bay, 1743 and Notes and Observations on a Book Entitled "A Voyage to Hudsons Bay in the Dobbs Galley, 1749"* (Toronto, Ont., 1949), pp. 85–86.

33. Bernard DeVoto, *The Year of Decision: 1846* (Boston, 1943), p. 62; William P. Cumming (ed.), *The Discoveries of John Lederer With Unpublished Letters By and About Lederer to Governor John Winthrop, Jr. . . .* (Charlottesville, Va., 1958), p. 42; Abel (ed.), *Tabeau's Narrative,* p. 171.

34. Robert Campbell to Hugh Campbell, Nov. 16, 1833, in Charles Eberstadt (ed.), *The Rocky Mountain Letters of Robert Campbell* (n.p., 1955), pp. 16–17.

CHAPTER 8

1. Edward Arber (ed.), *Capt. John Smith, of Willoughby by Alford, Lincolnshire; President of Virginia, and Admiral of New England. Works. 1608–1631* (Birmingham, Eng., 1884), p. 65; E. E. Rich (ed.), *Journal of Occurrences in the Athabasca Department By George Simpson, 1820 and 1821, And Report* (Toronto, Ont., 1938), p. 376.

2. Alice Bay Maloney (ed.), *Fur Brigade to the Bonaventura, John Work's California Expedition, 1832–1833 for the Hudson's Bay Company* (San Francisco, Calif., 1945), pp. 62, 75; K. G. Davies (ed.), *Peter Skene Ogden's Snake Country Journal, 1826–27* (London, 1961), p. 71; [Peter Skene Ogden], *Traits of American Indian Life & Character By a Fur Trader* (modern ed.; San Francisco, Calif., 1933), p. 4.

3. Elliott Coues (ed.), *New Light on the Early History of the Greater Northwest: The Manuscript Journals of Alexander Henry and of David Thompson* (New York, 1897), II, 790–810; J. V. Huntington (ed. and

trans.), Gabriel Franchère's *Narrative of a Voyage to the Northwest Coast of America in the Years 1811, 1812, 1813, and 1814 or the First American Settlement on the Pacific* (New York, 1854), p. 217.

4. Alexander Ross, *Adventures of the First Settlers on the Oregon or Columbia River: Being a Narrative of the Expedition Fitted out by John Jacob Astor . . .* (London, 1849), pp. 270–71; John McLoughlin to Jedediah S. Smith, Sept. 12, 1828, in Maurice S. Sullivan (ed.), *The Travels of Jedediah Smith: A Documentary Outline Including the Journal of the Great American Pathfinder* (Santa Ana, Calif., 1934), pp. 109–11; E. E. Rich (ed.), *The Letters of John McLoughlin From Fort Vancouver to the Governor and Committee: Second Series 1839–44* (Toronto, Ont., 1943), p. 116; St. Louis *Missouri Republican,* Oct. 15, 1823.

5. W. S. Wallace (ed.), John McLean's *Notes of a Twenty-five Years' Service in the Hudson's Bay Territory* (Toronto, Ont., 1932), p. 24.

6. James Mackay to John Evans, Jan. 28, 1796, in A. P. Nasitir (ed.), *Before Lewis and Clark: Documents Illustrating the History of the Missouri, 1785–1804* (St. Louis, Mo., 1952), II, 412; Pierre Menard Papers (MSS in the Illinois Historical Survey of the University of Illinois, Urbana), Menard to William Gillise, Feb. 21, 1833; American Fur Company Papers (MSS in the New York Historical Society Library; microfilm copy in the Missouri Historical Society, St. Louis), Charles W. Borup to [William] Morrison, Jan. 22, 1839; John Lawe Papers (MSS in the Chicago Historical Society, Chicago), Ramsay Crooks to Lawe, March 7, 1835.

7. Samuel Hearne, *A Journey From Prince of Wales's Fort in Hudson's Bay, to the Northern Ocean. Undertaken by Order of the Hudson's Bay Company . . .* (London, 1795), p. xliii; Peter Fidler, "Journal of a Journey with the Chepewyans or Northern Indians . . . in 1791 & 2" in J. B. Tyrrell (ed.), *Journals of Samuel Hearne and Philip Turnor* (Toronto, Ont., 1934), p. 535.

8. Anne McDonnell (ed.), "Original Journal of James H. Chambers, Fort Sarpy," *Contributions to the Historical Society of Montana,* X (1940), 114, 158; Daniel Greysolon DuLuth to ———, April 12, 1684, in *Collections of the State Historical Society of Wisconsin,* XVI, 114–25; Milo Milton Quaife (ed.), Charles Larpenteur's *Forty Years a Fur Trader on the Upper Missouri* (Chicago, 1933), p. 330.

9. E. E. Rich (ed.), *James Isham's Observations on Hudson's Bay, 1743 and Notes and Observations on a Book Entitled "A Voyage to Hudsons Bay in the Dobbs Galley, 1749"* (Toronto, Ont., 1949), p. 92; Henry H. Sibley Papers (MSS in the Minnesota Historical Society, St. Paul), Martin McLeod to Sibley, Aug. 20, 1846; Chouteau Collections (MSS in

the Missouri Historical Society, St. Louis), Ramsay Crooks to Pierre Chouteau, Jr., Nov. 16, 1832.

10. Diary of Ferdinand A. Van Ostrand (MSS in the North Dakota Historical Society, Bismarck); Bernard R. Ross, William L. Hardisty, and Strachan Jones, "Notes on the Tinneh or Chepewyan Indians of British and Russian America," *Smithsonian Institution Annual Report* (1866), p. 308. This citation refers to Ross's contribution; Thomas Simpson, *Narrative of the Discoveries on the North Coast of America; Effected by the Officers of the Hudson's Bay Company During the Years 1836–39* (London, 1843), pp. 335–36.

11. Lawrence Taliaferro Papers (MSS in the Minnesota Historical Society, St. Paul), Alexis Bailly to Taliaferro, Feb. 16, 1828; Peter Pond, "Narrative" in Charles M. Gates (ed.), *Five Fur Traders of the Northwest: Being the Narrative of Peter Pond and the Diaries of John McDonell, Archibald N. McLeod, Hugh Faries and Thomas Connor* (Minneapolis, Minn., 1933), pp. 34, 46; Hearne, *A Journey From Prince of Wales's Fort,* p. 309; J. N. B. Hewitt (ed.), Edwin Thompson Denig's "Indian Tribes of the Upper Missouri," *Bureau of American Ethnology Forty-sixth Annual Report* (1928–29), p. 459.

12. Hearne, *A Journey From Prince of Wales's Fort,* p. 351; "Journal of Jean Baptiste Truteau on the Upper Missouri, 'Première Partie,' June 7, 1794–March 26, 1795," *American Historical Review,* XIX (January, 1914), 308; Arthur T. Adams (ed.), *The Explorations of Pierre Esprit Radisson* (Minneapolis, Minn., 1961), p. 146.

13. Kenneth A. Spaulding (ed.), Alexander Ross's *The Fur Hunters of the Far West* (Norman, Okla., 1956), p. 211; cited in LeRoy R. Hafen and W. J. Ghent, *Broken Hand: The Life Story of Thomas Fitzpatrick, Chief of the Mountain Men* (Denver, Colo., 1931), p. 202.

14. T. C. Elliott (ed.), "Journal of John Work, June–October, 1825," *Washington Historical Quarterly,* V (April, 1914), 93.

15. George R. Brooks (ed.), "The Private Journal of Robert Campbell," *Missouri Historical Society Bulletin,* XX (October, 1963), 16; Coues (ed.), *New Light,* II, 727.

16. Robert Campbell to Hugh Campbell, Nov. 16, 1833, in Charles Eberstadt (ed.), *The Rocky Mountain Letters of Robert Campbell* (n.p., 1955), p. 16; Annie Heloise Abel (ed.), *Chardon's Journal at Fort Clark, 1834–1839* . . . (Pierre, S.D., 1932), p. 130; Annie Heloise Abel (ed.), *Tabeau's Narrative of Loisel's Expedition to the Upper Missouri,* trans. Rose Abel Wright (Norman, Okla., 1939), p. 143; Diary of Ferdinand A. Van Ostrand (MSS in the North Dakota Historical Society, Bismarck).

17. Ross, *Adventures of the First Settlers,* p. 168; Harold Hickerson (ed.), "Journal of Charles Jean Baptiste Chaboillez, 1797–1798," *Ethnohistory* (Summer, 1959), p. 267.

18. James Adair, *The History of the American Indians; Particularly Those Nations adjoining to the Mississippi, East and West Florida, Georgia, South and North Carolina, and Virginia* . . . (London, 1775), pp. 417, 423; J. B. Tyrrell (ed.), *David Thompson's Narrative of his Explorations in Western America, 1784–1813* (Toronto, Ont., 1916), p. 22; Clark Collection (MSS in the Missouri Historical Society, St. Louis), James Mackay, Notes on Indian Tribes.

19. American Fur Company Papers, Charles W. Borup to Ramsay Crooks, Nov. 16, 1840.

20. Abel (ed.), *Tabeau's Narrative*, pp. 207–8; Hewitt (ed.), Denig's "Indian Tribes of the Upper Missouri," p. 509.

21. John Rae to the Governor-in-chief, Governor, *etc.*, April 17, 1851; John Rae to Sir George Simpson, April 18, 1851, in E. E. Rich (ed.), *John Rae's Correspondence with the Hudson's Bay Company on Arctic Exploration, 1844–1855* (London, 1953), pp. 156–60.

22. For a revisionist view argued skillfully in defense of the Indian, see Frank G. Roe, *The North American Buffalo: A Critical Study of the Species in Its Wild State* (Toronto, Ont., 1951), pp. 601–70; Hearne, *A Journey From Prince of Wales's Fort*, pp. 77, 117; Simpson, *Narrative of the Discoveries*, pp. 75–76; Alexander Ross, *The Red River Settlement: Its Rise, Progress, and Present State. With Some Account of the Native Races and Its General History, to the Present Day* (London, 1856), p. 307; Rich (ed.), *Isham's Observations*, p. 81.

23. Abel (ed.), *Chardon's Journal*, p. 85; E. E. Rich (ed.), *A Journal of A Voyage from Rocky Mountain Portage in Peace River to the Sources of Finlays Branch and North West Ward in Summer 1824 (By Samuel Black)* (London, 1955), p. 56.

24. John C. Ewers (ed.), Edwin Thompson Denig's *Five Indian Tribes of the Upper Missouri: Sioux, Arickaras, Assiniboines, Crees, Crows* (Norman, Okla., 1961), pp. 94–95; Rich (ed.), *Journal of Occurrences in the Athabasca Department*, pp. 387–88.

25. George Simpson to Andrew Colvile, May 20, 1822, in Frederick Merk (ed.), *Fur Trade and Empire: George Simpson's Journal* . . . (Cambridge, Mass., 1931), pp. 182–83; J. N. B. Hewitt (ed.), "Journal of Rudolph Friederich Kurz . . . ," trans. Myrtis Jarrell, *Bureau of American Ethnology Bulletin*, CXV (1937), 176–77.

26. Spaulding (ed.), Ross's *Fur Hunters of the Far West*, p. 87; E. E. Rich (ed.), *Cumberland House Journals and Inland Journal 1775–82: First Series, 1775–79* (London, 1951), pp. 47, 67.

27. Tyrrell (ed.), *Journals of Hearne and Turnor*, p. 419; E. E. Rich (ed.), *Peter Skene Ogden's Snake Country Journals, 1824–25 and 1825–26* (London, 1950), p. 190.

28. Adair, *History of the American Indians*, pp. 9–10; Spaulding (ed.),

Ross's *Fur Hunters of the Far West*, p. 37; Washington Irving, *Adventures of Captain Bonneville, or Scenes Beyond the Rocky Mountains of the Far West* (London, 1837), II, 70–74. This comment apparently came from Campbell's correspondence with Irving. Because Irving placed it in quotes, I am assuming that the words are Campbell's.

29. Spaulding (ed.), Ross's *Fur Hunters of the Far West*, p. 72.

30. Ross, *Red River Settlement*, pp. 316–17.

31. Tyrrell (ed.), *Journals of Hearne and Turnor*, p. 419; Tyrrell (ed.), *David Thompson's Narrative*, p. 82; Rich (ed.), *Isham's Observations*, p. 92.

32. Rich (ed.), *Isham's Observations*, p. 81; Dugald Mactavish to Letitia Mactavish, Sept. 7, 1834, in G. P. deT. Glazebrook (ed.), *The Hargrave Correspondence, 1821–1843* (Toronto, Ont., 1938), pp. 153–54.

33. Ross, *Adventures of the First Settlers*, pp. 236–37; Daniel W. Harmon, *A Journal of Voyages and Travels in the Interior of North America* (New York, 1922), p. 242; Ewers (ed.), Denig's *Five Indian Tribes of the Upper Missouri*, p. 97; Hearne, *A Journey From Prince of Wales's Fort*, p. 77.

34. Ewers (ed.), Denig's *Five Indian Tribes of the Upper Missouri*, p. 52; Abel (ed.), *Tabeau's Narrative*, p. 180.

35. Rich (ed.), *Isham's Observations*, p. 80; Coues (ed.), *New Light*, I, 326; II, 515; Rich (ed.), *Journal of Occurrences in the Athabasca Department*, p. 79.

36. Tyrrell (ed.), *David Thompson's Narrative*, pp. 234–35; Duncan Cameron, "The Nipigon Country, 1804—With Extracts from His Journal" in L. R. Masson, *Les bourgeois de la Compagnie du Nord-Ouest, recits de voyages, lettres et rapports inédits relatifs au nord-ouest Canadien. . . .* (New York, 1960), II, 263; McDonnell (ed.), "Journal of James Chambers," p. 107.

37. Edward Umfreville, *The Present State of Hudson's Bay. Containing a Full Description of that Settlement, and the Adjacent Country; and Likewise of the Fur Trade . . .* (London, 1790), pp. 180–81.

CHAPTER 9

1. [Peter Skene Ogden], *Traits of American Indian Life & Character By a Fur Trader* (modern ed.; San Francisco, Calif., 1933), p. 10.

2. Henry A. Boller Papers (MSS in the North Dakota Historical Society, Bismarck), Boller to mother and sister, Sept. 27, 1858; Boller to Col. F. J. Boller, Aug. 18, 1858; Eric Goldman, "The Years of the Unraised Eyebrow," St. Louis *Post-Dispatch*, Oct. 11, 1959 (reprinted from *Princeton Alumni Weekly*).

3. J. B. Tyrrell (ed.), *David Thompson's Narrative of his Explorations*

in Western America, 1784–1813 (Toronto, Ont., 1916), p. 350; Henry H. Sibley Papers (MSS in the Minnesota Historical Society, St. Paul), Henry H. Sibley, Incidents of Indian Warfare (undated miscellaneous item in Sibley's handwriting); J. N. B. Hewitt (ed.), Edwin Thompson Denig's "Indian Tribes of the Upper Missouri," *Bureau of American Ethnology Forty-sixth Annual Report* (1928–29), p. 511.

4. Quoted in Merle Curti, *The Growth of American Thought* (2nd ed.; New York, 1951), p. 496.

5. Henry Brevoort to Washington Irving, June 28, 1811, in George S. Hellman (ed.), *Letters of Henry Brevoort to Washington Irving together with other unpublished Brevoort Papers* (New York, 1918), p. 26; Henry Brevoort to Washington Irving, July 14, 1811, in *ibid.*, pp. 40–41.

6. Edward Arber (ed.), *Capt. John Smith, of Willoughby by Alford, Lincolnshire; President of Virginia, and Admiral of New England. Works. 1608–1631* (Birmingham, Eng., 1884), p. 73; Bernard R. Ross, William L. Hardisty, and Strachan Jones, "Notes on the Tinneh or Chepewyan Indians of British and Russian America," *Smithsonian Institution Annual Report* (1866), p. 311.

7. Simon Fraser, "Journal of a Voyage from the Rocky Mountains to the Pacific Coast, 1808" in L. R. Masson, *Les bourgeois de la Compagnie du Nord-Ouest, recits de voyages, lettres et rapports inédits relatifs au nord-ouest Canadien. . . .* (New York, 1960), I, 182–83; Duncan Cameron, "The Nipigon Country, 1804—With Extracts from His Journal," in *ibid.*, II, 254; William P. Cumming (ed.), *The Discoveries of John Lederer With Unpublished Letters By and About Lederer to Governor John Winthrop, Jr. . . .* (Charlottesville, Va., 1958), p. 14.

8. Milo Milton Quaife (ed.), Charles Larpenteur's *Forty Years a Fur Trader on the Upper Missouri* (Chicago, 1933), p. 202; quoted in George Bryce, *The Remarkable History of the Hudson's Bay Company . . .* (London, 1902), p. 404.

9. "A Selection of George Croghan's Letters and Journals Relating to Tours into the Western Country—November 16, 1750–November, 1765" in Reuben Gold Thwaites, *Early Western Travels, 1748–1846 . . .* (Cleveland, Ohio, 1904–7), I, 100–70; William L. Clements (ed.), "Rogers's Michillimackinac Journal," *Proceedings of the American Antiquarian Society* (new series), XXVIII (1918), 224–73; James Sullivan *et al.* (ed.), *The Papers of Sir William Johnson* (Albany, N.Y., 1921–57).

10. Fred A. Crane, "The Noble Savage in America, 1815–1860: Concepts of the Indian, with Special Reference to the Writers of the Northeast" (Ph.D. dissertation, Yale University, 1952), p. 47.

11. Robert Campbell to Hugh Campbell, July 20, 1833, in Charles Eberstadt (ed.), *The Rocky Mountain Letters of Robert Campbell* (n.p., 1955),

p. 13; Ross Cox, *The Columbia River; or, Scenes and Adventures During a Residence of Six Years on the Western Side of the Rocky Mountains* . . . (3rd ed.; London, 1832), II, 21; "Extracts from 'The Substance of a Journal . . .' By John West," *State Historical Society of North Dakota Collections*, III (1910), 457.

12. Clements (ed.), "Rogers's Journal," pp. 234–39; Hewitt (ed.), Denig's "Indian Tribes of the Upper Missouri," pp. 596–97.

13. Hewitt (ed.), Denig's "Indian Tribes of the Upper Missouri," pp. 597–602.

14. *Ibid.*

15. Peter Grant, "The Sauteux Indians, about 1804" in Masson, *Les bourgeois*, II, 325–26; Daniel W. Harmon, *A Journal of Voyages and Travels in the Interior of North America* . . . (modern ed.; New York, 1922), p. 247; Alexander Mackenzie, *Voyages From Montreal on the River St. Laurence* [*sic*], *through the Continent of North-America, to the Frozen and Pacific Oceans* . . . (3rd American ed.; New York, 1803), p. 105.

16. Hewitt (ed.), Denig's "Indian Tribes of the Upper Missouri," p. 509; Samuel Hearne, *A Journey From Prince of Wales's Fort in Hudson's Bay, to the Northern Ocean. Undertaken by Order of the Hudson's Bay Company* . . . (London, 1795), pp. 66–67; Quaife (ed.), Larpenteur's *Forty Years a Fur Trader*, p. 335; K. G. Davies (ed.), *Peter Skene Ogden's Snake Country Journal, 1826–27* (London, 1961), p. 21; John Porteous Papers (MSS in the Burton Historical Collection, Detroit Public Library, Detroit), John Porteous to James Porteous, n.d. [1762].

17. W. S. Wallace (ed.), John McLean's *Notes of a Twenty-five Years' Service in the Hudson's Bay Territory* (Toronto, Ont., 1932), p. 273; "Journal of Occurrences at Fort William . . . ," in [Simon M'Gillivray], *A Narrative of Occurrences in the Indian Countries of North America Since the Connexion of the Right Hon. the Earl of Selkirk with the Hudson's Bay Company* . . . (London, 1817), pp. 82–83; E. E. Rich (ed.), *A Journal of A Voyage from Rocky Mountain Portage in Peace River to the Sources of Finlays Branch and North West Ward in Summer 1824* (*By Samuel Black*) (London, 1955), p. 74.

18. James Adair, *The History of the American Indians; Particularly Those Nations adjoining to the Mississippi, East and West Florida, Georgia, South and North Carolina, and Virginia* . . . (London, 1775), pp. 426–27; George Simpson, *Narrative of a Journey Round the World During the Years 1841 and 1842* (London, 1847), I, 109; Hewitt (ed.), Denig, "Indian Tribes of the Upper Missouri," pp. 525–26.

19. Thomas Simpson, *Narrative of the Discoveries on the North Coast of America; Effected by the Officers of the Hudson's Bay Company During the Years 1836–1839* (London, 1843), p. 35; Tyrrell (ed.), *David Thompson's Narrative*, p. 81; [Ogden], *Traits of American Indian Life*, p. 98.

20. J. N. B. Hewitt (ed.), "Journal of Rudolph Friederich Kurz . . . ," trans. Myrtis Jarrell, *Bureau of American Ethnology Bulletin,* CXV (1937), 154.

21. Arthur S. Morton (ed.), *The Journal of Duncan M'Gillivray of the North West Company at Fort George on the Saskatchewan, 1794–5* (Toronto, Ont., 1929), p. 60; "Memoir of DeGannes Concerning the Illinois Country" in Theodore C. Pease and Raymond C. Werner (ed.), *The French Foundations, 1680–1693* (Springfield, Ill., 1934), p. 355; [Ogden], *Traits of American Indian Life,* p. 64.

22. Elliott Coues (ed.), *New Light on the Early History of the Greater Northwest: The Manuscript Journals of Alexander Henry and of David Thompson* (New York, 1897), I, 209; Mackenzie, *Voyages From Montreal,* pp. 228–29; Wallace (ed.), McLean's *Notes,* p. 50.

23. Quaife (ed.), Larpenteur's *Forty Years a Fur Trader,* p. 335; Hearne, *A Journey From Prince of Wales's Fort,* pp. 66–67, 307.

24. Hewitt (ed.), Denig's "Indian Tribes of the Upper Missouri," p. 525.

25. Quoted in Frank Edgar Farley, "The Dying Indian," in *Anniversary Papers by Colleagues and Pupils of George Lyman Kittredge . . .* (Boston, 1913), p. 251; John C. Ewers (ed.), *Adventures of Zenas Leonard Fur Trader* (Norman, Okla., 1959), p. 150; Adair, *History of the American Indians,* pp. 393–94; Cox, *The Columbia River,* I, 213–14.

26. Adair, *History of the American Indians,* p. 5; Clark Collection (MSS in the Missouri Historical Society, St. Louis), James Mackay, Notes on Indian Tribes; Sibley Papers, Martin McLeod to Sibley, Aug. 20, 1846; Bartholomew Berthold to B. Pratte & Co., Nov. 14, 1823, in Dale L. Morgan (ed.), *The West of William H. Ashley . . .* (Denver, Colo., 1964), p. 62.

27. "Journals and Correspondence of John McLeod, Senior, Chief Trader, Hudson's Bay Company, who was one of the Earliest Pioneers in the Oregon Territory, from 1812 to 1844" (MSS copied from the originals in the Dominion Government Archives by R. E. Gosnell; unpublished typescript in the Library of Congress), John Stuart to John McLeod, March 2, 1834, pp. 185–86; Harold Hickerson (ed.), "Journal of Charles Jean Baptiste Chaboillez, 1797–1798," *Ethnohistory* (Summer, 1959), p. 293 (Fall, 1959), p. 384; American Fur Company Papers (MSS in the New York Historical Society Library; microfilm copy in the Missouri Historical Society, St. Louis), Jean Baptiste DuBay to Ramsay Crooks, Feb. 11, 1837; Peter Garrioch Collection (MSS in the Public Archives of Manitoba, Winnipeg), Peter Garrioch Diary, 1843–47.

28. John Spencer Bassett (ed.), *The Writings of "Colonel William Byrd of Westover in Virginia Esqr."* (New York, 1901), p. 162.

29. Coues (ed.), *New Light,* II, 737; [Ogden], *Traits of American Indian Life,* p. 12; Grant, "The Sauteux Indians," pp. 348–49; John C. Ewers (ed.), Edwin Thompson Denig's *Five Indian Tribes of the Upper*

Missouri: Sioux, Arickaras, Assiniboines, Crees, Crows (Norman, Okla., 1961), p. 89.

30. Simpson, *Narrative of the Discoveries on the North Coast of America,* pp. 336–37; E. E. Rich (ed.), *Cumberland House Journals and Inland Journals 1775–82: Second Series, 1779–82* (London, 1952), pp. 263, 265, 275.

31. Harold E. Driver, *Indians of North America* (Chicago, 1961), p. 373; Chouteau Collections (MSS in the Missouri Historical Society, St. Louis), William Laidlaw to Kenneth McKenzie, Feb. 15, 1832, Fort Tecumseh and Fort Pierre Letterbook; Boller Papers, miscellaneous, undated item in Henry Boller's handwriting; J. L. Burpee (ed.), "Journal du Yukon 1847–48 par Alexander Hunter Murray," *Publications des Archives Canadiennes,* no. 4 (1910), p. 99.

32. Frederick Merk (ed.), *Fur Trade and Empire: George Simpson's Journal* . . . (Cambridge, Mass., 1931), pp. 97–98; Tyrrell (ed.), *David Thompson's Narrative,* p. 93; Morton (ed.), *Journal of M'Gillivray,* p. 63.

CHAPTER 10

1. John C. Ewers, "When the Light Shone in Washington," *Montana: The Magazine of Western History,* VI (Autumn, 1956), 2–11.

2. *Ibid.;* John C. Ewers (ed.), Edwin Thompson Denig's *Five Indian Tribes of the Upper Missouri: Sioux, Arickaras, Assiniboines, Crees, Crows* (Norman, Okla., 1961), pp. 86–88.

3. Ewers (ed.), Denig's *Five Indian Tribes of the Upper Missouri,* p. 114.

4. Milo Milton Quaife (ed.), Charles Larpenteur's *Forty Years a Fur Trader on the Upper Missouri* (Chicago, 1933), pp. 343–44.

5. Samuel Hearne, *A Journey From Prince of Wales's Fort in Hudson's Bay to the Northern Ocean. Undertaken by Order of the Hudson's Bay Company* . . . (London, 1795), pp. 80–83; Alexander Ross, *Adventures of the First Settlers on the Oregon or Columbia River. Being a Narrative of the Expedition Fitted out by John Jacob Astor* . . . (London, 1849), p. 328.

6. W. F. Wentzel, "Letters to the Hon. Roderic McKenzie, 1807–1824" in L. R. Masson, *Les bourgeois de la Compagnie du Nord-Ouest, recits de voyages, lettres et rapports inédits relatifs au nord-ouest Canadien.* . . . (New York, 1960), I, 108.

7. John Spencer Bassett (ed.), *The Writings of "Colonel William Byrd of Westover in Virginia Esqr."* (New York, 1901), pp. 98–99; Henry A. Boller Papers (MSS in the North Dakota Historical Society, Bismarck), Boller to sister, July, 1858 (continued on Aug. 7, 1858) and undated letter of requisition to family; [Peter Skene Ogden], *Traits of American Indian Life & Character By a Fur Trader* (modern ed.; San Francisco, Calif.,

1933), p. 2; Robert Michael Ballantyne, *The Wild Man of the West. A Tale of the Rocky Mountains* (Philadelphia, n.d.), p. 154.

8. Charles MacKenzie, "The Mississouri Indians, A Narrative of Four Trading Expeditions to the Mississouri, 1804–1805–1806" in Masson, *Les bourgeois,* I, 318; Theodore C. Blegen (ed.), *The Unfinished Autobiography of Henry Hastings Sibley Together with a Selection of Hitherto Unpublished Letters From the Thirties* (Minneapolis, Minn., 1932), p. 15.

9. Alexis Bailly Papers (MSS in the Minnesota Historical Society, St. Paul), Personal memorandum book 1821–30; James McKenzie, "The King's Posts and Journal of a Canoe Jaunt through the King's Domains, 1808" in Masson, *Les bourgeois,* II, 421; Thomas Simpson, *Narrative of the Discoveries on the North Coast of America; Effected by the Officers of the Hudson's Bay Company During the Years 1836–39* (London, 1843), p. 17.

10. Documents Historiques années 1818–1866 (MSS in the Archdiocesan Archives, Archbishop's Residence, St. Boniface, Manitoba), Alexander Fisher to Harry Munro [Henry] Fisher, April, 1826; McKenzie, "The King's Posts," p. 421.

11. E. E. Rich (ed.), *Journal of Occurrences in the Athabasca Department By George Simpson, 1820 and 1821, And Report* (Toronto, Ont., 1938), pp. 224, 290–93; W. S. Wallace (ed.), John McLean's *Notes of a Twenty-five Years' Service in the Hudson's Bay Territory* (Toronto, Ont., 1932), pp. 378–79.

12. John Askin Papers (MSS in the Burton Historical Collection, Detroit Public Library, Detroit), Askin to Mr. Catterson, June 17, 1778, Letterbook, April 28, 1778, to July 7, 1778; Ross Cox, *The Columbia River; or, Scenes and Adventures During A Residence of Six Years on the Western Side of the Rocky Mountains* . . . (3rd ed.; London, 1832), II, 305.

13. Documents Historiques, Alexander Fisher to Harry Munro [Henry] Fisher, April, 1826; Alexander Fisher to Henry Fisher, March 15, 1832; Alexander Fisher to Henry Fisher, March 15, 1833; Alexander Fisher to Henry Fisher, March 15, 1837; Alexander Fisher to Henry Fisher, March 15, 1838; Dun:[can] Finlayson to Henry Fisher, Dec. 27, 1839; Alexander Fisher to Henry Fisher, July 13, 1840.

14. Archibald MacDonald to Edward Ermatinger, April 1, 1836, in William S. Lewis and Naojiro Murakami (ed.), *Ranald McDonald: The Narrative of his early life on the Columbia . . . and his great Adventure to Japan* . . . (Spokane, Wash., 1923), pp. 26–28.

15. Archibald MacDonald to Edward Ermatinger, March 10, 1839; Archibald MacDonald to Edward Ermatinger, April 2, 1840; Archibald MacDonald to Edward Ermatinger, March 5, 1841; Archibald MacDonald to Edward Ermatinger, March 30, 1842, in Lewis and Murakami (ed.), *Ranald McDonald,* pp. 31–36. In spite of the warning, Ermatinger did "lose sight" of the boy. Happily, however, young MacDonald proved

an exception to the rule that traders' sons were doomed to failure or worse. This, I do not believe, detracts any from the relevance of the evidence embodied in his father's letters.

16. Kenneth A. Spaulding (ed.), Alexander Ross's *The Fur Hunters of the Far West* (Norman, Okla., 1956), pp. 191, 196.

17. Wallace (ed.), McLean's *Notes*, p. 132.

18. Elliott Coues (ed.), *New Light on the Early History of the Greater Northwest: The Manuscript Journals of Alexander Henry and of David Thompson* (New York, 1897), II, 452; cited in Richard Glover, "Introduction" in E. E. Rich (ed.), *Cumberland House Journals and Inland Journals 1775–82: Second Series, 1779–82* (London, 1952), p. xxvii; J. B. Tyrrell (ed.), *David Thompson's Narrative of his Explorations in Western America 1784–1813* (Toronto, Ont., 1916), p. 282; Wallace (ed.), McLean's *Notes*, p. 196.

19. Alexander Mackenzie, *Voyages From Montreal on the River St. Laurence [sic], through the Continent of North-America, to the Frozen and Pacific Oceans . . .* (3rd American ed.; New York, 1803), p. 86; J. N. B. Hewitt (ed.), "Journal of Rudolph Friederich Kurz . . . ," trans. Myrtis Jarrell, *Bureau of American Ethnology Bulletin*, CXV (1937), 30.

20. Arthur S. Morton (ed.), *The Journal of Duncan M'Gillivray of the North West Company at Fort George on the Saskatchewan, 1794–5* (Toronto, Ont., 1929), pp. 30, 72; J. B. Tyrrell (ed.), *Journals of Samuel Hearne and Philip Turnor* (Toronto, Ont., 1934), p. 171; Wallace (ed.), McLean's *Notes*, p. 50; Coues (ed.), *New Light*, I, 209.

21. Mackenzie, *Voyages From Montreal*, pp. 228–29; Francois-Victor Malhiot, "Journal du Fort Kamanaitiquoya a la Rivière Montréal, 1804–1805" in Masson, *Les bourgeois*, I, 238; Duncan Cameron, "The Nipigon Country, 1804—With Extracts from His Journal" in Masson, *Les bourgeois*, II, 248–49, 263.

22. Quaife (ed.), Larpenteur's *Forty Years a Fur Trader*, p. 37; J. N. B. Hewitt (ed.), Edwin Thompson Denig's "Indian Tribes of the Upper Missouri," *Bureau of American Ethnology Forty-sixth Annual Report* (1928–29), p. 530; Hearne, *A Journey From Prince of Wales's Fort*, pp. 272, 310; Mackenzie, *Voyages From Montreal*, pp. 105–6; Cox, *The Columbia River*, I, 291; J. V. Huntington (ed. and trans.), Gabriel Franchère's *Narrative of a Voyage to the Northwest Coast of America in the Years 1811, 1812, 1813, and 1814 or the First American Settlement on the Pacific* (New York, 1854), p. 241.

23. Frederick Merk (ed.), *Fur Trade and Empire: George Simpson's Journal . . .* (Cambridge, Mass., 1931), p. 109.

24. Chouteau Collections (MSS in the Missouri Historical Society, St. Louis), Kenneth McKenzie to D. D. Mitchell, Feb. 14, 1832; Pierre

Chouteau to General Dearborn, Secretary of War, Nov. 19, 1804, Pierre Chouteau Letter Book, Oct. 18, 1804, to April 25, 1809; American Fur Company Letter Book, Dec. 16, 1816, to June 22, 1819 (MSS in Astor House, Mackinac Island; photocopy in Wisconsin Historical Society, Madison), Ramsay Crooks to John Jacob Astor, June 23, 1817; Lawe Papers (MSS in the Chicago Historical Society, Chicago), Ramsay Crooks to John Lawe, Feb. 15, 1835; David Lavender, *Bent's Fort* (Dolphin paperback; Garden City, N.Y., 1954), pp. 159–60. In "The Fur Traders in Northern Indiana, 1796–1850" (Ph.D. dissertation, Indiana University, 1953), Bert Anson wrote: "It is certain that much of the corruption of the Indians through whiskey was accomplished by nameless squatters, rather than by licensed traders . . ." (p. 276).

25. Cameron, "The Nipigon Country," p. 248; Morton (ed.), *Journal of M'Gillivray,* pp. 60–61.

26. Arthur Alphonse Ekirch, Jr., *The Idea of Progress in America, 1815–1860* (New York, 1951), pp. 13, 41–46, 267.

27. Roy Harvey Pearce, *The Savages of America: A Study of the Indian and the Idea of Civilization* (Baltimore, Md., 1953), pp. 48, 49, 89, 232.

28. *Ibid.,* pp. 58, 85, 136–46, 151, 160.

29. Henry Nash Smith, *Virgin Land: The American West as Symbol and Myth* (Vintage paperback; New York, 1957), pp. 55, 83, 135, 267, 303.

30. John William Ward, *Andrew Jackson: Symbol for an Age* (New York, 1955). See, especially, chapter III, "Nature's Nobleman."

31. Charles L. Sanford, *The Quest for Paradise: Europe and the American Moral Imagination* (Urbana, Ill., 1961), pp. vi, 15, 18, 93, 108.

32. Leslie Fiedler, "Montana: Or the End of Jean-Jacques Rousseau," in *An End to Innocence: Essays on Culture and Politics* (Beacon paperback; Boston, 1957), p. 132.

33. Pearce, *The Savages of America,* p. 240; Clark Collection (MSS in the Missouri Historical Society, St. Louis), James Mackay, Notes on Indian Tribes; George Simpson, *Narrative of a Journey Round the World During the Years 1841 and 1842* (London, 1847), II, 19; Pearce, *The Savages of America,* p. 127; quoted in Henry R. Schoolcraft, *Historical and Statistical Information Respecting the History, Condition and Prospects of the Indian Tribes of the United States . . .* (Philadelphia, 1851–57), I, 261.

34. Irvin Wyllie, "Social Darwinism and the Businessman," *American Philosophical Society Proceedings* (Oct. 15, 1959); Culbertson Collection (MSS in the Missouri Historical Society, St. Louis), journal of Major Alexander Culbertson of the American Fur Company; [Ogden], *Traits of American Indian Life,* p. 104.

35. Bailly Papers, Alexis Bailly, Personal memorandum book and

miscellaneous accounts, 1823; Askin Papers, diary, history notes, and essays of Hugh Heward; Boller Papers, Boller to sister, July 15, 1859; Percy G. Adams, *Travelers and Travel Liars, 1660–1800* (Los Angeles, Calif., 1962), p. 198; Edward Umfreville, *The Present State of Hudson's Bay. Containing a Full Description of that Settlement, and the Adjacent Country; and Likewise of the Fur Trade* . . . (London, 1790), p. 29.

36. Grace Lee Nute (ed.), "The Diary of Martin McLeod," *Minnesota Historical Bulletin,* IV (1921–22), 390.

CHAPTER 11

1. *Report of the Select Committee on the Hudson's Bay Company* (London, 1857), p. 42; Seymour Dunbar and Paul C. Phillips (ed.), *The Journals and Letters of Major John Owen* . . . (New York, 1927), I, 262.

2. Milo Milton Quaife (ed.), Charles Larpenteur's *Forty Years a Fur Trader on the Upper Missouri* (Chicago, 1933), p. 352.

3. Christopher Carson, "Report" in *Report of the Commissioner of Indian Affairs* (1857), p. 568; Reuben Gold Thwaites (ed.), John Long's *Voyages and Travels of an Indian Interpreter and Trader* . . . (Cleveland, Ohio, 1904), p. 116.

4. John C. Ewers (ed.), Edwin Thompson Denig's *Five Indian Tribes of the Upper Missouri: Sioux, Arickaras, Assiniboines, Crees, Crows* (Norman, Okla., 1961), pp. 94–95; Thomas Simpson, *Narrative of the Discoveries on the North Coast of America; Effected by the Officers of the Hudson's Bay Company During the Years 1836–39* (London, 1843), p. 17; Alexander Ross, *The Red River Settlement: Its Rise, Progress, and Present State. With Some Account of the Native Races and Its General History, to the Present Day* (London, 1856), p. 276.

5. Bernard DeVoto, *Across the Wide Missouri* (Boston, 1947), pp. 200–202.

6. J. V. Huntington (ed. and trans.), Gabriel Franchère's *Narrative of a Voyage to the Northwest Coast of America in the Years 1811, 1812, 1813, and 1814 or the First American Settlement on the Pacific* (New York, 1854), p. 261; Simpson, *Narrative of the Discoveries,* pp. 17–18. Simpson probably never saw the far West tribes. Thus, this comment probably reflects fur-trade consensus rather than his personal opinion; K. G. Davies (ed.), *Peter Skene Ogden's Snake Country Journal, 1826–27* (London, 1961), p. 21.

7. DeVoto, *Across the Wide Missouri,* p. 202; Maurice S. Sullivan (ed.), *The Travels of Jedediah Smith; A Documentary Outline Including the Journal of the Great American Pathfinder* (Santa Ana, Calif., 1934), pp. 72–73.

8. See "Introduction" to Richard Glover (ed.), *David Thompson's Narrative, 1784–1813* (Toronto, Ont., 1962); J. B. Tyrrell (ed.), *David Thompson's Narrative of his Explorations in Western America 1784–1813* (Toronto, Ont., 1916), p. 498.

9. Ewers (ed.), Denig's *Five Indian Tribes,* pp. 61–62.

10. Philip Ashton Rollins (ed.), *The Discovery of the Oregon Trail: Robert Stuart's Narratives of His Overland Trip Eastward From Astoria in 1812–13* (New York, 1935), p. 62.

11. J. N. B. Hewitt (ed.), "Journal of Rudolph Friederich Kurz . . . ," trans. Myrtis Jarrell, *Bureau of American Ethnology Bulletin,* CXV (1937), 295–96; Donald Mackenzie to Governor Simpson, July 27, 1823, in Cecil W. Mackenzie, *Donald Mackenzie "King of the Northwest": The Story of an International Hero of the Oregon Country and the Red River Settlement at Lower Fort Garry (Winnipeg)* (Los Angeles, Calif., 1937), pp. 141–42.

12. Quoted in LeRoy R. Hafen and W. J. Ghent, *Broken Hand: The Life Story of Thomas Fitzpatrick, Chief of the Mountain Men* (Denver, Colo., 1931), p. 259.

13. Alexander Ross, *Adventures of the First Settlers on the Oregon or Columbia River: Being a Narrative of the Expedition Fitted out by John Jacob Astor* (London, 1849), pp. 130–31.

14. Lawrence Taliaferro Papers (MSS in the Minnesota Historical Society, St. Paul), Alexis Bailly to Taliaferro, Feb. 16, 1828; quoted in Hafen and Ghent, *Broken Hand,* p. 259.

15. Frederick Merk (ed.), *Fur Trade and Empire: George Simpson's Journal* . . . (Cambridge, Mass., 1931), p. 108.

16. Christopher Carson, "Report" in *Report of the Commissioner of Indian Affairs* (1858), p. 547; Simpson, *Narrative of the Discoveries,* p. 222; Ross, *Adventures of the First Settlers,* p. 335; Ross, *The Red River Settlement,* p. 80.

17. J. N. B. Hewitt (ed.), Edwin Thompson Denig's "Indian Tribes of the Upper Missouri," *Bureau of American Ethnology Forty-sixth Annual Report* (1928–29), p. 625; Ross, *The Red River Settlement,* pp. 305–6.

18. Governor Simpson to Gov. J. H. Pelly, Feb. 1, 1837, in Merk (ed.), *Fur Trade and Empire,* pp. 335–36; see *ibid.,* pp. 102, 106, 135; James B. Marsh, *Four Years in the Rockies; or, The Adventures of Isaac P. Rose . . . Being One of the Most Thrilling Narratives Ever Published* (Columbus, Ohio, n.d.), p. 109. In *Across the Wide Missouri,* pp. 224–25, Bernard DeVoto recounted this incident, but his assessment of the Indians' actions differed markedly from Rose's.

19. Robert Michael Ballantyne, *The Wild Man of the West. A Tale of the Rocky Mountains* (Philadelphia, n.d.), pp. 100–101, 214–17.

20. [Peter Skene Ogden], *Traits of American Indian Life & Character By a Fur Trader* (modern ed.; San Francisco, Calif., 1933), p. 85.

21. Ross, *Adventures of the First Settlers,* pp. 332–33; quoted in Henry R. Schoolcraft, *Historical and Statistical Information Respecting the History, Condition and Prospects of the Indian Tribes of the United States* . . . (Philadelphia, 1851–57), I, 263.

22. John Work to Edward Ermatinger, Oct. 24, 1839, in "Old Letters from Hudson Bay Company Officials and Employes from 1829 to 1840," *Washington Historical Quarterly,* II (April, 1908), 263; Martin McLeod Papers (MSS in the Minnesota Historical Society, St. Paul), McLeod to Rev. Mr. Potter, missionary, Sept. 25, 1849; this document is evidently a rough draft.

23. Alexis Bailly Papers (MSS in the Minnesota Historical Society, St. Paul), Personal memorandum book, 1821–30; George Simpson to Andrew Colvile, May 20, 1822, in Merk (ed.), *Fur Trade and Empire,* p. 181; Ross, *The Red River Settlement,* p. 283.

24. R. F. Harding to James Hargrave, June 23, 1843, in G. P. deT. Glazebrook (ed.), *The Hargrave Correspondence, 1821–1843* (Toronto, Ont., 1938), p. 444; Ross, *The Red River Settlement,* pp. 322–23.

25. Hewitt (ed.), Denig's "Indian Tribes of the Upper Missouri," pp. 491, 594.

26. Ross, *The Red River Settlement,* p. 304; Quaife (ed.), Larpenteur's *Forty Years a Fur Trader,* pp. 355–56; Hewitt (ed.), Denig's "Indian Tribes of the Upper Missouri," pp. 624–25.

27. Carson, "Report" (1857), p. 567.

28. Henry A. Boller Papers (MSS in the North Dakota Historical Society, Bismarck), Journal of a Trip to, and Residence in, the Indian Country. Commenced Saturday, May 22^d 1858; William Woodbridge Papers (MSS in the Burton Historical Collection, Detroit Public Library, Detroit), Robert Stuart to Woodbridge, Nov. 11, 1841; Tyrrell (ed.), *David Thompson's Narrative,* pp. 142, 241.

29. Tyrrell (ed.), *David Thompson's Narrative,* pp. 142, 301.

30. Charles MacKenzie, "The Mississouri Indians, A Narrative of Four Trading Expeditions to the Mississouri, 1804–1805–1806" in L. R. Masson, *Les bourgeois de la Compagnie du Nord-Ouest, recits de voyages, lettres et rapports inédits relatifs au nord-ouest Canadien* . . . (New York, 1960), I, 331.

31. Davies (ed.), *Ogden's Snake Country Journal,* p. 54; Quaife (ed.), Larpenteur's *Forty Years a Fur Trader,* pp. 359–60.

BIBLIOGRAPHY

BIBLIOGRAPHICAL WORKS

Cuthbertson, Stuart, and John C. Ewers (compilers). "A Preliminary Bibliography on the American Fur Trade." (Typescript.) St. Louis: U.S. Department of the Interior, National Park Service, Jefferson National Expansion Memorial, 1939.

Dockstadter, Frederick J. *The American Indian in Graduate Studies: A Bibliography of Theses and Dissertations.* New York: Museum of the American Indian, Heye Foundation, 1957.

Fenton, William N., L. H. Butterfield, and Wilcomb E. Washburn. *American Indian and White Relations to 1830: Needs & Opportunities for Study.* Chapel Hill, N.C.: University of North Carolina Press, 1957.

Field, Thomas W. *An Essay Towards an Indian Bibliography. Being a catalogue of books, relating to the history, antiquities, languages, customs, religion, wars, literature, and origin of the American Indians, in the library of Thomas W. Field. With bibliographical and historical notes, and synopses of the contents of some of the works least known.* New York: Scribner, Armstrong, and Co., 1873.

Matthews, William, and Roy Harvey Pearce (compilers). *American Diaries: An Annotated Bibliography of American Diaries Written Prior to the Year 1861.* (University of California Publications in English, Vol. XVI.) Berkeley: University of California Press, 1945.

Vail, R. W. G. *The Voice of the Old Frontier.* Philadelphia: University of Pennsylvania Press, 1949.

Wagner, Henry R. *The Plains and the Rockies: A Bibliography of Original Narratives of Travel and Adventure.* Revised by Charles L. Camp. Columbus, Ohio: Long's College Book Company, 1953.

GENERAL WORKS

Books

Adams, Percy G. *Travelers and Travel Liars, 1660–1800.* Berkeley: University of California Press, 1962.

Benedict, Ruth. *Patterns of Culture.* Boston: Houghton Mifflin Company, 1934.

――――. *Race: Science and Politics.* New York: Modern Age Books, 1940.

Bissell, Benjamin. *The American Indian in English Literature of the Eighteenth Century.* (Yale Studies in English, Vol. LXVIII.) New Haven, Conn.: Yale University Press, 1925.

Bryce, George. *The Remarkable History of the Hudson's Bay Company Including that of the French Traders of North-Western Canada and of the North-West, XY, and Astor Fur Companies.* London: Sampson Low Marston & Company, 1932.

Chittenden, Hiram Martin. *The American Fur Trade of the Far West: A History of the Pioneer Trading Posts and Early Fur Companies of the Missouri Valley and the Rocky Mountains and of the Overland Commerce with Santa Fe.* 2 vols. New York: The Press of the Pioneers, Inc., 1935.

Commager, Henry Steele. *The American Mind: An Interpretation of American Thought and Character Since the 1880's.* New Haven, Conn.: Yale University Press, 1950.

Curti, Merle. *The Growth of American Thought.* 2nd ed. New York: Harper & Brothers, 1951.

Davidson, Gordon Charles. *The North West Company.* (University of California Publications in History, Vol. VII.) Berkeley: University of California Press, 1918.

DeVoto, Bernard. *Across the Wide Missouri.* Boston: Houghton Mifflin Company, 1947.

――――. *The Course of Empire.* Boston: Houghton Mifflin Company, 1952.

――――. *The Year of Decision: 1846.* Boston: Little, Brown and Company, 1943.

Driver, Harold E. *Indians of North America.* Chicago: University of Chicago Press, 1961.

Ekirch, Arthur Alphonse, Jr. *The Idea of Progress in America, 1815–1860.* Reprint. New York: Peter Smith, 1951.

Erasmus, Desiderius. *The Praise of Folly.* Translated by Leonard F. Dean. Chicago: Packard and Company, 1946.

Fairchild, Hoxie Neale. *The Noble Savage: A Study in Romantic Naturalism.* New York: Columbia University Press, 1928.

Gorer, Geoffery. *The American People: A Study in National Character.* New York: W. W. Norton & Co., 1948.

Hafen, LeRoy R., and W. J. Ghent. *Broken Hand: The Life Story of Thomas Fitzpatrick, Chief of the Mountain Men.* Denver, Colo.: The Old West Publishing Company, 1931.

Hagan, William T. *American Indians.* Chicago: University of Chicago Press, 1961.

Hazard, Lucy Lockwood. *The Frontier in American Literature*. New York: Thomas Y. Crowell Company, 1927.

Howard, Joseph Kinsey. *Strange Empire: A Narrative of the Northwest*. New York: William Morrow and Company, 1952.

Joad, C. E. M. *Decadence: A Philosophical Inquiry*. London: Faber and Faber Limited, 1948.

Keiser, Albert. *The Indian in American Literature*. New York: Oxford University Press, 1933.

Kroeber, A. L. *Cultural and Natural Areas of Native North America*. (University of California Publications in American Archaeology and Ethnology, Vol. XXXVIII.) Berkeley: University of California Press, 1939.

Lavender, David. *Bent's Fort*. Garden City, N.Y.: Doubleday & Company, Inc., 1954.

Lovejoy, Arthur O., and George Boas. *Primitivism and Related Ideas in Antiquity*. Vol. I of *A Documentary History of Primitivism and Related Ideas*. Edited by Arthur O. Lovejoy, Gilbert Chinard, George Boas, and Ronald S. Crane. Baltimore, Md.: The Johns Hopkins Press, 1935.

Morison, Samuel Eliot, and Henry Steele Commager. *The Growth of the American Republic*. 2 vols. 4th ed., rev. and enl. New York: Oxford University Press, 1954.

Morton, Arthur S. *Sir George Simpson, Overseas Governor of the Hudson's Bay Company: A Pen Picture of a Man Of Action*. Portland, Ore.: Oregon Historical Society, 1944.

Parkman, Francis. *The Conspiracy of Pontiac*. 2 vols. New York: Everyman's Library edition, 1908.

Pearce, Roy Harvey. *The Savages of America: A Study of the Indian and the Idea of Civilization*. Baltimore, Md.: The Johns Hopkins Press, 1953.

Phillips, Paul Chrisler. *The Fur Trade*. Norman: University of Oklahoma Press, 1961.

Prucha, Francis Paul. *American Indian Policy in the Formative Years: The Indian Trade and Intercourse Acts 1790–1834*. Cambridge, Mass.: Harvard University Press, 1962.

Rich, E. E. *The History of the Hudson's Bay Company, 1670–1870*. 2 vols. (Publications of the Hudson's Bay Record Society, Vols. XXI and XXII.) London: The Hudson's Bay Record Society, 1958.

Roe, Frank Gilbert. *The North American Buffalo: A Critical Study of the Species in Its Wild State*. Toronto, Ont.: University of Toronto Press, 1951.

Sanford, Charles L. *The Quest for Paradise: Europe and the American Moral Imagination*. Urbana: University of Illinois Press, 1961.

Smith, Henry Nash. *Virgin Land: The American West as Symbol and Myth.* New York: Vintage Paperback, 1957.

Stevenson, Burton. *The Home Book of Proverbs, Maxims and Familiar Phrases.* New York: The Macmillan Company, 1948.

Taylor, Archer, and Bartlett Jere Whiting. *A Dictionary of American Proverbs and Proverbial Phrases 1820–1880.* Cambridge, Mass.: The Belknap Press of Harvard University Press, 1958.

Tinker, Chauncey Brewster. *Nature's Simple Plan: A Phase of Radical Thought in the Mid-Eighteenth Century.* Princeton, N.J.: Princeton University Press, 1922.

Turner, Frederick Jackson. *The Character and Influence of the Indian Trade in Wisconsin: A Study of the Trading Post as an Institution.* (The Johns Hopkins University Studies in Historical and Political Science, Vol. IX, Nos. XI-XII.) Baltimore, Md.: The Johns Hopkins Press, 1891.
———. *The Frontier in American History.* New York: Henry Holt and Company, 1920.

Vestal, Stanley. *Kit Carson, the Happy Warrior of the Old West: A Biography.* New York: Houghton Mifflin, 1928.

Ward, John William. *Andrew Jackson. Symbol for an Age.* New York: Oxford University Press, 1955.

Wissler, Clark. *Indians of the United States: Four Centuries of their History and Culture.* Garden City, N.Y.: Doubleday & Company, Inc., 1954.

Wright, Louis B. *Culture on the Moving Frontier.* Bloomington: Indiana University Press, 1955.

Articles and Essays

Burt, A. L. "If Turner Had Looked at Canada, Australia, and New Zealand When He Wrote about the West," in Walker D. Wyman and Clifton B. Kroeber (ed.), *The Frontier in Perspective.* Madison: University of Wisconsin Press, 1957.

Ewers, John C. "When the Light Shone in Washington," *Montana: The Magazine of Western History,* VI (Autumn, 1956), 2–11.

Farley, Frank Edgar. "The Dying Indian," in *Anniversary Papers by Colleagues and Pupils of George Lyman Kittredge, presented on the completion of his twenty-fifth year of teaching in Harvard University, June, MCMXIII.* Boston: Ginn and Company, 1913.

Fiedler, Leslie. "Montana: Or the End of Jean-Jacques Rousseau," in Fiedler, *An End to Innocence: Essays on Culture and Politics.* Boston: Beacon Paperback, 1957.

Geyl, Pieter. "Huizinga as Accuser of His Age," in *History and Theory: Studies in the Philosophy of History,* II, no. 3 (1963), 231–62.

Goetzmann, William. "The Mountain Man as Jacksonian Man," *American Quarterly,* XV (Fall, 1963), 402–15.

Goldman, Eric. "The Years of the Unraised Eyebrow," St. Louis *Post-Dispatch,* Oct. 11, 1959 (reprinted from *Princeton Alumni Weekly*).

Howay, F. W. "Indian Attacks upon Maritime Traders of the North-West Coast, 1785–1805," *The Canadian Historical Review,* VI (December, 1925), 287–309.

Krutch, Joseph Wood. "The Infatuation with the Primitive," *Saturday Review,* XLV (Sept. 29, 1962), 14–16.

Le Suer, Meridel. "The First Farmers' Revolt," *Mainstream,* XV (March, 1962), 21–26.

Lovejoy, A. O. "The Supposed Primitivism of Rousseau's *Discourse on Inequality,*" *Modern Philology,* XXI (1923), 165–86.

McKay, Douglas. "Men of the Old Fur Trade: Peter Skene Ogden," *The Beaver: A Magazine of the North,* Outfit 269 (June, 1938), no. 1, pp. 7–9.

MacLennan, Hugh. "By Canoe to Empire," *American Heritage,* XII (October, 1961), 4–7, 94–101.

Nute, Grace Lee. "The Papers of the American Fur Company: A Brief Estimate of their Significance," *American Historical Review,* XXXII (April, 1927), 519–38.

Peckham, Howard H. "Indian Relations in the United States," in John Francis McDermott (ed.), *Research Opportunities in American Cultural History.* Lexington: University of Kentucky Press, 1961.

Wyllie, Irvin. "Social Darwinism and the Businessman," *American Philosophical Society Proceedings,* Vol. CV (Oct. 15, 1959).

FUR TRADE ACCOUNTS AND WORKS CONTAINING FUR TRADE ACCOUNTS

Books

Abel, Annie Heloise (ed.). *Chardon's Journal at Fort Clark, 1834–1839: Descriptive of Life on the Upper Missouri; of a Fur Trader's Experiences Among the Mandans, Gros Ventres, and Their Neighbors; of the Ravages of the Smallpox Epidemic of 1837.* Pierre, S.D.: Published under the auspices of Lawrence K. Fox, 1932.

———— (ed.). *Tabeau's Narrative of Loisel's Expedition to the Upper Missouri.* Translated by Rose Abel Wright. Norman: University of Oklahoma Press, 1939.

Adair, James. *The History of the American Indians; Particularly Those Nations adjoining to the Mississippi, East and West Florida, Georgia, South and North Carolina, and Virginia: Containing An Account of their Origin, Language, Manners, Religion etc. etc.* London: Printed for Edward and Charles Dilly, in the Poultry, 1775.

Adams, Arthur T. (ed.). *The Explorations of Pierre Esprit Radisson.* From the original manuscript in the Bodleian Library and the British Museum. Minneapolis, Minn.: Ross & Haines, Inc., 1961.

Arber, Edward (ed.). *Capt. John Smith, of Willoughby by Alford, Lincolnshire; President of Virginia, and Admiral of New England. Works. 1608–1631.* Birmingham, Eng., 1884.

Ballantyne, Robert Michael. *Hudson Bay; or, Everyday Life in the Wilds of North America, During Six Years' Residence in the Territories of the Hon. Hudson Bay Company.* London: Thomas Nelson and Sons, 1876.

———. *The Wild Man of the West. A Tale of the Rocky Mountains.* Philadelphia: Porter & Coates, n.d.

Barker, Burt Brown. *The McLoughlin Empire and Its Rulers Doctor John McLoughlin Doctor David McLoughlin Marie Louise (Sister St. Henry): An account of their personal lives, and of their parents, relatives and children; in Canada's Quebec Province, in Paris, France, and in the West of the Hudson's Bay Company.* (Northwest Historical Series, Vol. V.) Glendale, Calif.: The Arthur H. Clark Company, 1959.

Bassett, John Spencer (ed.). *The Writings of "Colonel William Byrd of Westover in Virginia Esqr."* New York: Doubleday, Page & Co., 1901.

Beauchamp, William N. (ed.). *The Life of Conrad Weiser As it Relates to His Services as Official Interpreter Between New York and Pennsylvania and as Envoy Between Philadelphia and the Onondaga Councils.* Syracuse, N.Y.: Onondaga Historical Association, 1925.

Beckwourth, James P. *The Life and Adventures of James P. Beckwourth, Mountaineer, Scout, and Pioneer, and Chief of the Crow Nation of Indians.* Written from his own dictation by T. D. Bonner. New York: Harper & Brothers, 1856.

Biggar, H. P., *et al.* (ed.). *The Works of Samuel De Champlain.* 6 vols. (Publications of the Champlain Society.) Toronto, Ont.: The Champlain Society, 1922–36.

Blegen, Theodore C. (ed.). *The Unfinished Autobiography of Henry Hastings Sibley Together with Selection of Hitherto Unpublished Letters from the Thirties.* Minneapolis, Minn.: The Voyageur Press, 1932.

Boller, Henry A. *Among the Indians. Eight Years in the Far West: 1858–1866. Embracing Sketches of Montana and Salt Lake.* Philadelphia: T. Ellwood Zell, 1868.

Burpee, Lawrence J. (ed.). *Journals and Letters of Pierre Gaultier de Varennes de la Vérendrye and his Sons with Correspondence Between the Governors of Canada and the French Court, Touching the Search for the Western Sea.* (Publications of the Champlain Society, Vol. XVI.) Toronto, Ont.: The Champlain Society, 1927.

Burrage, Henry S. (ed.). *Early English and French Voyages Chiefly from Hakluyt, 1534–1608.* New York: Charles Scribner's Sons, 1906.

Camp, Charles L. (ed.). *James Clyman American Frontiersman, 1792–1881: The Adventures of a Trapper and Covered Wagon Emigrant as Told in his Own Reminiscences and Diaries.* Definitive ed. Portland, Ore.: Champoeg Press, 1960.

Conard, Howard Louis. *"Uncle Dick" Wootton The Pioneer Frontiersman of the Rocky Mountain Region: An Account of the Adventures and Thrilling Experiences of the Most Noted American Hunter, Trapper, Guide, Scout, and Indian Fighter Now Living.* Chicago: W. E. Dibble & Co., 1890.

Coues, Elliott (ed.). *New Light on the Early History of the Greater Northwest: The Manuscript Journals of Alexander Henry and of David Thompson.* 3 vols. New York: Francis P. Harper, 1897.

—————— (ed.). *The Journal of Jacob Fowler Narrating an Adventure from Arkansas through the Indian Territory, Oklahoma, Kansas, Colorado, and New Mexico to the Sources of the Rio Grande del Norte, 1821–22.* New York: Francis P. Harper, 1898.

Cowie, Isaac. *The Company of Adventurers: A Narrative of Seven Years in the Service of the Hudson's Bay Company During 1867–1874 on the Great Buffalo Plains.* Toronto, Ont.: William Briggs, 1913.

Cox, Ross. *The Columbia River; or, Scenes and Adventures During A Residence of Six Years on the Western Side of the Rocky Mountains among Various Tribes of Indians hitherto unknown; together with A Journey Across the American Continent.* 2 vols. 3rd ed. London: Henry Colburn and Richard Bentley, 1832.

Cumming, William P. (ed.). *The Discoveries of John Lederer: With Unpublished Letters By and About Lederer to Governor John Winthrop, Jr. and an Essay on the Indians of Lederer's Discoveries by Douglas L. Rights and William P. Cumming.* Charlottesville: University of Virginia Press, 1958.

Dale, Harrison C. *The Ashley-Smith Explorations and the Discovery of a Central Route to the Pacific 1822–1829.* Rev. ed. Glendale, Calif.: The Arthur H. Clark Company, 1941.

Davies, K. G. (ed.). *Peter Skene Ogden's Snake Country Journal 1826–27.* (Publications of the Hudson's Bay Record Society, Vol. XXIII.) London: The Hudson's Bay Record Society, 1961.

Doughty, Arthur G., and Chester Martin (ed.). *The Kelsey Papers.* Ottawa, Ont.: The Public Archives of Canada and the Public Record Office of Northern Ireland, 1929.

Douglas, David. *Journal Kept By David Douglas During His Travels in North America 1823–1827: Together With A Particular Description Of Thirty-Three Species of American Oaks And Eighteen Species of Pinus: With Appendices Containing A List of the Plants Introduced by Douglas and an Account of his Death in 1834.* Reprint. New York: Antiquarian Press Ltd., 1959.

Douglas, R. (ed.). *Nipigon to Winnipeg: A Canoe Voyage through Western Ontario by Edward Umfreville in 1794. With Extracts from the Writings of Other Early Travellers through the Region.* Ottawa, Ont.: Commercial Printing, 1929.

———, and J. N. Wallace (eds. and trans.). *Twenty Years of York Factory 1694–1714: Jérémie's Account of Hudson Strait and Bay.* Ottawa, Ont.: Thorburn and Abbott, 1926.

Douglas, Walter V. (ed.). Thomas James's *Three Years Among the Indians and Mexicans.* St. Louis: Missouri Historical Society, 1916.

Drumm, Stella (ed.). John C. Luttig's *Journal of a Fur-Trading Expedition on the Upper Missouri, 1812–1813.* St. Louis: Missouri Historical Society, 1920.

Dunbar, Seymour, and Paul C. Phillips (ed.). *The Journals and Letters of Major John Owen Pioneer of the Northwest 1850–1871 Embracing his Purchase of St. Mary's Mission; the Building of Fort Owen; his Travels; his Relation with the Indians; his Work for the Government; and his Activities as a Western Empire Builder for Twenty Years.* 2 vols. New York: Edward Eberstadt, 1927.

Dunn, John. *The Oregon Territory, and the British North American Fur Trade. With an Account of the Habits and Customs of the Principal Native Tribes on the Northern Continent.* Philadelphia: G. B. Zieber & Co., 1845.

Eberstadt, Charles (ed.). *The Rocky Mountain Letters of Robert Campbell.* n.p. Printed for Frederick W. Beinecke, 1955.

Ellison, William Henry (ed.). *The Life and Adventures of George Nidever 1802–1883.* Berkeley: University of California Press, 1937.

Ewers, John C. (ed.). *Adventures of Zenas Leonard Fur Trader.* Norman: University of Oklahoma Press, 1959.

——— (ed.). Edwin Thompson Denig's *Five Indian Tribes of the Upper Missouri: Sioux, Arickaras, Assiniboines, Crees, Crows.* Norman: University of Oklahoma Press, 1961.

Flint, Timothy (ed.). *The Personal Narrative of James O. Pattie, of Kentucky, During an Expedition from St. Louis, Through the Vast Regions between that Place and the Pacific Ocean, and Thence back through the City of Mexico to Vera Cruz, During Journeyings of Six Years; in which He and his Father, who accompanied him, Suffered unheard of hardships and dangers, had various conflicts with the Indians, and were made captives, in which captivity his father died; together with a description of the country, and the various nations through which they passed.* Cincinnati, Ohio: E. H. Flint, 1833.

Garrard, Lewis H. *Wah-To-Yah and the Taos Trail or Prairie Travel and Scalp Dances, with a Look at Los Rancheros from Muleback and the Rocky Mountain Campfire.* Introduction by A. B. Guthrie, Jr. Modern ed. Norman: University of Oklahoma Press, 1955.

Gates, Charles M. (ed.). *Five Fur Traders of the Northwest: Being the Narrative of Peter Pond and the Diaries of John MacDonell, Archibald N. McLeod, Hugh Faries and Thomas Connor.* Minneapolis: University of Minnesota Press, 1933.

Glazebrook, G. P. deT. (ed.). *The Hargrave Correspondence, 1821–1843.* (Publications of the Champlain Society, Vol. XXIV.) Toronto, Ont.: The Champlain Society, 1938.

Glover, Richard (ed.). *David Thompson's Narrative, 1784–1813.* Toronto, Ont.: The Champlain Society, 1962.

Hafen, LeRoy R. (ed.). *Ruxton of the Rockies.* Collected by Clyde and Mae Reed Porter. Norman: University of Oklahoma Press, 1950.

———, and Ann W. Hafen (ed.). *Rufus B. Sage: His Letters and Papers 1836–1847 with an annotated reprint of his "Scenes in the Rocky Mountains and in Oregon, California, New Mexico, Texas, and the Grand Prairies."* 2 vols. Glendale, Calif.: The Arthur H. Clark Company, 1956.

———, and ——— (ed.). *To the Rockies and Oregon 1839–1842 With diaries and accounts by Sidney Smith, Amos Cook, Joseph Holman, E. Willard Smith, Francis Fletcher, Joseph Williams, Obadiah Oakley, Robert Shortess, T. J. Farnham.* Glendale, Calif.: The Arthur H. Clark Company, 1955.

Hamilton, W. T. *My Sixty Years on the Plains Trapping, Trading, and Indian Fighting.* From the original edition by E. T. Sieber. Introduction by Donald J. Berthrong. Norman: University of Oklahoma Press, 1960.

Hargrave, Joseph James. *Red River.* Montreal, Quebec: Printed for the author by John Lovell, 1871.

Harmon, Daniel W. *A Journal of Voyages and Travels in the Interior of North America between the 47th and 58th degree of North latitude, extending from Montreal nearly to the Pacific Ocean, a distance of about 5000 miles, including an account of the Principal occurrences during a residence of nearly nineteen years in different parts of that country To which are added A Concise Description of the face of the Country, Its Inhabitants, their manners, customs, laws, etc.* Originally edited in 1820 by Daniel Haskell. New York: Allerton Book Co., 1922.

Hearne, Samuel. *A Journey From Prince of Wales's Fort in Hudson's Bay, to the Northern Ocean. Undertaken by Order of the Hudson's Bay Company, for the Discovery of Copper Mines, a North West Passage, &c. In the Years 1769, 1770, 1771, & 1772.* London: Printed for A. Strahan and T. Cadell, 1795.

Hellman, George S. (ed.). *Letters of Henry Brevoort to Washington Irving together with other unpublished Brevoort Papers.* New York: G. P. Putnam's Sons, 1918.

Henry, Alexander. *Travels and Adventures in Canada and The Indian Territories between the Years 1760 and 1776.* 2 parts. New York: I. Riley, 1809.

Hubbard, Gurdon Saltonstall. *The Autobiography of Gurdon Saltonstall Hubbard Pa-Pa-Ma-Ta-Be "The Swift Walker."* Introduction by Caroline M. McIlwaine. Chicago: R. R. Donnelley & Sons Company, 1911.

Huntington, J. V. (ed. and trans.). Gabriel Franchère's *Narrative of a Voyage to the Northwest Coast of America in the Years 1811, 1812, 1813, and 1814 or the First American Settlement on the Pacific.* New York: Redfield, 1854.

Irving, Washington. *Adventures of Captain Bonneville, or Scenes Beyond the Rocky Mountains of the Far West.* 3 vols. London: Richard Bentley, 1837.

Jameson, J. Franklin (ed.). *Narratives of New Netherland 1609-1664.* New York: Charles Scribner's Sons, 1909.

Johansen, Dorothy O. (ed.). *Robert Newell's Memoranda: Travles in the Teritory of Missourie; Travle to the Kayuse War; together with A Report on the Indians South of the Columbia River.* Portland, Ore.: Champoeg Press, Inc., 1959.

Kellogg, Louise Phelps (ed.). *Early Narratives of the Northwest, 1634–1699.* New York: Charles Scribner's Sons, 1917.

Kenney, James F. (ed.). *The Founding of Churchill Being the Journal of Captain James Knight, Governor-in-chief in Hudson Bay, from the 14th of July to the 13th of September, 1717.* Toronto, Ont.: J. M. Dent and Sons Ltd., 1932.

Lewis, William S., and Naojiro Murakami (ed.). *Ranald McDonald: The Narrative of his early life on the Columbia under the Hudson's Bay Company's regime; of his experiences in the Pacific Whale Fishery; and his great Adventure to Japan; with a sketch of his later life on the Western Frontier, 1824–1894.* Spokane, Wash.: The Inland-American Printing Company, 1923.

———, and Paul C. Phillips (ed.). *The Journal of John Work, A chieftrader of the Hudson's Bay Co. during his expedition from Vancouver* to the Flatheads and Blackfeet of the Pacific Northwest, with an account of the Fur Trade in the Northwest and Life of Work. Cleveland, Ohio: The Arthur H. Clark Company, 1923.

McDonnell, Alexander. Narrative of Transactions in the Red River Country from the Commencement of the Operations of the Earl of Selkirk, till the Summer of the year 1816. With a Map, Exhibiting Part of the Route of the Canadian Fur Traders in the Interior of North America, And Comprising the Scene of the Contest between Lord Selkirk and the North-West Company. London: Printed for B. McMillan, 1819.

M'Gillivray, Simon. A Narrative of Occurrences in the Indian Countries of North America, since the Connexion of the Right Hon. the Earl of Selkirk with the Hudson's Bay Company, and his attempt to establish a colony on the Red River; with a detailed account of his lordship's military expedition to, and subsequent proceedings at Fort William, in Upper Canada. London: Printed by B. McMillan, 1817.

Mackenzie, Alexander. Voyages from Montreal on the River St. Laurence [sic], through the Continent of North-America, to the Frozen and Pacific Oceans: In the Years 1789 and 1793. With a Preliminary Account of the Rise, Progress, and Present State of the Fur Trade of that Country. 3rd American ed. New York: Published by Evart Duyckinck, 1803.

Mackenzie, Cecil W. Donald Mackenzie "King of the Northwest": The Story of an International Hero of the Oregon Country and the Red River Settlement at Lower Fort Garry (Winnipeg). Los Angeles, Calif.: Ivan Deach, Jr., 1937.

McLeod, Malcolm (ed.). Peace River. A Canoe Voyage from Hudson's Bay to Pacific, by the Late Sir George Simpson; in 1828 Journal of the late Chief Factor, Archibald McDonald, who accompanied him. Ottawa, Ont.: J. Durie & Son, 1872.

Maloney, Alice Bay (ed.). Fur Brigade to the Bonaventura, John Work's California Expedition, 1832–1833 for the Hudson's Bay Company. San Francisco: California Historical Society, 1945.

Margry, Pierre. Memoires et documents pour servir a l'histoire des origines francaises des pays d'outremer: decouvertes et etablissements des français dans l'ouest et dans le sud de l'Amerique septentrionale. Vol. VI. Paris: Maisonneuve et Ch. LeClerc, 1888.

Marlatt, Helen Stuart Mackay-Smith (ed.). Stuart Letters of Robert and Elizabeth Sullivan Stuart and their Children 1819–1864, With an Undated Letter Prior to July 21, 1813. 2 vols. n.p. Privately Printed, 1961.

Marsh, James B. Four Years in the Rockies; or, The Adventures of Isaac P.

Rose, of Shenango Township, Lawrence County, Pennsylvania; Giving His Experience As a Hunter and Trapper in That Remote Region, and Containing Numerous Interesting and Thrilling Incidents Connected with his Calling. Also Including his Skirmishes and Battles with the Indians—his Capture, Adoption and Escape—Being One of the Most Thrilling Narratives Ever Published. Reprint. Columbus, Ohio: Long's College Book Company, n.d.

Masson, L. R. *Les bourgeois de la Compagnie du Nord-Ouest, recits de voyages, lettres et rapports inédits relatifs au nord-ouest Canadien. Publiés avec une esquisse historique et des annotations par L. R. Masson.* 2 vols. Reprint. New York: Antiquarian Press Ltd., 1960.

Meek, Stephen Hall. *The Autobiography of a Mountain Man 1805–1889.* Introduction and notes by Arthur Woodward. Pasadena, Calif.: Glen Dawson, 1948.

Moberly, John Henry. *When Fur Was King.* In collaboration with William Bleasdell Cameron. New York: E. P. Dutton & Co. Inc., 1929.

Mooso, Josiah. *The Life and Travels of Josiah Mooso: A Life on the Frontier among Indians and Spaniards, not Seeing the Face of a White Woman for Fifteen Years.* Winfield, Kan.: Telegram Print, 1888.

Morgan, Dale L. (ed.). *The West of William H. Ashley: The International struggle for the fur trade of the Missouri, the Rocky Mountains, and the Columbia, with explorations beyond the Continental Divide, recorded in the diaries and letters of William H. Ashley and his contemporaries 1822–1838.* Denver, Colo.: The Old West Publishing Co., 1964.

Morton, Arthur S. (ed.). *The Journal of Duncan M'Gillivray of the North West Company at Fort George on the Saskatchewan, 1794–5.* Toronto, Ont.: The Macmillan Company of Canada Ltd., 1929.

Nasatir, A. P. (ed.). *Before Lewis and Clark: Documents Illustrating the History of the Missouri, 1785–1804.* 2 vols. St. Louis, Mo.: St. Louis Historical Documents Foundation, 1952.

Nute, Grace Lee. *Caesars of the Wilderness: Medard Chouart, Sieur des Groseilliers and Pierre Esprit Radisson, 1618–1710.* New York: D. Appleton-Century Company, 1943.

[Ogden, Peter Skene]. *Traits of American Indian Life & Character By A Fur Trader.* Modern ed. San Francisco, Calif.: The Grabhorn Press, 1933.

Pease, Theodore C., and Raymond C. Werner (ed.). *The French Foundations 1680–1693.* (Illinois State Historical Library *Collections,* Vol. XXIII.) Springfield, Ill., 1934.

Phillips, Paul C. (ed.). Warren Angus Ferris' *Life in the Rocky Mountains: A Diary of Wanderings on the sources of the Rivers Missouri,*

Columbia, and Colorado from February 1830, to November, 1835. Denver, Colo.: The Old West Publishing Company, 1940.

Quaife, Milo Milton (ed.). *The John Askin Papers.* 2 vols. Detroit, Mich.: Detroit Library Commission, 1928.

—— (ed.). Kit Carson's *Autobiography.* Chicago: The Lakeside Press, R. R. Donnelley & Sons Co., 1935.

—— (ed.). Alexander Henry's *Travels and Adventures in Canada and the Indian Territories between the Years 1760 and 1776.* Chicago: The Lakeside Press, R. R. Donnelley & Sons Co., 1921.

—— (ed.). Charles Larpenteur's *Forty Years a Fur Trader on the Upper Missouri.* Chicago: The Lakeside Press, R. R. Donnelley & Sons Co., 1933.

Rich, E. E. (ed.). *Colin Robertson's Correspondence Book September 1817 to September 1822.* (Hudson's Bay Company Series of the Publications of the Champlain Society, No. 2.) Toronto, Ont.: The Chaplain Society, 1939.

—— (ed.). *Cumberland House Journals and Inland Journal 1775–82.* First series, 1775–79; second series, 1779–82. (Publications of the Hudson's Bay Record Society, Vols. XIV and XV.) London: The Hudson's Bay Record Society, 1951, 1952.

—— (ed.). *James Isham's Observations on Hudson's Bay, 1743 and Notes and Observations on a Book Entitled "A Voyage to Hudsons Bay in the Dobbs Galley, 1749."* (Hudson's Bay Company Series of the Publications of the Champlain Society, No. 12.) Toronto, Ont.: The Chaplain Society, 1949.

—— (ed.). *John Rae's Correspondence with the Hudson's Bay Company on Arctic Exploration 1844–1855.* (Publications of the Hudson's Bay Record Society, Vol. XVI.) London: The Hudson's Bay Record Society, 1953.

—— (ed.). *A Journal of A Voyage from Rocky Mountain Portage in Peace River to the Sources of Finlays Branch and North West Ward in Summer 1824 (By Samuel Black).* (Publications of the Hudson's Bay Record Society, Vol. XVIII.) London: The Hudson's Bay Record Society, 1955.

—— (ed.). *Journal of Occurrences in the Athabasca Department By George Simpson, 1820 and 1821, And Report.* (Hudson's Bay Company Series of the Publications of the Champlain Society, No. 1.) Toronto, Ont.: The Champlain Society, 1938.

—— (ed.). *The Letters of John McLoughlin From Fort Vancouver to the Governor and Committee.* First series, 1825–38; second series, 1839–44; third series, 1844–46. (Hudson's Bay Company Series of the

Publications of the Champlain Society, Nos. 4, 6, 7.) Toronto, Ont.:
The Champlain Society, 1941, 1943, 1944.

———— (ed.). *London Correspondence Inward From Eden Colvile 1849–1852.* (Publications of the Hudson's Bay Record Society, Vol. XIX.)
London: The Hudson's Bay Record Society, 1956.

———— (ed.). *Moose Fort Journals 1783–85.* (Publications of the Hudson's
Bay Record Society, Vol. XVII.) London: The Hudson's Bay Record
Society, 1954.

———— (ed.). *Part of Dispatch From George Simpson ESQ' Governor of
Ruperts Land to the Governor & Committee of the Hudson's Bay
Company London March 1, 1829, Continued and Completed March 24
and June 5, 1829.* (Hudson's Bay Company Series of the Publications
of the Champlain Society, No. 10.) Toronto, Ont.: The Champlain
Society, 1947.

———— (ed.). *Peter Skene Ogden's Snake Country Journals 1824–25 and
1825–26.* (Publications of the Hudson's Bay Record Society, Vol. XIII.)
London: The Hudson's Bay Record Society, 1950.

Robson, Joseph. *An Account of Six Years Residence in Hudson's-Bay,
From 1733 to 1736, and 1744 to 1747.* London: Printed for J. Payne
and J. Bouquet, 1752.

Rollins, Philip Ashton. *The Discovery of the Oregon Trail: Robert Stuart's
Narratives of His Overland Trip Eastward From Astoria in 1812–13.
From the Original Manuscripts in the Collection of William Robertson
Coe, Esq. To which is added: An Account of the Tonquin's Voyage and of
Events at Fort Astoria (1811–12) and Wilson Price Hunt's Diary of his
Overland Trip Westward to Astoria in 1811–12.* New York: Charles
Scribner's Sons, 1935.

Ross, Alexander. *Adventures of the First Settlers on the Oregon or
Columbia River: Being a Narrative of the Expedition Fitted out by
John Jacob Astor to Establish the "Pacific Fur Company"; with an
account of some Indian Tribes on the Coast of the Pacific.* London:
Smith, Elder and Co., 1849.

————. *The Red River Settlement: Its Rise, Progress, and Present State.
With Some Account of the Native Races and Its General History, to the
Present Day.* London: Smith, Elder and Co., 1856.

Russell, Osborne. *Journal of a Trapper; or, Nine Years in the Rocky
Mountains 1834–1843 Being a General Description of the Country,
Climate, Rivers, Lakes, Mountains, Etc., and a View of the Life Led
by a Hunter in those Regions.* Boise, Ida.: Syms-York Company, Inc.,
1921.

Ruxton, George F. *Life in the Far West.* Edinburgh: William Blackwood
and Sons, 1868.

Sage, Rufus. *Rocky Mountain Life; or, Startling Scenes and Perilous Adventures in the Far West.* Boston : Estes and Lauriat, 1880.

Schoolcraft, Henry R. *Historical and Statistical Information Respecting the History, Condition and Prospects of the Indian Tribes of the United States: Collected and prepared under the direction of the Bureau of Indian Affairs per act of Congress of March 3rd 1847.* 6 parts. Philadelphia : Lippincott, Grambo & Co., 1851–57.

Simpson, George. *Narrative of a Journey Round the World During the Years 1841 and 1842.* 2 vols. London : Henry Colburn, 1847.

Simpson, Thomas. *Narrative of the Discoveries on the North Coast of America; Effected by the Officers of Hudson's Bay Company During the Years 1836–39.* London : Richard Bentley, 1843.

Spaulding, Kenneth A. (ed.). Alexander Ross's *The Fur Hunters of the Far West.* Norman : University of Oklahoma Press, 1956.

Sullivan, James, *et al.* (ed.). *The Papers of Sir William Johnson.* 12 vols. Albany, N.Y. : The University of the State of New York, 1921–57.

Sullivan, Maurice S. (ed.). *The Travels of Jedediah Smith; A Documentary Outline Including the Journal of the Great American Pathfinder.* Santa Ana, Calif. : The Fine Arts Press, 1934.

Thwaites, Reuben Gold (ed.). *John Long's Journal.* Vol. II of *Early Western Travels 1748–1846: A Series of Annotated Reprints of some of the best and rarest contemporary volumes of travel . . . during the Period of Early American Settlement.* Edited by Reuben Gold Thwaites. 32 vols. Cleveland, Ohio : The Arthur H. Clark Company, 1904–7.

Tyrrell, J. B. (ed.). *David Thompson's Narrative of his Explorations in Western America, 1784–1813.* (Publications of the Champlain Society, Vol. XII.) Toronto, Ont. : The Champlain Society, 1916.

———— (ed.). *Documents Relating to the Early History of Hudson Bay.* (Publications of the Champlain Society, Vol. XVIII.) Toronto, Ont. : The Champlain Society, 1931.

———— (ed.). *Journals of Samuel Hearne and Philip Turnor.* (Publications of the Champlain Society, Vol. XXI.) Toronto, Ont. : The Champlain Society, 1934.

Umfreville, Edward. *The Present State of Hudson's Bay. Containing a Full Description of that Settlement, and the Adjacent Country; and Likewise of the Fur Trade, with Hints for its Improvement, &c. &c. To which are added, Remarks and Observations made in the Inland Parts, During a Residence of Near Four Years; A Specimen of Five Indian Languages; and a Journal of a Journey from Montreal to New York.* London : Printed for Charles Stalker, 1790.

Victor, Frances Fuller. *The River of the West. Life and Adventure in the Rocky Mountains and Oregon; Embracing Events in the Life-time of a*

Mountain-man and Pioneer: With the Early History of the North-western Slope, including an Account of the Fur Traders, etc. Hartford, Conn.: Columbian Book Company, 1870.

Wallace, J. N. *The Wintering Partners on Peace River From the Earliest Records to the Union in 1821 With a Summary of the Dunvegan Journal, 1806.* Ottawa, Ont.: Thorburn and Abbott, 1929.

Wallace. W. S. (ed.). John McLean's *Notes of a Twenty-Five Years' Service in the Hudson's Bay Territory.* (Publications of the Champlain Society, Vol. XIX.) Toronto, Ont.: The Champlain Society, 1932.

———— (ed.). *Documents Relating to the North West Company.* (Publications of the Champlain Society, Vol. XXII.) Toronto, Ont.: The Champlain Society, 1934.

White, M. Catherine (ed.). *David Thompson's Journals Relating to Montana and Adjacent Regions 1808–1812.* (Montana State University Studies, Vol. I.) Missoula: Montana State University Press, 1950.

Articles, Serials, Bulletins, and Special Publications

Abel, Annie Heloise (ed.). "Trudeau's Description of the Upper Missouri," *Mississippi Valley Historical Review,* VIII (June–September, 1921), 149–79.

Allan, George T. "Journal of a Voyage from Fort Vancouver, Columbia River, to York Factory, Hudson's Bay, 1841," *Transactions of the Ninth Annual Re-Union of the Oregon Pioneer Association for 1881. And the Annual Address Delivered by Hon. W. C. Johnson, Together with the Occasional Address by Hon. Medorum Crawford, and Other Matters of Interest.* Pp. 38–55.

"Extracts from Chief-Factor James Anderson's Arctic Journal," *Royal Geographical Society Journal,* XXVII (1857), 321–28.

"Letter from Chief Factor James Anderson, to Sir George Simpson, F. R. G. S., Governor in Chief of Rupert Land," *Royal Geographical Society Journal,* XXVI (1856), 18–25.

"Personal Narrative of Capt. Thomas G. Anderson," *Wisconsin State Historical Society Collections,* IX (1882), 137–206.

Bagley, Clarence B. (ed.). "Journal of Occurrences at Nisqually House, 1833," *Washington Historical Quarterly,* VI (July, 1915), 179–97; VI (October, 1915), 264–78; VII (January, 1916), 59–75; VII (April, 1916), 144–67.

Barton, Richard, and Grace Lee Nute (ed.). "A Winter in the St. Croix Valley, 1802–03," *Minnesota History,* XXVIII (March, 1947), 1–14; XXVIII (June, 1947), 142–59; XXVIII (September, 1947), 225–40.

Beauregard, Mrs. H. T. (ed.). "Journal of Jean Baptiste Trudeau among the Arikara Indians in 1795," *Missouri Historical Society Collections,* IV (1912), 9–48.

Brooks, George R. (ed.). "The Private Journal of Robert Campbell," *Missouri Historical Society Bulletin,* XX (October, 1963), 3–24; XX (January, 1964), 107–18.

Burpee, Lawrence J. (ed.). "Journal of Matthew Cocking, from York Factory to the Blackfeet Country, 1772–73," *Royal Society of Canada Proceedings and Transactions* (Third Series), Vol. II, Section 2 (1908), pp. 89–121.

———— (ed.). "Journal of a Journey Performed by Anthony Hendry, To Explore the Country Inland, And to Endeavour to Increase the Hudson's Bay Company's Trade, A.D. 1754–1755," *Royal Society of Canada Proceedings and Transactions* (Third Series), Vol. I, Section 2 (1907), pp. 307–64.

———— (ed.). "Journal du Yukon 1847–48 par Alexander Hunter Murray," *Publications des Archives Canadiennes,* No. 4 (1910).

"Correspondence of Robert Campbell 1834–1845," *Missouri Historical Society Glimpses of the Past,* VIII (January–June, 1941), 3–65.

Carter, Clarence E. (ed.). "Observations of Superintendent John Stuart and Governor James Grant of East Florida on the proposed Plan of 1764 for the Future Management of Indian Affairs," *American Historical Review,* XX (July, 1915), 815–31.

Cassell, Abraham (compiler). "Notes on the Iroquois and Delaware Indians. Communications from Conrad Weiser to Christopher Saur in the Years 1746–1749 in his Newspaper printed at Germantown, entitled 'The High German Pennsylvania Historical Writer, or a Collection of Important Events from the Kingdom of Nature and the Church' and from his (Saur's) Almanacs," translated by Miss Helen Bell, *The Pennsylvania Magazine of History and Biography,* I, 163–67; 319–23.

"Notes of Auguste Chouteau on Boundaries of Various Indian Nations," *Missouri Historical Society Glimpses of the Past,* VII (October–December, 1940), 119–40.

Clements, William L. (ed.). "Rogers's Michillimackinac Journal," *American Antiquarian Society Proceedings* (New Series), XXVIII (1918), 224–73.

Dee, Henry Drummond (ed.). "The Journal of John Work, 1835: Being an Account of His Voyage Northward from the Columbia River to Fort Simpson and Return in the Brig *Lama,* January–October, 1835," *British Columbia Historical Quarterly,* VIII (April, 1944), 127–46; VIII (July, 1944), 227–44; VIII (October, 1944), 307–18; IX (January, 1945), 49–69; IX (April, 1945), 129–46.

Delanglez, Jean (ed.). "The 1674 Account of the Discovery of the Mississippi," *Mid-America: An Historical Review* (n.s.), XV (October, 1944), 301–24.

—— (ed.). "The Voyage of Louis Jolliet to Hudson Bay in 1679," *Mid-America: An Historical Review* (n.s.), XV (July, 1944), 221–50.

—— (ed.). "Tonti Letters," *Mid-America: An Historical Review* (n.s.), X (July, 1939), 209–38.

"Daniel Greysolon DuLuth to —— April 12, 1684," *Collections of the State Historical Society of Wisconsin,* XVI, 114–25.

Elliott, T. C. (ed.). "John McLoughlin to Edward Ermatinger Fort Vancouver February 1, 1836," *Oregon Historical Society Quarterly,* XXIII (December, 1922), 368.

—— (ed.). "Journal of Alexander Ross—Snake Country Expedition, 1824," *Oregon Historical Society Quarterly,* XIV (December, 1913), 366–88.

—— (ed.). "Journal of David Thompson," *Oregon Historical Society Quarterly,* XV (March, 1914), 39–63; XV (June, 1914), 104–25.

—— (ed.). "Journal of John Work, November and December, 1824," *Washington Historical Quarterly,* III (July, 1912), 198–228.

—— (ed.). "Journal of John Work, June–October, 1825," *Washington Historical Quarterly,* V (April, 1914), 83–115; V (July, 1914), 163–91; V (October, 1914), 258–87.

—— (ed.). "Journal of John Work; July 5–September 15, 1826," *Washington Historical Quarterly,* VI (January, 1915), 26–49.

—— (ed.). "Journal of John Work, April 30th to May 31st, 1830," *Oregon Historical Society Quarterly,* X (September, 1909), 296–313.

—— (ed.). "Journal of John Work, Covering Snake Country Expedition of 1830–31," *Oregon Historical Society Quarterly,* XIII (December, 1912), 363–71; XIV (September, 1913), 280–314.

—— (ed.). "Journal of Peter Skene Ogden: Snake Expedition, 1826–27," *Oregon Historical Society Quarterly,* XI (June, 1910), 204–22.

—— (ed.). "Journal of Peter Skene Ogden: Snake Expedition, 1827–1828," *Oregon Historical Society Quarterly,* XI (December, 1910), 355–79.

—— (ed.). "Journal of Peter Skene Ogden: Snake Expedition, 1828–1829," *Oregon Historical Society Quarterly,* XI (December, 1910), 381–96.

—— (ed.). "Letter of Donald Mackenzie to Wilson Price Hunt," *Oregon Historical Quarterly,* XLIII (September, 1942), 194–97.

—— (ed.). "Narrative of the Expedition to the Kootenae @ Flat Bow Indian Countries, on the Sources of the Columbia River, Pacific Ocean, by D. Thompson on behalf of the N. W. Company 1807," *Oregon Historical Society Quarterly,* XXVI (March, 1925), 28–49.

"Edward Ermatinger's York Factory Express Journal, Being a Record of

Journeys Made Between Fort Vancouver and Hudson Bay in the Years 1827–1828," *Royal Society of Canada Proceedings and Transactions* (Third Series), Vol. VI, Section 2 (1912), pp. 66–132.

Forsyth, Thomas. "Journal of a Voyage from St. Louis to the Falls of St. Anthony, in 1819," *State Historical Society of Wisconsin Collections*, VI (1908), 188–215.

Fox, J. Sharpless (ed.). "Letters on the Fur Trade By William Johnston," *Historical Collections and Researches made by the Michigan Pioneer and Historical Society*, XXXVII (1909–10), 132–207.

———— (ed.). "Narrative of the Travels and Adventures of a Merchant Voyageur in the Savage Territories of North America Leaving Montreal the 28th of May 1783 (to 1820) by Jean Baptiste Perrault," *Historical Collections and Researches made by the Michigan Pioneer and Historical Society*, XXXVII (1909–10), 508–619.

"First Journal of Simon Fraser from April 12th to July 18th, 1806," Dominion of Canada, *Report of the Public Archives for the Year 1929*, pp. 109–45.

"Letters from the Rocky Mountains from August 1st, 1806, to February 10th, 1807 By Simon Fraser," Dominion of Canada. *Report of the Public Archives for the Year 1929*, pp. 147–59.

Frost, Donald McKay. "Notes on General Ashley, The Overland Trail, and South Pass," *American Antiquarian Society Proceedings*, LIV (1944), 161–312.

"Diary of Nicholas Garry, Deputy-Governor of the Hudson's Bay Company from 1822–1835. A detailed narrative of his travels in the Northwest Territories of British North America in 1821. With a portrait of Mr. Garry and other illustrations," *Royal Society of Canada Proceedings and Transactions* (Second Series), Vol. VI, Section 2 (1900), pp. 72–204.

Giraud, Marcel (ed.). "Etienne Veniard De Bourgmont's 'Exact Description of Louisiana,' " *Missouri Historical Society Bulletin*, XV (October, 1958), 3–19.

Hazlitt, Ruth (ed. and trans.). "The Journal of Francois Antoine Larocque from the Assiniboine River to the Yellowstone—1805." (State University of Montana Historical Reprints.) *Sources of Northwest History*, No. 20.

Hewitt, J. N. B. (ed.). Edwin Thompson Denig's "Indian Tribes of the Upper Missouri." *Bureau of American Ethnology Forty-sixth Annual Report* (1928–29).

———— (ed.). "Journal of Rudolph Friederich Kurz: An Account of His Experiences Among Fur Traders and American Indians on the Mississippi and the Upper Missouri Rivers During the Years 1846 to 1852."

Translated by Myrtis Jarrell. *Bureau of American Ethnology Bulletin,* CXV (1937).

Hickerson, Harold (ed.). "Journal of Charles Jean Baptiste Chaboillez, 1794–1798," *Ethnohistory,* VI (Summer, 1959), 265–316; VI (Fall, 1959), 363–427.

Leader, Herman (ed.). "A Voyage From the Columbia to California in 1840 From the Journal of Sir James Douglas," *California Historical Society Quarterly,* VIII (June, 1929), 97–115.

"The Journal of Charles Le Raye," *South Dakota Historical Collections,* IV (1908), 150–80.

Lewis, William S., and Jacob A. Meyers (ed.). "John Work's Journal of a Trip from Fort Colvile to Fort Vancouver and Return in 1828," *Washington Historical Society Quarterly,* XI (April, 1920), 104–14.

McDonnell, Mrs. Anne (ed.). "Original Journal of James H. Chambers, Fort Sarpy," *Contributions to the Historical Society of Montana,* X (1940), 100–187.

—— (ed.). "The Fort Benton Journal, 1854–1856," *Contributions to the Historical Society of Montana,* X (1940), 1–99.

M'Gillivray, Duncan. "Some Account of the Trade Carried on by the North West Company," Dominion of Canada, *Report of the Public Archives for the Year 1928,* pp. 56–73.

Marks, Constant R. (ed.). "Letellier's Autobiography," *South Dakota Historical Collections,* IV (1908), 217–53.

Marshall, Thomas Maitland (ed.). "The Journal of Jules DeMun," translated by Mrs. Nettie H. Beauregard. *Missouri Historical Society Collections,* V (1927–28), 311–26.

"More Reports of the Fur Trade and Inland Trade to Mexico 1831," *Missouri Historical Society Glimpses of the Past,* IX (July–September, 1942), 43–86.

Morgan, Dale L. (ed.). "The Diary of William H. Ashley, March 25–June 27, 1825: A Record of Exploration West Across the Continental Divide, Down the Green River and into the Great Basin," *Missouri Historical Society Bulletin,* XI (October, 1954), 9–40; XI (January, 1955), 158–86; XI (April, 1955), 279–302.

Nasatir, Abraham P. "Jacques D'Eglise on the Upper Missouri, 1791–1795," *Mississippi Valley Historical Review,* XIV (June, 1927), 47–56.

Nute, Grace Lee (ed.). "A Description of Northern Minnesota by a Fur-Trader in 1807," *Minnesota Historical Bulletin,* V (February, 1923), 28–39.

—— (ed.). "The Diary of Martin McLeod," *Minnesota Historical Bulletin,* IV (1921–22), 351–439.

"Old Letters from Hudson Bay Company Officials and Employes [*sic*] from 1829 to 1840," *Washington Historical Quarterly*, I (July, 1907), 256–66; II (October, 1907), 40–43; II (January, 1908), 161–68; II (April, 1908), 254–64.

O'Neil, Marion (ed.). "The Peace River Journal, 1799–1800," *Washington Historical Quarterly*, XIX (October, 1928), 250–70.

Partoll, Albert (ed.). "Anderson's Narrative of a Ride to the Rocky Mountains in 1834," *Frontier and Midland*, XIX (Autumn, 1938), 54–63.

"The Reminiscences of General Bernard Pratte, Jr.," *Missouri Historical Society Bulletin*, VI (October, 1949), 59–70.

Quaife, M. M. (ed.). "Extracts from Capt. McKay's Journal—and Others," *Wisconsin Historical Society Proceedings* (1915), pp. 186–210.

"Reports of the Fur Trade and Inland Trade to Mexico 1831," *Missouri Historical Society Glimpses of the Past*, IX (January–June, 1942), 3–39.

Robinson, Doane (ed.). "Fort Tecumseh and Fort Pierre Journal and Letter Books," *South Dakota Historical Collections*, IX (1918), 69–239.

Ross, Bernard R., William L. Hardisty, and Strachan Jones. "Notes on the Tinneh or Chepewyan Indians of British and Russian America," *Smithsonian Institution Annual Report* (1866), pp. 303–27.

"Five Letters of Charles Ross, 1842–44," *British Columbia Historical Quarterly*, VII (April, 1943), pp. 103–18.

Sage, W. N. (ed.). "Peter Skene Ogden's Notes on Western Caledonia," *British Columbia Historical Quarterly*, I (January, 1937), 45–56.

Scaglione, John (ed.). "Ogden's Report of his 1829–1830 Expedition," *California Historical Society Quarterly*, XXVIII (June, 1949), 117–24.

Scott, Leslie M. (ed.). "John Work's Journey from Fort Vancouver to Umpqua River, and Return, in 1834," *Oregon Historical Society Quarterly*, XXIV (September, 1923), 238–68.

Thwaites, Reuben Gold (ed.). "A Selection of George Croghan's Letters and Journals Relating to Tours into the Western Country—November 16, 1750–November, 1765," in Vol. I of Reuben Thwaites (ed.), *Early, Western Travels 1748–1846 A Series of Annotated Reprints of some of the best and rarest contemporary Volumes of Travel . . . during the Period of Early American Settlement*. 32 vols. Cleveland, Ohio: The Arthur H. Clark Company, 1904–7.

———— (ed.). "A Wisconsin Fur-Trader's Journal, 1803–4 By Michel Curot," *Collections of the State Historical Society of Wisconsin*, XX (1911), 396–471.

———— (ed.). "The Fur-Trade in Wisconsin—1812–1825," *Collections of the State Historical Society of Wisconsin*, XX (1911), 1–395.

"Journal of William Fraser Tolmie—1833," *Washington Historical Quarterly,* III (July, 1912), 229–41.

"Journal of Jean Baptiste Truteau on the Upper Missouri, 'Première Partie,' June 7, 1794–March 26, 1795," *American Historical Review,* XIX (January, 1914), 299–333.

Volwiler, A. T. (ed.). "William Trent's Journal at Fort Pitt, 1763," *Mississippi Valley Historical Review,* XI (December, 1924), 390–413.

"Extracts from 'The Substance of a Journal During a Residence at the Red River Colony, British North America, and Frequent Excursions Among the North-West American Indians in the Years 1820, 1821, 1822, 1823' By John West," *State Historical Society of North Dakota Collections,* III (1910), 439–90.

Wilson, James Grant (ed.). "Arent Van Curler and His Journal of 1634–35," *American Historical Association Annual Report* (1895), pp. 81–101.

Young, F. G. (ed.). "The Correspondence and Journals of Captain Nathaniel Wyeth 1831–6," *Sources of the History of Oregon,* Vol. I (1899), parts 3–6.

GOVERNMENT DOCUMENTS

Great Britain. Parliament. House of Commons. Select Committee on Aboriginal Tribes. *Report.* London, 1837.

———. ———. ———. Select Committee on the Hudson's Bay Company. *Report.* London, 1857.

U.S. Congress. Senate. "Annual Report," by Christopher Carson, in *Report of the Commissioner of Indian Affairs of 1857.* 35th Cong., 1st sess., S. Exec. Doc. 11. Washington, D.C., 1858. Serial no. 919.

———. ———. "Annual Report," by Christopher Carson, in *Report of the Commissioner of Indian Affairs of 1858.* 35th Cong., 2nd sess., S. Exec. Doc. 1. Washington, D.C., 1859. Serial no. 974.

———. ———. "Annual Report," by Christopher Carson, in *Report of the Commissioner of Indian Affairs of 1859.* 36th Cong., 1st sess., S. Exec. Doc. 2. Washington, D.C., 1860. Serial no. 1023.

———. ———. "Annual Report," by Christopher Carson, in *Report of the Commissioner of Indian Affairs of 1860.* 36th Cong., 2nd sess., S. Exec. Doc. 1. Washington, D.C., 1861. Serial no. 1078.

———. ———. *Message from the President of the United States, in compliance with a resolution Concerning the Fur Trade, and Inland Trade to Mexico.* 22nd Cong., 1st. sess., S. Exec. Doc. 90. Washington, D.C., 1832. Serial no. 213.

———. ———. "Report," by Thomas Fitzpatrick, in *Report of the Commissioner of Indian Affairs of 1850.* 31st Cong., 2nd sess., S. Exec. Doc. 1. Washington, D.C., 1851. Serial no. 587.

———. ———. "Report," by Thomas Fitzpatrick, in *Report of the Commissioner of Indian Affairs of 1851.* 32nd Cong., 1st sess., S. Exec. Doc. 1. Washington, D.C., 1852. Serial nos. 612–13.

———. ———. "Report," by Thomas Fitzpatrick, in *Report of the Commissioner of Indian Affairs of 1853.* 33rd Cong., 1st sess., S. Exec. Doc. 1. Washington, D.C., 1853. Serial no. 690.

MANUSCRIPTS

Abbott Family Papers. Burton Historical Collection. Detroit Public Library. Detroit, Michigan.

Abert Papers. Missouri Historical Society. St. Louis, Missouri.

American Fur Company Letter Book, 1816–19. State Historical Society of Wisconsin. Madison, Wisconsin.

American Fur Company Papers. Burton Historical Collection. Detroit Public Library. Detroit, Michigan.

American Fur Company Papers. Chicago Historical Society. Chicago, Illinois.

American Fur Company Papers (microfilm copy of original MSS in the New York Historical Society). Missouri Historical Society. St. Louis, Missouri.

Anderson, Meriwether Lewis, Collection. Missouri Historical Society. St. Louis, Missouri.

Askin, John, Papers. Burton Historical Collection. Detroit Public Library. Detroit, Michigan.

Bailly, Alexis, Papers. Minnesota Historical Society. St. Paul, Minnesota.

Bailly de Messein, Honoré Gratien Joseph, Papers. Indiana State Library. Indianapolis, Indiana.

Bardon, John A., Papers. Minnesota Historical Society. St. Paul, Minnesota.

Boller, Henry A., Papers. North Dakota State Historical Society. Bismarck, North Dakota.

Cass, Lewis, Papers. Burton Historical Collection. Detroit Public Library. Detroit, Michigan.

Chouteau Collections. Missouri Historical Society. St. Louis. Missouri.

Clark, William, Collection. Missouri Historical Society. St. Louis, Missouri.

Crooks, Ramsay, Letters, 1813–43. Burton Historical Collection. Detroit Public Library. Detroit, Michigan.

Culbertson Collection. Missouri Historical Society. St. Louis, Missouri.

Dickson, Robert, Papers. Minnesota Historical Society. St. Paul, Minnesota.

Documents Historiques années 1818–66. Archdiocesan Archives. Archbishop's Residence. St. Boniface, Manitoba.

Dousman Papers. Ayer Collection. Newberry Library. Chicago, Illinois.

Edgar, William, Papers. Burton Historical Collection. Detroit Public Library. Detroit, Michigan.

Ewing, William G. and George W., Papers. Indiana State Library. Indianapolis, Indiana.

Fur Trade Collection. Public Archives of Manitoba. Winnipeg, Manitoba.

Fur Trade Papers. Missouri Historical Society. St. Louis, Missouri.

Garrioch, Peter, Collection. Public Archives of Manitoba. Winnipeg, Manitoba.

Grignon, Lawe, Porlier Papers. State Historical Society of Wisconsin. Madison, Wisconsin.

Hubbard, Gurdon Saltonstall, Letters. Chicago Historical Society. Chicago, Illinois.

Hudson's Bay Company Papers. Minnesota Historical Society. St. Paul, Minnesota.

Juneau, Solomon, Correspondence. Chicago Historical Society. Chicago, Illinois.

Kaskaskia Papers. Missouri Historical Society. St. Louis, Missouri.

Laughton, Bernardus, Collection. Chicago Historical Society. Chicago, Illinois.

Laut Transcripts. Ayer Collection. Newberry Library. Chicago, Illinois.

Lawe Papers. Chicago Historical Society. Chicago, Illinois.

McKenzie, Roderic, Papers. Minnesota Historical Society. St. Paul, Minnesota.

MacKintosh Family Papers. Burton Historical Collection. Detroit Public Library. Detroit, Michigan.

"Journals and Correspondence of John McLeod, Senior, Chief Trader, Hudson's Bay Company, who was one of the Earliest Pioneers in the Oregon Territory, from 1812 to 1844" (typescript copied from the original MSS in the Dominion Government Archives by R. E. Gosnell). Library of Congress. Washington, D.C.

McLeod, Martin, Papers. Minnesota Historical Society. St. Paul, Minnesota.

Menard, Pierre, Papers. Illinois Historical Survey of the University of Illinois. Urbana, Illinois.

Menard Collection. Illinois State Historical Library. Springfield, Illinois.

Menard Family Collection. Illinois State Historical Library. Springfield, Illinois.

Porteous, John, Papers. Burton Historical Collection. Detroit Public Library. Detroit, Michigan.

Ramsay, Alexander, Papers. Minnesota Historical Society. St. Paul, Minnesota.

Rice, Henry M., Papers. Minnesota Historical Society. St. Paul, Minnesota.

Sibley, Henry H., Papers. Minnesota Historical Society. St. Paul, Minnesota.

Taliaferro, Lawrence, Papers. Minnesota Historical Society. St. Paul, Minnesota.

Van Ostrand, Ferdinand A., Diary. North Dakota State Historical Society. Bismarck, North Dakota.

Woodbridge, William, Papers. Burton Historical Collection. Detroit Public Library. Detroit, Michigan.

THESES AND DISSERTATIONS

Anson, Bert. "The Fur Traders in Northern Indiana, 1796–1850." Unpublished Ph.D. dissertation, Indiana University, Bloomington, 1953.

Crane, Fred A. "The Noble Savage in America, 1815–1860: Concepts of the Indian, with Special Reference to the Writers of the Northeast." Unpublished Ph.D. dissertation, Yale University, New Haven, Conn., 1952.

Kennedy, Sister Mary Joseph. "The Pioneer Fur Traders of Northwestern Indiana." Unpublished Master's thesis, De Paul University, Chicago, 1932.

Little, Margaret E. "Early Days of the Maritime Fur Trade, 1785–1794." Unpublished Master's thesis, University of British Columbia, Vancouver, 1934.

Parker, Robert J. "The Iroquois and the Albany Fur Trade, 1609–1701." Unpublished Ph.D. dissertation, University of California, Berkeley, 1932.

Russell, J. C. "The Reputation of the Plains Indians as Reported by Hunters, Trappers, Travelers, Army Officers, and Indian Agents." Unpublished Master's thesis, Colorado State Teacher's College, Greeley, Colo., 1930.

Tevebaugh, John Leslie. "Merchant on the Western Frontier: William Morrison of Kaskaskia, 1790–1837." Unpublished Ph.D. dissertation, University of Illinois, Urbana, 1962.

Todd, Edgeley Woodman. "Literary Interest in the Fur Trade and Fur Trapper of the Trans-Mississippi West." Unpublished Ph.D. dissertation, Northwestern University, Evanston, Ill., 1952.

Wiese, Bernard R. "The Interpretation of the Indian in American Historiography." Unpublished Master's thesis, University of South Dakota, Vermillion, 1955.

NEWSPAPERS

Missouri Republican (St. Louis), Oct. 15, 1823; June 7, 1827.

INDEX